HOW TO RUN THE
COUNTRY
MANUAL

Haynes

First published in March 2015

A catalogue record for this book is available from the British Library

ISBN 978 0 85733 800 6

Published by Haynes Publishing,
Sparkford, Yeovil, Somerset BA22 7JJ, UK
Tel: 01963 442030 Fax: 01963 440001
Int. tel: +44 1963 442030 Int. fax: +44 1963 440001
E-mail: sales@haynes.co.uk
Website: www.haynes.co.uk

Haynes North America Inc.
861 Lawrence Drive, Newbury Park,
California 91320, USA

Printed in the USA by Odcombe Press LP,
1299 Bridgestone Parkway, La Vergne, TN 37086

Acknowledgements

SPECIAL THANKS TO:
Sid Smith for heroic editing and Drew Buchan for the World Cup blog quote in the Introduction.

Thanks also to the following inspirational writers and economists: Will Hutton, Alex Brummer, Ruth Sunderland, Ha-Joon Chang, Stephen King, Kevin McKenna, Julian Knight, Anthony Sampson, Larry Elliot, Jeremy Warner, Simon Capewell, Poly Toynbee, Suzanne Moore, Peter Oborn, Owen Jones, Frazer Nelson, Andrew Rownsley, Seamus Milne – not forgetting of course the giants on whose shoulders we stand and scribble: J.M. Keynes, M. Friedman and C.S. Lewis.

AUTHORS	Kevin Albertson	Ian Rock
	James Meadway	Chris Fox

PROJECT MANAGER
Louise McIntyre

EDITORS
Sid Smith, Ian Rock

PAGE DESIGN
James Robertson

PHOTOGRAPHY
Shutterstock, Alamy (pages 96, 105 and 144)

CARTOONS
Kathryn Lamb

HOW TO RUN THE COUNTRY
MANUAL

Kevin Albertson   Ian Rock

James Meadway   Chris Fox

CONTENTS

PART 1 – ECONOMICS

Images of Britain: The Edinburgh Military Tattoo. But nearly half of all Scots now feel they'd be better off outside the UK.

INTRODUCTION

We live in interesting times. Mistrust in politicians is on a scale not seen since the Peasants' Revolt. Our elected representatives seem to be asleep while the cracks in the nation's structure grow larger. The United Kingdom is anything but united, recently coming within a whisker of losing a third of its land mass and a tenth of its people; by a slim margin Scottish voters granted the union a reprieve.

So how did it come to this? Not so long ago we were proud of our achievements as a country and of our extraordinarily rich national inheritance.

To sum up what's wrong, just look at our performance in the last World Cup. Three home nations – Scotland, Wales and Northern Ireland – failed to qualify. Then, following England's humiliating early exit, this perceptive comment was posted online:

> Britain is a country living off other people's talent,
> skills and money.
> We want instant success, so we bring in foreign
> players.
> We can't educate our people, so we bring in
> immigrants.
> We can't sustain any competitive industries, so we
> outsource or sell them.
> We can't make anything the world wants, so we
> manage and hide other people's money.
> We have nothing left to sell except our
> housing stock.

If you boiled this down to one overriding malady it would be short-termism. The players in Germany's 2014 World Cup-winning side learnt their craft under a *long-term* plan of nurturing home-grown talent. The same country's world-beating industries have long adopted a similar approach: 'patient capitalism'.

Where Britain has applied similar methods, we shine. Think Team GB: in recent years British athletics has come from nowhere to podium triumph. When we do things properly we are unbeatable. And if those in power utilised Team GB as a template for managing the nation's fortunes, a prosperous future would seem assured. But before getting too carried away, a lot needs to be done to stop the rot.

Losing it

Visitors arriving at Heathrow airport often head eastward into the capital by road. Shortly after the M4 flyover rises above suburban rooftops it snakes between two giant glass and steel showrooms dedicated to a single purpose – the flaunting of German automotive

Mass disenchantment 1381 style. The Peasants' Revolt witnessed unpopular politicians, the Chancellor and Treasurer, being beheaded by the mob.

supremacy. Not so long ago this same route was straddled by an art deco tower celebrating Jaguar, MG and Triumph. Once a world leader, today Britain is the only major Western nation without its own car industry. The country that developed the Harrier jump jet and (with France) the supersonic Concorde today subcontracts for EU and US manufacturers. Great Britain may have once ruled the waves but our latest ocean liners – the *QE3* and *Queen Mary 2* – are built in France and Italy, while UK shipyards stand idle; even some Royal Navy ships are contracted to Korean yards (see page 46). Today, pride in what we design and build as a nation is in short supply. Instead the City of London is king – yet its achievements are tarnished by sagas of greed, unjustified rewards for failure, rigged markets and state bailouts.

What's good?

Sometimes merit can be obscured by familiarity. The American-born writer Bill Bryson provided a humorous tonic with his bestseller *Notes from a Small Island*, published in 1996, observing:

> *Here is a country that fought and won a noble war, dismantled a mighty empire in a generally benign and enlightened way, created a far-seeing welfare state – in short, did nearly everything right – and then spent the rest of the century looking on itself as a chronic failure. The fact is that this is still the best place in the world for most things – to post a letter, go for a walk, watch television, buy a book, venture out for a drink, go to a museum, use the bank, get lost, seek help, or stand on a hillside and take in a view.*

Of course much (privately run) water has passed under the bridge since this was written. But in essence this rousing description still rings true. The problem is that most of the best stuff is firmly in the past.

Being British

The United Kingdom of Great Britain and Northern Ireland – to give it its full name – is a country with a broad personality, being a composite of four home nations. We all enjoy dual nationality, depending on which

---

WHAT BRITAIN HAS GIVEN THE WORLD

There's hardly a field of human endeavour where Britain has not made an enormous contribution.

As well as giving the world the English language, our forebears came up with just about every sport worth playing – including football, rugby, cricket, hockey, badminton, polo and bobsleighing, and some idiosyncratic activities such as curling, conkers, shin-kicking, cheese-rolling and, at least in celluloid form, quiddich. And with them the concept of fair play. We led in the abolition of slavery, and are the country of Shakespeare, Newton, Burns, Dickens, Turner, Darwin, Hardy and Austen.

Landmark British inventions include the television, the world wide web, the computer, the modern bicycle and pneumatic tyre, the light bulb, penicillin, the limited company, electric motors, railways, tanks, hovercraft and the jet engine, not forgetting those indispensables of modern life - the toothbrush, the flushing toilet, lawnmowers and tin cans. And if all that wasn't enough, we enjoy a rich heritage of regional accents, glorious countryside and wonderful architecture.

As for British qualities – a subject of some debate – surely we still cling to notions of honesty and decency. And despite a tendency towards grumpiness we generally manage a degree of courtesy: we open doors for others, queue fairly, and brake promptly at pedestrian crossings.

---

part of the kingdom, or the wider world, we were born in. As the award winning writer Jonathan Freedland has pointed out, this concept has been hugely successful, not least for minorities who have found living in a country defined by its plurality easier than in most places. The word 'British' works well next to an unseen hyphen – Welsh British, Nigerian British, Muslim British. It would be a tragedy to lose it, in the event of a future Yes vote in an independence referendum, causing the country to fragment and shrink into its component parts.

Complaints Dept

If Britain had a Complaints Dept, the grievances might resemble those aired in the recent Scottish referendum. Many supporters of the Yes campaign felt that inequality was rising and must be tackled. Many warmed to the idea of more social democracy and less unregulated free market.

Either way, there's one thing for sure: nothing succeeds in uniting a nation like success, and nothing fractures it like failure. After decades of decline under uninspiring leadership, many voters are disenchanted, and some want the exit. The only real surprise is why it took so long.

One reason many have lost faith is that over the last 30 years we have lost national assets. Our railways and utilities have been sold. The post-war public-service ethos has been smothered. We have lost many of our great companies and there is lingering resentment at the demise of British industries and the communities they sustained. In their place we have rising inequality and low wages.

Many feel that we run a daily gauntlet of legalised scams and mis-selling from manipulative banks, and giant utility, energy and telecoms companies. Protecting consumers seems the least of politicians' priorities.

Why a Haynes manual?

Haynes manuals are traditionally about fixing mechanical things like cars and motorbikes. But what if the country needs fixing? For too long politics and economics have been the preserve of learned folk, many of whom would struggle to wire a plug. This book aims to cut through the waffle and explain how the machinery of state that governs our lives actually works. Hopefully it will answer some of the big questions that concern people – the ones which politicians rarely give straight answers to. Anyone who's ever used a Haynes manual to solve a mechanical problem can get to grips with the national control panel.

Money, Power and People

The UK's control panel has three main parts: Money, Power and People. Or, if you prefer, Economics, Politics and Society. Hence this book is presented in three sections. But which should come first? You might argue that we should start by deciding what kind of society people want to live in, and then use money and power to make it happen.

But, after much deliberation, Economics became Part 1 – on the grounds that a successful economy is needed for the cash to create the society we want. A successful economy should also generate well-paid jobs. Politicians know that voters will be swift to punish them if the supply of money dries up, hence the temptation to max out the nation's credit card.

Most people want to be part of a nation that's on the way up, and they are willing to help make it happen.

Economics

Britain is sinking deeper into debt. The 'national debt' is a frightening £1.4 trillion. Luckily, we can still borrow from the markets at favourable rates of interest, but we need to get serious about making our own money.

Another way the sums can be made to add up for a while is by selling assets. But fans of *Downton Abbey* might recall Lord Grantham criticising nearby estates for 'chipping away at your land until there's nothing viable left'.

Meanwhile, switching TV channels, the business guru Alex Polizzi declares, 'The reason big companies get bigger and more successful is because they strategise.' The same is true for countries. Without long-term strategies they risk floundering, outmanoeuvred by competitors and global markets.

The first rule of economics is that the finances of nations don't operate like a household budget. Britain puts great store in global free-market economics, something we explore in Part 1, but one of the ironies of the free market is that some of its staunchest supporters are those who profit by rigging and hindering its workings. Rather than winning new markets, large companies here perhaps prefer an inward-looking 'toll-booth economy' in which they capture essential services – such as water, energy, trains – and replace the market with state-endorsed monopolies, charging extraordinary fees that we have to pay.

Politics

In Part 2 we strip politics bare. Groucho Marx quipped, 'Politics is the art of looking for trouble, finding it everywhere, diagnosing it incorrectly and applying the wrong remedies.' Peter Hitchins regards it as 'a mild form of mental illness', referring to politicians as the 'inmates of the political asylum'. This may seem harsh, but it chimes with the public mood. We might at least agree with George Orwell, who characterised this country as 'a family with the wrong members in control'.

Many people feel that Westminster politics is little more than a party game, with MPs squabbling over how to spend diminishing

© Tupungato / Shutterstock.com

amounts of (largely borrowed) money. Are politicians no more than rogue traders who went to a good school? Certainly, most of those at the top of politics are comfortably off: should their schemes fail, they will never feel the draught personally.

Political initiatives seem to largely consist of debating in the media what 'message' to 'communicate' to win round voters – what to say rather than what to do. There seems little interest in formulating intelligent strategies as to how Britain might generate prosperity. This may explain why so many voters feel disenchanted.

Yet out of mass disenchantment, something new is rising in British politics – a revolt against established parties, increasingly despised as the 'Westminster elite'. For now they stagger on, kept alive by a voting system designed to bar newcomers. Voters have concerns about key issues, such as job security, low wages, the NHS and decent schools. Many have to grapple with pressures on services brought about by austerity and immigration. Running the country is about pulling the right levers. Yet no one seems quite sure which levers to pull, reacting with panic rather than thinking things through properly. This is a recipe for failure, yet rarely are those in power held to account.

Politics needs to offer a belief that it can improve our lives. But can the old parties adapt to the new environment, rather than clinging on until they are unseated through mass voter dissatisfaction or social unrest?

Society

This country has long believed that hard work and talent can take you anywhere. Yet it is harder now than at any time in living memory to climb the ladder. Conversely, it's rare for the very rich to slip down. In the UK, more than in most advanced economies, if you're born poor you stay poor.

No matter how gifted, a young person's prospects increasingly depend on what family they're born into. For many, wages have fallen, work is more insecure and a house is the stuff of dreams. Over the past 30 years competition between businesses at national and international level has been passed down as competition between individual workers. In Part 3 we look at what can be done to bring unity again.

Declining fortunes

Even today the UK punches above its weight. In old atlases about a quarter of the globe was coloured pink. As the world's only superpower Britain commanded the greatest empire in history. But two world wars in the 20th century virtually bankrupted the country. In the post-war period the empire's member states matured, with power gradually devolving, in most cases without a war of independence. Most of these new nations today participate in the Commonwealth. Meanwhile the US was expanding its influence, now joined by China.

By the end of the 1940s Britain was 'a country which had run out of money; a country whose achievements were vast and largely in the past, and whose present was one of being in hock to the Americans for ever more' (to quote author Nigel Fountain), with mountainous debts from the Second World War. But Britain was years ahead in technologies such as jet engines, computing, aerospace and nuclear power, and its manufacturing exports generated foreign currency. Government drove the national resurgence and established the NHS and the welfare state. In the 1970s, despite major Commonwealth trading partners like Canada, Australia and New Zealand, Britain decided that it could only retain influence on the world stage as part of the Common Market (today's EU).

Today Britain is in slow decline. In 2014, as the Chinese premier Li Keqiang and his wife began their state visit with the Queen at

Over the last 30 years or so, power at the top has shifted. Some groups have got their hands on greater wealth, prestige and influence, others have lost out. Briefly, here's what's up and what's down:

- **Going up** The rising powers include the prime minister, the Treasury and the City. The media, advertising, lobbyists and PR firms are all more powerful, as are bankers, multinational corporations, secretive hedge funds and private equity houses. As government has become more dependent on private funding and party donations, a new kind of establishment has taken power. Today, media-savvy masters of the free market and 'Branson-omics' have taken over from the old aristocracy and squirearchy. Lobbyists hawk political friendships for profit, offering wealthy clients access to those in power. But with greater value placed on profit and less on public service, this new elite is united by little more than a desire for personal enrichment.
- **Going down** The ideal of the understated British gentleman has disappeared (although there remains a lingering admiration in public life for qualities like decency, modesty and self-control). The old nobility have mostly lost their seats in the Lords. The old order – the landed gentry and colonels, with a sprinkling of industrialists and academics – have been put out to grass. Parliament and Cabinet have been marginalised. Archbishops and clergy have slipped down the charts along with once-powerful institutions such as the monarchy and universities. Trade unions and the public sector are smaller. Nationalised industries have almost disappeared. Home-grown industrialists are thinner on the ground; former national champions like Cadbury, Rolls-Royce Motor Cars, ICI, EMI, Jaguar Land Rover, GEC and Rowntree have either been broken up or sold to foreign corporations.
- **Respect** Those retaining the public's trust include the armed forces, doctors, judges, barristers, professors, teachers and civil servants. Conversely, trust in MPs, bankers, corporate CEOs, tabloid journalists and energy companies has plummeted.

Windsor Castle, the official Chinese newspaper *The Global Times* took a swipe at Britain saying, 'A rising country such as China should understand the embarrassment of an old declining empire which resorts to eccentric acts to hide its embarrassment.'

The visit confirmed which nation was in the ascendant. Contracts were signed allowing Chinese firms to own and operate a Chinese-designed nuclear power station and to build and operate high-speed rail lines in Britain, despite their mixed safety record. Prime Minister Cameron proudly declared, 'Britain is playing a part in the rise of China.'

Website

Can't get enough politics and economics? The website for this book – www.howtorunbritain.com – has useful additional content and some interesting links, including source material behind the facts and figures quoted here. You can even download some of the unabridged text, prior to its editing. It's also worth noting that the four authors of this book don't necessarily agree with every word written by their bedfellows. (It's that kind of subject.) If all else fails, let's just blame the government!

ECONOMICS

Chapter 1

WHAT'S SO IMPORTANT ABOUT ECONOMICS?

Not so long ago, we believed in the future of Britain. Outpourings of technical genius reassured us that the UK was ahead of its rivals. Many of the world's coolest bands, fashions and films were home-grown. James Bond drove the world's most desirable car – not a Ferrari but an Aston Martin DB5. Britons routinely chalked up international sporting victories and broke records on land, sea and air.

But underpinning our faith in tomorrow was the belief that younger generations would be better off than their parents, and so would their children. With free higher education and plentiful well-paid jobs, the future was bright. And what made all this possible was the economy.

Today our economic faith has evaporated. What went wrong, and how do we fix it?

The economy

At the heart of any successful economy is its ability to produce goods and services. But large developed economies like the UK also have knowledge and investment from centuries of hard work: for example, our roads, railways and energy networks were built at huge expense and still benefit us today.

But economies can rear up and bite their supposed masters – the politicians and economists. One reason the economy sometimes appears to have a mind of its own is that we live in a 'market society', dependent on millions of decisions made by individual citizens. This means the supply and demand of most things, from cars to Cornish pasties, determines movements in prices. It also helps to determine 'who gets what' – or as economists put it, how we distribute society's resources.

However, we don't live in a pure market economy. The government supplies massive services, such as the NHS, defence and state education, and it buys huge amounts of our resources. The

TWO BIG LEVERS – FISCAL AND MONETARY

The control panel that government ministers sit in front of has two main economic policy levers:

- **Fiscal policy** There are two main controls here: taxes and spending. Depending whether government wants to speed up or slow down the economy, it imposes more or less taxation and boosts or cuts its spending. Higher taxes and lower government spending suck money out: useful if inflation is pushing up prices. Lower taxes and higher spending pumps up demand, a good way to ease recession.
- **Monetary policy** The lever marked 'Interest Rates' particularly matters to people with mortgages or savings. This isn't the only lever to influence how we spend or save, but it's the one that has mattered most. In recent years interest rates have been used by the Bank of England to try to control inflation – which has been targetted at a comfortable 2% since 1997. We look at the dangers of inflation – rocketing prices – on page 27.

There is a third lever, monetary activism, that for many years was labelled Do Not Touch. This has recently been pulled hard. The most prominent example of monetary activism has been Quantitative Easing (QE): what we might call printing money (see page 28). Following the 2008 crash and the subsequent recession, this has flooded the system with cash in a bid to get everyone spending.

Governments can drive with more than one hand. The two main levers – fiscal and monetary policy – have been used in tandem to target inflation and unemployment. Since the 1980s, however, governments have been less active in economic management, perhaps conscious of past errors at the controls. But the 2007–8 crash required a major emergency response with tools such as QE.

state also sets the laws and regulations, allowing for contracts and quality standards and establishing ownership.

The national tool box

Governments have levers for managing the economy: how skilled politicians are at deploying them is a matter of debate. Governments extract money in the form of tax. They adjust interest rates – to boost the economy by controlling demand for credit, or to rein it in if it starts to get too excitable. Sometimes they try to influence the value of the currency (so with any luck your holiday money might stretch a little further).

Money collected by the taxman might be used to redistribute wealth within society or to invest where the market can't or won't – such as major infrastructure projects like rail, road and sewers.

Where we work

Our economy is heavily focused on services – far more than our major competitors. We make most of our money from activities that don't involve either making stuff (manufacturing) or 'primary industries' like agriculture or mining. This is how Britain earns its living:

- **Services** A whopping 80% of the economy, employing more than 8 out of every 10 people in work.
- **Manufacturing** This has steadily fallen to less than 10% today
- **Raw materials production** Things like mining: 5%
- **Construction** Around 6%
- **Agriculture** Just 1% of the economy, down from 6% in 1948, employing around 1% of the workforce.
- **Government spending** Producing 19% of added value. The public sector employs around 5.4 million people, down a million from 2008 (partly reflecting Royal Mail posties who moved into the private sector with the ongoing privatisation).

The risk takers

Private businesses are the legal structures through which most work is organised. The limited company was a British invention – one that paved the way for our worldwide supremacy. A company has a defined ownership, inspiring confidence in those who deal with it. But it's the concept of 'limited liability' that allows owners to take risks, since they are personally protected against loss. (There are other forms of ownership, such as partnerships, where this limited liability does not hold.) The ability to take risks is key to economic success because growth depends on investing.

Running the economy

There are a number of bodies within (or accountable to) government with hands on the controls.

- **The Treasury** At the centre of the nation's economic management is HM Treasury. This institution dates back to the 12th century when it managed the monarch's treasure. Today it has around 1,000 staff. Under the Chancellor of the Exchequer, it controls taxing and spending – the government's 'fiscal policy'. Criticisms include that it's too active, too indolent, or both. Recently Chancellor George Osborne has launched the Office for Budget Responsibility to ensure that government economic

NUMBER CRUNCHING

How many people work in Britain?

Around 30.6 million. Approximately 2 million people are classified as unemployed, but around 9.6 million are of working age and not actively seeking work – perhaps because they can afford not to, or they've given up, are students or they duck and dive under the state radar.

How many firms are there?

2.26 million firms are registered for VAT, and the number has risen steadily since 2008. Most are very small and 20% are one-man-bands. Partnerships account for another 10%. Three-quarters employ fewer than five people. That leaves a miniscule 0.4%, less than 10,000 firms, employing more than 250 staff.

forecasts were independent, removing the temptation for politicians to massage figures.

- **The Bank of England** 'The Old Lady of Threadneedle Street' was established in 1690 to oversee loans to government, mostly to finance wars with France. The Bank gradually transformed into one of the first central banks, with exclusive rights to issue coinage and to act as a 'lender of last resort' to other private lenders. This latter role is particularly important, since banks are prone to collapse and a hefty backstop is necessary if trust in the banking system is to be maintained.

As the UK's central bank, the Bank of England's priority is the security of the banking system. But it plays a big part in influencing how money circulates. Traditionally, this has been achieved by moving interest rates. But since 2008 the Bank of England has employed devices such as the £375 billion Quantitative Easing programme, and has taken a more direct role in the oversight of the financial system, together with the new Prudential Regulation Authority and the Financial Conduct Authority who report back to it.

Although the Bank is publicly owned it's not an arm of the Treasury, since former chancellor Gordon Brown made it independent in 1997. The Bank works largely through the Monetary Policy Committee (MPC), a panel appointed by the

From the end of the 1940s to the early 1970s, Britain enjoyed unprecedented prosperity – as did much of the developed world. That growth meant improvements for most people including full employment, mass consumption, a welfare state and the NHS. The poverty and inequality that had scarred the country over previous decades was steadily eased. By 1957, a Conservative prime minister, Harold Macmillan, could claim that most of us had 'never had it so good'. How did Britain achieve this?

- **'Economic miracles'** occurred in the defeated countries of Germany, Italy and Japan – the latter averaging an eye-watering 9% annual growth from 1953 to 1965, and then a stellar 8% through to the mid-1970s. This provided a market for British exports.
- **Technological advances** such as jet engines, nuclear power, aerospace, radar, computers – many pioneered during and before the war – became widespread. In most of them Britain was a leader.
- **Government was trusted** (it had just helped to win the war) and this helped to legitimise economic decision-making. Voter turnout at elections has never regained such dizzy heights.

- **The redistribution of wealth** through taxes and spending – providing ordinary people with decent medical care, housing and jobs – took the sting from lingering class conflict over the dire poverty of the interwar years.
- **Economic stability** was underpinned by the capacity of the United States to sustain both an enormous arms expenditure and to support the world monetary system via the dollar's link to gold.

Heading south

It was too good to last. The UK was hit by economic crises from the end of the 1960s. The era of rapid growth was mired in political and economic conflict. Keynesian techniques of economic management were by the mid-1970s found wanting in both the US and the UK. Governments across the world switched tack, some under IMF pressure, stressing the importance of low taxes and reduced public spending. Neoliberalism demanded a limited role for the government and greater freedom for the owners of firms and assets to behave as they wished. Yet the dynamism and confidence of the post-war period has never been recaptured.

governor (who is appointed by the chancellor) with a remit to set interest rates – the 'base rate' – at a level that steers the economy to the government's inflation target.
- **HM Revenue and Customs** Formed from the merger of the Inland Revenue with Customs & Excise – the nation's internal tax people combining with those whose focus is on external revenues. HMRC collects taxes and comes under the wing of the Treasury. Taxes provide income to government, but they're also used to influence behaviour – such as the excise duty on cigarettes. More recently, HMRC has adopted some social security functions through its operation of the tax credits system, beefing up the earnings of those on low incomes.
- **The Department for Business, Innovation and Skills** The BIS is the department for economic growth – funding university and higher education, supporting innovation (such as publicly funded research) and giving general 'support for enterprise'.
- **International organisations** These range from purely reporting institutions, such as the OECD, to those that directly influence the economy, like the IMF. The biggest influence, thanks in part to its law-making powers, is the EU. These are discussed in more detail on page 114. The OECD (Organisation for Economic Co-operation and Development), based in Paris, has been described as the rich countries' club, being limited to 34 high-income economies. Founded to help oversee the post-war Marshall Plan to get Europe back on its feet, today it's a forum to share economic experiences. It publishes reliable data and is regarded as the West's leading economic think tank. It is notably independent: a 2014 report dismissed a core economic orthodoxy, that of 'trickle-down' economics. It found that the UK economy would have been more than 20% bigger had the gap between rich and poor not widened since the 1980s.
DEFINITION: 'Trickle down economics' suggests policies which promote the wealth of the already wealthy on the assumption that this affluence is shared with the rest of us by 'trickling down'. This has been one of the central planks of government economic policy

for the last 30 years. For example the 'non-domicile' tax rule allows around 120,000 super-rich foreign residents to legitimately avoid paying tax in Britain on income from overseas assets. However, renowned economists like Thomas Piketty and Ha-Joon Chang have found no evidence to substantiate whether 'trickle down' economics actually works in practice.

The British economy is odd, perhaps dangerously so. As we have seen, there's been a shift away from manufacturing and we are dominated by services – far more than most of our competitors. Ours is also an internationalised economy. It is the sixth largest exporter by value, but also the sixth largest importer. This international focus is particularly strong in financial services, with London vying with New York as the world's financial centre. The UK handles 42% of the $4 trillion traded daily on foreign exchange markets around the world. And Britain is more unequal than most developed economies, although in the 1970s we were one of the most equal.

There is another way

- **East Asia's 'tiger economies'** enjoyed rapid industrialisation with state support. Governments directed and subsidised entire new industries resulting in huge global corporations such as Samsung and Hyundai.
- **Germany** has a more consensual system in the workplace, with staff representatives on the boards of large companies. Germany is now the world's largest exporter.
- **Finland** transformed itself into a world-leading high-technology exporter through a government-led innovation strategy.

There are many other examples of state support bringing enormous dividends. There are real alternatives to the preferred option of most UK politicians – sitting on their hands.

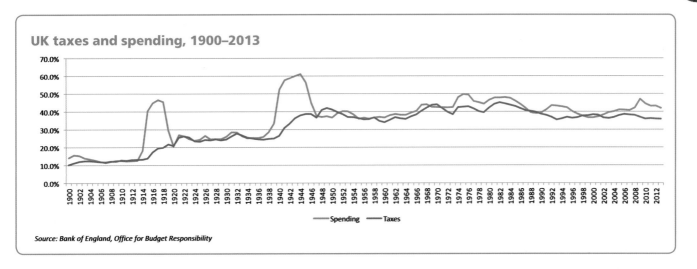

UK taxes and spending, 1900–2013

Source: Bank of England, Office for Budget Responsibility

— Spending   — Taxes

Tax

Twin weapons – tax and spending

The really high-profile role of government is its power to levy taxes. Tax is what pays for the government's activities, but the range of its activities has expanded hugely.

It's interesting to see how much money the government takes and how it is spent. The chart below shows taxes and spending as a share of the economy – of the Gross Domestic Product (GDP – see Chapter 2).

The two big blue spending blips on the graph point to one very obvious conclusion – wars are expensive (we're still paying for WW2). Since WW2, government spending has levelled. UK governments of any stripe have tended to spend around 40% of GDP. This is typical for a developed country. True, UK spending as a share of GDP has fallen since the 1970s, but governments in the OECD spend around 45% of GDP.

Since WW2 there have been three main periods when government spending has shot up, mirrored by taxes falling: recessions. This is the nightmare of governments paying out more in benefits (notably for unemployment) while taxes dry up. As a result, the fiscal deficit widens. But the period since the crash of 2008 looks like a break with the pattern we're used to.

Tax – where does it all go?

In 2013–14, the government took £722 billion in taxes. The pie chart below shows how this was spent.

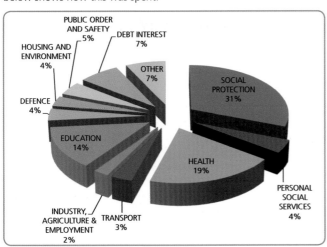

One expense leaps off the page: 'social protection' is by far the largest single item. What is it? Although it includes welfare payments, these only comprise a fraction of the £222 billion total. The largest item is pensions, accounting for 47% (£104 billion). Housing benefits are 12% (£26 billion), and payments for unemployment are just 2.2% (£4.9 billion). The big number includes 'transfer payments' – simply taking money from one group and giving it to another.

Which taxes rake in most money?

What are the biggest sources of revenue to support all this spending?

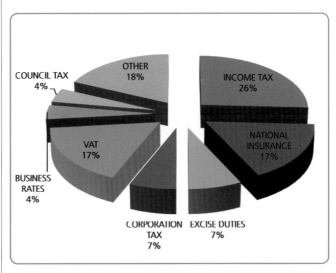

Income tax is the greatest single contribution. This is followed by that rather odd 'tax in disguise', National Insurance.

Who pays the most income tax – rich or poor? The largest contributions by value come from those with higher incomes: 25% of the total £167 billion in income tax revenue is coughed up by the richest 1%. However, the tax system hits the poorest hardest; they pay proportionally more tax out of their earnings. This is due to 'indirect' taxes, like VAT and excise duties, which tax us all at a flat rate. Prince or pauper, you pay 20% VAT on petrol (plus fuel duty); this might take a big chunk out of a low-paid carer's earnings, but bankers filling up their Porsches hardly notice it. The richest 10% contribute 34% of their income in taxes, while people in the middle (the 'median') pay 37% of their income in tax.

Chapter 2

THE BIG PICTURE

Looking down at Planet Earth from outer space reminds us that Britain is a small island in a global world. To try and understand how this big picture all fits together, economists wear 'special glasses' that help detect all the money, goods and services sloshing around. Welcome to the world of 'macro-economics'. Trying to take in an entire national economy in one enormous mouthful is a pretty ambitious task – one that's likely to lead to indigestion. But let's give it our best shot, Gaviscon at the ready.

To get some idea of how the UK economy works, we can think of it as a gigantic eBay. Every day the popular online marketplace handles millions of transactions by millions of eBayers, all free to act economically as they wish. Star ratings allow buyers and sellers to earn trust which, combined with a few house regulations, ensures that the system runs pretty smoothly. In a similar way, 65 million UK citizens interact with seven billion people across the world. But as well as the simple business of buying and selling, there are factors such as financial services, health care and retirement to consider – against a background of international competition.

All the trading we do (together with the laws and regulations to protect consumers) form markets. And markets can automatically allocate resources according to supply and demand: when things are in short supply, the price will increase. So decision-making is spread among millions of people, businesses and institutions, who are free to buy or work or do nothing at all.

GOOD CAPITALISM v. COWBOYS Inc

The tactics used by businesses to get our money include:
- **Excellence** The service or product is so good that customers want to come back, telling their friends and generating repeat business (e.g. Amazon, John Lewis, Bentley).
- **Trickery** Firms put traps in the small print of phone contracts, utility bills, airline bookings, bank accounts. Similarly, deliberately over-complex tariffs can trap users, for example through train fares which are higher for same-day travel, or higher charges for non-online customers, or websites that trick us with mandatory extras, or misleading supermarket labelling and confusing offers. Payday lenders have been accused of legalised exploitation of vulnerable customers.
- **Monopoly or market power** Customers faced with price rises sometimes have little choice but to pay – because there is no effective competition so all the providers might decide to raise their prices together. Our reluctance to switch providers may be due to our belief that they're each as bad as the rest. Cartels might collude to raise prices or to speculate in key futures markets, exacerbating price fluctuations in commodities such as oil, wheat, coffee and chocolate.
- **Abuse** Firms might resort to illegal activity, seeing possible fines as merely the price of doing business. These might include PPI mis-selling, banks rigging currency markets and utility providers switching off customers without consent. The supermarket horsemeat scandal resulted from long supply chains with ample scope for fraud.

Many of us, as consumers, have experienced all the above. But many politicians seem to think that excellence is inevitable if only regulation can be of a sufficiently light touch, with a cutting of red tape and a rolling back of the state. The problem is that excellence isn't easy – otherwise every transaction we make would be wonderful. Therefore, if legal loopholes allow it, lazy or incompetent operators may be drawn to making quicker profits by less honest means. Clearly someone needs to protect consumers from corrupt firms, while allowing the good ones to thrive. Prevention is better than learning lessons afterwards.

Sin taxes

We may not like some of the sharper practices, or unhealthy products, in the market, but clamping down isn't the only option. 'Sin taxes' can boost NHS funding, for example. As well as taxing tobacco and alcohol, cash could be generated by taxes on foods loaded with sugar and salt, since obesity is a large and growing burden on the NHS.

'THERE'S BEEN A SERIOUS BREAKDOWN IN FINANCIAL REGULATION'

With millions of people doing their own thing – buying, selling, working, investing – the economy is far too complex to be fully planned: there is no 'Fat Controller' behind the scenes. Of course a lot of it looks after itself. But this doesn't mean markets shouldn't be shaped. The more freedom people have, the more important it is for the market to be regulated. eBay's success depends on behind-the-scenes regulation that promotes trust, honest descriptions and prompt delivery and payment – and that chucks out dodgy members intent on abusing the rules. The trick is to channel the naked power of market forces so they work well for everyone.

Amazingly out of the fog of these millions of individual decisions an order emerges in a well-constructed market. Studying the economy is about making sense of this seeming chaos – trying to understand how the system fits together. And the best way to make sense of it is by following the money.

What is money?

Every market trade or deal is done for money (bar the odd small-scale swap). Work is done for money, and taxes are paid in money. Money itself is centralised: in this case the 'Fat Controllers' are the governor of the Bank of England, the Bank itself and the Treasury. For a modern economy to function, its money must be used and accepted by everyone, and so money needs to be controlled. We can't have just anyone printing £20 notes, for example. To understand how the rest of the economy operates, we need to poke our noses into other people's finances: what could be more fun?

There's more to life

Many of the things we value have nothing to do with money: love, country walks, freedom, the smell of autumn. We don't pay our family or our friends simply for being there. For economists, such 'non-market transactions' mess up the calculations about the economy. What is the value of a meal cooked at home from vegetables grown in your garden and served to your family? We don't know. Gross Domestic Product (GDP) is a measure of national income, but by counting only market transactions it ignores important things like environmental damage. In traditional economic theory, a tree cut down is worth more than a tree standing.

GDP also excludes unpaid work – such as housework or carework, which is essential for society; since this kind of work is often undertaken by women, it's not unreasonable to conclude that GDP is gender-biased.

Despite these inconvenient truths, the money-first approach is useful in two ways. First, it's easy to get a grip of. The monetary economy is so big you can't miss it: there are more hours devoted to working for money than just about any other activity. Second, the money economy provides a universe, a handy framework, that other activities can be seen in relation to. Money regulates pretty much everything, directly or indirectly. Even our leisure is structured around its demands. Because money allows us to put a price on just about everything, everything can be dragged into its orbit. Everything can be a commodity. Which in some ways rather misses the point. The money-dominated world of GDP tells us next to nothing about what really matters in people's lives – happiness.

The story of money

For something so central to our lives and societies, money is poorly understood – not least by economists. The general consensus is that money came about because the alternative – swapping and bartering – is so awkward. It would take a long time to find someone who would swap a room for the night in exchange for this book. Or suppose I want some bacon and have a hen to swap, in a 'barter economy' I would need to find someone who not only wanted my hen, but also had some bacon to exchange. So money facilitated trade. Instead of waiting for your wants to coincide with someone else's it's simpler to swap a token.

DOWNFALL

One five-letter word underpins all successful economies: trust. If people trust each other they are more likely to trade, thereby generating economic growth.

Heightened levels of trust mean less need for rules, regulations and legal enforcement. And markets work efficiently; savers, for example, put their money into projects believing they will be fairly treated.

Banking depends on credit-worthiness ('credit' is derived from the Latin 'credere', meaning to trust or believe). Bankers were trusted pillars of the community, but the financial services industry has recently been mired in scandal, with some banks factoring the probability of relatively low regulatory fines as a cost of doing business.

Without trust the legal and moral anchors of markets erode. In societies where economic development is slow, the problem is often corruption and a lack of trust.

What happens when this lubricant of economic systems dries up?

- As people start to eye each other with suspicion, business activity slows. If suppliers fear they won't get paid, the result is empty shops and aircraft un-refuelled on the tarmac. Sellers demand pre-payment, buyers are wary. As fears grow, the incentive to cheat rises, reducing trust still further. Mistrust leads creditors to demand their money, suspecting that debtors may soon lose the ability to pay.
- Good loans turn bad. Money flees to havens abroad. The haves and have-nots fight over the diminishing spoils, leading to fear rather than co-operation.
- Government's ability to fix the economy gets harder as global markets no longer trust a tottering nation. Few now trust the political class.
- Bank runs cause instability. Cash machines stop working.
- Reforms seem to reward some at the expense of others. Rather than binding society together, they tear it apart, leading to the law of the jungle.
- The army is on the streets.

Moral

As citizens we should value politicians who espouse honesty and integrity rather than spin and profiteering. We might insist on government transparency and effective regulation to restore trust and stamp out market abuse.

This all makes sense, except that money actually came about not as currency but as a record of debts and as a way to settle them – in effect 'putting it on the slate'. In ancient agricultural societies, exchanging food, goods and services was done on credit. Early versions of money probably existed in the form of a number chalked up on an ancient 'overdraft' long before coins and notes were invented. So traders didn't invent money: bankers got there first!

Starting as an ancient record of debt, money also became a store of wealth and power and a means of making payments – to buy things, pay taxes, settle debts. In fact fulfilling these three functions is the very definition of money.

In gold we trust

For much of history, coins had an intrinsic value, being made of precious metals such as silver or gold. (Silver was only removed from British coins in 1947; before 1920 they were 92.3% silver, then 50%.) But the notes and coins in our pockets today are intrinsically worthless. Instead money depends on trust: we trust, and we believe that so do others. If this belief collapses, so will the financial system – bringing hyperinflation like that suffered by Germany in the 1920s or Zimbabwe today.

We can see trust at work on a £5 note. In flowery writing, the governor of the Bank of England declares 'I promise to pay the bearer on demand the sum of five pounds'. So although this note is an *asset* for you – since it's your money and you can make a payment of £5 with it – it is a *liability* for the Bank of England, because they potentially have to cough up if someone queries its value. In other words, it is what bankers call a 'financial instrument' – an asset for one person, a liability for another, as on a company balance sheet. If we trust that the Bank of England will not collapse, this cash can be accepted as payment – in effect it's 'as safe as the Bank of England' (if not 'as good as gold').

Cashless society

Notes and coins only comprise a fraction of the money in our economy. Around 97% of the money in the UK is in the form of bank deposits – money in your bank account. This is different from notes and coins, although we use it in the same way when we make a payment using a debit card or cheque. Although the funds in our bank account are still our assets, the liability is no longer the Bank of England's: it's the high street bank or building society that has to 'promise to pay'. And, rather unsettlingly, money in this form isn't yours: it's 'your' bank account, but the money belongs to the bank. By opening a bank account and paying money into it we are lending the bank our money, at our own risk. Left to the market, such seemingly mundane actions can have troubling consequences.

The banking trick (or treat)

As we saw with Northern Rock in 2007, if customers no longer trust a bank then panic sets in – causing a run and putting the bank at risk of collapse. Since banks depend on trust and trust can evaporate in an instant, perhaps sparked by a malevolent rumour, banks are always at risk of collapse. This is why the firm hand of the nation's central bank matters so much. It was one of the deciding factors in the Scottish referendum, where worries about the pound trumped many folk's desire to be rid of Tory rule.

It seems crazy that banks are central to the nation's economy and yet at such high risk; to maintain trust therefore takes a huge backstop. Without the reassurance of big government to support

banks, there is a danger of panics and bank failures. However, with the Bank of England as a guardian of the UK banking system, bankers might be tempted to take advantage of the fact that the government will bail them out.

Losing confidence

Bank runs are dangerous because the balance that modern, commercial banks hold day-to-day in their deposit accounts is far greater than the amount they hold in cash. Normally this doesn't matter because not all customers want to withdraw money at the same time. However, if there is a fear the bank might collapse, everyone wants to withdraw their money to safeguard their savings. A run can thus become self-fulfilling: after a few large withdrawals, a bank's reserves will have disappeared, leading to its collapse. Fortunately, because such runs are based on perception, they can be halted rapidly.

Following a BBC report in September 2007, many Northern Rock depositors believed that it might fail to meet their claims, and they rushed to withdraw cash. Queues formed outside branches in the first bank run in the UK since 1866. But swift intervention by the government, reassuring savers their deposits would be guaranteed by the state, ended the panic and prevented the run spreading to other banks – even if, by that point, Northern Rock was a dead duck. To prevent runs a government-backed 'deposit guarantee' is in place. This makes the Financial Conduct Authority responsible for guaranteeing all deposits held in banks up to a particular value (currently £85,000 per person per bank). This is a subsidy from the taxpayer to the banking sector – because banks are deemed too big to be allowed to fail.

But banks today do more than take deposits and make loans. They sit at the centre of global finance – of which the UK's financial industry is an important part. We look at the scary implications of this on page 30.

WHAT DO BANKS DO?

We tend to think of banks as like a big piggybank. Some people put their money in, some people take their money out, and sometimes people borrow money (and usually repay it). Of course these days most transactions are electronic, with no physical cash changing hands. But we might imagine that behind the online banking façade somewhere there must be vaults full of money, perhaps guarded by the Bank of England itself.

The reality is far more peculiar. Banks are uniquely privileged institutions. As we have seen, cash is largely valueless in itself. We only regard notes and coins, and our electronic bank accounts, as valuable because of our trust in the system. Banks came about because someone figured out how to exploit this trust. Banking in Europe developed from goldsmiths' shops. They were trusted to take and store gold and savings (for a fee), and to use these deposits to lend money.

But as they expanded their money-lending, the alchemy of banking became clear – that actual savings were not necessary to make loans. As long as the goldsmiths' promises were accepted, they could lend more than they held. This was known as 'fractional reserve banking', where reserves (a bank's holding of money) would only need to be a fraction of total lending.

The system worked as long as people trusted it – and didn't take all their gold back at once. If they did not trust the system, savers would demand their money and the bank would collapse.

Banking today stretches this principle further. Modern banks create money on demand, without the need for large reserves of cash on the premises. They can do this because as long as assets and liabilities on a balance sheet match each other, an institution will be officially solvent – it can meet all the demands made on it for payment.

When a modern bank makes a loan, it does two things simultaneously. On one side it creates an asset: the loan is a 'promise to repay' the money, with interest, back to the bank. On the other, it creates a liability: the new sum of money, created out of nothing, is placed in the borrower's account. As the two sides balance each other out, the bank will be solvent.

On this basis, banks have hugely expanded their lending in recent decades. But as we know this ended with the 2007–8 crisis because some people the banks lent money to could not repay. This dragged the entire financial system into crisis.

HOW INCOME FLOWS

Each pound you spend is a pound earned by someone else. Money flows around the economy through spending decisions that result in earnings. Sounds simple doesn't it? But this insight into the workings of the economy was critical to the great economist John Maynard Keynes. He labelled this procession of purchases and sales the 'circular flow of income' (although other economists, including Karl Marx, had the same idea).

Things are more complex because not everyone immediately spends the money they've just earned. They might park some in a savings account – which takes it out of the 'circular flow'. Or they might spend it on goods and services from abroad. Or a business might send its money overseas to avoid paying taxes here.

There are many ways that revenue can leak from the local or national flow. And these leaks make economic management far harder – like keeping a punctured tyre inflated while the car's moving.

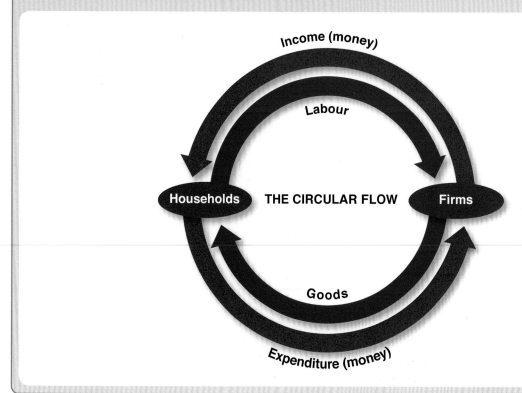

Splashing the cash – buying and spending

Money flows around the system as different demands for payment are created and met, rather like Toytown cash swilling around a Monopoly board. One day we get paid, the next we might treat ourselves by spending on goodies, or on essentials like food and rent, or to repay our debts. Debts are a claim on our future income made by others, usually charging interest, like credit cards or payday loans.

Should there be cash left over we might save it, which removes the money from circulation. But what if too many people decide to save? When people aren't buying the economy slows, or even slips into recession. Too much saving is bad – something economists label 'the paradox of thrift'.

Money, then, has a dual nature: it can be spent as a 'flow of payments' or it can be squirreled away as savings. But imagine how this would look if you could take a step back and watch millions of people spraying money around or building up their savings – it would reveal how the economy as a whole functions, the flow of income.

Who gets what?

So if we imagine money flowing around the economy in a circle, where is the start and finish? Answer: we can dive in anywhere, make a start at any point, and still see how the economy works.

There are two different actions in the circular flow: buying and selling. So we could start by looking at how the economy operates from the point of view of people who are buying – or perhaps from the seller's perspective. These are just two different ways of looking at the same thing. This principle is built into official statistics.

Measuring economic muscle

Gross Domestic Product (GDP) is the number that depicts a nation's economic muscle. It attempts to sum up everything in the economy. It's usually calculated by adding up the value of everything bought and the value of everything sold. These two values – minus (in both cases) the costs of producing them – should come to the same thing. You can't buy more than is sold and you can't sell more than is bought.

This raises a key question: who gets what in our economy? And, for that matter, who contributes what? By and large, we want to see an economy operate on fair principles, rather than being exploitative. As we'll see later, blatant unfairness can also have economic consequences.

Who ate the pie?

Sticking with the image of the economy as a pie, imagine a bunch of hungry people who want to bake and divide the pie among themselves. These people might have contributed different amounts of ingredients. There's no rule saying that the biggest slices should go to those who contributed the most. Perhaps someone has contributed very little because they're too ill or old to get to

the shops. Someone else might have brought loads of stuff because they've inherited a well-stocked garden from their parents.

Similarly, in the real economy, the size of the slices is determined by the claims of ownership of different people and institutions. Their claims may have very little relationship to their economic contribution.

GDP

As we've seen already in Chapter 1, the economy divides into different activities. Most of Britain's output is from the services sector. Manufacturing ('primary production') makes up a relatively small part. Of the total output, measured as GDP, 65% is consumed by households. Another 21% is consumed in services provided by

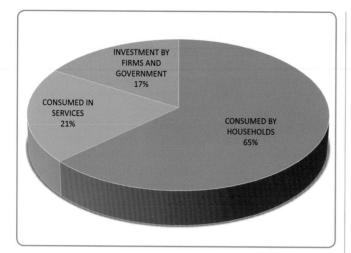

Pie chart:
- INVESTMENT BY FIRMS AND GOVERNMENT 17%
- CONSUMED IN SERVICES 21%
- CONSUMED BY HOUSEHOLDS 65%

government (both local and national) – everything from cleaning the streets to running the NHS. Total investment by firms and government is 17%.

Sharp-eyed readers may be scratching their heads because the total comes to more than 100%. There's a clue in the name 'GDP': it's the Gross *Domestic* Product. It's about what the national economy does inside our borders; but of course a national economy also trades with the rest of the world. And by doing this, the UK can consume more than it produces domestically. Later on we'll look at some of the problems this causes.

Corn today or corn tomorrow?

We know what happens to the goods and services we consume (or which the government consumes on our behalf, such as defence). Once we've eaten the food, gone to the cinema, driven the car till it's running on empty – that's pretty much it. The stuff we bought has been used up. It plays no immediate further part in the monetary economy. Consumption of any sort has this slightly sad quality of finality, even where consuming it has other consequences: driving the car uses up fuel – but it also requires insurance and the exhaust pollutes the air.

Postponing pleasure

Unlike consumption, where perhaps you might gobble something up right now, you might instead choose to put money aside for a rainy day. Investment is special because it is intended to have longer-term economic consequences. By denying yourself pleasure now, you hope to get even juicier goodies in the future: a return on the investment. Or perhaps we can foresee a time when we will be too old to work, and therefore need to put something aside to tide us over.

By placing some of your money aside, it should be possible to reward yourself by receiving more back in future, or to use it to generate income payments over a period of time. There's a sort of magic to investing; it doesn't exactly make money grow on trees, but it can make economic growth happen. So millions of people deciding to invest or not invest is critical to the whole economy.

Imagine a society that has only a single product: corn. You've got two options with corn. It can be eaten today, or planted to grow more in the future. Clearly on one level it's desirable to eat

today, but if all the corn is consumed today, none can be planted. We will eventually starve. So a balance needs to be struck between consumption today and consumption in the future.

As with corn, so with money. As a nation we allocate our resources between consumption today and investment for the future. But only about 17% of the British GDP is saved. This makes us a 'low-investment economy', especially compared to fast-growing middle-income countries like China, where investment savings top 40%. But we're even a low-investment economy relative to the French and Germans, and have been for at least a century. This has consequences for the kind of economy and society we live in. See Chapter 5.

There is another complication. Although we can measure the country's total (aggregate) investment as a share of GDP, much depends on millions of citizens deciding separately whether to save or spend. We don't all meet up as a nation and decide how we intend to invest. Also, the reasons people choose to invest for the years ahead – their motivation for postponing 'jam until tomorrow' – is more sophisticated than a simple desire to eat in the future. People invest because they want to get something back in the years ahead, and their decision to invest will be driven by how much they expect those future returns to be. However, being prudent isn't without its risks: the company we invest in might go bust or the returns promised by the sharp-suited salesman might disappear.

Where best to invest?
- **Equity** Stocks and shares are a claim of direct ownership (*eg* owning a small 'share' of a listed company). Or you might own a property, perhaps with some borrowed mortgage money secured on it.
- **Debt** You might lend money, perhaps by putting it in a building society savings account, in return for getting paid interest.
- **Partnership** Businesses can adopt different legal structures, for example where partners own part of the firm.

K.J.Lamb

'HERE'S A LITTLE SOMETHING FOR YOU TO PUT TOWARDS YOUR FUTURE DEBTS '

Depending on how these various investments ('claims on ownership') pan out, the returns they generate will be paid to you in different ways, for example as dividends, interest payments, or assets going up in value and generating a capital gain.

Unlike commodities – the stuff we buy and then consume (so they play no further part in the economy) – investment plays a part in the future, for good or ill. If we think back to the national pie, where people were either taking slices or contributing ingredients, we said that both should add up to the same thing. There can't be more taken out of the pie than has been put in (allowing for the balance of foreign trade). Yet investment seems to break this rule. It is a slice from the pie, and yet can also act as a future ingredient. It's as if the investors were taking a slice from the pie now, but instead of eating it they use it as an ingredient in a new pie.

But there's something we've overlooked: who provides the pie dish? Suppose there's only one available, owned by someone in town. Although it won't cost them anything to lend us their pie dish, they might want to charge something: they could argue it's their contribution. So we could pay them back with a slice, even if they have contributed no ingredients as such. Similarly the person who originally patented the delicious recipe might demand a royalty for every pie that's made in future.

The secret ingredient

Let's leave pies for a moment. In the real economy, investment as an 'ingredient' is made in the form of capital. This might comprise things like machinery and buildings, or infrastructure such as roads. Basically it's the stuff that's not entirely used up during economic activities. It's a fixed part of the process that's still there after everyone's gone home. It can also take less tangible forms, such as patents and trademarks (intellectual property). Despite the fact that it doesn't get used up too quickly, capital can still be regarded as an ingredient. But because it lasts over time, it has future economic consequences. Once capital is brought into the mix, something is left over afterwards. The office remains standing after all the workers have gone home – or even if they are all made redundant.

The important idea here is that because capital isn't wholly used up over time, it grants the owner a claim against what the economy produces in future – in the form of returns on that capital. These might appear as share dividends or as 'capital gains', such as rising share prices, or perhaps a house you rent out has gone up in value. You might receive interest payments where you've saved money, or in the form of a savings bond. By bringing capital into the process, investors get a particular kind of future return paid back to them based on ownership.

Raw materials

To make the economy function, you need more than just capital. You need people to work in offices, design things, promote things, drive lorries and operate machinery. We've seen how capital gets paid for its contribution. Labour, too, is paid for its services through wages or (if you're middle class) a salary. So far we've got the factory and machinery (capital), and the people to make it all work (labour), but there's still one thing missing: raw materials such as eggs and flour, steel and energy. Raw materials have a short life because participating in the work uses them up. And the labour you might contribute as an employee is also used up. If you work for eight hours on Monday that time has gone. Capital is long-lasting, though it doesn't last forever: the van that's used to deliver the sandwiches your business makes will wear out, a problem known as depreciation.

But something else is going on here. Economies aren't all about money. They also have a physical existence. The way money swishes around the economy is also influenced by who has ownership of the economic processes that make the economy work. Money makes the economic processes of the world go round. But it is not the same thing as those processes.

There are three ways money facilitates trade and economic processes:

- **As a price tag** – a measure of the relative value of stuff
- **As a store of wealth and power** – it doesn't have a shelf life, or go mouldy
- **As a handy means of payment** – making it easier to sell what you produce and to buy materials.

Rising inequality and unproductive wealth

The national pie isn't distributed evenly. Let's see how the size of the slices differs between those who sell their labour (most of us), and those who own capital and buy labour.

It might not seem fair that a person who hasn't contributed work gets a share of the output, just because they're lucky enough to own capital. But if we save a few quid of our own and invest our money

wisely we hope it will produce a money return without us having to do anything productive.

Capital ownership has changed a lot over the years – see graph. Today it is strongly concentrated in a few well-manicured hands. Most people own few assets beyond their house: few of us own shares, even indirectly through a pension fund. Even home ownership is currently falling. Net housing wealth (the value of the house minus the value of the mortgage) is around £27,000 for the median UK household. For the poorest 30% it's zero; for the top 1% it's £1.2 million. But, as we shall see in a minute, owning a house to live in isn't the same as owning 'productive capital'.

The evidence points towards an increase in inequality in recent decades (see Thomas Piketty's bestselling book *Capital in the Twenty-First Century*). Wealth and therefore power is becoming concentrated in fewer hands. The UK has moved from being one of the most equal countries in western Europe in the 1970s to about the most unequal today – to the point where the 12 richest families hold the same wealth as half the population.

Piketty claims that, left to its own devices, there is an inbuilt bias in capitalism towards rising inequality. He argues that some assets in the economy produce a higher rate of return than the rate the economy overall grows. If owners of wealth get a higher rate of return than the rate of economic growth then those who don't own many assets (most of us) will be squeezed. Those who sell their labour are tied (at best) to the general rate of growth, not the rate of return on assets. Those holding key assets will therefore grab a greater and greater share of the pie, as has happened over the last 200 years or so, with the exception of the so-called golden years of capitalism from around 1945 to 1980.

Piketty may be the 21st century's rock star economist, but Winston Churchill beat him to it, memorably pointing out, 'The inherent vice of capitalism is the unequal sharing of blessings.' This does not mean we should dispense with capitalism. We would not chop down an apple tree simply because, although it was good at producing apples, it did not distribute them appropriately.

And *wealth* is not the same thing as *capital*. You need not have contributed work to get paid a share of economic output in the form of money. For example, we need houses to live in but

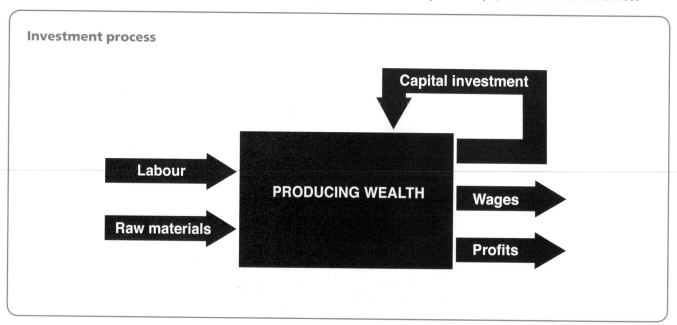

Investment process

Capital investment

Labour

Raw materials

PRODUCING WEALTH

Wages

Profits

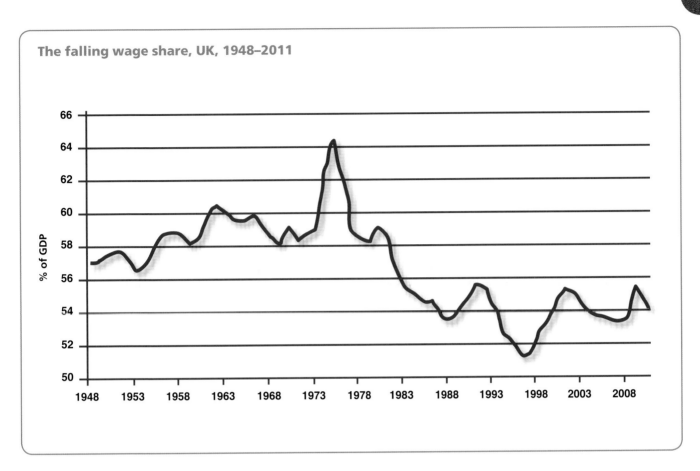

The falling wage share, UK, 1948–2011

(y-axis: % of GDP)

the buildings don't enter into any sort of production process. We consume housing by living in a home, so it counts as a 'consumer good'. But housing can also be used in another way: as a source of wealth. As the owner of a property you could earn an income from it by renting it out. Or it may go up in value, earning you a capital gain.

Some other goods can similarly be switched between uses. A computer used for games counts as a 'consumer good'. But the same computer used in a business would become a 'capital good'. What matters is not the thing itself, but the way it's used. Later we'll look at the implications of seemingly unproductive activities producing financial returns for people.

Sharing

The output of Britain's economy is shared among different groups. What they get depends on what claims of ownership they hold. Consumption is a one-off thing, with nothing left over afterwards. You eat a sandwich and it's gone. Similarly, raw materials and labour are used up in making stuff (with labour it's the time spent doing the job). But capital hangs around – lasting a long time. This allows its owners to make a special claim to get a greater share of the fruits of the economy.

Inflation

When we hear about 'runaway inflation' it tends to be in the context of house prices. Galloping property values are generally welcomed by the media and homeowners since everyone with a stake in the game starts to feel richer. When homes are rising in value by a larger

amount than most people can earn in a job, it induces a general feel-good factor – for those lucky enough to own property

But there is a darker side to inflation, one that's highly destructive. The Germans are especially sensitive about such risks since social collapse brought on by hyper-inflation in the 1920s paved the way for Nazism. Crazy tales abound of small purchases, such as a coffee, requiring a wheelbarrow of cash.

In Britain in the 1970s prices in the shops jumped week to week, peaking at an alarming 25% per annum in 1975. This precipitated waves of strikes as workers sought equally dramatic increases in wages to keep up.

But some quietly benefit from such conditions, since rising prices have the effect of shrinking debts. Suppose your mortgage is £100k but your house is only worth £90k: you live in fear of repossession and being overwhelmed by debt. If on the other hand your house rises in value to £200k, you're free to move house or take out some of the equity to spend. The mortgage debt is fixed while the asset grows in value. The only downside is the risk of dearer mortgage payments, since interest rates tend to be raised along with inflation.

Getting the measure of it

Inflation today is at exceptionally low levels, around 0.5 to 2%. But how do we come up with this figure? Each month people at the ONS (Office of National Statistics) calculate the price of a basket of goods and services on which consumers typically spend their money – about 700 items in all. They then work out how much this basket goes up in price each month. Of course, different goods increase in price at different rates: food prices have rocketed by a stonking 40% in the last few years. The government's preferred measure is based on the

Consumer Price Index (CPI), and items in the basket are changed from time to time to reflect modern lifestyles.

Items recently added to the inflation basket include flavoured milk, Netflix, canvas shoes, mixer drinks, fruit snackpots, hired suits and bird seed (someone knows how to have a good time!). In a sign of changing consumer habits, out have gone wallpaper paste, gardeners' fees and DVD recorders.

Controlling the beast

Traditionally if prices looked a bit 'toppy' governments would reach for the lever marked 'interest rates' – the main tool for managing inflation. Forcing interest rates up would act as a brake, making borrowing money more expensive and pushing up business costs and monthly mortgage payments. This would dampen demand, lowering inflation. Conversely, stepping on the accelerator by pushing rates down made it cheaper to borrow, ultimately creating a boom.

In the UK, inflation has only become a persistent issue since WW2. Before that, prices would also move downwards in recessions: during the 1930s, for example, house prices steadily reduced amid a boom in construction and homebuying. This persistence has come about because the banking system today has the capacity to create money as it is needed. Extra money can be pumped into the economy where it will chase the same amount of available goods, thereby pushing up prices.

A certain amount of inflation isn't a bad thing: it can help resolve 'conflicts over income distribution' – arguments about wage increases. If your boss gives you a pay rise, the extra money makes you feel a bit better off (even though it might be largely eaten up by higher prices in the shops). But rising incomes can swiftly turn into rising prices, ratcheting up a spiral of wage claims and price rises. But at present, unlike in the 1970s, these sorts of 'distributional conflicts' are very weak, keeping inflation down. But what happens if it goes too low?

Devilish deflation

Inflation in reverse – falling prices – may sound like a good thing. But if things in the shops are getting cheaper month by month, the temptation is to postpone the purchase. If the whole country does this it freezes the economy – leading to wage cuts, closures and job losses. So ever-cheaper stuff isn't always a good thing. In fact deflation can be devastating.

Debts may be fixed: the amount you owe on your mortgage should stay the same (unless you repay some or borrow more). But if wages are dropping in line with falling prices, you have less money to spend; and if your house shrinks in value it may be worth less than your mortgage. The same is true for heavily indebted economies like the UK's: this 'debt deflation' would mean more and more resources being spent on repaying debts rather than funding productive activity. This is currently considered a particularly serious risk inside the eurozone.

Printing money: Quantitative Easing

Cutting interest rates was traditionally one of the big ways governments tried to get the economy moving: cheaper loans motivated people to go out and buy stuff, while discouraging saving. But with the base rate today stamped into the ground (in early 2009 it dropped to an historically low 0.5%), the scope for further cutting is pretty limited, short of actually paying borrowers to take loans – known as 'negative interest rates'.

So to kickstart economic activity after the crash something

more powerful was needed. Quantitative Easing involved the Bank of England issuing lots of new money, simply by creating it electronically. You might think that the obvious thing to do with all this 'hot money' would be to drop it from a helicopter – or as tax cuts – so we all get some of the benefit and promptly rush out and spend. That would get the economy going. But no. It is spent on buying government debt (bonds) owned by the big banks and other City institutions (some fresh from being bailed out by the taxpayer).

To date an eye-watering £375 billion of new QE money has been created. This was supposed to work by increasing how much Bank of England money the other banks held and inducing them to lend more – therefore stoking up growth in the wider economy.

No one's sure where all the money wound up. We do know that lending by banks to small businesses fell and first-time buyers still find it difficult to obtain a loan. Hardly the outcome predicted. Indeed the Bank of England's own evidence suggests that QE ended up boosting asset prices such as shares and property, and may have pushed inflation up a little.

It also means, since the Bank of England is government-owned, that the government has been buying its own debt and pays interest to itself – a distinctly odd situation – with no clear way, as yet, to resolve it. Helpful suggestions should be sent to: The Governor, c/o Bank Of England.

The big wide world

Every country's economy has relationships with the rest of the world, through trade and people owning businesses or property abroad. As we saw earlier, Britain has for a long time consumed more than it produces – by being a net importer of goods.

If Britain exports Land Rovers or sells legal services to people in other countries, we earn revenue in return. Conversely, if we buy BMWs or Ferraris our money mostly ends up in German and Italian coffers (after the cut taken by car dealers in the UK). These flows of money in and out of the country define where we stand economically in relation to the rest of the world.

And Britain's 'balance of trade' – the difference between what we export and what we import – has long been smothered in red ink. Compare this with a country like Japan which exports a lot more than it imports, thereby clocking up a healthy balance of trade surplus. The UK, on the other hand, runs a 'trade deficit'. (Incidentally, both goods and services are known as 'commodities', but goods are called 'visibles' because you can physically see and touch them, and services are 'invisibles'.)

Fortunately there are other things we can sell abroad to generate flows of income into the country. For example, if you live in the UK but own a kebab shop in Iceland, you probably hope to receive rent from your investment overseas. This rent coming in from abroad goes towards the UK balance of payments. Trouble is, it works the other way too: people abroad who own investments here, perhaps a new luxury flat, are similarly paid a return on those investments.

But owning stuff abroad needn't take the form of direct ownership of assets, such as property; you might have bought shares in Samsung and thus earn dividends, or perhaps you lent money overseas on which you earn interest. A country either has to earn enough to cover its expenses, or it has to borrow (or sell off the family silver). The major difference between economic activities at home and overseas is that the latter affect the relationships between Britain and other countries.

Exchange rate

Anyone who travels abroad knows about the exchange rate – how many dollars (or whatever) you get for your GBP. As well as affecting how much spending money you have on holiday, it's also of critical importance to the UK economy. By raising or lowering the price of the goods we export, it makes British goods more or less competitively priced (and hence desirable) to buyers around the world.

An exchange rate *appreciation* is when the value of the pound rises relative to other currencies. This makes our exports more expensive to the rest of the world, but makes imports cheaper. The result is likely to be a decline in exports and an increase in imports. In other words, when the exchange rate appreciates, our trade deficit gets worse.

A *depreciation* of the exchange rate is when the pound falls in value. Our exports then become cheaper abroad and hopefully more desirable, but imports will become more expensive, squeezing domestic purchasing power (and potentially pushing up price inflation). Some politicians argue that a strong pound – a pound that is appreciating – is good for the country. Well, it all depends on whether we are trying to export or import. At present, if the balance of trade is anything to go by, we ought to be trying to export more.

All countries need to earn a living in the world. Most employ a mix of methods so that all their eggs aren't in one basket (eg being dependent upon fluctuating oil prices). Some options are more conducive to long-term prosperity, or more in keeping with human dignity and community sustainability. So nations may pay their way through:

- **The exports of manufactured goods** Local industries that design, build and export products to other countries bring foreign exchange into the local economy. Successful manufacturing economies include Japan, South Korea, Germany, China, USA.
- **The trade in 'invisibles'** Exports of banking and financial services and insurance can help nations pay their way (eg USA, Switzerland, UK), as can royalties from books, music and other intellectual property.
- **The sale of entertainment** Creative nations sell cultural output such as music, films, TV programmes and books (eg Hollywood in the USA and the BBC in the UK).
- **Sovereign wealth funds and foreign investment** Where individuals or states invest overseas, profits may be brought back to the home nation. Some nations benefit from large state-owned property portfolios (eg Norway, Qatar) from the proceeds of which they fund their domestic policies.
- **Exporting natural resources** Countries often have a ready market if blessed with reserves of oil, gas or minerals (eg Australia, Russia, Canada, Qatar, Norway, Saudi Arabia). However, such resources can be a mixed blessing. Sometimes large volumes of natural resource exports can harm other sectors of the economy.
- **Exports of food products** Farmers and fishers may contribute to the balance of trade through exports of food and drink (Canada, New Zealand, France, Italy).
- **Tourism & leisure** We may earn foreign funds from those who holiday in our country (Greece, Spain, France, UK).
- **'Branch office' investment** Inward investment from foreign multinationals who build subsidiary factories and offices (UK, Ireland, Belgium). At some stage in the future, however, perhaps the parent company might want to take the profits out or close the branch office down.
- **Brains and education** Universities and R&D centres attract revenues, investment and foreign students (USA, UK).
- **Property** We may also generate foreign exchange by exporting the title deeds to our property. London property, in particular, is often sold overseas. Selling state assets may similarly generate short-term gains.
- **Tax havens** Nations which offer a lower rate of corporation tax than their neighbours can use the complexities of internal taxation law to their benefit, picking up the tax which results from multinationals operating in other parts of the world (Ireland, Gibraltar, Bahamas, Luxembourg).
- **Hosting foreign military bases** A friendly overseas power may pay to rent bases in another sovereign territory.
- **Dirty work** Poorer nations may resort to sex tourism, the reprocessing or dumping of toxic waste, or even providing havens for criminal activity such as smuggling, sex trafficking, racketeering or illegal logging.

Most independent countries issue their own currency. (The obvious exception is the eurozone, and there are some 'dollarised' nations like Panama that use the US dollar as their own.) Because each national currency is the only accepted form of money within its own borders, there arose a need to change one currency into another so that countries could trade.

The rate at which currencies can be changed from one to another – the exchange rate – sets the price of each country's goods and services to other countries. So how these rates are set is of enormous importance. But does someone control them, or is it just left to chance? This is a subject that people have long argued about.

Back in the 19th century, right up until WW1, exchange rates were fixed relative to the price of gold – a system known logically enough as the Gold Standard. Each country's central bank maintained the price of its currency by managing its gold reserves. Britain ran the show – with the whole system resting on the belief that the Bank of England would ensure its smooth functioning. But things began to fizzle out with the decline in British power after WW1. Several nations, including Britain, opted out of the Gold Standard when it proved unstable, provoking severe loss of competitiveness and high unemployment. The Gold Standard failed because it was too rigid, causing politicians to respond to recession by imposing austerity measures, deflating their economies when they should have been stimulating growth. (There are echoes here of today's eurozone.)

Only after a further world war was a new system devised. Under the Bretton Woods Agreement, exchange rates were fixed relative to the US dollar, which in turn was fixed against the price of gold, the US government promising to maintain this price. But as the US economy came under increasing strain by the 1960s, this system also broke down, president Richard Nixon unilaterally declaring its end in 1971.

Since then, most exchange rates have floated freely – the rate being set by the demand and supply for a currency. Just like anything else, from oil to peanuts to chocolate, when demand for a foreign currency is high the price of that currency (the exchange rate) will rise. Demand will be high when a country's goods, services or assets are much sought-after elsewhere in the world, and will fall when they are not. So the exchange rate for a national currency depends to a large degree on how robust the country's economy is (or is perceived to be). So demand in years gone by for Mercedes and VWs tended to push the German currency (then the Deutschmark) higher, making VWs more expensive outside Germany.

But there are other ways that exchange rates can be manipulated. Governments can influence them by changing the supply of a currency – selling our own reserves of pounds, for instance. Alternatively, it can be influenced by governments (or central banks) moving the interest rate. High interest rates in Britain make our financial assets more desirable for foreigners. However to buy those assets foreigners need local currency, and so overseas money flows into the country, pushing up the pound (and vice versa for low rates). So if we want to export less than we import, we can get our hands on the money to do it by enticing foreigners to send their money here by putting up interest rates.

However, the interest rate lever doesn't always work. To make matters worse, wobbles in exchange rates attract short-term speculators, with financial markets piling in to profit from changes in currency prices. This happened in 1992 when John Major's government joined the old European Exchange Rate Mechanism (ERM). The ERM required that different currencies floated within certain limits in relation to each other – a sort of flexible early version of the euro. So when the value of the pound sank below its floor, the government pushed interest rates up from 10% to 15% in a single day (in the process giving mortgage holders heart attacks) – all to no avail. The pound fell below its lowest allowed ERM rate and in September 1992 it crashed out on 'Black Wednesday'. Many foreign exchange speculators made a killing. On the plus side, the experience caused us to look long and hard at the euro when it came along. One lesson from all this is that continually pushing up the exchange rate by borrowing more and more is unsustainable in the long term or, in this case, even in the short term.

Export or die

Every year since 1983, the UK has run a deficit on its trade in goods – in effect leaking money. For three decades, we have imported more goods than we have exported. As well as shed loads of manufactured stuff (much of it made in Japan, Korea and China) the total includes imports of raw materials and energy. (Despite exporting North Sea oil and gas, Britain became a net importer of oil again in 2005.) Interestingly, 45% of the goods we import come from the eurozone. Either way, we have a problem. Currently, our deficit in goods stands at a massive £110 billion a year. One reason for this shocking performance is that successive governments have allowed UK manufacturing to shrink; because manufactured goods are more likely to be sold abroad than services, Britain's exports have collapsed.

You might wonder why the exchange rate didn't automatically adjust, so that UK exports became cheaper overseas, restoring competitiveness. Part of the reason is that some of the shortfall was made up by exporting services.

Selling services abroad is a bit trickier than exporting things like jet engines: very few film stars might be willing to fly their British hairdresser to Hollywood for a do. Nonetheless, there are some services that can be traded internationally, and Britain is quite good at business services like management consultancy, finance and law. Much of this is produced in the UK's financial powerhouse, the City of London. The result of all this service trade is that the UK runs a surplus in services of £70 billion (2013 figures), clawing back over half our horrendous deficit in trade.

Finally, there is another possible factor able to make up the difference. Big international investments by UK institutions have traditionally earned returns from overseas. Meantime, foreign firms began to steadily invest in the UK, bringing capital into the country and keeping up the exchange rate. Unfortunately, the tide is now turning. Today those foreign investments in the UK are starting to pay out increasing sums overseas. The figures fluctuate quite vigorously but the trend seems to be that payments going out are no longer outweighed by investment earnings coming into the country. But then we could not reasonably expect that foreigners would invest here without, at some point, wanting to take their profits home.

The bottom line

Britain today runs an astronomical trade deficit in goods. This used to be a lot less (or even positive) and was largely compensated for by large surpluses on services or investment income. It may not have entirely bridged the gap but it hid the worst of it. The UK's total current account deficit (adding up goods, services and net incomes) came to an eye-watering £72.4 billion last year. Compared to the total income of the nation – the GDP – it weighs in at a whopping 4.2%. This is just *one year's* worth of losses, a record level in money terms (and close to the highest-ever deficit in GDP terms: 4.7% in 1989 at the height of the 'Lawson Boom'). And if you thought it couldn't get any worse, the overall deficit now seems to be ballooning ever larger.

The sad truth is, Britain has lived with a current account deficit every single year since 1994. So how come no one's blown the whistle? The mystery is how any country, year after year, can run such a large deficit. It seems we're getting something for nothing from the rest of the world – which is perfectly happy to sell us more stuff than we have the money to buy. The risk is that one day, foreign investors will take their money home again, leaving a gaping hole; the politicians are just hoping this doesn't happen while they're in power.

The difference between what we can sell overseas and what we require from overseas has to be made up. This has been managed by politicians and economists. First, to finance the persistent deficit, they have borrowed astronomical sums from the rest of the world. Second, huge British assets have been sold overseas. The UK's external debt – that's the total amount we owe – now stands at around 400% of GDP – or four times our national income. This is a shocking sum, the highest of any major developed economy. The worrying implication of funding a persistent current account deficit in this way is that the rest of the world has bigger and bigger claims against UK assets and incomes, whether through direct ownership (privatised utilities, for instance) or rising levels of debt. The interest on this debt must be paid out every year to overseas owners.

Natural healing

There is an alternative. Countries which run huge, unsustainable deficits with the rest of the world usually wake up to find their currency has been pummelled – in our case this would entail a sharp fall in the value of the pound. As we just saw, a falling currency – exchange rate depreciation, as economists would call it – would make Britain's exports cheaper and imports more expensive. This is a mixed blessing: the bad news is that we might have to pay more for imported goods; the good news is that this should then make it easier for UK firms to export more. But even the bad news isn't too bad because of the depreciation: we'd be likely to buy fewer imports since they've gone up in price. All of which helps reduce the current account deficit. But we must stop borrowing from overseas and exporting the title deeds to our nation.

A depreciation along these lines happened after the UK crashed out of the Exchange Rate Mechanism (ERM) system in 1992 (see boxout opposite). The pound fell sharply in value and disaster turned to triumph; for a few years, the weak pound boosted British exports to the rest of the world. As a result, for the first and only time since the 1960s, employment in manufacturing rose as producers hired more labour to meet rising export demand. But as the economy recovered the pound started to rise, appreciating in value, once again making British exports more expensive and imports cheaper. The current account deficit reappeared, and has been with us ever since.

The drugs don't work

Following the 2007–8 crash, the pound declined by a stonking 25% or so. Disturbingly, the drug of depreciation failed to work its magic this time. The current account deficit has stubbornly failed to improve. This indicates far deeper problems. The early signs are that our years of selling off assets and borrowing from abroad are returning to haunt us. Even allowing for the weakness in demand for British exports in the eurozone countries (see boxout overleaf), we are being dragged down by past sell-offs and borrowing: the incomes we now have to pay to those in the rest of the world (because they own UK assets or we owe them debt), are now so large that they're overwhelming the incomes we get from the rest of the world. We have sold so much off and borrowed so much that we may meet a tipping point where it is no longer possible to run up further debt. However, if much of our country no longer belongs to us, the benefits of a return to growth (even if it were possible) might also largely accrue to our overseas landlords.

K.J.Lamb

'ONE MINUTE I'M UP, THE NEXT I'M DOWN...'

Booms, slumps and the business cycle

Meanwhile, back in Blighty, despite record levels of national debt, a ballooning trade deficit and government borrowing requirements spiralling, some maintain an optimistic outlook. Indeed, it would seem little can go wrong in our economy. To some extent diagnoses of the state of the UK economy depend on which economist you ask. Mainstream economics has long been dominated by ideas of 'laissez-faire' (free markets). Nothing has to be done; indeed intervening is positively harmful. This doctrine might be music to politicians' ears (although some might not relish their options being constrained). This sort of thinking provided the bedrock upon which Gordon Brown based his now-infamous claim that there would be 'no return to boom and bust'.

As we all know, this prediction turned out to be highly inaccurate. Industrialised capitalist economies still have booms and busts, and have done since they came into existence some 200 years ago. This ever-repeating cycle always begins with a period of sustainable growth. But somehow this morphs into wildly optimistic expansion fuelled by outrageous greed and excessive borrowing. Ever-crazier bank lending is justified by the belief that this time it's different – the mad assumption that expansion will continue forever. Having run up mountains of debt, the whole thing ends in tears as everyone bails out in terror, leading to recession. The cycle can be so regular that it seems as natural as breathing. But there is nothing natural here: it is a peculiar feature of our economy, and its occurrence is related to two fundamental parts of society.

Money mania

Money is essential to lubricate trade. But it allows the acts of buying and selling to be separated. I can offer something for sale, perhaps on eBay, but I might not find any buyers. They might really value what I have to offer, but can't afford it. Similarly, I might look for something I want to buy but there might not be any sellers on that day. Just like the primitive world of bartering, no one can trade without someone else wanting something in return. Money makes trading massively easier, but doesn't guarantee trade.

The problem arises because money is not just used to buy and sell. It's also something we might save. Perhaps, for example, people

EUROZONE CRISIS

The euro was established in 1999 with high hopes. Not only would it promote greater integration among the members states who'd signed up to it, but it would also restore much-needed dynamism to European economies by removing barriers to trade and allowing the free movement of capital.

For its first decade, it appeared to be fulfilling both hopes: not only was growth throughout the eurozone robust, it appeared that its weaker members, clustered particularly in southern Europe, were among those benefiting most. For the countries jovially labelled PIGS (Portugal, Ireland, Greece and Spain) growth was especially rapid and unemployment fell. Euro members had healthy government finances, running clear surpluses on their public expenditure. The supporters of the single currency project appeared vindicated. Even in cynical Britain there were growing calls to join, with then-Prime Minister Tony Blair as cheerleader.

The global financial crisis of 2008–9 changed everything. At the heart of the euro was a fatal flaw, identified by economists of both left and right but glossed over by the euro's supporters. Entry into the single currency effectively fixed the exchange rate of the members relative to each other. Germany entered at a relatively low rate but southern Europe entered much higher; this provided Germany (and northern Europe generally) with a permanent export advantage inside the eurozone, its goods appearing much cheaper abroad. Germany developed a huge trade surplus inside the eurozone, while southern Europe ran an equally gargantuan deficit.

This southern deficit was financed, in part, by borrowings from German and other northern eurozone banks. To maintain fixed exchange rates, the German surplus had to be recycled as debt, allowing imbalanced trade to continue. Debts piled up in southern Europe – public debt in Greece, private debt in Spain and Portugal. The Irish Republic had an unsustainable housing bubble. The southern eurozone nations were doing what Britain has been doing: propping up their exchange rates through borrowing from abroad. In their case, they had to do this to maintain their fixed exchange rate inside the eurozone.

When the crisis broke, there was an initial period of calm when it was believed euro members could not default. But the full horror of the Greece debt was exposed in late 2009. A default – or worse, a series of defaults – was entirely possible. And since it was banks in northern Europe holding southern European debt, they were directly threatened. The whole castle came close to tumbling down. Resolving the crisis has so far proved impossible, with the EU, ECB and IMF insisting on austerity while attempting to shore up European banks. Where will it all end? Watch this space.

want to send their money overseas to put it into a bank account in a tax haven. The money is thus removed from circulation, meaning that the circular flow of transactions (work being done and goods and services traded) breaks down. If I stop or reduce my spending, someone else will be earning less. If this happens in the economy as a whole, we have a recession.

Breakdown

This was the mechanism behind the recession of 2008–9. In response to the financial crash, banks pulled back their lending. Households and businesses, in turn, fearful of the future, stopped spending. Thus, less stuff was being bought and fewer people were employed to make and sell it all. World GDP fell by 30%. In the UK, it fell by over 5%. By 2011, cross-border flows of capital were still down a crushing 60% on their 2008 peak.

The crash of 2008 was exceptionally bad. The most serious recessions tend to be those associated with financial crises across the whole world – and recovery is much slower. In response many nations seek to become net exporters to build up their own economy. However, it is logically impossible for all nations to export more than they import. As every economy seeks to buy less from abroad and to sell more abroad, over-supply increases. The modern financial system in some ways makes things worse – amplifying the decline in spending and economic activity, much as it exaggerates it in the opposite direction during booms. The impact of the 2007–8 crash has been particularly long-lasting, and there are good reasons to think that true recovery is still some way off.

Creative destruction

The way booms alternate with slumps has a lot to do with another fundamental feature of our economy: its decentralisation. Much as

politicians might pretend otherwise, there is no grand overall plan, and in any case there is no single authority that could implement it. Instead, the economy operates on millions of decisions made by firms, individuals and governments.

These decisions are supposedly coordinated by the famous self-correcting market, but there are features that generate an up and down rhythm to the capitalist economy. There are periods of great excitement, with investment surging ahead, employment and wages rising. But when markets expand rapidly they can overextend themselves – beyond the point at which all the output made can be sold. Buoyed by the thought of ever-expanding profits and speculative gains, industry, individuals and governments can overextend their levels of debt. When it all goes pop, investments that had appeared sound now look ludicrous. We know this because booms and busts have been a regular occurrence for centuries – from the canal mania of the late 18th century to the dot.com boom of the early 2000s. Companies go bust, there are redundancies and short-time contracts. The economy sinks into recession.

But this hangover after the wild party is part of the recovery process. As firms go bankrupt, their assets sold off for knock-down prices, the path is cleared for further growth. By writing off previous investments, it is possible to invest again at new, lower prices. The dot.com boom may have ended in tears but what was salvaged from the wreckage provided much of the infrastructure of today's Internet, with giants like Google and Amazon establishing themselves. By clearing the decks, crisis can pave the way for recovery. The Austrian economist Joseph Schumpeter called this process 'creative destruction': only through destroying older accumulations of capital is progress made and innovation introduced.

Chapter 3

THE ENGINE ROOM

Don't take off your 'money glasses' quite yet, because we're going to look at how Britain earns its living in the world and how this affects us all as citizens, for good or ill. Although none of us can actually see the macroeconomy, we all take part in it. To understand how the nation's engine room works, we now need to zoom in.

Industry and commerce

If you take a train journey north from London, you get a pretty good sense of Britain's economic geography – how different parts of the country generate wealth. But something slightly odd is apparent from the start. London is disproportionately huge – home to one-sixth of the UK population. The capital sprawls out over the South East, a mass of housing and economic activity but with precious little manufacturing. This suburban expanse seems to embrace nearby towns, but eventually, as the buildings and population thin out, the green of the British countryside beckons and agriculture becomes more apparent. Occasionally, the further we head away from London, industry can be spotted in the distance.

But the same journey north would have told quite a different story when Britain was the world's richest economy, over a century ago. The Industrial Revolution saw growth and prosperity focused on booming cities like Glasgow, Birmingham, Leeds and Manchester.

Who works where?

Britain's population was one of the first to overwhelmingly live in cities. But what's so striking today is the extraordinary concentration of the population in and around London – and its absence elsewhere. Hopping off the train at one of the many towns across the country might reinforce this point: while many larger city centres have been redeveloped over the last decade and exude a feeling of prosperity, many smaller towns can appear melancholic. Years of austerity brought on by recession have hit these places hard.

The graph opposite shows the wealth produced in each EU member state (relative to the EU-wide average, fixed at 100). Within each country, the wealth is spread from the poorest regions on the left of the bar, to the richest on the right. At a glance, it's clear that something very peculiar is happening with the UK.

Of course all countries have poor areas and rich areas. But the spread between the two extremes in Britain is massively larger than all the rest. Central London on the far right of the UK bar turns out to be the richest single area in the entire European Union – by a huge margin. Yet within the same country, the Welsh Valleys and

---

WHO OWNS OUR LAND?

Traditionally it was the aristocracy, the Church and the royal family who owned the majority of Britain. But many old aristocratic families have been ruined by 'drink, debt and divorce' (according to *Country Life* magazine). And the Church of England is now no longer even in the top ten, having sold off nearly all its land.

Today the largest landowner in Britain is the Forestry Commission, with about 2.5 million acres. After that it's the National Trust, with about 820,000 acres (including Scottish NT) and the MOD with about 590,000 acres. Next come pension funds and privatised utilities and water companies with around half a million acres, followed by the Crown Estates on behalf of the monarch (most of the income generated goes to the Treasury) at around 360,000 acres. (Constitutionally the Crown is the ultimate owner of all land in England and Wales.) Next in line, perhaps surprisingly, is the RSPB with around 320,000 acres.

The most recent change has been a trend for big corporations to invest in land because it retains its value in times of recession and is likely to become more expensive as concerns about climate change and food security grow. In future, more land is likely to end up in the hands of businesses and foreign investors.

Only about 7% of the UK's total land area is classified as urban (in England it's 11%). As well as supporting agriculture, the rest has uses ranging from woodland (around 12%) to unspoilt countryside.

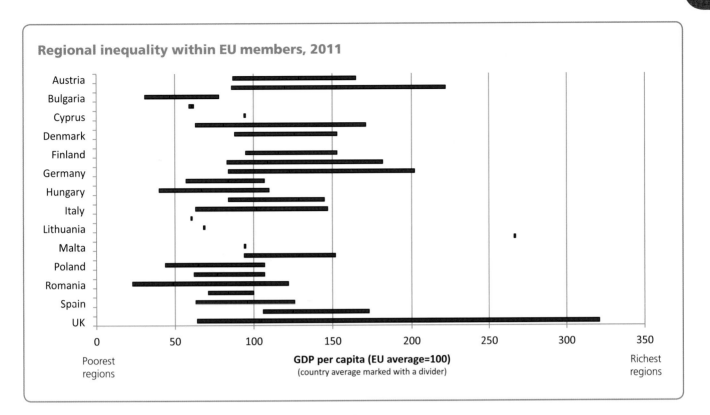

Regional inequality within EU members, 2011

GDP per capita (EU average=100)
(country average marked with a divider)

Poorest regions — Richest regions

Austria, Bulgaria, Cyprus, Denmark, Finland, Germany, Hungary, Italy, Lithuania, Malta, Poland, Romania, Spain, UK

the Wirral are comparable in terms of wealth to the EU's poorest members such as Bulgaria and Romania.

Of course, richer parts of the country help subsidise poorer regions. Central government raises taxes across the country and its spending helps redistribute the money (although less so today).

Things look a little more worrying when you consider that this data is based on *incomes*. And it's perfectly possible to earn an income while making no economic contribution to the country, such as through an overseas hedge fund. But there's another issue: although London appears to be enormously rich its wealth is held in few hands, rather than by a lot of moderately well-off citizens. In fact London is the most unequal city in the OECD.

Where have all the factories gone?

There was something missing on our journey out of London. We were hard pushed to spot any industry. Around the capital itself manufacturing was thin on the ground – just 2.4% of people working in London are involved in manufacturing. The East Midlands, by contrast, still has 12% of its employed people working in industry.

INDUSTRIAL RELATIONS

When you turn on BBC news and hear the announcement, 'And now we're going over to our industry correspondent,' the relevant item is generally negative, such as a strike. Similarly the phrases 'industrial action' and 'industrial relations' conjure up images of walkouts and disruption. However, in other developed economies 'industrial action' would relate to a positive story about manufacturing activity. It seems that the loss of industry in Britain has extended beyond the physical closure of factories – even into the language itself.

And Wales, the North of England and the East Midlands still have more than one in ten jobs in manufacturing.

Britain's northern towns were the first in the world to industrialise. Back then, these towns, along with Wales and Scotland, generated the nation's prosperity, with the South lagging behind, still dominated by agriculture – although London was a global hub for trade and finance. Today, Britain has been busy deindustrialising.

The number of people in Britain working in industry peaked in the mid-1960s – reaching close to 40% of the working population. Since then, manufacturing employment has fallen to less than 8%. Manufacturing has plummeted from seven million jobs in 1979 to under three million today. So it's hardly surprising that manufacturing's share of national output has nearly halved over the last 20 years, sinking to a paltry 11% of GDP today – the lowest since records began.

This situation isn't unique to the UK – most major developed countries have gone through a similar process since 1970, with manufacturing steadily declining as a share of both output and employment. But for most of our competitors manufacturing employment has been relatively stable over the last 20 years at around 16%.

But countries vary: the US was among the earliest to deindustrialise, with manufacturing employment declining to around 9% today; Japan, by contrast, was one of the last, at around 16% employed in industry.

Wipe out

The decline in the UK has been far more severe than our competitors. From one of the most industrialised economies on the planet, today we are one of the least industrialised. Although manufacturing employment was already in slow decline, the 1979–81 recession dealt a killer blow: around a third of British manufacturing capacity was wiped out. How did this happen?

Following exploratory drilling in the 1960s, the first barrels of North Sea oil were landed with great fanfare in 1975. Despite urgings by the then-energy secretary Tony Benn to establish an 'oil fund', saving at least some of the revenues generated, the Labour Cabinet followed Civil Service advice in using oil tax revenues to pay for current expenditure.

The Conservative government of 1979 inherited this situation, and chose to maintain it. With the oil-price spike of the same year, and production from new fields gushing, North Sea revenues hit a peak in 1984–85 generating a windfall of £22 billion. Between Margaret Thatcher's arrival in office and her exit in 1990, total North Sea tax revenues (even in the relatively lax North Sea regime) came to an exceptionally bountiful £166 billion.

Without the foresight to put any of this wealth aside, these revenues were spent by the politicians of the day. With the loss of a million manufacturing jobs between 1979 and 1984, unemployment was skyrocketing and pushing four million by the mid-1980s. So successive Thatcher governments sorely needed the tax revenues. At the same time, rising oil exports continued to push up the value of the pound, squeezing manufacturing still further (a problem known as 'Dutch disease').

In effect, North Sea oil was used to pay for deindustrialisation. Meanwhile rising stars like Germany and South Korea were heading in the opposite direction, strengthening their industries.

Without the windfall, there was no realistic chance of the government at the time being able to bear the costs of exceptionally high, and sustained, unemployment. But the comparison with Norway, which established an oil fund, is sobering: that country today has $700 billion stored away, more than enough to fund future investments and provide all its citizens with a decent pension.

It was thanks to a uniquely unfavourable set of circumstances. First a global recession hit demand. Then came the combination of rising North Sea oil production and government attempts to control inflation with steep interest-rate increases. North Sea oil was exported, while high interest rates attracted capital from the rest of the world.

Both factors massively pushed up the value of the pound, making British exports far more expensive, inducing a profound shock. Accordingly, Britain's trade in goods collapsed into deficit in 1983 and it has remained in the red every single year since.

Unemployment

The exceptional rise in unemployment in the Thatcher era, to levels unheard of since the Great Depression of the 1930s, was largely paid for through direct taxation. Of course governments of all colours are masters at massaging figures to make them look better. And, sure enough, some long-term unemployment was discreetly massaged into invisibility through disability benefits. The other classic way of mopping up private-sector job losses is by boosting state-funded jobs, and from 1979 to 1987 public-sector employment expanded with 650,000 new jobs created.

'HOW'S YOUR OUT-OF-WORK / LIFE BALANCE ?'

Defining 'declining'

A *relative* decline in manufacturing should not be confused with an *absolute* decline. There was an upside to the 1980s carnage that decimated our industries. Whether by luck or judgement it had the effect of driving up productivity. By squeezing manufacturing so hard, with high interest rates and a high-value pound, less efficient producers were killed off. The only plants and firms left standing were the strongest ones that could survive the squeeze. As a result, manufacturing productivity increased over the period and has remained high since. Of course many markets, once retreated from, remained lost to our foreign competitors for good. But the relatively few British manufacturers that remain today are focused on exports, often highly specialised, and many are among the most productive in the world.

Rising from the ashes?

Let's take one dramatic example: UK car manufacturing peaked in 1972, with 1.92 million cars produced. It then went into freefall. But by 2013 1.6m cars were made here, growing especially sharply in the last few years. Current forecasts suggest that the peak of the 1970s will soon be topped; and, while in the 1970s more than half of British-made cars were produced for the home market, today close to 80% are sold abroad, with half going to the EU (although we buy more imported vehicles for the home market). In 2012, the UK ran a surplus on the exports of finished cars for the first time since 1976. And that surplus has been maintained.

But there are some stark differences with Britain's past auto industry. With the sale of Rover Group to BMW in 1994, not a single UK-owned mass-producer of cars remained, its reincarnation as MG Rover collapsing in 2005. It's a similar story with commercial vehicles.

Despite the recovery in output, productivity gains mean there are far fewer jobs in the industry. In the 1950s, over half a million people were employed in UK vehicle production, but by 2014 this number was 130,000. At one point, a single UK producer, British Leyland, employed 200,000 people at 46 factories, claiming 30% of the domestic market. Formed through a series of government-sponsored mergers, culminating in its nationalisation, the company last turned a profit in 1978, consuming state aid totalling more than £2.9 billion ahead of its privatisation in 1988.

Today, productivity measured in output per worker has improved immensely. This is down to automation – robots and technology. But it's also thanks to much better management – an efficient 'Toyota-ist' approach, with foreign-owned plants introducing good management techniques.

The opening of Nissan's Sunderland plant in 1986 marked a break with the past. Alongside a no-strike agreement with the plant's single union, Nissan's new methods included:

■ **'Just-In-Time' production** Frequent deliveries from suppliers kept costly stocks of components to a minimum.
■ **The 'Kaizen' system** A spirit of social equality on the shop floor

MANAGEMENT v. UNIONS

Anyone who can recall the days of 'Red Robbo' leading impromptu walkouts and strikes at car plants in the 1970s might have little sympathy for the unions of the day. The Midlands motor industry was plagued with lousy industrial relations, which damaged the quality of cars. But poor industrial relations were combined with poor management and low investment. The old 'them and us' style of British management contrasts with today's Japanese approach. Damned in the 1970s, unions are still present throughout the industry yet strike days are a tiny fraction of earlier times.

What could be more British than Cadbury, Harrods and Heathrow airport? Yet all are foreign-owned. From the energy that heats our shower and the trains that convey us to work, the chances are the profits from running many UK operations will be heading overseas. Many British industries, companies and brands are no longer British-owned, including well-known items such as Jaffa cakes, Tetley tea bags and Branston pickle. Since 2004, over £400 billion worth of British companies have been sold abroad, far exceeding UK companies' shopping sprees in the other direction.

Britain is considerably more open than other major economies – far more so than the US, Germany and China. In contrast to the UK's willingness to permit the sale of crown jewels like Cadbury, the French government in 2005 blocked Pepsi Corporation's takeover bid for food giant Danone (yoghurt and Evian water); although Paris agreed to US giant General Electric's buyout of the Alstom energy business, it was on the condition of securing a 20% stake in the combined operation for the nation.

Why does this matter?

Perhaps the most obvious contrast with our government's relaxed attitude to corporate assets is our love of property ownership. A 'home-owning democracy' has enormous appeal for two main reasons. First, as individuals we like the security this gives us – no one can suddenly decide to liquidate our main asset and boot us out. Second, owning property is an investment for the future. Yet when it comes to the UK owning its industries we, inexplicably, adopt a totally different approach.

The takeover of Cadbury by Kraft Foods in 2010 left many thinking that it has become too easy for foreign firms to snap up UK companies. Cadbury was known as a philanthropic employer for well over a century. It combined impressive international sales with generous benefits for its workforce. But loaded with debt following the takeover, Kraft closed the Somerdale plant near Bristol, reneging on prior assurances to keep it open (although the plant had earlier been threatened with closure). After the takeover the new owners declared a new tax base in Switzerland, a move reckoned to cost the British taxpayer millions each year (despite the fact that before the takeover Cadbury was already engaged in legitimate 'highly aggressive' tax avoidance) The new owners even axed the tradition of sending retired workers Xmas cards and a pensioner's hamper (despite the chief executive having received a 31.5 per cent pay rise to nearly £19 million). Some years earlier, when Cadbury wanted to buy US rival Hershey it was blocked by its American owners.

Infrastructure

More than a third of UK infrastructure (eg water, power stations and transport) is foreign-owned, including four of the 'Big Six' energy companies and several train operators. Ironically, a share of the profits from Thames Water today ends up in the coffers of the Chinese Communist Party – hardly the legacy Mrs Thatcher envisaged. The *Daily Mail*'s Alex Brummer (author of *Britain For Sale*) points out that such companies 'are part of the fabric of the nation, and . . . the people who bought them did so with big debts, running them for profit, not for the long-term benefit of the British people'.

Investment can be good

Inward investors can of course be a good thing, enhancing our industrial base and skills, such as the car factories built and run by Toyota and Nissan. Similarly, where failed British products are revived by foreign

Many well-known, quintessentially British brands are no longer in UK ownership.

firms (such as BMW and the Mini), it is obviously a better outcome than insolvency. But the disposal of world-class national champions like Pilkington Glass (sold in 2006 to its smaller rival, Japanese Nippon) appears short-sighted. As the *Daily Mail* city editor, Ruth Sunderland, has observed , the danger of becoming 'branch office Britain' is that the brains of the operation end up abroad. Overseas parents will naturally prioritise employment and the smart stuff like R&D in their domestic market, particularly in times of downturn. But even where this is not the case, inventions made by British subsidiaries will primarily benefit the parent company, so the UK can never gain competitive advantage. One major reason Germany has maintained its standing as an industrial nation is because it does not give primacy to short-term shareholder value over the long-term national interest.

Stephen King, the chief economist at HSBC (and author of *When the Money Runs Out*) points out that, 'If a country sells off its assets and companies to foreign investors, the profits that come from those asset sales then accrue to other people, not the people in the UK. There has been a generational shift – the older generation sells its assets not to the younger generation but to foreign investors. That leaves the younger generation only as workers, without the benefits of a stream of profits that might otherwise accrue to them.'

But in an era of globalisation, even nominally British companies like BP or Marks & Spencer may not be quite what they seem. Twenty years ago, just 13% of shares in top listed UK companies were foreign-owned. Today it is more than half. With shareholding increasingly dominated by global asset management groups that trade shares as casino chips, a country isn't likely to grow the national champions it needs. Leaving ourselves unquestioningly 'open for business' may not always be in Britain's best interests.

Source material: Alex Brummer, Ruth Sunderland, Channel 4

This UK Nissan plant is among the most efficient in the world.

whereby every employee is encouraged to come up with small improvements to the process.

◼ **Regular job rotation** To overcome fatigue and help employees appreciate each other's jobs.

Clearly, intelligent management – engaging with employees and treating staff decently – gets results. The Nissan plant today, like Honda at Swindon and Toyota at Burnaston, is among the most efficient in the world. The shock of the 2008 crash, whose subsequent recession hit the motor industry particularly hard, was overcome thanks to the workforce accepting flexible hours, and through direct aid from government. After falling below a million in 2009 for the first time in decades, car production rebounded, rising 50% over the next five years.

Chain reaction

Despite the UK's success in attracting inward investment, industry has suffered from familiar British business failings: declining expenditure on research and investment. This is particularly marked when compared to manufacturers elsewhere in Europe. But great new products stem from investment, especially in R&D. Could this be because some foreign-owned plants do the brainy stuff in their home countries?

There is another problem. Of the components used to produce cars at UK plants, only around 40% by value is sourced from Britain. This compares with 60% or higher in Germany and France. Politicians brag about how we're exporting more cars than ever, and the value of *finished* cars being exported is greater than imports. But

most of the raw materials and components that the cars are made of first have to be imported. So once the components are taken into account, it turns out we're still running a trade deficit in cars.

This is a feature of British manufacturing generally, large swathes of which are foreign-owned. So as many of our indigenous firms have been lost, UK supply chains have been hollowed out. British auto component producers like Lucas, Girling, Dunlop and Smiths were broken up or sold. Foreign ownership of car manufacturing increases this tendency, with large multinationals seeking to reduce their costs by extending their supply chains across national borders. This is driving Britain into a permanent current-account deficit.

The rise of services

As we have seen, when, in 1992, the pound came crashing out of the Exchange Rate Mechanism (see boxout on page 30), its subsequent drop in value eased the pressure on British export industries and manufacturing employment rose. This expansion, however, was short-lived. When another housing boom gathered pace (from around 1996), the pound shot up in value. Low interest rates were intended to encourage investment, but alongside easy money from deregulated finance they ended up stoking a credit bubble, with a boom in prices from the early 2000s.

This environment was influenced by the decision of the American Federal Reserve to slash US interest rates to exceptionally low levels. The rising value of the pound meant cheaper imports, but British exporters struggled to sell abroad. Cheap credit combined with low-cost manufactured goods flooding in from China and elsewhere (which were improving in quality) pushed the balance of trade deep into deficit. Predictably, more jobs were lost in UK manufacturing, albeit at a slower pace than in the disastrous 1980s. And this time the damage was masked by apparent economic expansion – with 1.76 million jobs created in the public sector between 1987 and 2008.

The big shift

By the mid 2000s, the huge shift away from manufacturing had become apparent. But who cared? We were now living in the 'post-industrial' society – in conditions of rollicking prosperity – or so it seemed. Politicians talked up the 'knowledge economy' – so much cooler than factories. Britain was viewed as having a specialism in 'knowledge-intensive services', selling its expertise to the world. Indeed, in contrast to our dismal balance of trade in goods, Britain has generated a consistent surplus in services (financial services to the fore), although not enough to make up the difference. Traditional occupations and jobs-for-life were so last century; a flexible labour market offered exciting fresh opportunities.

This mid-2000s enthusiasm – tied up with notions of Cool Britannia and a new 'creative class' – obscured some big problems. Yes, Britain's exports of knowledge-intensive services was the largest of any large developed economy as a share of total exports. And our loosely-defined creative industries such as TV production, the music industry and the arts employed 1.68 million people by 2012. But even this only represented 5.6% of UK employment.

The chill factor

It became clear, post-crash, that service industries did not promote a more equal and meritocratic society, as had been hoped. Instead, the disappearance of manufacturing jobs sacrificed occupations that had provided good pay and job security. While a few service-sector jobs, mostly in financial services, were highly paid, most were not. The new flexible labour markets have seen a rise in 'zero-hours' working with minimal security. Between 1997 and 2006, growth in employment mostly took place in the lowest-paid 20% of jobs – which increased by 5%. New jobs offering average wages dropped by 4% – although high-paying jobs at the top increased by a similar amount.

Who's to blame?

Low wages and growing income inequality (the 'polarisation' of the labour market) have been blamed on a number of things:

- **The global financial crisis** The recession brought on by the financial crisis was the most significant factor behind the decline in most people's standard of living, at least as measured in pay since 2008.

GLOBALISATION

Britain is part of an increasingly globalised and interconnected world. Inevitably there are winners and losers, benefits and dangers. The trick is to get the best and leave the rest.

What is globalisation?

Globalisation refers to the movement across national boundaries of knowledge, goods and services, culture and finance, plus the migration of people. We are witnessing, for good or ill, the extension world-wide of the market forces which exist within countries or regions. Basic economic theory suggests that global markets mean greater possibilities for goods, labour and finance to become better matched and more specialised. It is claimed that this will maximise economic efficiency, leaving us all better off.

The three aspects of globalisation

Knowledge There's no real downside to the march of knowledge. Globalisation of communications is not a recent phenomenon; the invention of the telegraph in the Victorian era was arguably a greater force for change than the Internet. The telegraph, the telephone, radio and the online search engine allow us, at effectively zero marginal cost, to connect socially and vocationally with global communities. What's not to like?

Culture The global spread of culture, through movies, TV and radio, has been more of a mixed bag. Many would argue that, in a world of global culture, it's good that we can choose whatever we prefer. However, this ignores the impact of 'soft-power' – that is, the power to influence people's opinions or actions through repetition, attraction and co-option. In a networked and multi-media world, a dominant nation or corporation can project its own version of truth and culture. A small nation is less able to produce TV and radio content, movies and computer games. So its language and culture – indeed, its very history – may become buried through the relentless spread of culture from a more powerful player. For example the Hollywood movie 'U-571' had no qualms about blatantly rewriting history, portraying intrepid US forces capturing a crucial Nazi enigma code machine, glossing over the truth that this was actually a Royal Navy operation (before the United States had even entered the war). But future generations will most likely only know the movie version. However, in the world-wide culture wars Britain has one distinct advantage: English is our national language and the international language of choice. But this is a two-way street and we tend to import more culture than we export. So if the UK wishes to retain control of its culture it must retain control of its media. Otherwise, the version of culture promoted as being the most attractive may come to mean that which is of most benefit to major international movie studios or overseas corporations.

Trade No nation in the world has all the resources to sustain a modern society, so they all need to trade with other countries. Britain has prospered as a trading nation because international commerce offers the potential for economic and social growth. 'Trade not aid' is said to provide the basis for nations and regions to prosper – and this is no less true for Cornwall or East Anglia (for example) than for any other part of the world. This is because, in practice, money follows trade.

Britain is facing economic headwinds because for many years it hasn't been able to pay its way. If a country cannot balance its trade (selling as much or more than it buys), its stock of money will leak away and it will be unable to provide for its citizens. Where a nation does not control its own currency, the potential exists to lose out to a larger, more economically powerful neighbour. Consider the southern European nations and how they have suffered since losing their own currencies. The same logic applies to national regions, except that the central government may recycle some of the wealth generated in richer areas to support poorer regions. Hence 'United' Kingdom.

Globalisation has helped to reduce inequality between countries, but it has also added to inequality within countries, as skilled workers benefit from new markets while low- and medium-skilled workers compete with cheaper workers in emerging countries.

- ■ **New technology** In recent years many routine tasks have become automated – from cash registers to ATM machines. Yet research suggests that job polarisation has been underway since the 1950s, long before IT consultants took over the world. And of course technology, in the form of computers, smartphones and the Internet, has opened up many new opportunities. Changes in technology are as likely to produce new forms of employment as to de-skill existing work.

- ■ **Immigration** Debate centres on 'benefit tourism' imposing burdens on the public purse, and conversely on worries about new workers taking jobs from residents, undermining pay and conditions. Net migration (the difference between those leaving the country and those arriving) has averaged a surplus of 200,000 a year over the 2000s; at present it's around 260,000. Research suggest that over the last decade migrants from the EU contributed £22 billion more in taxes than they took in public services or received in welfare payments. (These numbers, though, exclude some hidden costs, such as benefits for native workers who might have been put out of a job.) Migrants have been generally young and healthy, placing fewer demands on public services, and they have worked and paid taxes.

So what is the effect of immigration on employment? Greater competition for jobs and a supply of labour willing to work for lower rates of pay would seem likely to push down wages, but evidence for this is inconclusive. Certainly some low-paying sectors like care work have seen downward pressure on wages. On the other hand, a higher-skilled immigrant, such as an entrepreneurial IT expert, may create new jobs down the supply chain.

Migrant workers have responded to the kind of economy that has been created in Britain, with its increased numbers of service-sector occupations, both at the top and bottom of the spectrum. Our economy looks like this because of long-standing government policies, including the maintenance of a high-value pound, easy access to credit and low interest rates. Businesses here have, in turn, responded to this environment.

Immigration is explored in more detail on page 148.

Global finance

The aspect of globalisation which can potentially wreak the most damage is the most neglected – the free flow of capital. While the benefits of global trade, knowledge and culture are generally accepted (although there are downsides), the benefits of the flow of capital are more difficult to pin down, at least at a national level. Some economists have argued that gains to national economies from the free flow of capital are insignificant; however its threats are substantial – sometimes to the point of undermining a nation. We know from the 2007–8 crash that global finance has a lot in common with fire – a good servant but a bad master.

Foreign investment may bring us net benefits by starting a UK subsidiary or reviving a failing British business. However, foreign owners can buy UK companies merely to close them down. But there are other more damaging repercussions that can result from the inflow of funds.

The pound sterling gives us a flexible exchange rate: the price of foreign currencies can fluctuate in value against the pound. But big inflows of foreign exchange (*eg* when companies or other major assets are sold to overseas buyers) will cause the pound to increase in value. This stronger pound makes foreign imports cheaper and our exports more expensive: our manufacturing and service sectors become less competitive.

It is estimated that £440 billion of British companies have been sold abroad since 2004. This inflow of capital comes on top of the inflows resulting from the sale of property to foreigners; in the three years ending 2012, overseas investors bought 65% of Central London office space. There is no way of calculating how much our exports have been crowded out of world markets because of this, but if we wish to reduce our trade deficit we should reduce the capital inflow. Our governments' penchant for selling off the family silver is an obstacle to us paying our way in the world with manufacturing exports.

Travel and migration

International travel affords us enormous opportunities to broaden our experience. Freedom to take vacations, or to choose where we might live and work, can substantially improve our lives – at least for those who can afford it. However, there are potential downsides. For people living in host communities, high levels of immigration may threaten jobs, culture and social stability. There are also issues for the poorer countries that migrants leave behind. Outward migration of talented people can disrupt communities, stretching family relationships to breaking point, and erode local knowledge and proud traditions ('cultural capital').

Global crisis management

Economists warn about the destabilising effects of tsunamies of hot money sloshing about the world. Major financial players may one day invest in a nation then suddenly dis-invest. Yet Westminster politicians have a tendency to believe that freedom is always for the best.

The globalisation of the world economy might allow all nations to share the good times. But they also share the bad. Of course, the individuals who benefit most from a booming global economy are usually not the people who eventually put their hands in their pockets to bail the system out.

Economic crises will occur every now and then, but the UK's embrace of globalisation increases our exposure to risks from other nations. We should not cut ourselves off from the world – but neither should we fail to prioritise what is best for our nation. If the benefits of globalisation are as some claim, there should be enough money put aside in the boom years to tide us over the bust years.

Certainly, if you ever hear a politician claiming that boom-and-bust is laid to rest – then it's time to rush out and buy canned food and gold!

Conclusion

If we do not stand up for ourselves as a country no one else will. Large inflows of foreign capital can undermine our economy. As a nation, we want our businesses to be for the good of the people of this country – rather than that Britons should be employed (or remain unemployed) depending on what is best for foreign-owned businesses.

It's a small world

Britain's dramatic slide in manufacturing output is partly due to our economy being highly internationalised. Thanks to the legacy of early industrialisation and our worldwide empire, Britain acquired huge amounts of overseas investments – second only to the US throughout the post-war period. By 1978, we accounted for 11% of investment worldwide (Foreign Direct Investment), massively ahead of manufacturing powerhouses like West Germany (2.6%) and Japan (1.3%).

But this outward focus meant a consistently high value for the pound relative to other currencies. A high-value pound made UK assets such as property very valuable, which helped sustain the UK's financial sector. But export industries struggled with

TOP BRANDS

One way of judging a country's economic success is by the number of its brands that enjoy world recognition. Interbrand, the brand consultancy, publishes an annual list of the 100 most valuable global brands. The logos (see below) are instantly recognisable. America dominates the list, along with Japan and Germany. France, Italy and South Korea are also well represented, with one or two recent Chinese arrivals. UK brands in the 2014 top 100 are HSBC (33), Shell (65), Burberry (73), Johnnie Walker (86) and Land Rover (91).

Why does this matter? Because as the brand specialist Rita Clifton observes, 'He who owns the brand owns the wealth.' She goes on to ask, 'Why aren't British business leaders as ambitious to grow their businesses for the long term?' Some might suggest that if there were awards for enormous salaries, UK companies would dominate the charts.

See website for links to Interbrand top 100.

high prices and cheaper imports, losing sales and surrendering markets. And our overseas investments, offering high, short-term returns, left British industry starved of money. We became a 'low-investment economy'.

In recent decades capital has flooded into the UK from the rest of the world. Much of this comprises Foreign Direct Investment – overseas investors buying UK assets. Successive governments have encouraged this, seeing it as bringing benefits such as access to new technology, technical knowledge and better management, as well as creating markets for existing domestic firms. So when BMW developed the new Mini it revitalised the former Morris plant at Cowley in Oxford. However a less successful example would be the acquisition by Germany's MAN Truck & Bus group of the Cheshire-based commercial vehicle manufacturer ERF, which culminated in the closure of their UK factories.

Open for business

The apparent turnaround in the British motor industry's fortunes has been much heralded by successive governments keen to preserve the UK's traditional commitment to free trade and free markets. Politicians crow about a 'resounding success for inward investment' and an 'open economy'. But being a branch office at the end of foreign-owned global production chains also has its risks. International capital can leave as quickly as it came, and multinationals can dominate their supply chains. Apple, Nike and other well-known brands can choose from a vast range of low-cost, high-volume producers, many in East Asia. But what do suppliers do when squeezed? They, in turn, squeeze their workforces. Chilling stories of death-trap garment factories and suicide nets provided for workers speak of tough labour conditions behind some famous global brands.

UK governments since the early 1980s have argued that they should not, or could not, intervene when a multinational enterprise was acting against local interests. The closure of the Longbridge car plant in 2000 led to great local bitterness; this was followed a few years later by Ford's equally historic manufacturing plant at Dagenham in Essex. Ford also ceased production of its famous Transit van in Southampton, and LDV vans in Birmingham went under after the government rejected the request for bridging finance in the downturn. But the threatened collapse of major banks in the autumn of 2008 prompted the government to take swift action.

One of the dangers of Foreign Direct Investment (FDI) is that it can become addictive for governments bereft of alternative plans. Indeed FDI in the UK grew more than six times from 1990 to 2011, reaching a massive $1,199 billion. The 45,000 foreign affiliate firms located in the UK today are also relatively large; although representing only 2% of UK firms, they accounted for 36% of total turnover and 13% of employment.

When TV news features a British factory, the machinery often has a 1960s look; investment might be maintained in terms of directors' perks, but less so on the shop floor. Of course there are many successful and well-funded British firms, but foreign-owned manufacturers tend to be better managed and more likely to invest and innovate. (Domestic firms can learn from, or be pressured by, these well-run foreign companies.) UK governments try to attract foreign firms through low taxes and minimal regulation, but such subsidies are sometimes not offered to British-owned manufacturers.

Loss of control

Foreign managements have less concern about the local UK economy, and therefore less to lose by shutting up shop and relocating overseas. Wales heavily promoted FDI in the 1980s to compensate for the loss of traditional industries; despite being home to less than 5% of the UK population, it attracted 14% of all FDI in that decade. Politicians queued up to promote Wales as a stunning FDI success story. But EU expansion eastwards, and the shift of global manufacturing to the Far East, killed off Wales' cost advantages. In the decade to 2008, 171 plants closed there with the loss of 31,000 jobs. Perhaps the most notorious case was LG, which had been given £124 million to open a plant at Newport with the promise of 6,100 jobs; the plant closed after a decade, having employed no more than 2,000 workers at its peak.

Game changer

Apart from the risks of plant closure and the waste of public money, the longer-term threat is that global investment has fallen since the 2008 crash and still hasn't recovered; it was still down by about 60% as of 2013.

Not only has the volume of FDI fallen, but we are now competing for investment against many poorer nations. Since 2012, the share grabbed by the developing world has started to exceed that of the developed. The UK may have an historic advantage in attracting FDI, but we are up against fast-growing parts of the world.

Thus the crash has accelerated the shift in the world economy towards newer countries as producers – while reminding businesses of the importance of the home market. But it also revealed flaws in the tactic of UK firms moving production to lower-cost countries like China or India. Loss of control has caused supply problems for businesses like the model train maker Hornby. Last year, one in six UK manufacturers 'reshored', moving operations back to their home country – despite the higher cost of things like rents and energy.

Revolution in the East

The rapid industrialisation and economic growth over the last 20 years of the 'Asian Tigers' – East Asian countries such as Malaysia, China and South Korea – is due to many factors, not least state support and low-value currencies. But the cost of exporting their manufactured goods was also reduced by revolutions in transport and communications.

- **Containerised transport** slashed the costs of bulk exports
- **Shipping speeds** have increased, cutting the costs of getting goods to the consumer
- **International phone calls** are so cheap that some, such as Skype, are almost free

As a result, Western countries have sucked in huge amounts of Eastern goods, fuelled by cheap credit. Meanwhile the quality of the goods has improved – especially in advanced electronics.

These changes have produced a profound rebalancing of the world economy. The German economy has managed to adapt, yet the UK has tended to weakly declare that 'we can't compete with China' – an echo of the rise of Japan in the 1960s. Successive governments in the UK have readily accepted this new world order, urging other countries to become as open and as liberal as us. But is being open and liberal the best strategy?

THE SWING TO SERVICES

As far back as the 1960s, some economists were talking excitedly of the benefits for countries like Britain of shifting away from manufacturing. The thinking was that making stuff becomes easier and cheaper – meaning that it becomes tougher to stay profitable. In contrast it was claimed that the service sector doesn't change much: productivity stays the same. (This was before Amazon showed everyone how to do retailing better.) The widely quoted parable was that it takes just as many musicians to play a Beethoven string quartet as it always has, and musicians' wages keep rising: by contrast, the cost of making their records has collapsed. In short, the 'Baumol theory' suggests that an advanced economy will swing towards services and away from manufacturing.

Based on this, deindustrialisation in the West might be regarded as a reasonable choice founded on a belief in globalisation and free trade. However, economies based largely on low-wage services make for a poorer population than export-focused nations – which of course was the original source of Britain's wealth.

ARM AND INNOVATION

Based in Cambridge, ARM (Advanced RISC Machines) is one of the world's leading supplier of microchip designs. The company's designs are used in 95% of the world's mobile phones and a significant number of notebooks. ARM chips use little power and produce little heat – essential for smartphones. ARM does not manufacture, instead designing and selling its intellectual property to manufacturers such as Apple and Samsung. Its revenues are around £700 million, and it employs some 2,000 people, mostly in the Cambridge area.

ARM originally stood for Acorn RISC Machines, a technology developed by Acorn Computers, makers of the BBC Micro, a low-cost personal computer from the mid-1980s. Acorn was broken up in 1998 but its work on RISC (reduced instruction set computer) processors has proved to be an enduring and highly profitable legacy.

FREE TRADE

Free markets. Free trade. Free bananas. Surely anything free must be a good thing. We may think of globalisation as a modern phenomenon, but the 19th century also enjoyed worldwide trade and finance, with the UK at its heart.

As top dog, it suited Britain that other countries tore down trade barriers to allow our manufactured goods access to their markets. UK industry reigned supreme in everything from trains to toffees. However, rising nations such as the US and Germany imposed tariff barriers to protect their home industries. More recently, South Korea and Japan sheltered their industries until they were strong enough to compete openly.

So who benefits from the UK being so open?

Sorry – we got it wrong

The days of bountiful free markets seem to be over. The steady march of progress, in which rising trade and freely flowing capital advanced hand in hand around the globe, benevolently breaking down national barriers, now looks like a rose-tinted fantasy.

Instead, since the crash we have seen the re-assertion of state control in the global economy. Worldwide, government interventions in 2008–9 to support the financial system came to an extraordinary $11.9 trillion (source IMF). In countries like the US and UK, governments printed vast amounts of (electronic) money in the form of Quantitative Easing programmes in a bid to boost stalled economic activity.

The pre-crash doctrine espoused by fans of unfettered globalisation demanded that countries create 'level playing fields' – by breaking down trade barriers to facilitate free competition. State intervention was the work of the devil, only to be practised where obvious market failures demanded it. But many countries are now acting strategically by making the most of their economic strengths. This may not bode well for future global co-operation.

Industrial strategy

If you want to irritate a Westminster politician, just mention the words 'Industrial Policy'. The chances are it will provoke a violent allergic reaction.

Governments across the world have long supported their industries by means such as easy access to funding and by targeting sectors they want to grow, such as renewable energy or defence. A few decades ago, Britain did likewise. But this idea has fallen out of favour. 'Industrial policy' became associated with the perceived failures of the 1970s – British Leyland being the most spectacular example. Instead, governments since the early 1980s have favoured 'competition policy' – the provision of fair conditions for free markets. This might typically involve minimal regulation and more congenial legal systems, such as ending restrictions on ownership. Funding might also be provided for workers' education and training. The term 'picking winners' is still used sarcastically by politicians as something governments should avoid because it results in 'picking losers' – or at least that's the version of history that's been handed down.

Selective memory

The notion that government attempts to support British business always ended in failure is misplaced. Poor results were often achieved, but this was often because intervention was done in a panic rather than as part of a thought-through plan. In other words, governments have not had an intelligent industrial strategy for some time.

In the post-war period, British governments had long-term strategies for economic development. But these were often blown off course by short-term politics. Harold Wilson's 'National Plan' of 1965 died in the devaluation crisis of 1966–67. The 'Industrial Strategy' of 1975 was ripped up as the government bailed out near-bankrupt Chrysler UK. And, as we have seen, the income from North Sea oil was used for boosting tax revenues.

Perhaps the ultimate pragmatic intervention to support British business came with the 2008 bailout of the banking system – although this actually reflected a long tradition of government support for the financial sector.

CASE STUDY: TRIUMPH MOTORCYCLES

Like so many industries Britain once dominated, motorcycle production collapsed in the face of Japanese competition, largely due to poor management and a lack of investment. In 1983 the abandoned Triumph factory in Meriden, Coventry, was bought by a housing developer, demolished and redeveloped. And that would have been that, had this developer not been someone quite remarkable.

John Bloor had already turned his construction company from a one-man-band into a multi-million-pound operation – Bloor Homes. And when the factory's assets were sold he also acquired the patents, manufacturing rights and trademarks. Bloor's money, drive and vision took Triumph from an initial 12 workers in a shed to worldwide success, with factories in the UK and overseas.

Over the next eight years Bloor spent around £100 million developing a new range of motorbikes, and went on investing for another 13 years until he saw a profit in 2004. Today Triumph products are highly regarded, and it has six high-tech factories around the world and 750 dealers in 35 countries. Around 80% of its products are sold outside the UK. By 2008, production topped 50,000 units a year.

Triumph is well-financed and devotes huge sums to investment. It is privately owned, without shareholder pressure to extract short-term profits. The brand name gave international recognition, but with it came a reputation for oil leaks and unreliability. Its success is due to excellent products, such as the 2.3 litre Rocket III, the world's largest-capacity production bike.

Triumph's resurgence has since seen other defunct marques such as Norton and Ariel revive, albeit on a smaller scale. If anyone in government wants to know how to revive a great British industry, look no further.

HMS FALSE ECONOMY

During the recent Scottish referendum campaign, the UK's defence secretary intimated that, should Scotland leave the UK, the Royal Navy would reconsider its commitment to shipbuilding on the Clyde.

The contract for the new Type 26 frigates is worth £4 billion and up to 11,000 skilled jobs. Maintaining such skills is key to the capacity of the UK to arm itself. However, in 2012 a £452 million contract to build four Royal Fleet Auxiliary refuelling and supply vessels was given to Daewoo of South Korea on the grounds that it was cheaper. But was this such a good deal for the UK?

Offshoring

A decision to go offshore should be balanced against the 30% of local wages that would come back to the government through taxes. And most workers spend their wages locally rather than, say, stashing them in an offshore tax haven. This means money flowing to the economy, creating prosperity, reducing social problems and generating taxes such as VAT.

Who decides?

Of course it is not the job of the Royal Navy to consider the economic good of the UK. Its concern is the cost and specification of the ships. And when budgets are devolved, there is no incentive for one government department to consider the bigger picture. But these huge sums of taxpayers' money can create lots of good jobs. In competitor countries public spending is undertaken to bring maximum benefit to the country. Why not in Britain?

One of the reasons stated for handing the shipbuilding contract to South Korea was that, as a result of past underinvestment, UK shipyards might not have the capacity to build such ships (although BAe soon afterwards announced the closure of its modern Portsmouth yard). If true, this would be a prime opportunity to start a revival of British shipbuilding. It also suggests that offshoring damages the UK's ability to supply its own naval needs.

Outsourcing government

If naval contracts are awarded on the grounds of cost minimisation, why stop with shipbuilding? The Houses of Parliament requires £4 billion in structural work over the next decade or more. We might ask why politicians have to work in the Palace of Westminster rather than, for example, in an office building in Stoke, where rents are lower.

Of course, no one is suggesting this as a serious option. It might make sense economically, but there are issues of national pride and tradition. Yet perhaps shipbuilding should be as much a source of pride as the Houses of Parliament. When governments are considering procurement, perhaps they should consider the 'triple bottom line' – economic, social and environmental sustainability. Nothing beats decent jobs for building strong communities and social sustainability: it's how most towns grew up. And constructing at a local level minimises environmental costs.

A simple 'What's cheapest?' approach short-changes the nation.

Government support (whisper it)

UK governments may have given limited support for British industry, but we certainly do have an industrial strategy – in two landmark sectors where national need trumped immediate economic issues.

Britain's aerospace industry is by some measures the second-largest in the world. Airbus, a joint European venture, has major plants in the UK and is one of only two large civil aircraft manufacturers globally, the other being US-based Boeing. In what turned out to be a strategic error, in 2006 BAe Systems disposed of its 20% share in Airbus. Britain was left without a stake in this hugely successful business, ceding control to the French and German senior partners (who had the backing of their governments). However, Rolls-Royce remains the world's second-largest manufacturer of aircraft engines. Employment in the industry has fallen from 250,000 in 1980 to around 100,000 today, but productivity has rocketed: each worker added £55,000 of value in 1980, but £159,000 by 2006.

This is an industry which has benefited from government intervention. Rolls-Royce was saved from bankruptcy in 1971 by being nationalised by a Conservative government. British Aerospace was formed in 1977 from the nationalisation and merger of the UK's two major manufacturers, Hawker Siddeley and BAC, themselves the product of a government-led merger in 1960. British Aerospace was privatised in 1981 and Rolls-Royce was sold back to the market in 1987.

Since then, government support has been consistent, as a result of defence contracts which make up about half of the industry's revenues. The UK has exceptionally high defence spending, and the wisdom of close relationships between government defence procurers and the industry that supplies them can be legitimately questioned. But government support, provided consistently over a long period of time for a presumed national interest, has created a successful industrial strategy for aerospace. The US defence industry has similarly benefited from state involvement, but on a gargantuan scale.

Healthy – and wealthy

Defence isn't the only arena where government support has nurtured world-class British companies. The prioritisation of health care, and the NHS in particular, by successive governments has helped foster an environment in which 23% of the top 75 drugs sold globally are made by UK pharmaceutical companies. Over a third of all private-sector research spending in the UK is made by pharmaceuticals, while the industry's contribution to the balance of trade is the largest of any sector apart from North Sea oil.

UK pharmaceutical manufacturers have benefited from long-standing government funding for medical research. Universities and publicly funded research centres have provided scientific breakthroughs and the staff that private companies rely on. Another huge benefit provided by the state is the NHS, which is worth a staggering £9 billion a year. This massive, long-term market is of exceptional value to manufacturers. It is reinforced by pricing regulations (the Pharmaceutical Price Regulation Scheme), which sets fair prices for drugs and makes allowances for the manufacturers' appropriate profits.

In other words, government support appears at both ends of the pharmaceutical production line. At the start it provides valuable raw research and skilled individuals. At the end it provides a stable market for the industry's products.

On the basis of this public support the British pharmaceutical industry remains a world leader. Yet this pre-eminence comes under periodic threat, such as the recent closure of US-based Pfizer's research centre at Sandwich in Kent. There was also the recent threat of a takeover of AstraZeneca (one of only two remaining UK-owned pharmaceutical companies), also by Pfizer. This bid, motivated substantially by the perceived tax advantages of the UK, with further cost-saving closures of labs and factories in the pipeline, was rejected by AstraZeneca's board as predatory and damaging to the company's (and hence Britain's) longer-term interests. But the takeover bid was initially supported by the government, whose default position is an 'open for business' stance. Perhaps they should have been mindful of the broken promises by the US food group Kraft during its takeover battle for Cadbury just a couple of years earlier.

Innovation in the UK

The economist Mariana Mazzucato has challenged 'hands-off' Westminster politicians by pointing out that the state can achieve huge success when it gets involved with industry in an intelligent way. Overseas governments have made targeted interventions that helped develop new products and processes – even whole new industries. Examples include steel, railways, air travel, microchip manufacturing, car making, biotechnology, the Internet and nanotechnology.

In most advanced economies – France, Italy, Brazil, Germany, India – governments consider it their normal function to help grow world-class industries. Silicon Valley is often heralded as the pinnacle of US free-market innovation, but it was developed on the back of government funding. Its high-tech firms grew up in southern California because it was home to much military research spending, and Google's core search algorithm was developed with funding from a National Science Foundation grant.

Just not cricket

Despite all this evidence, UK governments over the last three decades have believed that free markets alone will deliver sufficient innovation and therefore growth. Doing nothing is often easier and safer for politicians. But it is worrying that government funding for scientific research has plummeted as a share of GDP since its peak under Harold Wilson's 1966 government. Far from supporting the 'white heat' of the technological revolution (as Wilson declared), governments since the late '70s have varied from indifference to a grudging acceptance of the need to correct market failures. But private businesses will often not fund pure research, whose returns are uncertain and long-term.

R&D famine

The UK has a long and distinguished history of scientific research, not least in medicine. But the free-market doctrine means that today the UK spends surprisingly little on science. We spend even less on developing new ideas from science – commercialising scientific breakthroughs into new products. Research and development (R&D) spending in Britain – both public and private – accounted for 1.7% of GDP in 2012, far below the OECD average of 2.3%, and blown away by countries like Germany (2.9%) and Japan (3.4%). And guess which countries enjoy the most success in world markets?

Since the 2008 financial crisis, R&D spending by private business has fallen and is mostly carried out by a handful of leading firms, such as Dyson. The top 10 highest-spending firms accounted for 44% (£7.7 billion) of business R&D spending in the UK. Government, meanwhile, has wound down its own research arm, with funding for the Public Sector Research Establishments like Porton Down or the Met Office falling by 19% in real terms since 1995. Instead, public sector research funding has increasingly been allocated to private businesses or universities.

Graphene and patents

UK governments may be reluctant to spend on R&D – yet, per pound spent, the UK gets more scientific citations (quotes in scientific papers) than any other major developed country.

Britain is home to world-class universities and research facilities, and English is the language of scientific research. The structure of DNA was first described at a publicly funded lab in Cambridge. More recently, graphene (sheets of carbon only a single atom thick) was first efficiently extracted at Manchester University.

So the spirit of the Bletchley Park codebreakers lives on. But as a nation we are famously bad at deriving commercial success from British inventions. Take graphene. China holds 2,200 patents relating to the material. The US has 1,700. South Korea holds 1,200. And the UK, the country that showed how to extract it, has just 50. Of course, the quantity of patents says nothing about their quality (and there are solid arguments against *over*-patenting), but British businesses don't seem interested in applications from pure research – even where the research was conducted in the UK.

Previous efforts by government to encourage entrepreneurial research (emulating US universities like Stamford) have not been entirely successful. Spending on applied research is significantly lower here than in our competitor countries, and that has translated into a weakness in turning new discoveries into new products.

One reason for the UK's low level of research spending is that our economy is increasingly skewed towards sectors that don't spend much on research. So the decline of R&D spending here (down from around 4% of GDP in the 1960s) is another downside of deindustrialisation.

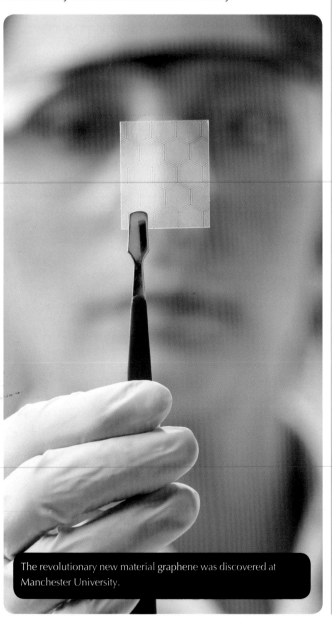

The revolutionary new material graphene was discovered at Manchester University.

Tomorrow's commercial success depends on today's investment in R&D.

There is one redeeming feature however: a fair amount of innovation gets under the official radar. Some apparently low-innovation sectors, such as oil and gas or house construction, can foster commercial creativity, often based around improved delivery of a service. For example new houses are increasingly built with prefabricated and hi-tech components such as timber I-beam floor joists. Innovation in insulation has been driven by the Building Regulations' focus on energy efficiency.

Big hitters

The UK's business research spending ranks a pitiful 21st in the world and is still falling, despite direct government support, notably in the form of R&D tax credits. (These tax credits have grown 1,111% to £1.1bn since their introduction in 2000, but critics say that much of this growth is because smart accountants have exploited them as a loophole.)

One side-effect of the loss of British manufacturing capacity is the disappearance of company research laboratories. In 2011 Pfizer shut down its Sandwich research centre (where Viagra was discovered); Shell closed its Thornton base in 2012, with the loss of 280 jobs; ICI's research centre in Blackley, Manchester, (where polyester was invented) was sold in 1993 and is now a business park. ICI – that British industrial champion – was broken up and sold off. Large conglomerates like ICI could undertake long-range research, being big enough to bear the costs and risks, but the disappearance of the nearby cotton and clothing industry that the Blackley site supported meant there was little incentive to remain.

With manufacturing in Britain now so shrunken and specialised, fruitful relationships between researchers and industry have decayed – although aerospace and the pharmaceutical industry retain some decent R&D capacity. While nations like Germany have expanded their range of exported products, the diversity of our exported products has withered as we retreat to a handful of major specialist sectors.

Short-sighted

The sort of businesses that have grown in Britain suggests why research isn't a priority. In real terms, R&D spending across gas, water and electricity sectors fell by 37% following privatisation. A Cabinet Office report from 2002 attributed this decline to 'a focus on short-term commercial goals rather than long-term investment'. Today less than 0.5% of the utilities' turnover is spent on R&D. As a result, public expenditure on energy research has shrunk precipitously, from around £1.2 billion in 1980 (in real terms) to £60 million or less today. Despite the perceived dangers from climate change, and commercial opportunities in developing renewables, the UK government spends over five times more on nuclear weapons research (around £327 million a year) than on energy research.

The UK as a global financial centre

There was, during the 2000s, assumed to be one outstanding, world-class hotspot for innovation in the UK. In the summer of 2007, everything seemed to be going right for financial services.

'The financial services sector in Britain,' the then-Chancellor Gordon Brown said in his last Mansion House speech, 'is a great example of a highly skilled, high-value-added, talent-driven industry that shows how we can excel in a world of global competition.

Britain needs more of the vigour, ingenuity and aspiration that you already demonstrate is the hallmark of your success.'

Brown's speech went down well with the City bankers at the dinner. After all, between 1997 and 2007 the sector grew by 5% a year, way ahead of the national economy's 3.2% growth rate – itself far above the historical average. The alchemy of the City wove its hypnotic spell over those who should have known better. Politicians adopted a pitying tone towards our European neighbours who hadn't been clever enough to adopt modern methods of economic management: light-touch regulation, privatisation and openness to international trade and investment. If only they could blow away the cobwebs, even high-unemployment, low-growth Germany could aspire to be more like the UK.

In the City

Naturally the Blair government was keen to sweep away perceived obstacles in the bankers' paths. The Bank of England was made independent in the first few days after Brown arrived in Number 11, a move praised in the City and elsewhere as promoting low inflation. Meanwhile the new regulatory body, the Financial Services Authority (FSA), was a dependable partner in delivering continued prosperity with the lightest of light touches. Fears that a Labour government might hobble the financial sector were rapidly dispelled. Corporation taxes were cut again and again; tax loopholes were either opened wider or left as they were – from the small ('taper relief' on capital gains tax) to the huge (tax havens in Jersey and the other Crown Dependencies).

Yet none of this was new. The financial sector, with the City of London at its centre, had for more than a century been at the heart of the UK's economic structure. A dense network of City firms, partnerships and institutions had developed to manage the flows of money from empire. This gentleman's capitalism depended on personal relationships. It was a self-governing world where good practice was maintained with minimal need for lawyers – in tune with the London Stock Exchange motto 'My word is my bond'. This may sound a million miles from the modern 'Wall Street On Thames', but what hasn't changed is that the City was immensely profitable for those involved.

However, what's good for the City isn't necessarily good for Britain. Because financiers in London would rather invest abroad than at home, seeking the highest and quickest returns possible, the domestic economy was deprived of investment. One reason Britain led the Industrial Revolution in the 18th century was its networks of local and regional banks – which is still one of the factors behind Japanese and German industrial success. Yet these local banks were starved of funds, and eventually put out of business, by international finance capital in London, which sucked in available funding. As far back as the 1930s, the Macmillan Committee was complaining about the apparent inability of the UK's financial system to fund small businesses.

Countdown to lift-off

After the Second World War, finance became sedate. Bankers supposedly followed the 3-6-3 rule: borrow at 3%, lend at 6%, on the golf course by 3pm. But the seeds of its later undoing could be discerned. Harold Wilson, then president of the Board of Trade, allowed the creation of the 'Eurodollar' market in 1950 for those seeking to borrow and lend dollars outside America's control: one customer was the West's arch-enemy, the USSR. This offshore centre began to exert pressure on governments across the world, making it more difficult for them to regulate markets. Then two things happened that caused these unrestricted offshore centres to explode: the breakdown of restrictions on currency exchange rates (Bretton Woods), and the binning of national capital controls – freeing money to slosh around the globe. Post-war regulations designed to maintain stability were condemned as financial repression. The era of conducting business on the basis of reputation, golf and G&Ts was ending.

The Big Bang

The Thatcher government dealt a final blow to gentlemanly capitalism with the Big Bang of 1986, removing some of the remaining barriers to trading financial products. Noisy, crowded trading floors populated by blazer-wearing stockbrokers and jobbers were reincarnated as computerised dealing rooms. Big US investment banks bought British merchant banks, introducing a new aggressive way of doing business.

At the same time came a de-restriction of consumer borrowing. Skyrocketing borrowing by the US government brought in a ballooning market for government and corporate debt. A credit boom in the late 1980s, under Chancellor Nigel Lawson, collapsed into recession by 1990. The boom had been driven by increases in house prices, fuelled by deregulated borrowing and the transfer of council housing to the private sector, sold off at huge discounts.

Labour, arriving in office in 1997 after an 18-year absence, inherited this deregulation and ran further with the Conservatives' financial regime, encouraging extraordinary levels of borrowing. A besotted government, the sweeping away of regulation and ready access to dollars encouraged 'financial innovation'. Banking corporations devised increasingly complex financial products – with the aid of massive computing power and the recruitment of some of the brightest minds in the country.

Yet as long as the financial sector seemed to be growing, politicians were unworried. They might have asked why so little employment was being created amid this expansion, apart from a few extra sandwich makers and taxi firms. Financial services of the kind we have in the UK do not create jobs. In 1997, at the start of the boom, UK financial services employed one million people. A decade later it still employed one million people, despite growing

'HUGE BONUS FOR YOUR THOUGHTS'

K.J.Lomb

from 6% of GDP to nearly 10%. Yet this was the horse that governments chose to bet the house on.

What counts?

The value of financial services isn't as easy to pin down as say, haircuts or motorcycle manufacture. It's hard enough to say 'Collateralised Debt Obligations' let alone monitor such financial exotica. Even those in the industry had difficulties comprehending what was going on – as we discovered in 2008.

As we saw earlier, modern banks function by the creation of money and loans. But if you or I make a loan, this doesn't get added to GDP. It is regarded, more correctly, as a transfer payment. No new value is created, since we are shuffling money from one place to another. Yet if a bank makes a loan, this *does* count towards its output, and it appears in GDP. Odd, isn't it? Nothing in the rest of the economy will have changed, but the more loans banks make the more their output will appear to grow.

What's so shocking is that all the apparent spectacular growth of financial services over the 2000s may have been a mirage. The banks' much-trumpeted contribution to rising productivity, and its addition to GDP, may have amounted to little more than a form of double-counting.

Financial services perform financial transactions. For some unknown reason we privilege this, rather than treating it as merely shifting around bags of money. In the words of Adair Turner, former head of the Financial Services Authority, much of the sector's activities are socially useless – even if hugely well-rewarded.

Dragons' den

Bankers might counter that they encourage innovation in the economy by planting venture capital. That may appear to be the case when Kelly Hoppen dispenses wads of notes in the TV show *Dragons' Den*. But this sort of funding is a tiny and declining part of the UK's capital markets. Of the £10 billion invested by venture capital firms in the UK in the last year, just 10% went to companies in the early stages of growth. Much of the rest went on operations like management buy-outs (44% of total funding in 2013). This sort of funding has, in any case, shrunk from £33 billion in 2007, just prior to the crash.

So who benefits? The value of financial services appears to accrue to that small section of their workforce engaged in the most lucrative financial transactions. This has little effect on the wider economy. Banks mostly benefit bankers – and big banks especially. One third of the richest 1% in the UK is employed in financial services compared to just 4% of the whole workforce.

True, in the six years to 2008, at the height of the boom, financial services coughed up £193 billion in all forms of tax. But this is only half the £378 billion paid to the state by manufacturing over the same period. And it pales into insignificance next to the £289 billion of direct costs, and £1,270 billion of indirect costs, that we all had to pay to clean up the bust after the boom (IMF estimates).

So maintaining the UK as a global financial centre imposes costs on the rest of us. It distorts economic outcomes across the country. Its major purpose is to fund our chronic current account deficit. At the centre of global financial flows, it can cover the UK's deficit by selling assets and mobilising credit. Without the City of London, our current account deficit could not have been sustained, as it has been, for decades.

Chapter 4

PROBLEMS AND CURES

Governments hope to get elected as an economic recovery is taking hold in order to claim the credit. In theory they see their task as taking the edges off the peaks and troughs. In practice, though, they are less keen on moderating booms – reluctant to be seen as spoiling the fun. And they have often proved incapable of halting downturns.

Smoothing the cycle

In the post-war period economists employed demand-management techniques: 'Keynesianism'. It was believed that by increasing spending during a recession and cutting it during a boom, governments could regulate the business cycle. This 'counter-cyclical' balancing mechanism would, it was hoped, set a limit to both slumps and booms.

From the late 1940s to the early 1970s, this seemed to work. For the UK, the problem throughout this post-war period was the current account – a deficit of imports over exports. In periods of economic growth, with people feeling richer, we sucked in imports – buying more than we sold. This trade gap would then threaten to bring down the value of the pound, which was fixed against the dollar under the Bretton Woods Agreement. So governments would apply the brakes, either by raising taxes and cutting spending (fiscal policy) or pushing up interest rates (monetary policy). But as the economy slowed a bit too hard, they'd have to step on the throttle to re-stimulate. This became known as the 'stop-go' cycle.

Boom city rollers – the 1970s

The early 1970s witnessed a downturn after a long boom, so the Keynesian remedy was duly applied. President Richard Nixon declared that 'we're all Keynesians now' when seeking to reflate the US economy. But these efforts seemed in vain. Demand management by government could only generate short-lived growth – like Britain's 'Barber Boom' of the early 1970s, named after the then-chancellor. More troublingly, each attempt to kickstart the economy appeared to produce inflation. Keynesian demand management appeared to no longer work. Increasing inflation, even as the economy was slowing, was the worst of both worlds. This combination of inflation and stagnation was labelled 'stagflation'.

Handbags at dawn – the 1980s

In both the UK and the US, a fresh concept known as monetarism was wheeled out to fight inflation. Monetarism was a variant on the ideas of Milton Friedman – Mrs Thatcher's favourite economist. It claimed that inflation is always and everywhere a monetary phenomenon; if governments regulated the amount of money in circulation (known as 'the growth of the money supply') inflation could be painlessly squeezed out. Indeed, governments might only need to 'commit' to doing this to cool inflationary urges.

When governments on both sides of the Atlantic followed this new course interest rates soared. This in turn ramped up exchange rates and worsened the recession. And, for Thatcher's new government, control of the money supply was proving elusive. The suppliers and dealers in money – principally the large commercial banks – paid lip service to government but continued to do as they wished to satisfy the demand for money. The money supply oscillated wildly during the early 1980s, until the policy was quietly abandoned. By the middle of the decade, inflation was somewhat under control following years of cuts and recession (having been falling in 1979 on Thatcher's arrival in office). But things were about to get out of hand once more.

The deregulation of credit markets was now allowing consumers easier access to borrowing. Combined with low real interest rates, generous income tax cuts and the growing willingness of the banking system to give credit, this generated the 'Lawson Boom' – with good times for a couple of years until it turned sour in 1989. Meanwhile inflation shot up, reaching 12% by the time Mrs Thatcher left office. With the collapse of the housing bubble the economy slipped back into prolonged and deep recession.

Autopilot – the 1990s

Through the excitement of the 1980s and early 1990s, government commitment to economic intervention and 'demand management' had been largely abandoned. In the event of recession, the plan was to allow the 'automatic stabilisers' of rising unemployment and welfare payments to operate. John Major's government saw a significant widening of the deficit in the early 1990s as a result. The arrival of New Labour didn't shift the consensus that governments should not intervene. Indeed, from 1997 management of the interest rate lever was passed from the Treasury to a newly independent Bank of England, with the government merely setting an inflation target for the Bank to aim at.

With governments sworn not to touch the big *macroeconomic* levers, attention instead focused on *microeconomic* interventions: ensuring markets could function effectively, providing a supply of appropriately skilled labour and providing infrastructure such as roads. Enterprise Zones were launched in deprived areas, backed up by grants and freezes on business rates.

Desperate measures – the 2000s

Labour aimed for a further restraint on government spending through the 'Golden Rule' – that public debt should not rise above 60% of GDP. It also introduced the balanced budget rule: that the deficit should remain around zero over the course of the business cycle. Both were thrown into disarray by the 2007–8 crisis which required huge bailouts for the banks and the operation of the 'automatic stabilisers' on a grand scale. This set a floor to the crash, sustaining at least some economic activity as the economy shrank rapidly and lending dried up, and helped to prevent the far greater evil of economic collapse.

But enormous amounts of new borrowing ramped up the government's debt, nearly doubling it in a single year. Moreover, the crash was followed by efforts to drive the Bank of England's base rate to near-zero levels, and saw a radical new weapon: Quantitative Easing.

All these exceptional measures introduced after the banking crash remain in place today. But the levers have been pulled so hard that there's not much further they can go. The enormous government deficit, it is argued, has made fiscal policy unworkable because borrowing money for tax cuts and state spending would increase the nation's debt pile. The other big lever, interest rates, cannot be moved from its near-zero level until the recovery has been locked in place. When the governor of the Bank of England hints at interest rate rises to come, the financial markets tremble – and they never quite arrive. Some speculate that this state of affairs might be the new normal.

Age of austerity: 2010 onwards

The Coalition government which arrived in May 2010 took a different approach. After bailing out the banks, government debt was enormous but would be restored to health – said the Coalition – through austerity. This meant the sharpest cuts in public spending for generations. The new Office for Budget Responsibility (OBR) within the Treasury (with a mandate to produce independent economic forecasting), provided a routemap declaring that after a few years of hardship the economy would rebound to the greatest boom in British peacetime history, with enthusiasm for the government's economic programme restoring confidence.

This didn't happen. In early 2010, just as the economy seemed to be turning the corner, austerity pushed it into recession for the next two years. The most dramatic cut was on capital investment by government, which fell around 50% (such cuts being easier to hide). There followed a near-unprecedented double-dip recession, which by late 2012 seemed headed for a possible triple-dip.

Who could predict it?

As the downturn took hold, business investment fell spectacularly short of expectations: forecasters had said it would rise more than 35% by 2014, but the actual rise was just under 1%. The OBR had also predicted an export boom, but the current account deficit continued to widen and at the time of writing stands at 6.5% – close to the worst gap since records began.

And while real wages were predicted to increase by over 3% a year, living standards have fallen consistently for the last six years. Pay increases have struggled to keep pace with today's very low rates of inflation. But the biggest and most damning error was that the OBR forecast the government deficit to be around £40 billion and falling in 2014: at £91 billion the deficit is more than twice that prediction. (The 'structural deficit', once the effect of the business cycle is removed, was supposed to be in balance by 2014.) The government has had to extend its austerity programme by several years.

But with government imposing so many cuts, shouldn't its fiscal deficit be getting smaller? Instead it's still widening. The solution to this riddle is down to two things. First, although local councils have seen cuts of up to a third in their funding – with the loss of half a million public-sector jobs – central government spending is still high. Second, the government is taking in less revenue. The deficit is the difference between what the government spends and what it earns through taxes. Even where public spending has been pushed down, tax revenues have also fallen, or at least failed to keep pace with economic growth. The result has been a widening of the deficit and an increase in the government's borrowing needs.

Weak taxes

The decline in tax revenue is particularly worrying because some of the damage has been self-inflicted. Corporation tax revenues are down around 14% since 2008, with government cutting corporation tax every year, so that the UK's headline rate is now among the lowest in Europe. If UK companies paid as much tax as they did in the last year of Mrs Thatcher's reign, the country would be £30 billion a year better off. There would still be a deficit, but the fiscal situation would be transformed.

Another self-inflicted wound is the increase in the personal allowance – the amount we can earn before income tax is paid. There is less revenue from both business and individuals.

Research from the LSE and the University of Essex has revealed that recent tax cuts (including the lopping of the 50p top rate for those earning more than £150,000) matches the amount saved by government spending cuts. In other words, the tax cuts and benefit cuts have been fiscally neutral, making no difference to the government's deficit. But because tax cuts have mainly benefited the wealthy while spending cuts have mainly hurt the poor there's been a redistribution from the poor to the rich.

Low wages

The weakness in the amount of tax raised reflects weaknesses in the economy. With incomes falling, there has been less income to tax and a growing deficit. But while it's relatively simple for governments to reverse tax cuts, turning around the unprecedented slide in incomes won't be easy. In fact this appears to be the worsening of a long-standing trend. Meanwhile, the government has become increasingly reliant on indirect taxes; the VAT increase to 20% in 2010 has seen VAT revenues up by 32%. But indirect taxes hit the poorest hardest.

'NO, ROGER – LESS IS **NOT** MORE '

Just to make matters worse, the growth in lower-paid jobs has sucked tax credits out of the kitty. Tax credits were established by the Labour government to remove disincentives to work: low incomes would be topped up by payments that taper off as more is earned. However, because incomes have fallen, the bill for these credits is some £5 billion higher than forecast, running at around £31 billion a year.

'Decoupling' and falling incomes

It wasn't meant to be like this. As recovery from recession kicked in, no one anticipated falling incomes and the creation of so many low-paid jobs. Since 2008 average real earnings have fallen by around 12%. Remarkably, six million people defined as 'in poverty' are actually employed.

Only 1 in 40 jobs created recently is full-time. Self-employment is rising from an average over the last 20 years of 12% of the workforce to an unprecedented 15%. This is unlikely to simply reflect an entrepreneurial spirit since average earnings from self-employment are down 22% since 2008. But perhaps the biggest source of job insecurity is 'zero-hours contracts', under which people have no contracted hours of work, leaving the employer free to cut their hours at will. Around a million workers are currently on such contracts, almost doubling since 2012. Many landlords refuse to accept a zero-hours tenant on the grounds that their income will not be reliable. It's estimated that 1 person in 12 in the labour force is in 'precarious employment' – a huge rise.

There are some other signs that conditions are worsening. Unpaid internships, intended to provide work experience, are stretching to two or three years in some industries. Some might call this exploitation.

Growth or no growth?

Weirdly, all this damage to the individual's standard of living is taking place in an economy with a relatively swift increase in GDP. Although this issue has become more pronounced since the crash, it's not unprecedented. Is there a problem in the way things are measured?

GDP is widely accepted as a measure of economic health. At least two generations have associated an improvement in GDP with an improvement in their quality of life. But over the past 15 years or so, this relationship appears to have weakened, if not completely broken down. In the five boom years leading up to 2008, average real incomes started to flatline – actually falling in some regions outside London – despite economic growth consistently hitting more than 3% a year, significantly above the historic trend. Personal budgets squeezed by rising prices for essentials like gas and food were partially eased by the falling price of imported manufactured goods. Thankfully, the situation in the UK is nowhere near as bad as in the US, where stagnating average earnings have left real pay today no higher than it was in 1979; since the crash, stagnation has turned into outright decline – despite consistent economic growth since 2013.

Low productivity

Why the shrinking wages? First, the crash hit productivity. Without productivity increases, the scope for business owners to pay staff more is limited, since there's no extra value that can be shared. And rising inequality means that most extra value produced falls into the hands of the comfortably off, rather than the workers. (Of course, a small section of workers have seen rapid increases in their earnings, notably those in financial services.)

But the status of most workers has been weakened over a long period. Unemployment is still relatively high, unemployment benefits have been reduced and many people are lumbered with significant debts. And trade unions have a lot less clout. So we could wait a long time for even a few pence in the pound to be diverted into our pockets unless there is government intervention.

The debt crisis

Despite many people's incomes remaining stagnant during the 2000s, there was rising consumer expenditure.

The explanation is debt. Our financial system, let off the leash from the end of the 1970s, expanded its lending to households. By the early 2000s, the US central bank, the Federal Reserve, drove interest rates to historic lows in response to a mild recession on the back of the dot. com crash, the East Asian crisis and the later 9/11 attacks. It then kept rates low in a bid to boost activity. But the ensuing boom was fuelled by cheap credit. This closed the gap between real incomes and what suppliers wanted to sell. It was underpinned, especially in the US and the UK, by rapidly rising house prices. With mortgages cheaply available, demand for housing was sustained.

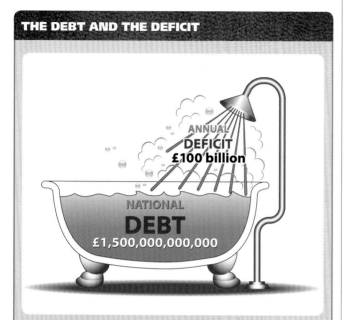

THE DEBT AND THE DEFICIT

The debt

The national debt is the total amount that Britain owes – accumulated over many years but massively added to by the bank bailout. It's gigantic, currently nearly £1.5 trillion. Our total economy (GDP) is around £1.7 trillion. The greater the debt the greater the deficit, because of interest payments.

The deficit

This is the amount the government is borrowing. The yearly amount is around £100 billion – money the UK is borrowing so that government can keep spending. Britain's borrowing is more than almost any other country in Europe.

Government is spending £263 million a DAY more than it gets in tax. This is more than we spend on defence. According to *The Spectator*, 'you could disband the military, fire diplomats, close the prisons, fire every police officer, cancel all aid – and still not be able to balance the books'.

Big debts mean big interest payments. Paying for borrowing is the third-largest cost to the government after welfare and health. And that drain will grow larger with increases in interest rates. The more we borrow now, the less future generations can spend on public services – and the higher their taxes.

So who do we owe the money to? Hard to say. To finance its debt, the state issues bonds (IOUs), which are bought by a set of authorised banks. It pays interest on these bonds which the banks sell on the global financial markets. Who ultimately owns these titles is one of the world's best-kept secrets.

One potential ray of light is the fact that the deficit is roughly equivalent to the estimated amount lost to HMRC through tax avoidance and evasion. Some argue that by also addressing this, together with the implicit annual subsidy to the banking sector, we might even be able to run a surplus.

'BRING OUT YER DEBT'

K.J.Lamb

Debtor nation

Between 2001 and 2008, UK household debt went from less than 100% of household disposable income to a peak of 163% – the highest of any major developed country. In cash terms the amount we owed more than doubled.

The UK is by some distance the most heavily indebted large economy on the planet – taking into account debts held by the government, households, firms and financial businesses. For around a decade, we enjoyed growth fuelled by all this debt. The wheels of commerce were kept turning by borrowing: debt expanded faster than the economy. An enormous consumer boom ensued, but it was built on sand.

Between 2001 and 2008, we turned our homes into cash machines through a spate of remortgaging. During this period, borrowing by households against the increased value of their houses ('housing equity withdrawal') was bigger than the sum of economic growth. This brings to mind something we talked about earlier – the dilemma of eating corn now or planting it for the future. Meanwhile, as a share of GDP, investment in the UK slumped from 16% in 2000 to just 11% by 2008.

An accident waiting to happen

What caused the 2007–8 crash? Increasing borrowing by households in the 2000s enabled financial firms to leverage this borrowing, using increasingly complex risk-management techniques. Assisted by light-touch regulation, banks expanded their operations on the back of limited reserves and capital, exploiting looser and looser definitions of suitable reserve assets. By 2007, British banks had an astonishing £3,900 billion worth of risky assets balanced on just £120 billion of shock-absorbing equity (about 3%). For Chancellor Gordon Brown, this expansion represented 'a new golden age for the City of London', and most MPs agreed.

The graph shows the full horror of this debt. Interestingly, government debt is a relatively small part of the picture, even after 2008.

MINSKY'S DEATH SPIRAL

One day you may be happy, prosperous and secure. But your apparently sound financial position – perhaps your business or household – could be exposed to shocks elsewhere in the economy. The economist Hyman Minsky explained this hidden danger as follows.

Banks create loans and offer them to customers who want to borrow money. At first, banks lend only to very safe bets – to those of their customers they judge are most likely to repay their debts. But after a while, these customers (large businesses, say) have all the credit they want. So banks look for somewhat-less-safe bets – smaller businesses, higher-risk companies, prime mortgages. These, too, eventually borrow all the money they want.

But banks, to make profits, must continually expand their lending: they depend on interest payments to generate returns. So they look for even riskier prospects, and so on until they find themselves lending money, as with US sub-prime mortgages, to those who may have no job or assets. By this stage, bankers may also resort to illegal activities such as rigging markets or swindling customers with bogus products such as PPI.

Thus the whole system has become financially fragile: over-extended and liable to collapse with only the smallest of knocks.

Minsky's theory suggests that high debts relative to income, regardless of how apparently well-managed they are, are more risky than lower debts. This applies not only to banks but to nations.

Of course, these liabilities were balanced by assets. But the assets were increasingly risky, notably for banks that had lent to the US sub-prime mortgage market. These were mortgages offered to people derisively known as 'NINJAs' – because they had No Income, No Job and no Assets. Sub-prime lending in the US rose by 232% in the

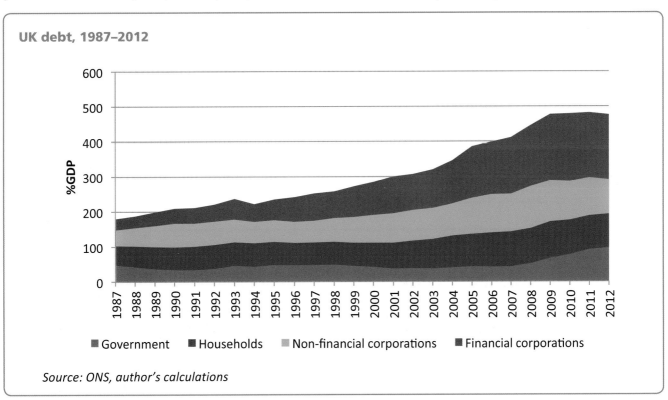

UK debt, 1987–2012

%GDP

■ Government ■ Households ▨ Non-financial corporations ■ Financial corporations

Source: ONS, author's calculations

seven years to 2007, reaching $1.7 trillion. You might well ask what the regulators were doing.

Such high-risk lending made sense for the creditor banks if, and only if, house prices kept rising. When house prices started to turn in 2006, the sub-prime business model collapsed as homeowners defaulted and homes were repossessed. By then, sharp operators had already made big personal fortunes. The reason this was so contagious was because these 'sucker loans' had been resold in increasingly complex packages, culminating in the notorious Collateralised Debt Obligations (CDOs). Somehow, these loans ended up on the balance sheets of major banks as seemingly high-value assets, sanctified by major credit ratings agencies. As the number of people defaulting spread, the value of these financial assets collapsed and that, in turn, threatened the solvency of major banks.

The first hint of this for the British was the failure of Northern Rock in November 2007 (see Chapter 2). The crisis continued over 2008, defaults and failures spreading through the financial system until eventually they consumed the giant Lehman Brothers, America's third-largest investment bank, which filed for bankruptcy on 18 September 2008. At this point, the global financial system was, in the words of the normally sober director of the IMF 'on the verge of systemic meltdown'.

Tangled up in red

In 2008 Britain was close to the financial abyss and social collapse. The UK was more deeply entangled in the financial system than any other country. Consumer borrowing at home had enabled UK banks (and other financial institutions operating here) to massively expand their operations across the world. Their balance sheets grew formidably. But with their financial assets failing, some becoming worthless, they were heavily exposed. As funding fled from the interbank system, they could no longer finance their operations. That would have meant closing bank branches and shutting down cash-points. Prime Minister Gordon Brown had to avoid the daunting prospect of putting the army on the streets to quell civil unrest. He therefore opted to bail out the banking system. The direct and indirect costs came to an astonishing £1.27 trillion, or around 90% of GDP – proportionately more than any other large economy. Lloyds and Royal Bank of Scotland had to be partially nationalised and their operations placed under a new group of mandarins and senior bankers: UK Financial Investments.

Since the crash, major economies have attempted to pay down their huge debts. Households and firms have similarly deleveraged, while austerity has been adopted by governments here and in the eurozone. By paying debts, however, they are not spending in the rest of the economy. Without spending, the economy slows down.

This slowdown in growth since the crash, at least among high-income countries, has caused a revival of the concept of 'secular stagnation' – the trend that, with rising inequality in the economy, a greater share of society's income goes to people who are less inclined to spend it: the rich. Following Keynes' argument, this will lead to a slowdown in growth: a secular stagnation.

Rising inequality in Britain has led to falling relative wages, and hence demand falls. To keep consumers buying, the temporary solution has been to offer debt in compensation for falling wages. In the long run this is suicidal. Debt must be repaid, with interest, at some point. But if incomes are falling or stagnant, people's ability to repay is diminishing. The risk of crisis increases, particularly if interest rates rise. And real long-term growth has been slowing in Britain for decades, as it has elsewhere.

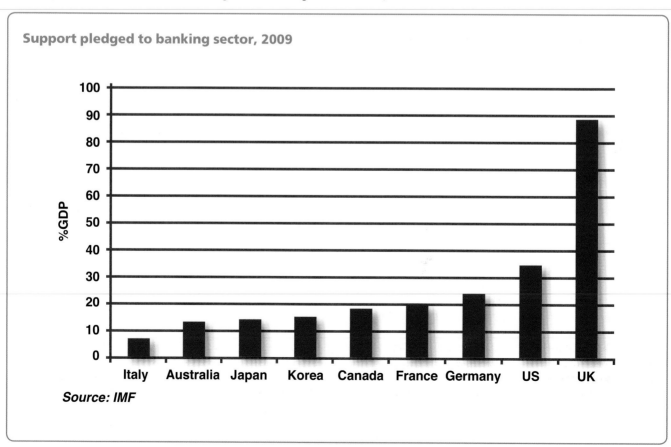

Support pledged to banking sector, 2009

%GDP

Italy　Australia　Japan　Korea　Canada　France　Germany　US　UK

Source: IMF

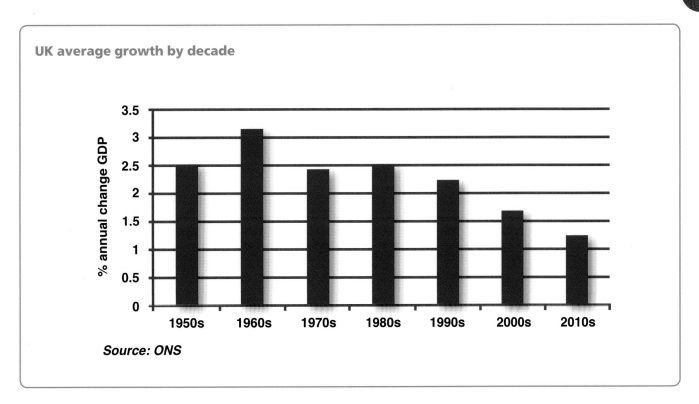

UK average growth by decade

Source: ONS

Growing pains

The UK economy has been growing quite strongly, relative to much of the developed world, since early 2013. Yet this has produced no rise in real incomes for most of us. As in the run-up to the crash, we are relying on debt to rescue us – filling the gap left by flat or falling real incomes. 'Unsecured lending' by households (basically all loans except mortgages) has been rising by an astounding £1 billion a month. This includes credit card debts, store credit and, ominously, high-interest payday lending. It's no surprise that this figure more or less matches the increase in consumer spending. Housing equity withdrawal has yet to take off, so there may be scope for homeowners to load up with even more debt. We can add to the mix PPI compensation (from mis-sold credit card insurance) which provided a one-off £25 billion boost for consumers.

But there are signs that inequality is rising sharply again, with the richest 1,000 Britons doubling their wealth in the last four years. Luxury goods sales have risen across the world. But economic growth based on rising debts and falling incomes isn't sustainable. Either real incomes must increase or the economy will fall over again – and this time we may not be so lucky. The army may yet need to be deployed on the streets.

The current account trap

First we complain that incomes aren't rising. Now we're going to flag up the risks when wages finally take off.

As the economy has grown since 2013, the pound has risen in value. This has reduced the cost of imports but made our exports more expensive. Meanwhile the current account deficit – our trade with the rest of the world – has necessitated, as we saw in Chapter 2, more borrowing from overseas and the selling off of more assets.

However, debts require interest payments and assets produce financial returns. When these payments are made to the owners abroad, they are counted as a debit against the current account – a flow of money out of the country. Over the 2000s, the UK was in a happier position (as it long had been) of earning more income from owning assets and debt in the rest of the world than it paid out to the rest of the world. That situation has changed. Foreign-owned UK assets, and debt we owe abroad, is so large that we are paying more to the rest of the world than we are earning from it. This has worsened the current account deficit, meaning that we need to borrow more to plug the gap.

Solutions

There are three quick solutions to this income problem.

- **A recovery in incomes from abroad** This will depend on rapid growth in the rest of the world, but with the majority of UK-owned assets located in the eurozone, this is unlikely.
- **Defaulting on debt or nationalising foreign-owned assets** Highly unlikely.
- **A sterling crisis** The value of the pound might drop. This happened in 1947, 1967, 1976, 1992 and, at a slower rate, in 2008–9. But keeping sterling at a high value has been essential to maintaining the desirability of UK assets and debts for the rest of the world. This, in turn, has made borrowing at low rates to cover the current account deficit possible.

The old enemy: short-termism

As we saw earlier, investment in the UK is low relative to similar economies and has been since at least the 1870s, when competition from the US and Germany began to be felt. This is often associated with short-termism and the desire of our substantial financial sector to seek quick and high returns.

On one level this is a strength: the UK is good at attracting investment from abroad, the flipside to being good at investing

After the 2008 crash it was widely agreed that we needed to rebalance the economy towards manufacturing. Wealth creation was to be based on investment and exports, rather than consumer spending on the back of house-price inflation. But the UK today is still the only major Western country without a coherent industrial policy. Westminster politicians' horror of long-term strategy, and their insistence that manufacturing didn't matter, allowed other nations, among them Japan, Korea, Taiwan and Germany, to sprint ahead.

By slashing corporate taxes, government hopes that the UK can continue to attract foreign direct investment. But this means competing with many other countries, such as Ireland, all just as keen to lure multinationals with ever-lower taxes. To reduce reliance on this begging bowl strategy, we might want to emulate countries that have rebuilt their industrial base. The *Daily Mail* city editor, Ruth Sunderland, points out that manufacturing creates real assets, not illusory ones that exist only on computer screens or in footnotes to bank reports. It creates high-value jobs, in the regions as well as in the City.

There is a lot of ground to make up. The UK now ranks 19th in global manufacturing out of 26 countries, having sunk behind the Czech Republic, Poland, Thailand and Australia as well as powerhouses such as the US, China, Germany and South Korea. UK industry accounts for a mere 3% of global exports, down from 4.4% at the turn of the millennium; we are a net importer of industrial products, food and energy.

Ha-Joon Chang, the Cambridge professor of economics, believes that Britain needs to identify industries and technologies for the future motor of the economy, and to provide them with support, including subsidies for R&D, loan guarantees for small firms or preferences in government procurement. Primarily these should be targeted at strategic industries.

Support might take the form of:

- **Co-ordinated investment** Major infrastructure investments such as new factories must be co-ordinated with the broader industrial strategy, customised to industries we want to grow.
- **Education and skills** Without a national strategy, it is difficult for educators to know what kinds of engineers or technicians to produce, and for students to know what skills to acquire.
- **A joined-up strategy** Strategies need to be hammered out in consultation with the major parties – private-sector firms, trade unions, universities and research institutes.

Nurturing seedlings

As soon as there's a glimmer of success, UK companies are tempted by buyouts. But if promising UK saplings aren't allowed to grow, we will never breed tomorrow's national champions – the UK's Googles, Microsofts and Apples. This requires government to promote a longer-term focus and to support entrepreneurs.

To build an export-focused economy, we must encourage innovation. Much can be learnt from countries like the USA, Malaysia and South Korea.

The basic infrastructure required includes:

- **The rule of law**, for example in patenting new technology
- **Funding** for small and medium-sized businesses
- **A skilled workforce**
- **Good facilities** such as buildings, power and transport

- **A culture** that promotes and rewards enterprise
- **An economic system** that nurtures long-term growth and provides protection from hostile takeovers

German lessons

German industry is the export champion of the world. Much of the credit is due to the large numbers of family businesses, collectively known as the 'Mittelstand'. Key to their success is a willingness to plan for the long term. The Mittelstand thrives because it has a degree of support largely unknown in Britain. Technical and vocational education is valued in Germany and co-ordinated with the needs of industry. A network of 428 savings banks supports local businesses, with the backing of state investment banks. Both the banks and the workforce are represented at board level.

JCB – the world famous digger manufacturer – is one of the few successful British firms in the mould of Germany's Mittelstand companies. Its chairman, Sir Anthony Bamford, points out that 'Germany has had a proper industrial policy for many years because they understand they have to export to live. In contrast we have not had an industrial policy in the last 50 years. Politicians by their nature have their minds on short-term things, even though manufacturing is the backbone of a successful economy.'

A plan to strengthen manufacturing might include tax breaks for research and development, low rents and business rates, a bank dedicated to manufacturing plus a powerful manufacturing 'tsar' in government. But to revive UK export earners, regain lost markets and beat our competitors will require passionate, intelligent, long-term government support. Rival manufacturing nations see this as an essential plank of industry. For example, 70 per cent of Chinese manufacturers rank government support for technology, science and innovation as their top advantage.

In advanced manufacturing, it is not enough to argue that rolling back the so-called 'dead hand of the state' will allow entrepreneurs to magically appear. Industries such as renewable energy involve long-term projects with high levels of risk and large investments. Manufacturers need long-term finance which banks with a short-term mentality can't provide.

The UK must reshape its economy so that we can pay our way without relying on debt-driven pseudo-growth. There is no reason why Britain cannot be a great manufacturing nation again – if government has the will and puts the right policies in place.

Source material: Will Hutton, Ruth Sunderland, Ha-Joon Chang.

elsewhere. But it has grown into a damaging reluctance to invest in our own industries, particularly in longer-term projects such as infrastructure. The economist Dieter Helm estimates that to bring the UK's infrastructure up to western European standards will require £500 billion of investment over the next decade or so.

Some of the decisions by governments over the last 30 years appear to have reinforced this short-sighted attitude. As noted earlier, energy privatisation slashed our investment in energy research, but it has also meant a neglect of strategic capacity. Britain, for example, has gas storage of just 4% of national demand, compared to 20% in Germany and 50% in Austria.

And British management is, by international standards, often less than brilliant. The business pages are full of stories of outrageous pay awards for CEOs and directors. Too many big companies excel at cost-cutting through factory closures, retreats from markets and selling themselves to the highest bidder. A 2012 Department for Business report noted that, 'The UK falls behind key competitor nations such as the US and Germany in terms of leadership and management capability.' It estimates that over £19 billion is squandered every year in lost working time due to poor management.

Surveys of managers reveal a lag in managerial competence relative to Sweden, the US, Germany and Japan. While the UK has some exceptionally well-managed plants, usually foreign-owned, there are many poor performers. Training for managers is limited and haphazard. Worse, there is little long-term thinking at many firms. Businesses that plan ahead and invest in research and development tend to do well.

Some of this poor management is due to the financial structure: City pressure for short-term profits comes at the expense of investment in future products. Some CEOs are so fixated on reporting what the markets want to hear that they will do almost anything to improve their quarterly figures – even at the cost of long-term success. Is it coincidental that successful companies like Dyson, JCB and Triumph Motorcycles are privately owned?

However, large companies, unlike small businesses, fund most of their investment from retained earnings rather than borrowing. And companies in the UK are sitting on enormous piles of cash: around £650 billion. Profits, outside the North Sea producers, are at record levels, dividend payments to shareholders are up and corporation taxes have fallen. So a lack of cash for the large companies is not a problem. The challenge is encouraging them to invest in product development.

The productivity puzzle

Why is the UK starved of investment when big firms have so much money? Economists have labelled this the 'productivity puzzle'. Productivity is the rate at which the economy can turn the ingredients – raw materials, labour and capital – into output. Productivity is usually measured by output per worker: how many sausages each employee produces, or how many sausages per hour worked.

The UK's productivity has tended to lag behind our competitors', although things looked up during the 2000s as this so-called 'productivity gap' started to close. Since the crash, productivity has fallen. Output per hour is lower than it was in 2008. This is not unexpected. In a downturn, when most of us are feeling the pinch, consumer demand falls and hence less stuff is sold by firms. If they're

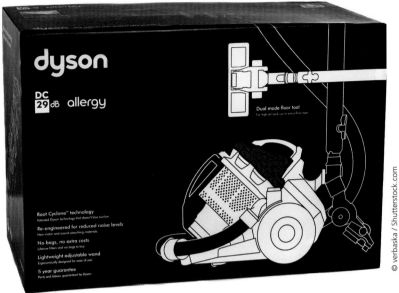

selling less stuff, the value of their output is also likely to decline. With the same number of staff, this brings productivity down. Yet while our competitor countries have mostly recovered, the UK productivity per worker is 22% lower than the OECD average.

For a developed economy like the UK, improved productivity increases the scope for bigger pay packets and rising living standards. Falling productivity means the opposite.

The causes of this drop in performance are not clear. It may be that some of the productivity gains in the 2000s weren't quite what they appeared and may even have been illusory, since they were heavily influenced by the expanding financial services. But part of the problem more recently is due to weak investment. Without investment, we cannot install new machinery and build factories and offices. Hence we're likely to lag behind in new technology.

The end of growth?

There is low economic growth across the developed world. But this may not just be a blip. Some leading economists think it may be the result of a 250-year period of growth coming to an end. For most of human history, growth has scarcely been above zero. Then the Industrial Revolution drove immense productivity gains, largely through new technology. Although new technologies are still being created, they seem less fundamental. The washing machine, says Ha-Joon Chang, has transformed the world more than the iPod.

Perhaps we are heading in a new (or very old) direction – towards low growth. This idea has been around for a long time, mooted by famous names including John Stewart Mill and Karl Marx, and Robert Barro today.

So how do we feel about living in a low-growth world? Perhaps this is a change we need to make. Prosperity is still possible with low growth, as outlined in Tim Jackson's book *Prosperity Without Growth*.

Economic growth damages the environment. And we are unlikely to invent technologies over the next 50 years to reduce that impact – particularly on the climate. We may need to question the desire for unlimited growth and instead focus on different ways of achieving widespread prosperity: through simply working less, for instance.

Chapter 5

A STRONGER ECONOMY

We have completed our brief tour around the economy of the UK. The picture is mixed. We still have a handful of world-class industries and some historic strengths such as our science base. But these gems sit in a morass of problems, some of them long-standing. It's often said that when the economic tide goes out you see who's swimming naked.

Since 2008, a number of long running weaknesses in the UK economy have been bared – problems such as rising inequality and over-reliance on a bloated financial sector. And there are likely to be disruptions in the future such as those associated with excessive debt, energy supplies and climate change.

Where next?

Recognising problems is the first step to solving them. Let's now grapple with some ways these problems might be resolved. An economic policy needs to be part of a wider strategy – a series of joined-up policies with a story connecting them. So governments would need to formulate an intelligent routemap, rather than business as usual with a series of off-the-cuff tweaks aimed at scoring political points and grabbing tomorrow's headlines. Governments know that our biggest problem is the spending deficit and the enormous £1.5 trillion national debt.

Austerity, combined with improvements in productivity, is a possible strategy. But there are many issues facing the British economy. The table opposite shows some of the key ones. In each case, we have offered three possible solutions:

- **The first solution** is what today's politicians would probably opt for – the consensus view in British politics.
- **The second solution** would move the country in a more free-market direction – the right-of-centre view.
- **The third solution** would move the economy away from the free-market neoliberal tendency of recent years.

There is no reason to pick solely from one column. The real challenge is to prioritise the options, since the issues connect with each other in different ways. Nor are the options exhaustive; you could push the last two columns much further, or adopt a milder version.

Ownership matters

At the bottom of these issues lies the question of ownership – and hence the control of society's wealth and power. At present, the political bias is towards private ownership as the best possible form; witness, for example, the increased private sector involvement in the NHS and the transfer of the canal system and the East Coast main railway line to the private sector. But it isn't always privatised versus nationalised. There are other options:

- **Private ownership** Most assets in private hands. Private ownership is said to be more efficient, since (it is argued) the benefits of the ownership, in the form of profits, rents or other returns, accumulate directly to the owners, who therefore want to manage their assets effectively.
- **Public ownership** Governments still hold substantial assets, such as the military, Network Rail, the Bank of England and parts of some major banks. Arguments for public ownership stress the need for vital services to have long-term support. Because of their not-for-profit nature, greater investment can be ploughed back or lower charges levied on consumers.
- **Co-operative ownership** The collective ownership of assets by their customers or by employees goes back to the first modern co-operative shop in 1844. Today, the John Lewis Partnership and the Nationwide Building Society are famous and successful examples of co-operative or 'mutual' ownership. This method is said to provide the best of both worlds – greater efficiency and motivation compared to public ownership, and less need to maximise short-term profits for shareholders. This model is also suited for charitable work.
- **Community ownership** A community (however defined) owns an asset and receives its benefits. A modern example would be green energy micro-generation schemes, in which a small generator is owned by a local community, providing electricity directly or a monetary return from the sale of electricity.

THE ISSUE	THE PROBLEM	POSSIBLE SOLUTIONS		
		Business as usual	Free Market	Progressive
Business investment	Low, and declining over the longer-term	Cuts to corporation tax and other business taxes	Deep cuts to corporation tax and other business taxes	Government invests; change asset ownership to reduce short-termism; use QE money to invest
Debt	High in every sector, and rising	Austerity to reduce government debt	More rapid austerity; selective debt write-offs	Increase real wages; selective debt write-offs
Inequality and falling wages	Rising, hurting tax revenues, potentially damaging growth	Small rises in the National Minimum Wage	Cut business and income taxes and taxes on investment	Large increase in minimum wage; wealth taxes
Productivity	Relatively low, damaging growth	Some additional support for science; promote FDI	Remove barriers to establishing new businesses; promote FDI	Promote R&D; use broader measure of value; redistribute
Financial system	Large relative to GDP	Introduce better regulation of banks' activities; encourage financial services growth	Remove 'too-big-to-fail' subsidy	Break up banks, introduce regional and local banking; greater public control and oversight of finance; controls on cross-border capital
Current account deficit	Rising, threatening financial and economic stability	Promote British exports through government programmes; develop high-tech industry	Allow pound to devalue rapidly	Reduce dependency on imports; industrial strategy for key sectors

Arguments for this form of ownership hinge on the ability of a local community to take greater care of an asset than a (perhaps distant) private or public body.

Economics and values

Economics was defined by Adam Smith, the first modern economist, as a 'moral science'. Like physics, chemistry or biology, it was analytical and based on evidence – but there was an important difference. Human behaviour muddied the water and human involvement meant that there had to be a moral element based on values (see page 143).

The kind of economy we live in will be defined by things such as our country's history and the resources we can mobilise – talented people, oil wealth, fertile land, seas brimming with fish and so on. But how the economy operates within these limits is a matter for public debate.

For 30 years, this debate has largely settled in favour of neoliberalism – the belief that free markets are best left alone to organise production and distribution, with minimal government regulation. But this is not the only choice. In the years since the crash of 2008 we have encountered some of the problems involved with that choice – not least the crash itself.

In the end, the economy we want will be determined by the society we want.

WELSH WATER AND CO-OPERATIVE OWNERSHIP

Water supplies were privatised across England and Wales in 1989, with the ten publicly owned regional water authorities sold on the stock market, shares trading at a heavy initial discount. Each water authority was left as a monopoly supplier in its original area, and £4.5 billion of debt was written off to help the new companies on their way.

Welsh Water was established as a private business in the same way. But, following what turned out to be an over-optimistic expansion plan by its new managers, and the imposition of a government windfall tax on high privatised utility profits, the new company got into difficulties and was bought by the subsidiary of a major US power company. When this parent company, too, faced financial difficulties, a management buyout of the company was arranged.

A new company, Glas Cymru, took over Welsh Water's assets, financed through substantial bond issuance and, unusually, a co-operative structure was adopted. Glas has no shareholders in the usual sense; instead, each customer receives a dividend, and a surplus is reinvested into the company. Glas Cymru has maintained a higher rate of investment than the private owners, resulting in the lowest water bills in the UK, while also seeing significant improvements in water quality – Wales' 'Blue Flag' awards rising from five in 1995 to forty a decade later, a third of the UK total.

PART 2 HOW TO RUN THE COUNTRY MANUAL

POLITICS

Chapter 6

WHAT'S IT ALL ABOUT?

We live in a time of enormous disenchantment with mainstream politics – and it's not hard to see why: headlines speak daily of scandals, corruption, petty squabbling, incompetence and spin. It seems that the most popular type of politics today is of a sort that promises the freedom of a clean break from the shackles of the old Westminster parties.

Why politics matters

Politics is about power. In all societies, someone has to be in charge, and politics is the means by which power is wielded over the rest of us. In a democracy – something that we in the West tend to take for granted – politics is the way in which politicians and parties convince us that they're the right people for the job; but crucially, this is a two-way street – it also gives ordinary people the means by which those in power can be booted out of the driving seat. In other regimes, politics is a sham: state power is seized by the barrel of a gun, rather than won at the ballot box.

What's the point of politicians?

Most people are detached from politics: less than 1% of people living in Britain are themselves members of a political party. Engrossed in their political games, the old Westminster parties have today lost

much of their appeal to the British public. But the fact remains that we need honest, competent people whom we can trust to pilot the nation toward the future.

The most important areas for which Members of Parliament (MPs) are responsible are as follows.

- **Ensuring defence of the country** In times of crisis, war, or pandemic, people look to politicians for leadership.
- **Managing the economy** If politicians want to be re-elected, they need to keep the economy going and boost people's standards of living.
- **Passing new laws** It's the job of MPs to introduce and vote on the laws that govern society. Laws are drafted and implemented by civil servants, and enforced by the police and the courts.
- **Working for the good of the country** Politicians are meant to do what's best for the national interests. When US multinational Pfizer proposed a potentially damaging takeover of Britain's AstraZeneca, for example, the British government was expected to uphold national interests.
- **Listening to constituents** In theory we, the public, have a hotline to those in power: MPs are elected to represent a particular locality. All MPs are supposed to run a weekly 'surgery' at which local people can present their problems. Local councillors are also supposed to represent the interests of constituents (by delivering decent local services efficiently).
- **Changing the way in which government works** Politicians can vote to change the British constitution, altering who does what in government.
- **Keeping it all together** Politicians are the 'invisible hand' that holds society together. By listening to the views of people, businesses and interest groups, they should be able to initiate appropriate policies. The government also oversees the Civil Service, with the power to fire those who underperform.

THE THREE BASIC ROLES OF A GOVERNMENT

- **To preserve security:** defending the country against invasion and keeping the peace among the citizens.
- **To balance people's individual rights and responsibilities:** ensuring that the level of 'give and take' works in the interests of citizens.
- **To provide basic welfare:** ensuring that citizens who are old, poor, or sick aren't left to die on the street – something better than the Victorian workhouse or food banks – the ideal is a free health service, a living wage and full employment.

Governments generally run into trouble if they put economic growth ahead of these three overriding objectives.

PULLING THE BIG LEVERS

How can governments ensure that conditions are right for the economy to grow?

- **Setting taxes** Lower taxes leave us with more money to spend or save – whoopee. But it also results in lower funding for health care, education and social security. Targeted tax rises can help to discourage socially damaging behaviour (binge drinking, smoking, gambling, etc). Giving generous tax breaks to encourage research and development or manufacturing can kick-start valuable new export industries.

- **Interest rates** Interest rates can slow or speed up the economy, affecting the cost of financing business and mortgages. The Bank of England sets Bank Rate, on which all other banks base their own interest rates. Although independent of government, the Bank works closely with HM Treasury.

- **Regulation** On the one hand, businesses must be regulated properly to protect wider society from cowboy operators – for example dumping waste and causing environmental and health damage. On the other hand, cutting unnecessary 'red tape' can make businesses more productive.

- **Targeted spending** Government spending accounts for around 40% of the UK's total economic output. Ensuring that government procurement policies favour British-made services and goods can boost home industries, employment and the balance of payments. (Most other countries already adopt 'patriotic purchasing' policies, the United States among them.)

- **Subsidies and incentives** Governments in competitor countries, such as Japan, Korea, the United States, France and Germany, adopt other policies geared toward supporting their national industries, such as funding for research and subsidies (sometimes in defiance of international trade law).

Peacekeeping duties

Inevitably, some groups in society will find themselves opposed to other groups: some might favour the construction of a ring road, while others favour protecting the rural landscape. So that they don't resort to armed combat and start massacring each other, they have access to politicians to argue their case. Politics can help release some of the steam from potentially nasty conflicts by providing a platform for peacefully airing views.

To resolve conflicts, some degree of compromise is usually needed, and people will normally accept an outcome even when they don't agree with it if they feel that it results from a political process that has been fair and legal. Politics plays an essential role in accommodating mediating among different interests, for example balancing the rights of residents against corporations lobbying for legislative changes to boost profitability.

Democracy

At its heart, politics is about putting democracy into action. But what exactly is democracy?

Churchill is widely credited with quipping: 'Democracy is the worst form of government except for all those other forms that have been tried from time to time.' Having been voted out of power after leading the country to victory in the Second World War, he had every reason to feel bitter, but instead chose to praise the system (and was duly re-elected in 1951). Equally famous is the definition of democracy as 'government of the people, by the people, for the

people' that is widely attributed to US President Abraham Lincoln, but was actually written by 14th-century scholar John Wycliffe, the first person to translate the Bible into English.

To be democratic, a nation must hold regular elections for both national and local government. Elections must be fair: no one must be pressurised into voting for one candidate (so ballots are cast anonymously), and the whole population must be eligible to vote, subject to a few exceptions (such as those under the age of 18 and those who are mentally incapable).

A referendum is another national vote, this time on only one question, the answer to which is usually 'Yes' or 'No', such as the recent independence referendum in Scotland. There has been no UK-wide referendum since the 1970s – then on whether people wanted to stay in the European Union. If you missed that one, watch this space – a re-run may be on the cards soon!

Pure democracy

Athens is famously the birthplace of democracy (although only a tiny minority of Athenians actually had the right to vote). Based on the original Athenian model, in a true democracy all citizens would vote directly on individual laws to be passed; in a nation with a population in excess of 65 million people, the practicalities of this would be fantastically complex. The next best thing is a 'representative democracy' in which people elect MPs or councillors, who are effectively subcontracted to vote on the people's behalf. One of the most democratic countries in the world today is Switzerland, which holds frequent referendums allowing people a direct vote on key issues.

How democratic is Britain?

We can inflate our chests with national pride because not only can Britain justly claim to be the 'mother of all parliaments' but we also fought valiantly to save Europe from Nazi dictatorship. Moreover, in 2014 Scotland delivered a lesson in how modern political democracy ought to function: To quote Kevin McKenna 'its battle over the subject of independence was as passionate, raw and emotional as any previously encountered in these islands – yet not a bullet was fired, nor were there physical casualties' (other than the occasional victim of grievous bodily egging).

However you can suck your chest back in when you think about our distinctly unrepresentative voting system, with the majority of votes not counting. Furthermore, surveys regularly report tales of mass disenchantment with the self-obsessed community of London-based politicians, lobbyists, and public relations and media people – the 'Westminster Village' – who are seen as preoccupied with spin and self-interest that has little positive impact on our everyday lives.

Democracy (not)

Back in the 1970s, Britain was a nation in the grip of violent price inflation, regular power cuts and incessant waves of strikes. Things had got so out of control that otherwise sensible voices were calling for a 'benign dictatorship' – that is, a firm hand to put things in order. Conventional wisdom has it that 'turkeys don't vote for Xmas' and that people would never voluntarily vote away their democratic rights – but history shows that, in certain circumstances, well-meaning citizens will support 'illiberal democracy'. Many people would vote for an illiberal government if it were to trump a greater evil, promising security against violence or hardship, protecting a way of life to which they're attached, restoring national pride, or even denying

VOTE FOR ME!

BLAH BLAH...

ME ME ME...

ME

PR

LOBBY LOBBY...

WESTMINSTER VILLAGE

There is a gap between the theory of British democracy and how power really works in practice, with many decisions taken by small, often unelected, groups. The overwhelming threat to democracy in the West today is from the 'capture' of government by powerful special interests, who seek immunity from punishment and privileges to which they are not entitled.

Clues that things are very wrong in Britain include a tax system that some suggest would embarrass Queen Victoria, an invisible climate policy, health care policies that have little to do with health, and essentials such as food, energy and housing that remain largely unregulated, with consequent risks to consumers. Add to this a financial system that has already caused great harm, yet remains unreformed in key areas. Yet our elected representatives appear oblivious to the idea that anything needs fixing.

Politicians generally like to be seen to be sticking up for 'strivers'; they also need to be on the alert for 'shirkers', whose power comes not from hard work, creativity and innovation, but from the manipulation of naive or corrupt politicians. By converting natural 'state monopolies' into highly profitable private monopolies, for example, shirkers secure wealth for themselves at the expense of taxpayers.

There are two schools of thought on how to tackle this: either larger governments must match the economic power concentrated in private hands, or smaller governments must make stronger laws, limiting that private economic power. The difficulty with the latter approach is that global corporate forces can run rings around nation states.

Corruption leads to loss of trust and to voters feeling that democracy is a charade, because they see that real power rests elsewhere. They lose faith in the political process and disengage. Participation thus declines – and policy starts to be driven by the extremists…

Source material: Lawrence Lessig & Rollingstone.com

freedoms to those whom they see as undeserving. Governments of countries such as Russia and Hungary (the latter an EU member state) are regarded as illiberal, yet their leaders enjoy huge popularity. Might local democracy in Britain be similarly vulnerable were a majority of voters in one area to support candidates standing on a militant theocratic ticket? Legal and constitutional freedoms have little force when majorities are hostile to liberal values.

France and the United States both proudly claim to be the first home of representative democracy – so it's a shame that we have to disappoint them: *Britain* has the oldest system, with a Bill of Rights dating from 1689. (The Isle of Man actually boasts the longest continually established parliament.)

The French claim is based on the French Revolution of 1789, which overthrew the king – until Napoleon became dictator a few years later and swept the country clean of democracy.

The Americans adopted their Bill of Rights in 1791, but large numbers of citizens were barred from voting (not least Native Americans), and the United States shamefully continued segregation (a form of apartheid) well into the 1960s.

Alternatives to democracy

'All those other forms of government' that didn't impress Churchill include the following.

■ **Autocracy/totalitarianism** North Korea is perhaps the best-known dictatorship today. In this type of state, all power is concentrated into the hands of a leader who can't be removed in an election. Laws are made or altered according to the leader's wishes. These are one-party states, with no official opposition permitted. China – although hugely powerful economically and now capitalist in all but name – is still run by the Communist Party, which tolerates no opposition and rules with an iron fist. One thing that dictators and democrats have in common is that their powers of persuasion often derive from personal 'charisma'; sustaining autocratic regimes, however, depends on the military and usually a brutal police force. Both right-wing and left-wing extremes – fascism and communism – are totalitarian in character. But the chilling roll call of dictators extends far beyond Stalin and Hitler: from Afghanistan to Zimbabwe, and from Cambodia's Pol Pot and Haiti's Baby Doc Duvalier to Chile's General Pinochet and the Burmese Military Junta – plus, of course, Middle Eastern tyrants such as Gaddafi, Assad and Saddam Hussein. Yet it is not unknown for Western governments to prop up such brutal regimes when it suits them, even to the extent of overthrowing democratically elected governments.

■ **Absolute monarchy** The reason why most countries no longer have a monarchy is that the people chose to replace it with an elected parliament – with the monarchy sometimes losing their heads in the process. The English Crown originally exercised absolute power, ordained according to the 'divine right of kings' (authority to rule drawn directly from God; the sovereign subject only to God and not to the law). Rule was effected through a mix of loyalty, faith, bribery and fear, with a powerful military subjugating those who dared transgress.

■ **Theocracy** In some societies, religion is such a compelling force that government is run strictly according to religious principles. One of the best-known examples is the Iranian regime run primarily by a group of Shi'ite clerics. Policy is dictated through interpretation of holy scripture and religious texts, but is essentially tribal, often violently excluding others who share the same religion. There are some groups present in the UK who support the idea of a militant theocracy, through establishment of *caliphates* and the application of *sharia law*. One concern about the rise of 'Islamic State' is that it is founded on belief, not nationality, and thus is global in its goals.

■ **Anarchism** Opposed to all forms of government (the ancient Greek *anarchia* means 'no ruler'), anarchists assert that people should be allowed to get on with their lives without interference – 'small government' and self-regulation at its most extreme! Anarchist groups have mounted demonstrations at meetings of G8 and G20 world leaders, which have sometimes erupted into violence (see Chapter 10).

Britain's transition from absolute monarchy to 'representative democracy' was marked with bloodshed and struggle – but more by evolution than revolution.

United nations

Of the four home nations of the British Isles, the largest, England, first grew increasingly powerful in trade and military might. Following political union, the UK went on to become a global superpower, spawning a worldwide empire that lasted nearly 300 years. Such unprecedented economic and military success exerted a strong 'motive force' – a powerful pull to the centre – helping to unify the four nations.

The history of Welsh ties with England goes back to the 13th century, the countries eventually being joined as a single legal state in 1542. The Crowns of England and Scotland were joined in 1603, and the parliaments united under the Act of Union in 1707 within the Kingdom of Great Britain. However, it was not until the Union of 1801 that the title the 'United Kingdom of Great Britain and Ireland' came into being.

It was not to last: following the First World War and the 1916 Uprising, (southern) Ireland became an independent state in 1922, with the six counties of Northern Ireland (Ulster) remaining within the union.

Scotland and Wales were granted devolved governments in 1999.

Magna Carta

The 'Big Charter' was the first major constitutional document in the Western world – pre-dating the US Declaration of Independence by some 550 years.

Back in 1215, the great barons of the land rose up in mutiny against the inept King John, forcing him to sign an agreement that limited the power of the monarch. Magna Carta was, in effect, a statement of basic rights that, in theory, bound the all-powerful king to act within the rule of law. Most notably, it established the right of *habeas corpus* (the right to appeal against imprisonment), effectively putting an end to kings imprisoning anyone whom they disliked without first trying them in a court of law. Or as Tony Hancock put it in 1959, pleading to the jury in his sketch 'Twelve Angry Men': 'Does Magna Carta mean nothing to you? Did she die in vain?!'

Goodbye Monarch – Hello King

The English Parliament was set up by Henry II in the 12th century as a way of raising taxes and governing the country more effectively. Its power gradually increased until the country became a republic, following the bloody English Civil War and the execution of the defeated Charles I in 1649. This lasted precisely 11 years under the austere rule of Oliver Cromwell (who famously banned Christmas celebrations). The Restoration of Charles II to the throne in 1660 marked the end of republican rule in England, but King William of Orange deposed successor James II in a bloodless coup (the 'Glorious Revolution'). In effect, power then shifted from a single monarch to members of an elected Parliament (and the unelected House of Lords). Parliament came into effect in 1689 and a Bill of Rights was drawn up, establishing the supremacy of Parliament once and for all, replacing the monarchy as the nation's supreme law-making body. All future monarchs had to bend to the will of Parliament.

The Big Split

The break with the Roman Catholic Church marked a major turning point in the power struggle between church and monarch. The Reformation saw the creation of the Church of England and the appropriation of enormous monastic wealth by the state. The 1534 Act of Supremacy confirmed the break from Rome, declaring Henry VIII to be supreme head of the Church. Today, the monarch remains head of the Church of England, but the title is largely nominal, with little real power.

The right to vote (the 'franchise')

If you were to step back in time a couple of centuries, one thing would immediately strike you (once you adjusted to the lack of toilet facilities): the fact that you would be unable to vote unless you were male and owned land or other property.

Fearing that violent revolution would sweep away the landed gentry, as had recently been the case in France, politicians grudgingly started to make concessions: in 1884, the right to vote was extended to all men aged over 21. But even by 1900 this still encompassed only 30% of the adult population and it wasn't until 1971 that the vote was extended to 18-year-olds.

Only after the First World War was the female half of the population finally granted the vote. Many Victorian MPs had dismissed the idea of women voting as 'madness'. But as the male franchise expanded, women mobilised 'suffrage' movements employing a mix of high-profile protests (chaining themselves to railings, firebombing the homes of politicians and throwing a banner over the king's horse at the Epsom Derby, which action resulted in Emily Wilding Davison's death). Women over the age of 30 were finally given the vote in 1918, which was later extended to the same terms as men in 1928 (those over 21) and 1971 (those over 18).

Putting the House of Lords in its place

Until the Parliament Act 1911, unelected peers sitting in the House of Lords had the power to block any laws drawn up in the Commons. Three years earlier, the Lords had vetoed a radical Budget that proposed the introduction of old-age pensions and some limited welfare payments for the less fortunate. The Act finally established the House of Commons as the key law-making body in Parliament, and today the House of Lords is little more than a debating chamber with the right to scrutinise proposed laws drawn up in the Commons.

The political parties

If you were to travel back to Georgian and Victorian times, there's one thing that would seem depressingly familiar: there were two main political parties, one of which was the Tories; the other, the Whigs. The Whigs believed in 'free' markets, rather like modern Conservatives, drawing support from industrialists and merchants; in contrast, the Tories drew support from wealthy landowners. From the mid-19th century, the Whigs slowly fragmented over issues such as free trade (unbridled competition was damaging British industry) and constitutional reform. Their collapse left the Tories centre stage until the surviving Whigs eventually morphed into the Liberal Party, forerunner to today's LibDems, and the Labour Party appeared on the scene in the early 1900s.

Today, this old order is facing challenges from newer parties, especially the Scottish National Party (SNP) and the UK Independence Party (UKIP).

Conservative (Cons)

How the French must laugh at election time when the printed names of Tory candidates and MPs are denoted with the bracketed abbreviation 'Cons' – which happens to be the Gallic word for 'idiots'.

Unfortunate as this may be, the origin of the word 'Tory' is hardly more prepossessing. The word dates from the 17th century and was originally a term of abuse based on the Irish word for outlaw, *tóraidhe*, used to describe English Catholics who supported the monarch over Parliament (such as Guy Fawkes). But despite such dubious linguistic baggage, the Conservative Party, founded in 1834, is today the longest surviving modern British political party, having enjoyed more years in government than any other.

Conservatives traditionally believed in 'conserving' things – that is, retaining what they saw as being best about Britain. Tory Prime Minister John Major captured the old ethos rather well when he spoke of 'a country of long shadows on county cricket grounds, warm beer, green suburbs, dog lovers, and old maids cycling to holy communion through the morning mist'. Add to this a pride in military tradition, with patriotic support for the armed forces and industrial prowess, and you can see how dramatically different this is from today's Conservative brand: modern Tories have more in common with the US Republicans, in bed with Wall Street, according to some.

As a party, the Tories tend to hold most sway in the densely populated south-east of England. Their strongest support tends to be in areas with high average incomes, where wealthier people want lower taxes and 'light touch' regulation. Its membership demographic tends to be older and yet some of its current policies are significantly different from traditional 'One Nation' Conservative

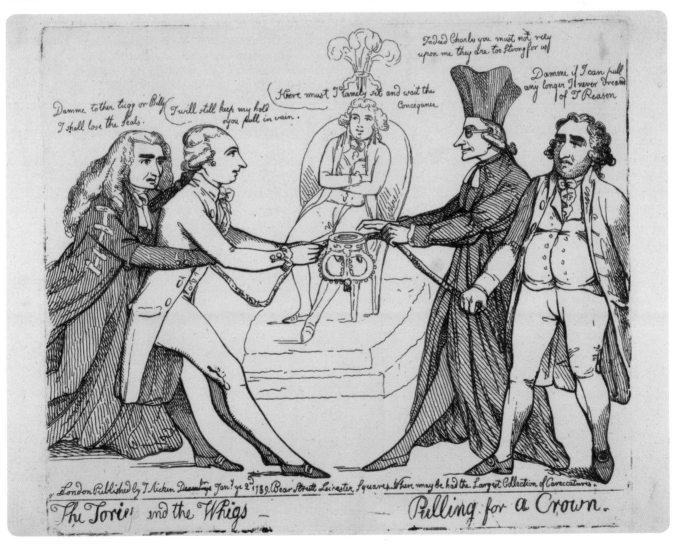

The Tories and the Whigs — Pulling for a Crown.

values. Prime Minister Cameron even famously characterised his party as the 'effing Tories', and Theresa May warned of voters perceiving them as the 'Nasty Party'. The Eurosceptics are the last bastion of old conservativism, defending the British way of life against perceived European domination, although the country that they're defending has in many ways become a satellite of the United States – but even this territory is being hijacked by newcomers UKIP, who have made a big splash in traditional Tory 'safe seats'.

If you were to ask a Conservative supporter what he or she holds dear politically, you would probably hear replies about 'being free to make money' (and to keep most of it) and wanting to hold on to 'what's best about Britain'. These principles have fairly broad appeal (defining the detail is trickier) and indeed are not particularly different from those of Labour. Strictly speaking, the Conservative Party may be right of centre and Labour, left, but these terms are increasingly irrelevant; hence the widespread feeling that the parties are 'all the same'. Both main parties are pro-consumerism and believe in the market economy, while the Conservatives tend to be more trusted than Labour when it comes to managing the economy, but less trusted on things such as running the National Health Service (NHS).

When it comes to economics, modern Conservative policies are rooted in the 1980s Chicago School of neoliberalism, which itself is based on 19th century 'free market' ideology. This informs policies such as:

- promoting 'free trade' and 'market solutions';
- deregulation;
- privatisation and outsourcing of state assets and public services – including utilities, transport, the prison service and the NHS;
- cutting public spending, including on the armed forces and police;
- an openness to foreign (US) involvement in the British military and defence;
- maintaining nuclear weapons capability;
- support for the financial sector;
- openness to ceding control of UK 'national champions' to overseas owners;
- reduced welfare support;
- low taxes, including for high earners and big business;
- disengagement from EU 'super state' ambitions;
- limits on immigration, where practicable; and
- a focus on law and order.

Labour (Lab)

Britain was the first industrial nation, and millions of newly urbanised workers made a major contribution to the nation's wealth. But without a vote, ordinary people had no ability to improve appalling working conditions or to push for a living wage, let alone to aspire to better education and even the most basic of health care. To help them to achieve some of these ambitions, workers formed unions – and the unions established the Labour Party in 1900 as a political wing to represent their members.

After the war in 1945, Labour and the Conservatives had very different ideologies, offering voters a real choice, with Labour's Clement Attlee forming the NHS and nationalising key industries, such as the railways and mines.

Labour used to be a 'moral crusade' – a movement as much as a party. But it remained dependent for funding and much of its membership on powerful trade unions, which rebuffed Prime Minister Harold Wilson's attempts in the 1960s and 1970s to moderate and modernise them. Then, during the 1978–79 'Winter of Discontent', galloping inflation, rampant strikes and power cuts culminated in the largest stoppage of labour since the 1926 General Strike. By the 1980s, the old socialist parties across Europe were losing their way, and many Labour voters were attracted by Thatcher's popular patriotism and promises of individual opportunity. After losing its fourth election in a row in 1992 and desperate for power at all costs, the Labour Party ditched its traditional principles (such as the hallowed 'Clause 4' commitment to nationalisation), transforming itself into 'New Labour' under Tony Blair. The rejuvenated party deployed enormous energy and expertise in marketing its new political 'brand', reducing its dependency on trade unions by appealing to wealthy donors.

'Blairism' propagated many of the reforms of Thatcher, effectively stealing the Tories' clothes, but with the broad aim of creating a fairer society. Yet it seemed easily dazzled by the super-rich and City bankers, spin doctor Peter Mandelson famously declaring New

Labour to be 'intensely relaxed about people getting filthy rich' (adding the less-quoted proviso that they must pay their taxes). After the attacks on the United States of 11 September 2001 ('9/11'), New Labour became more authoritarian and centralised, many former Cabinet ministers later going on to enjoy lucrative corporate directorships around the world.

Today's Labour Party follows broadly similar policies to those of the Tories, the main differences relating to:

- keeping the NHS predominantly in the public sector;
- quality public services and the need to fund them through taxation;
- a belief that those with the 'broadest shoulders' should contribute more tax;
- protecting consumers from abuses in poorly regulated markets such as energy, banking and railways;
- maintaining a more supportive welfare system; and
- fewer limits on immigration.

Because the Labour Party's bedrock support was traditionally rooted in the working class and the union movement, it has always tended to do better in parts of the country with industrial heritage, such as Scotland, Wales and the north of England. It also has strong support amongst public sector workers, as well as those on lower incomes. But today even traditional 'safe seats' are being eaten into by relative newcomers such as SNP, Plaid Cymru and UKIP. The unions may have created Labour and union members' subscriptions may still be a crucial source of party funding, but in recent years the relationship has become strained.

Scottish National Party (SNP)

The SNP dominates politics in Scotland. Despite being constrained by the relative size of its home population, the SNP also has a reasonable share of the overall UK vote, with sufficient muscle in Westminster to hold the 'balance of power' in a coalition government. The political stance is significantly more left of centre and social democratic than that of the main UK parties, supporting more effective regulation of the free market and a fairer society with well-funded public services, paid for by means of higher taxes if necessary.

The party's phenomenal success is thanks in no small measure to former First Minister Alex Salmond's drive and passion. Now led by Nicola Sturgeon, the SNP is currently in government in the Scottish Parliament. This marks a significant change in politics north of the border, where the appeal of Toryism is a distant memory. In 1979, one in three in the Scottish electorate voted Tory; then came the decline in manufacturing, rising unemployment and the introduction of the hated Poll Tax. Support for both Tories and Labour has since plummeted, as the numbers feeling disenfranchised have grown.

Plaid Cymru (PC)

It's a similar story in Wales, where Plaid Cymru has won a major share of the 60 seats in the National Assembly for Wales. As well as being a very big deal in the 'land of my fathers' (*Hen Wlad Fy Nhadau*), this Welsh nationalist party, like the SNP, is also becoming more significant in the overall UK political scene. Interestingly, the social democratic ethos and strong local popularity of both parties is in sharp contrast to right-wing, overtly nationalist parties in England, such as the British National Party (BNP), which have failed to make much headway.

Liberal Democrats (LibDems)

Traditionally the small third party in British politics, for several decades in the 20th century the LibDems had only a handful of MPs, never garnering enough support to make much impact. Popularity peaked in 2010, when the election produced a hung parliament (that is, essentially a draw) and the LibDems held the balance of power, opting to join the Conservatives in a coalition government. However, their willingness once in government to disregard loudly trumpeted election pledges, such as cutting tuition fees, together with their botched campaign for the alternative vote (AV) system and controversial privatisation of Royal Mail, has resulted in a collapse in votes amongst the electorate. Even elections for councils in which LibDems traditionally did well have lately shown a decline in support.

UK Independence Party (UKIP)

A relative newcomer, UKIP's focus is primarily on EU membership and immigration. 'Ukippers' want the UK to withdraw from the European Union because of concerns about loss of control to the European 'super state' and the extent of EU laws impacting on Britain. All EU citizens have the right to live and work in other member states, and high levels of immigration are perceived to have had consequences for wages and services in the UK. Free movement of workers is a key pillar of the Treaty on the Functioning of the European Union, so it's argued that if the UK were to control its borders, it would have to leave the Union.

Under the leadership of Nigel Farage, UKIP gained huge momentum in the 2014 European elections, and at the time of writing polls suggest that the party might command as much as 20% of the UK vote, albeit with only a handful of seats. Interestingly, polls of 'Ukippers' reveal that a majority are more social democratic than Tory on issues such as the NHS and the renationalisation of railways and energy companies, and support higher taxes on the rich and a hike in the National Minimum Wage – it is not clear whether such attitudes are supported by UKIP policy.

The Green Party (Greens)

Green parties have enjoyed major successes in Europe, for example they play a significant role in the coalition government in Germany. To a lesser extent, the Greens have had success in local elections in the UK and can attract a share of votes similar to that of the LibDems in general elections. At the time of writing, there is one Green MP (the redoubtable Caroline Lucas MP for Brighton Pavilion).

The Greens seem to have discovered the fire and passion that moved Labour so long ago: most policies are on the sensible side of socialist and focus primarily on environmental responsibility. Economic growth is regarded as less important than preserving the health of the planet – because being rich is pointless if sea levels are rising and lives are endangered. Government policy should actively try to change individual behaviour, towards minimising environmental damage, and big companies are viewed as needing regulation to control pollution and the using up of the planet's resources.

Other policies relate to:

- a living wage;
- renationalisation of the railways;
- a maximum pay ratio (that is, no executive should receive more than ten times the salary of the lowest-paid worker within the company);
- higher taxes for the wealthy; and
- open borders and few limits on immigration.

FRUITCAKERY AND NUTTERY: THE JOKERS

Election season in Britain sometimes resembles a village fête. One of its more entertaining aspects is the fact that anyone can form a party or stand as a candidate – which is an open invitation to eccentrics, comedians and other colourful characters. So why not vote for:
- the Monster Raving Loony Party, which promises a free bottle of gin for everyone;
- the Fancy Dress Party (the name says it all); or
- the Natural Law Party, which promises to solve crime and economic problems with yogic flying (don't ask)?!

Northern Ireland parties

The good people of Ulster have an Assembly that houses a coalition government, with leading figures from both communities sharing the top jobs. The Assembly has 108 elected members and powers over areas such as health, education and environmental policy, with Westminster retaining others.

Politics in Northern Ireland is deeply entwined with cultural and religious loyalties, and parties rooted in the communities hold sway. The main parties are as follows.

- **Democratic Unionist Party (DUP)** The DUP is the largest party in politics in Northern Ireland. It entered into a power-sharing agreement with ultra-nationalist Sinn Féin in 2007.
- **Ulster Unionist Party (UUP)** Formerly the biggest party and considered more moderate than the DUP, in the past the UUP held several seats in Westminster and was often called upon to support Tory or Labour governments struggling to gain a majority.
- **Social Democratic and Labour Party (SDLP)** Traditionally the biggest party representing the Catholic community, like the UUP the SDLP has recently been supplanted by a rival party.
- **Sinn Féin** Leading members are widely presumed to have been involved in the past in Irish Republican Army (IRA) terrorist activity, but the party was key in arranging a ceasefire and renouncing violence, leading to the Good Friday Agreement. It is now the biggest party among the Catholic community and presently shares power in government with the DUP.
- **Alliance Party** This party has cross-community appeal and seeks to break free of traditional 'tribal' loyalties, but has relatively limited support at present.

National government

In times of national crisis, politicians from all parties have the option of forming a national government, uniting to work together in coalition for the greater good. This happened twice during the last century: during the 1930s, in response to the Great Depression, and then again during the Second World War. The benefit of 'all for one' government is that it brings together the most talented politicians from all parties (like a broad coalition) and, thanks to an automatic majority in the House of Commons, new laws can be pressed through quickly. But this 'one-party state' is meant to be a temporary response to a crisis – not a nascent dictatorship.

Coalition: Holding the balance of power

Traditionally, one of the strengths of Britain's peculiar 'first past the post' (FPTP) voting system has been that it results in a clear winner, with sufficient majority to pass laws and to rule with confidence. But, in recent years, mass disillusionment with the two main parties has sparked 'hung parliaments' in which neither party is able to garner enough votes to win a majority of seats and hold power. In this event, if one of the big parties teams up with one (or two) of the smaller parties, the combined vote results in the required majority – as in the 2010 Con–LibDem coalition.

RODIN'S THE COALITION

The advantage of coalition government is said to be that a more diverse group of people represents a wider range of voters. The smaller party will normally want to extract a price for lending its support, including positioning some of its senior people as ministers holding key Cabinet posts and pushing for some of its policies to be adopted. Sometimes, however, the smaller partner caves in to pressure, abandoning its beliefs in exchange for a brief moment in the limelight, or the coalition may be short-lived and acrimonious. So if coalitions are now more likely in general elections, would it not make sense to adopt a voting system in which all votes count?

What do politicians stand for?

You don't hear the word 'ideology' much these days – and yet this was traditionally the thing that propelled many people into politics in the first place. Without any sort of belief in improving society or running the country better, we find ourselves with politicians driven by naked self-interest, ambitious for a spot of grandstanding on the national and world stages. 'Fighting the good fight' seems to have been exchanged for fiddling expenses.

The days in which one party supposedly represent the workers (Lab) and the other, the bosses (Cons), are long gone; today, the dividing line is often hard to make out. However, all parties do have policies based on broad beliefs – what you might call 'ideology-lite' – such as the Conservative drive to privatise state assets in the belief that they will be run more efficiently (the proceeds filling government coffers).

You can sometimes spot ideologies because they normally end in '–ism' (for example 'socialism'). But the media have a habit of tacking the suffix on to the names of prime ministers who've made a big impact – 'Thatcherism', 'Blairism', etc – which is more personality cult than ideology.

At heart, this boils down to the question of what works best for British people – and how to balance two contrasting beliefs:

- that 'greed is good' – that unbridled competition is desirable to motivate us as individuals to strive to acquire wealth that 'trickles down', benefiting society; and
- that people and society, as a whole, achieve more by working together and cooperating, not operating solely in pursuit of personal profit, with wealth 'welling upwards', benefiting society.

Freedom and liberalism

It's somewhat ironic that, in the self-proclaimed 'home of liberty' and 'land of the free' (the United States), the word 'liberal' is used as a term of abuse, often sandwiched between 'goddamn' and 'asshole'.

Paradoxically, 'liberalism' is the ideology that underpins our hard-won rights of British citizens. Britain is often referred to as a 'liberal democracy' because we stress individual freedoms and liberties. For example, you should be free to say and write pretty much what you like, as long as it's not inciting hatred or is slanderous or libellous (falsehood expressed as fact that harms an individual). You can travel where you please and have a say in who governs you. Add to this the fact that Brits enjoy the protection of a deep-rooted legal system and it's evident that we are among the freest people on the planet.

The main principles of liberalism are as follows.

- **Popular consent** A government should operate with the consent of the majority of the people.
- **Equality** All citizens should have the same voting rights and access to justice through the law.
- **Individual liberty** Citizens should have basic rights, such as freedom from imprisonment without criminal charges.
- **Economic freedom** Citizens should have the freedom to set up businesses and to create wealth.

Free-market capitalism/neoliberalism

'Neoliberal' economics is the dominant American 'free market' financial model adopted by the main UK parties for the last 30 years or so. Indeed, by the mid-1990s, neoliberalism (or 'market fundamentalism') had become the dominant doctrine followed by most countries around the globe.

In the UK, both main parties have enthusiastically adopted these core beliefs, which have become mainstream political thinking. This isn't surprising given the prosperity and material rewards with which consumerism has furnished many people of this generation, despite debt-laden storm clouds appearing on the horizon. Hence all main parties agree that government should leave people to get on with their lives and that everyone has the right to own property, which few people would object to. Both parties also prefer to let business 'self-regulate' rather than to impose regulation.

But there is a downside: the global financial crisis of 2008–09 illuminated the dangers of 'light touch' regulation. There's plenty of evidence that, without someone to enforce clear guidelines, less ethically minded businesses (some payday lenders and monopolistic utility companies) will act within the law to exploit consumers – one person's 'free market' becoming another's unregulated freedom to scam customers. Allowing enormously powerful investment banks and global insurance companies to self-regulate was supposedly a major factor behind the crisis. So it's really a matter of where you

TAX DODGEMS

However, the socialist aim of nationalising industries extended far beyond the reasonable state control of natural monopolies such as rail and utilities, into poorly planned enforced mergers in aerospace, shipbuilding and car manufacturing. The Thatcher government's privatisation of sclerotic state-owned businesses such as BP, Rolls-Royce and British Airways was therefore not particularly controversial.

As a political doctrine, socialism died when the Berlin Wall came down in 1989, and even the Labour Party disassociated itself with the ideology, morphing into a sort of 'Conservatives-lite', under Tony Blair's 'New Labour'. Today, the desire for a fairer society is about as close as politicians get. Rather than an alternative to capitalism, it's become a way of guiding and refining capitalism's rough edges to make it work better. Maybe a new '–ism' word is needed?

Today, the Green Party, the SNP and Plaid Cymru are probably the most 'socialist' parties, with policies such as:

- a more equal share of the wealth, so that land and industry is owned by the many rather than the few (which all sounds terribly 'lefty' until you consider the Thatcherite ideology of a property-owning shareholder democracy);
- a living wage and an end to 'zero hours' contracts, which unethical employers can use to exploit workers;
- more emphasis on sexual and racial equality;
- raising educational and health standards across the whole population, rather than only for the privileged few; and
- better organisation of society through rational government planning, rather than pure reliance on short-term market forces.

draw the line, so that the state can harness the power of markets rather than be controlled by them.

As respected economist Thomas Piketty demonstrates, naked neoliberalism can actually suffocate enterprise, replacing it with private monopolies, anti-competitive collusion and inherited wealth, resulting in plummeting social mobility. 'Small government' is all very well, but if it shrinks too much, it will lose the ability to govern – and without politicians, who will be accountable if things go wrong? To make government smaller, chunks of its operations are farmed out to private contractors such as Serco, G4S and A4E – and so 'small government' becomes 'big corporate'. And it will take more than simple faith in 'free markets' to stem the rising tides of climate change.

The tarnished reputation of socialism is largely a result of the dramatic failure of its more radical cousin communism. Globally, not so many people still live in communist regimes, in which it is believed that the government should own everything – land and industry – on behalf of the people. In effect, individuals direct their (demotivated) efforts towards raising living standards for everyone, rather than only for themselves. Former communist nations such as Cuba, Russia and China have today moved on, with varying degrees of success.

Socialism

Say the word 'socialism' to a Texan and their first instinct will be to reach for a handgun. Few words carry more baggage (other than perhaps 'Thatcherism'). Socialism arose in response to the massive inequalities brought about by totally unregulated capitalism in the Industrial Revolution. The welfare state and NHS that we take for granted today were built on basic socialist ideals: eliminating poverty and hunger. Its objective is a fairer society and an economy that benefits the majority.

Some of the major success stories for socialism in the UK include:

- the NHS;
- recognition of trade unions, and improved pay and conditions for employees;
- the provision of free state education for all children up to the age of 18;
- the availability of welfare benefits as a safety net; and
- the provision of affordable housing.

Thatcherism

Margaret Thatcher achieved landslide election victories in 1979, 1983 and 1987, but was a divisive figure in the country, sweeping away many traditional Conservative policies. The main tenets of 'Thatcherism' were:

- reducing the power of trade unions seen as overly dominant;
- encouraging individuals to own shares and property, and to start their own businesses;
- lower taxes and reduced government spending; and
- restoring national pride, with strong foreign policy and defence.

As far as most people at the time could see, these were laudable aims. However, the idea of Britain as a 'home-owning democracy' was nothing new, having been highly successful in the 1930s. Thatcher's Conservatives rode a wave of prosperity, benefiting from a North Sea oil bonanza, releasing personal ambition stimulated by tax cuts and a housing boom. But the

© David Fowler / Shutterstock.com

law of unintended consequences resulted in vast areas of Britain's industrial heartlands being lost, at a time when other countries were strongly investing to build up their manufacturing bases. Mass share ownership was a blip. And many of the privatised industries ended up being owned and run by foreign governments – hardly what had been envisaged! Just as nationalisation went too far under Labour in the 1950s and 1960s, many voters now believe that privatisation has today swung too far in the opposite direction, with polls showing clear majority support for renationalising the utilities and railways.

Thatcher talked the language of Churchillian patriotism, but believed in US-style individualism and money-making – beliefs that had broad appeal beyond the business community. She wanted a national renaissance characterised by a sense of duty, family values and enterprise, spawning world-class British industries; the irony is that the changes she unleashed ultimately moved society in a very different direction.

What's gone wrong?

Politics is facing a crisis. Disenchantment with politicians is nothing new, but voter mistrust has today reached a new low. Although similar complaints are being echoed in many countries around the world, including the United States and Europe, Britain has more than its fair share of unique problems.

The Telegraph, which exposed the MPs' expenses scandal, identifies one major problem behind the widespread feeling of mistrust: 'The last two decades have seen a terrifying decline in standards among the British governing elite. It has become acceptable for our politicians to lie and to cheat. An almost universal culture of selfishness and greed has grown up.'

Disillusionment

We're all familiar with the bad habits of politicians: telling untruths and half-truths; pretending that sparse policies have far-reaching effects; and ducking responsibility. But today there seems to be a whole new level of fakery. Politics has become the plaything of ambitious professional careerists and Ministerial posts are seen as springboards to nice little earners on corporate boards – so it's little wonder that the old Westminster parties are in long-term decline.

As *the Guardian* columnist Owen Jones has pointed out, disillusionment with political elites has been fuelled by a long list of unfortunate events, including the expenses scandal, the Iraq War, and a general culture in Westminster of spin and corruption. There's been the disappearance of industries that once supported cohesive communities, the shrinking of local government and unions, and a general fragmentation in society. And, to top it all, the main parties parked their tanks on political common ground, leaving nothing of substance to squabble over.

Yet from the seats at the back of the auditorium a roar of defiance is rising, channelled through new smaller parties, the leaders of which instinctively connect with the public. The SNP and UKIP both attract packed meetings, fuelled by the public's powerful sense that they've been abandoned. The Scottish referendum proved the Tories to be an endangered species north of the border, while Labour seemingly holds little appeal in much of the south. Both are losing 'market share' rapidly – and yet, because of the FPTP voting system, the gap between the popular vote and seats in Parliament (the difference between what people want and what they get) has widened to undemocratic levels.

Everything appears to be changing, except those at the top.

Chapter 7

ELECTIONS AND VOTING

The right to vote is at the heart of any democracy and, for politicians, election day is judgement day. The vote gives folk from all walks of life the opportunity to voice their concerns, booting out a failing government and voting in a better one.

At least, that's how it's supposed to work...

Campaign trail

Until recently, it was the prime minister who would decide when a general election should be called, within a five-year maximum time frame, and he or she would choose that moment with care. The Fixed-Term Parliaments Act 2011 changed all that: from 2015, general elections will now be held every five years (with certain exceptions).

TYPES OF ELECTION

- **General elections** These are the big ones for the UK Parliament, held every five years from 2015.
- **Devolved elections** Elections to the Scottish Parliament, Welsh Assembly and Northern Ireland Assembly also take place every five years.
- **By-elections** Local by-elections take place when a parliamentary seat becomes vacant between general elections, perhaps because the elected MP has died or has been forced to resign for some salacious reason.
- **Local government elections** Usually held during May in each year, local elections allow people to choose their councils or city mayors.
- **Police and crime commissioner (PCC) elections** These elections were introduced in 2012 in England and Wales, but are probably the least democratic and most unnecessary elections: only one in ten registered voters take part – with accusations of millions of pounds being wasted.
- **Euro elections** Every five years, the British public is asked to vote for members of the European Parliament (MEPs). Voter turnout tends to be low, at only 30–40%, and some use this as an opportunity to cast protest votes (see Chapter 6).

Parliament is 'dissolved' by the monarch (closed for parliamentary business) 25 days before an election, allowing MPs to focus on campaigning. Manifestos are drawn up: statements of policies that each party promises to pursue if elected. The media circus hits town, seizing the airwaves and populating the papers with political discussion until almost everyone's heartily sick of verbally incontinent suits. And, in case by some miracle you missed all the fun, hundreds of party workers are dispatched to canvass key marginal areas (areas in which two or more parties have similar levels of support) to drum up support.

Primaries: Picking winners

Where do MPs come from? The obvious answer, 'Dalek City on Planet Skaro', has yet to be scientifically proven. What we do know for sure is that candidates – aspiring MPs – are selected by their local branches on the basis of party loyalty and 'winning appeal' (although wealth and influence are sometimes rumoured to play a part). The effect of this is that our choice of potential MPs is limited to a carefully pre-screened list. When the Communist Party of China restricts choice on the ballot paper in Hong Kong to certain hand-picked people, we decry this as undemocratic; under the voting system in the UK (as we will see later), there are large numbers of 'safe seats' in which even Teletubby Tinky Winky would enter Parliament if the favoured party were to select him to stand.

Sometimes, candidates are selected at 'primary' meetings that are open to the public, but these are often crammed with supporters of one candidate. On very rare occasions, to boost their election chances, parties choose to give local residents a say, regardless of which party they may support, by holding 'open primaries'. In this instance, every voter receives a ballot paper in the post, along with the details of two or three candidates (likely to be well known in the local area). The advantage to the party of such a postal primary is that it can produce a popular candidate with local appeal. The main disadvantage is the expense (some £40,000 per primary), plus the fact that, once elected, such MPs tend to speak their own minds rather than toe the party line.

The art of persuasion

At a general election, parties employ a range of techniques to try to connect with the people and win votes. You'll be hard pressed to avoid:

- party-political TV broadcasts, plus televised interviews and debates;
- adverts on billboards and in newspapers;
- party members canvassing on your doorstep or by phone, plus contact by text or email;
- adverts and coverage online, including blogs and social media; and
- coverage of party leaders touring the country and holding rallies.

But it's arguable how much impact campaigns actually have on the result – particularly in areas with a lot of 'brand loyal' voters. And modern politics is as much about knocking the opposition (negative campaigning) as it is about positively promoting a party's own manifesto promises.

Perhaps most effective of all is a spot of legalised bribery. As the distinguished author Larry Elliot puts it: 'Parliaments have their own

rhythm and chancellors usually get heavy in the first couple of years, raising taxes and cutting spending so that they have a war chest to raid as polling day approaches.'

Party-political broadcasts

Each of the parties, including smaller contenders such as the Green Party, is entitled to air a number of political TV broadcasts. This applies to general, European and even some council elections. There are no awkward questions to answer and the party can promote

'To be born British is to win first prize in the lottery of life' – or it might have been in the days when Victorian empire builders such as Cecil Rhodes bestrode the globe. Today, you might be forgiven for thinking it's the booby prize – and not solely on account of the weather. But we are extraordinarily lucky compared with much of the world's population, who struggle for the basics of life or suffer under brutal dictatorships. We can breathe a sigh of relief that our fundamental rights and freedoms are enshrined in the law of the land (see Chapter 8).

Strictly speaking, however, there aren't actually any 'British citizens'; rather, we are all 'subjects of the Crown', which sounds a lot grander. One of the wonderfully quirky things about being a 'loyal royal subject' is the reassuring regal proclamation residing inside the front cover of British passports – an imperial warning formulated to ward off persons with the temerity to be of foreign persuasion: 'Her Britannic Majesty's Secretary of State requests and requires in the name of Her Majesty all those whom it may concern to allow the bearer to pass freely without let or hindrance and to afford the bearer such assistance and protection as may be necessary.'

Citizenship tests

People from EU member states are free to move, work and live anywhere they choose inside the European Union, without the need to apply for citizenship. But anyone from elsewhere wanting to live or work in the UK for more than a temporary period (on a visa) will normally need to secure British citizenship.

Over 50% of migration into the UK is from outside the Union and around 190,000 foreign citizens naturalise annually as British citizens, the largest groups being from India, Pakistan and Nigeria.

Until recently, handing out citizenship was a low-key affair: if you wanted to become an official denizen of these fair isles, you either had to be born here or have lived in the country for two years. Today, the residency requirement is five years – or three years if married to a UK citizen. Citizenship tests have been introduced, in line with the practice in most countries, to improve understanding of British culture. Although the multiple-choice test isn't generally considered to be too taxing, BBC's *Panorama* has highlighted fraudulent private exam bodies facilitating abuse. Nonetheless, to mark the occasion, successful new 'subjects' attend citizenship ceremonies at which they swear an oath of allegiance to their new home country and to the Crown.

Comparison with other countries

It's sometimes claimed that it's too easy to become a British citizen. Most countries set fairly tough conditions to qualify for such a valuable prize. Becoming a US citizen, for example, is a long and drawn-out process: first, you need to be a 'green card' holder (you must have secured employment, have a resident family member's sponsorship, or be getting married to a US citizen); then, you need to clock up continuous residency of five years, learn the language and history, and be of 'good moral character'. Italy and Spain set relatively high ten-year naturalisation periods, and Sweden, 12 years.

In Germany, citizenship cannot be obtained simply by marrying a genuine *Deutschlander*; instead, after a period of eight years' residency, you *may* be entitled to a German passport (subject to having adequate language skills, no criminal record and no dependency on welfare). Citizenship is normally determined by inheritance from parents and not by place of birth. Children with a German mother or father are automatically citizens at birth – but not all children born in Germany are automatically German.

its policies – yet many parties spend large parts of their ten minutes attacking opponents and promoting their leaders as 'stars' of some sort – without saying much about what they'd do themselves.

In recent years, live televised debates between party leaders have been broadcast, making headline news. These are riskier for the big parties, who have most to lose by jousting with smaller contenders. Arguments rage about which parties should be included, but on the basis of numbers of votes, it would seem democratic to cast the net far more broadly than the top three or four.

Who can vote?

Registering to vote is easy: the local council will write to you, asking you to register by post or online. Even the Queen gets a vote – but never actually puts pencil to ballot paper, because the monarch must be neutral, remaining above the sordid world of politics (or could it be voter apathy?)

At election time, you'll receive a polling card, alerting you to the date and the location of your local polling station – a town or village hall, or a temporarily converted school. At the polling station, you'll be asked to cast your vote in a 'ballot booth' designed to ensure that your vote is kept private.

Some people are unable to vote. This may be because they:

- are under the age of 18 (although there's an argument for this age to be lowered – as it was for the Scottish referendum – because 16-year-olds have other legal rights and obligations, such as to join the armed forces and paying tax);
- are mentally incapable;
- reside in prison;
- have been convicted in the past five years of voting fraud;
- sit in the House of Lords; or
- are foreign nationals – even if granted residency (although people from Commonwealth countries and Irish nationals living in the UK can vote in a UK general election).

Opinion polling

Opinion polls can provide a political barometer to show what the British people are thinking and can be surprisingly accurate at estimating support for parties – often within a 3% margin of error. Sometimes, newspapers and TV stations will commission polls as a device to generate stories about party popularity. In recent years, the Scottish Parliament has pioneered the emailing of 'snapshot polls' to MSPs to let them know what their voters are thinking.

EXPANDING OR SHRINKING BOUNDARIES

The map of local voting areas in which MPs have their 'seats' (constituencies) needs to reflect changes over time as the UK population grows or (in some areas) shrinks. Each party has a vested interest, knowing that boundary changes can work in their favour, so this is a job that can't be trusted to MPs. To resolve this problem impartially, a review of parliamentary seats is carried out every eight–ten years by four independent Boundary Commissions (one for each of the home nations), staffed by civil servants. If the Commission considers population to have grown significantly in a constituency, it may split that constituency into two; where local population has declined, two neighbouring constituencies may be merged.

EXCUSES

Politicians avidly read polls and will sometimes develop kneejerk policies in response. Most commonly, however, their stock answer to a predicted bad result is 'The only result that counts is the one on election day', or to blame media bias. This latter may indeed be a valid argument: national newspapers make no bones about their political allegiances. While they may claim merely to reflect the views of their readership, some would argue that the media sets the agenda, influenced by wealthy proprietors (who often aren't even UK nationals – see Chapter 9).

Who pays for it?

The big parties spend a lot of money on their campaigns: the Conservatives and Labour have huge promotional budgets totalling as much as £10 million. Money is raised from rich donors and from membership subscriptions, with Labour gaining additional support via trade unions. One concern is the potential corrupting influence of big donors on campaign contributions (see Chapter 6).

Come the big day

The vote itself is squeezed into a single day. Polling stations open at 7am and close at 10pm, with breathless broadcasters predicting the likely results based on 'exit polls' (asking emerging voters which party they voted for). Meanwhile, across the country, ballot boxes are collected, and the local returning officer (who plays the role of referee) oversees their counting into the early hours and beyond, before formally announcing the result for that constituency amidst a highly charged atmosphere.

Voting systems

On the face of it, the old blue–red two-horse race of British politics has now become a national contest between a whole bunch of parties: Conservatives, Labour and Liberal Democrats, plus the Greens (who are as popular as the LibDems), the Scottish National Party (SNP) and Plaid Cymru (threatening many former Labour strongholds), not to mention UKIP and Respect. Rarely has politics looked so fluid and unpredictable – except for one thing: the electoral system used for Westminster elections is very cruel to parties that amass many votes in many places, coming a strong second or third in lots of locations, but first in very few.

First past the post (FPTP): A 'single winner'

Elections to the UK Parliament and local councils use the long-standing 'first past the post' (FPTP) system, so-called because it resembles a race. We all know the drill: turn up at the polling station and boldly scrawl an 'X' by the name of the party/candidate you want to win; then, once all of the votes have been counted, the person with the highest number is declared the winner. The trouble is that the votes cast for all of the other candidates usually total more than those cast for the winner – and each of these votes has effectively been ignored. Across the country as a whole, the majority of votes are binned.

The party that gets to govern the country is the one that wins the highest number of local constituencies, each of which translates into a seat in the House of Commons. Securing a majority of seats means that the party can push through its agenda (assuming that its MPs toe the party line when voting in Parliament). In some instances, however, the winning party may have secured fewer than half of the total number of seats, and in this case it will struggle to govern effectively unless it makes deals with opposition parties to secure their support.

In the example given in Table 7.1, the Tory candidate won, despite getting less than 40% of the vote; more than 63% of the voters in Walmington-on-Sea actually voted for different candidates. If Sir Quentin had won with a much more comfortable margin of, say, 10,000 or more votes, this would be described as a 'safe seat'; in fact, he has only a small majority, so the seat would be referred to as 'marginal'.

ADVANTAGES

- **Community links** The winning candidate in an FPTP system is supposed to represent local voters in Parliament, which should mean in theory that people feel 'ownership' of their MP. In practice, it's not unusual for candidates with zero interest in the local area to be 'parachuted in' from party headquarters. It's also rare for MPs to put their constituents' interests ahead of those of their party and their own careers – although local MPs have been known to cynically join marches protesting their own party's plans to close a local hospital.

- **Strong government** The FPTP system is supposed to result in strong majorities for the winning party; hence 'strong government'. For example, in 2005, New Labour won some 36% of the votes cast, which translated into a massive majority of 66 seats in the House of Commons, giving the party a free hand to

Table 7.1   General election outcome, Walmington-on-Sea constituency

Candidate	Party	Votes	% of vote
Sir Quentin Fox-Hunter	Conservative	17,132	36.5
Red Soundbite	Labour	16,748	35.1
U. O'Sceptic	UKIP	8,213	17.5
Mr Pledge	LibDems	1,971	4.2
Lou Carbonera	Greens	1,831	3.9
	Others	1,314	2.8

RESULT: Sir Quentin Fox-Hunter (Cons) wins the seat by a margin of 384 votes.

pass its preferred legislation. More recently, we've ended up with a 'hung parliament' – effectively, a draw in which neither of the two biggest parties wins a decisive majority and one is forced to enter into coalition with one (or more) of the smaller parties.

DISADVANTAGES

- **Ignores the majority of voters** There is no winners' podium with silver and bronze medals. In 'winner takes all' systems, the most popular candidate under FPTP usually garners fewer votes than all of the runners-up combined, sometimes winning by a photo finish (only a handful of votes). This means that the victor is elected on a minority of the votes cast and that most voters end up with an MP whom they've actually voted against! If the winning party attracts less than half the votes cast, can it really claim to have been democratically elected? Today, more than a third of voters reject both main parties, with another third of the potential electorate declining to vote for anyone at all.
- **It's unfair** Under FPTP, governments get substantial majorities in Parliament that are vastly disproportionate to their share of the vote. For example, the 2005–10 New Labour administration had a parliamentary majority based on the support of only around a quarter of all eligible voters.
- **Keeps the same 'big two' parties in power** The FPTP system is designed to accommodate two big players: Labour and Tory. Since the end of the Second World War, each has held power for a similar amount of time, power switching incessantly between the two. The 1951 election was the high-water mark of two-party politics, splitting more than 96% of the vote. But although that share has substantially declined since and the old red–blue duopoly is now much weaker, smaller parties remain marginalised and, with only a handful of MPs at most, aren't able to promote their agendas.

Majority rule systems: 'Every vote counts'

The big advantage of 'majority rule' systems – systems in which a party wins only if it achieves more than half of the votes cast – is that the elected government has the support of a majority of voters. Each vote cast carries equal weight and no vote is ignored, because the wishes of all those voters whose chosen local candidate didn't win are still taken into account.

PROPORTIONAL REPRESENTATION (PR)

Proportional representation works very simply: political parties win seats according to the total percentage of votes that they've attracted nationwide. So, to get a majority of seats in the House of Commons, a party would need to poll more than half of the total votes cast. Under this system, people are voting for the party rather than for a local candidate – which, for most voters, makes little difference. Candidates who hope to be elected are selected from lists drawn up by the political parties, ideally with a good geographical spread to reflect all regions of the country.

ADVANTAGES

- **Fair and simple** Proportional representation is generally regarded as fair because every vote counts; hence it raises voter turnout and lowers apathy. It's a race in which every horse wins something in proportion to its popularity.
- **Proven track record** The system is already successfully used in countries such as Holland, Sweden, Switzerland and Germany.

- **Flexible** Proportional representation can be refined to combine local representation with national fairness (see below).
- **May benefit society** Countries with PR voting systems tend to score higher on the United Nations Human Development Index, demonstrating higher equality and better health care, education and environmental policies.

DISADVANTAGES

- **No local link** Because people are voting for the party rather than a local candidate, there's generally no link between MPs and voters (but see below).
- **Coalition governments** If no single party attracts a majority of the votes and so has no dominant majority in Parliament, there must be bargaining between parties. Decision making therefore tends to be slower, but policies are consequently likely to be properly considered rather than dictated from the top. Some suggest that coalitions prevent one party from pursuing extremist policies; they also have to behave like adults, rather than hurl insults at each other. Diverse opinions must be heard, with reason and discussion playing a greater role than bullying by whips (see Chapter 11). Most European countries have happily used this system for donkeys' years, although coalitions in Italy famously fizz with instability.
- **Opens the door to extreme parties** If a significant handful of people were to decide to vote for a fanatical Militant Nudists Freedom Party, in theory it could get a foothold in Parliament. To avoid this outcome, most PR systems set a minimum threshold (say, 5% of the vote locally or nationally), preventing the more extreme from obtaining seats in Parliament, while preserving democracy.

REFINING PR

The ideal voting system would combine the basic fairness of proportional representation with some sort of local representation, so that voters still feel a connection with the person elected to represent them.

Additional member (AM) system

The additional member system is already used successfully in the Scottish Parliament and Welsh Assembly, with a similar version (known as 'mixed-member proportional representation') well proven in New Zealand. Under the AM system, voters get two votes rather than one. The first is cast as in UK general elections: for a particular candidate who will represent the constituency in Parliament. The winning candidate, as under FPTP, is the one who has the most votes.

For the second vote, however, voters choose among parties, on a simple PR basis. These votes are then totted up *nationally* and additional seats awarded in proportion to a party's share. For example, if the SNP were to win 40% of all second votes, it would be granted 40% of what are called 'additional members' – MPs additional to those elected under the FPTP vote.

In Scotland, of 129 members of the Scottish Parliament (MSPs), 73 are elected via FPTP and 56 as additional members (known as 'list MSPs').

Local candidate list method

Under the 'local candidate list' method, a country is divided into local voting constituencies (bigger areas than we have at present, each with, say, 20 seats). Each party has several candidates standing for election. The votes cast in the region as a whole are counted and seats granted to the parties in proportion to the percentage of votes that each wins.

Suppose that Labour and Tory each were to win 35% of the vote, while the Greens, the LibDems and UKIP each win 10%: the big two would each get seven seats and the smaller parties, two each.

A variant of this – the 'd'Hondt method' – is used in Northern Ireland and in MEP elections.

Alternative vote (AV) system

The 'alternative vote' (AV) system is used already to elect the Mayor of London. Under this system, rather than mark 'X' next to your favourite local candidate, you list them in order of preference – writing '1', '2', '3', etc, next to your top choices. If one candidate turns out to be very popular and gets more than half the vote, then he or she wins and everyone can go home; if there's no clear winner, the least popular candidate is then eliminated and all of the second ('2') votes on those ballots are distributed among the appropriate

remaining candidates. This process continues until someone reaches the magic mark (more than 50%).

A similar 'ranked voting' system, known as the 'single transferable vote' (STV), is used in the Republic of Ireland.

Changing the system

The trouble with the present system is that it disregards the votes of the majority of UK citizens, which isn't particularly fair or democratic, resulting in voter apathy and seething resentment. As the big two parties become less popular, the present system begins to look even more unbalanced and unrepresentative. And yet, when the LibDems proposed introducing the relatively complex AV system to England in a referendum in May 2011, the Conservatives vigorously campaigned against it and the electorate duly rejected it, blowing the prospect of electoral reform out of the water for the next few years.

Voting: A downward trend

Not everyone with the right to vote bothers to turn up on election day. Unlike Australia, voting at UK general elections isn't compulsory. Indeed, voter turnout in the UK is among the lowest in Europe and has been declining for many years, from around 83% of people in the 1950s to some 60% today. A phenomenal 16 million people didn't vote at the last general election and, in some local areas, only four people in ten bother to show up. In European and local council elections, as few as one in three eligible people exercise their hard-won democratic right to vote. And while governments are fond of reminding us that they have a 'democratic mandate' to implement their policies, the fewer the people who vote, the less legitimate that claim.

Low turnout can be blamed on:

■ distrust – that is, widespread cynicism about politicians keeping their word or acting on behalf of their constituents, with many politicians seen as lacking in real-life experience or, worse, as being corrupt;

■ a feeling that 'they're all the same' – that the policies of the UK's big parties are substantially indistinguishable and that 'whoever you vote for, the government still gets in';

■ an absence of policies offering any real interest or the prospect of hope to make our lives better;

■ 'safe seats' in many areas, in which the winner is a foregone conclusion, leading voters to see no point in exercising what will be a wasted vote. (In marginal seats, voter turnout is higher, because people know that their votes are more likely to matter.)

The age of alienation

The UK prides itself on its democratic probity and cheating is negligible – but the system itself is warped. The established parties can slip into Downing Street on a barely legitimate 30% of the vote. And elections depend on swing votes in a diminishing number of marginal seats – which are plied with good things by politicians: no hospitals ever close in marginals. (Sources: Electoral Reform Society and Polly Toynbee)

As things stand, it seems we may be in for a long period of coalition governments where parties try to cobble together just enough votes to scrape them over the line into Number 10. It is

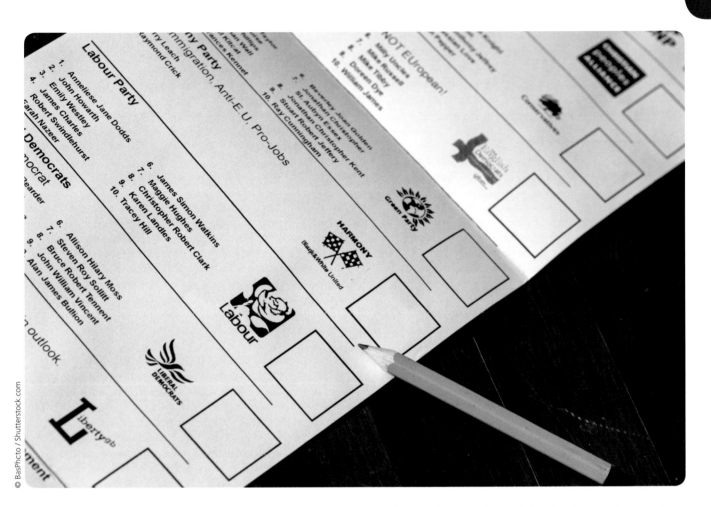

desperately unambitious and a recipe for getting a government without a solid mandate.

THE SNP: A LESSON IN VOTER ANIMATION

Judging by the tumultuous 85% turnout for the Scottish independence referendum, 'political apathy' is a myth. When something is worth voting for, people will queue into the night to add their names to the register. In 2014, Scotland came alive with packed public meetings, debates in pubs and gatherings on street corners.

The popular appeal of the SNP is in stark contrast to the faded appeal of stale Westminster politicians. A nationalist party open to all, with a firm pro-business stance, yet espousing social democratic policies, it blended together an agenda of patriotism, social justice and cultural self-confidence to create a clear and popular project that propelled huge numbers of people into the voting booths.

The SNP offered voters an alternative to neoliberal economics espoused by the main Westminster parties, with the chance to cut loose from a solar system in which the City of London is forever the sun. (This probably also accounts for some of the surge in support for UKIP south of the border.)

Critics point to the fact that the SNP promised voters large dollops of jam whilst campaigning against unpopular cuts, privatisation and taxes imposed by Westminster. But in doing so, the SNP summoned up feelings of hope, patriotism, passion and purpose among allegedly disengaged voters. *(Sources: BBC & Kevin McKenna)*

Local democracy

Turnout at council elections is about half that of general elections – often as low as 30%. Most of us haven't got a clue who our local councillors are, and councils are sometimes seen as unimportant and powerless to effect real change (not least because most of their funding comes from central government). Yet how well local councils perform can have a direct effect on the lives of local residents.

How many voters are there?

The UK population is around 65 million, rising by around a quarter of a million a year. By law, everyone aged 18 and over has to put their name on the electoral roll and around 46 million people are registered to vote (a difference largely comprising those without the right to vote, such as children). Nevertheless, it's estimated that as many as 8 million people in England, Scotland and Wales have not yet registered – mainly the disenfranchised young, those living in poverty, with chaotic lives, or those who want to keep a low

---

TACTICAL VOTING

If you live in a 'safe seat' area in which your preferred choice hasn't got a snowball's chance of entering Parliament, you could still try to prevent your least favourite party from winning. For example, as a Green voter, you might decide to vote Labour just to stop the 'effing Tories' getting in. This type of 'tactical voting' is unique to the British FPTP system.

profile for various reasons. This is more than 10% of the electorate – so there's a whole lot of law-breaking going on, which raises questions about the competency of the Home Office and UK Visas and Immigration (the rebranded Border Agency). Also, the number of Britons living abroad is around 5 million, with only a handful registered to vote in UK elections.

Reversing the decline

Low voter turnout is largely the result of disenchantment with politicians. Some more arrogant MPs openly hold their constituents in contempt: they like the power, but forget who voted them into office, shirking any sense of duty. But most MPs realise that they need to do more to engage with voters.

The Scottish independence referendum proved that the decline can be reversed. While politicians tend to focus on ways of making voting easier, they would be well advised to consider instead what might induce us to burst through the polling station doors at the crack of dawn.

- Parties need to inspire us by developing well-thought-out, credible strategies to drive the country forward. We need braver policies that grab the public imagination and inspired leadership. Who dares wins. Trust comes with enthusiasm for a cause.
- They might adopt an adult approach to politics, with honest people who know what they're doing and abide by a strict code of ethics. Perhaps we should allow citizens to sue the government for breach of contract if it fails to deliver on its manifesto promises? There could also be a lot more referenda for big decisions (such as the privatisation of the NHS).
- They might improve the quality of new MPs by setting minimum criteria for candidates, to ensure that they have a suitable depth of experience beyond the incestuous worlds of media and lobbying.
- Our forebears fought for the right to vote, so simply choosing not to do so is an insult. Since we're legally required to register to vote, might we take it a step further and (like several other

democracies) legally require every (eligible) person to vote in general elections? We might then choose to register a protest vote for an outsider, such as the Monster Raving Loony Party, or to 'spoil the ballot paper' – writing a 'helpful suggestion' or putting multiple crosses or doodles as a gesture of defiance.

- We might add a 'none of the above' option to ballot papers – and if this turns out to be the most popular choice, require all parties to forfeit their deposits and re-run with different candidates.
- Promotion: advertise the event in advance by hanging up huge voting signs to entice voters.
- Education: It might help if the reasons for voting and the process itself were explained more clearly in school citizenship classes.
- Busy people may not have time to visit a polling station. In New Zealand people can vote in any polling station, anywhere. Or keep polling stations open for more than one day.
- We might consider the potential for 'e-democracy', with mobile devices and online capabilities theoretically able to usher in a new golden age of ancient Athenian direct democracy, in which all citizens could vote on all issues.

The main problem of course is the nature of the mechanised party system which turns politicians into constipated chickens, afraid to utter anything meaningful, battered by media and Twitter for any slip ups. Off-the-leash speakers from the smaller parties are popular because they're free from such constraints. It would also help if local voters could have a say in the choice of party candidates instead of head office selecting on the basis of a party member's robotic obedience.

ISSUES WORTH VOTING FOR

Pollsters spend a lot of time asking the public *why* they vote and it seems that we look favourably on the party that offers the best plan for the following.

- **The economy** If the economy seems to be doing well and people feel reasonably confident about their finances and job prospects, it's good news for the party in power. If not, we're more likely to vote for change. Hence the temptation for politicians to stoke up debt-fuelled housing booms in the short term.
- **Tax cuts** Few of us are beyond the temptation of an extra few quid promised towards a good cause (our own).
- **Public services** People like to see hospitals and schools that are well funded and run efficiently. Hence the temptation for politicians to embark on expensive 'pay tomorrow' PFI schemes (see Chapter 9), forgetting that people may sometimes be persuaded to pay higher taxes in return for genuinely improved access to health and education.
- **Immigration** For the last 30 years or so, politicians have studiously avoided discussing the subject of immigration, for fear of being labelled racist. But with EU enlargement embracing low-wage eastern European countries and with the free movement of workers a central pillar of the European Union, this has now become a prominent issue.
- **Europe** The public are increasingly questioning the benefits of EU membership. The recent results in the 2014 European elections were largely seen as a protest against a loss of national autonomy, a lack of democracy in Brussels and the burgeoning

POLITICAL PLAYGROUND

cost of EU membership. The success of UKIP sees the larger parties scrabbling to present policies of their own that will tempt UKIP voters back to the fold.

- **Resurgence of UK industry** A recent YouGov poll found that a large majority of voters – some 85% – want the government to promote a stronger UK manufacturing base, with 62% believing that it will give the country more economic security. More than four out of five voters would like political parties to develop a clearer strategy to get Britain making and exporting more. Anger about deindustrialisation was a major driver in the Scottish 'Yes' campaign.
- **Military conflict** Wars can rapidly change political fortunes, as Margaret Thatcher found in 1982 with the successful campaign to defend the Falkland Islands against Argentina. In contrast, Tony Blair's disastrous decision to unquestioningly support the US invasion of Iraq in 2003 was hugely unpopular.
- **Local issues** Voting decisions aren't all based on national issues. One of the penalties for living on an overcrowded island is that new runways, roads, power stations, railways and housing estates cause massive discontent among local residents who cry 'Not in my back yard!' People generally believe that the local environment should be protected, and the threatened closure of local facilities such as a hospital can garner huge support for candidates opposed to the plan.

BROADENING PARTY APPEAL
Although both big parties can still rely on heartlands in which they can bank a strong core vote from 'natural supporters' ('We've *always* voted Labour'), the fact is that far fewer people today are blindly loyal to one big political brand. The key to electoral success is therefore appealing beyond this core vote base: Labour can't win if it doesn't gain some seats in the Tory stronghold of the south-east; the Tories need to win more seats in the north.

Appealing to moderate 'middle Britain' is often seen as the electoral holy grail. These are 'swing voters' who may shift their allegiances between parties, and tend to be people with middle-class lifestyles with home ownership, or even private schooling for their kids, who are usually wooed by:

- promises not to raise taxes;
- the absence of any ideology that the media might regard as 'extreme';
- the promise of decent public services; and
- the prioritising of national security issues.

Why do we vote?
A combination of factors affects how we vote, including age, class, sex, ethnicity and the area in which we live. In the UK, religion isn't thought to play a major role in how we vote, unlike in the United States, where 'God and guns' are a significant factor. If we're being honest, we can also be influenced by things such as gut instinct, what friends and colleagues think, and the views of the media (which are sometimes accused of 'dumbing down' debate).

CULT OF PERSONALITY
Human factors are enormously important to our vote – that is, whether we like individual politicians and party leaders, and how trustworthy and capable they appear. We naturally want the person in the hot seat to be up to the job. A leader with charisma who can communicate well on TV can be a huge bonus to a party, and as a nation we may have been guilty of voting in leaders such as Blair and Cameron on the basis of their personalities, rather than their policies. In fact, a charismatic leader hasn't always been a guarantee of success: Labour's Clement Attlee, despite being blessed with a quiet and reserved nature, won a stunning post-war victory against Sir Winston Churchill, on the basis of policies offering real hope and progress, such as a free national health care system, railways that were better operated and an export-focused industrial strategy.

CLASS
Traditionally, manual 'blue collar' workers tended to vote for Labour, whereas the better-off middle classes and office staff were more likely to vote Tory. Thatcher's Conservative brand of patriotism and popular capitalism changed that, holding broad appeal. Today, the rise of UKIP has again cut across traditional demarcation lines: as well as splitting the right-wing vote, it has appealed to some traditional Labour voters. Similarly, the SNP in Scotland has dramatically cut into Labour heartlands.

THE FEMALE VOTE
Women are considered to be more open to persuasion, with higher numbers of 'swing voters' who are less inclined to have a long-standing preference for a single party come hell or high water. Politicians take notice of influential women's websites such as Mumsnet, and believe that women are likely to value policies relating to health, education and family values.

The importance of female voters does, of course, beg the question: why aren't there more female MPs?

AGE
As a rule, younger people have tended to gravitate towards left-wing parties because of their message of equality and compassion for those less fortunate; as people get older, they tend to become more right-wing. The problem is that those who don't vote don't count – and at the last general election some 76% of over-65s voted, compared with only 44% of under-24s.

ETHNICITY
The makeup of the British population has changed over the years and ethnic minorities are expected to grow to around 20% of the UK population by 2051. Labour tends to do better amongst Britain's expanding ethnic groups, but different communities have different voting patterns.

WHERE YOU LIVE
It seems the further away from Westminster people live, the less they like the Tory message; hence, in Scotland, Wales and the north of England, Labour and the nationalist parties SNP and Plaid Cymru have broad appeal, to the extent that the Tories are an endangered species. Cornwall too has a strong and growing regional identity. The Tories do better in the south-east, where incomes tend to be higher. The south-west, being more rural and less affluent, was traditionally LibDem territory. The north–south divide is still very evident, with the unbalanced economy perpetuating a split between wealthier southern counties and former industrial heartlands further north. House prices tend to reflect this divide.

Chapter 8

POWER SYSTEMS

Power has a tendency to go to politicians' heads. To prevent deluded would-be despots grabbing control of the national steering wheel and enslaving the rest of us to their mad plans, there need to be some pretty hefty safety belts at the heart of any democracy. This is achieved by dividing the state into three branches, with robust firewalls to keep them separate from each other.

Splitting power

- **The executive** The epicentre of power lies at 10 Downing Street. The prime minister and Cabinet are responsible for formulating government policies, which the Civil Service implements.
- **The legislature** Parliament is the nation's decision-making headquarters, where the elected members from different parties scrutinise the actions of the executive. The job of the House of Commons (and of the devolved assemblies) is to debate proposed new law and policy, and to vote on whether or not it should be implemented.
- **The judiciary** The court system interprets the 'broad brush' laws created by Parliament and applies them to everyday situations in

the name of the state. But the courts' role is also to protect civil liberties, standing up for minorities (no matter how unpopular in the media) and challenging government when it passes legislation that threatens citizens' rights. All citizens, including politicians, are required to obey the decisions of the courts.

Unlike most countries, the UK has no written constitution that precisely lays out the terms of this separation of powers; instead, we rely on an 'unwritten' constitution embodied in the laws and decisions made over many centuries to protect civil liberties and to curb executive powers. But this means that there are grey areas…

TRUST ME … I'M A LAWYER

British people still trust judges far more than they do politicians or big business. Although the apparent remoteness of judges can make them easy targets, for example for lenient prison sentences, they are broadly respected for their independence and integrity. The 'judge and jury' system is one of the great safety mechanisms that prevent the state from behaving in an oppressive way. The object of any tyrant would be, first, to make Parliament subservient to his or her will, and then to abolish trial by jury. So it's rather strange that Britain entrusts the day-to-day running of the criminal justice system at its most basic level to magistrates – laypeople working part-time who need have no formal legal training.

Trust may be high in judges, but the profession of lawyers from among whom more senior judges are chosen is regarded with greater suspicion. Today's 'compensation' culture has led more of us to have dealings with lawyers, and ordinary clients are often exasperated by unnecessary fees and delays. Significant numbers of solicitors were found to be overcharging for work undertaken under 'legal aid' provisions (which has controversially now been severely cut). But it's the 'magic circle' of five giant law firms in the City, dealing with corporate clients and interlocked with US partners, which make the biggest money.

Sitting in judgment: The judiciary

To control the messianic tendencies of ambitious politicians, it's essential that there are independently powerful people capable of strimming them down to size. This role falls to the judiciary, who are 'servants of the monarch' and independent of government. The Supreme Court, as the highest court, is an important check on the power of Westminster.

The UK actually has three legal systems – one for England and Wales, one for Scotland and another for Northern Ireland – but they have a lot in common. Statutory law comprises Acts of Parliament and secondary legislation made to give detail to the Acts; because it cannot cover every eventuality and because statute is sometimes in need of interpretation, case law provides for its application in practice. The courts system is based on a hierarchy, with certain types of criminal and civil case being heard by certain types of court and tribunal, the judgments of which can be appealed on certain grounds to the higher courts – see page 88.

The growing power of European law

As a member state of the European Union, the UK agrees to adhere to its regulations (which are directly applicable) and directives (which require UK legislation to give them effect). Saying no isn't usually an option – since we have limited ability to 'derogate' (to refuse to apply a particular provision). This has had a profound effect on the British constitution, because laws passed by the European Parliament now have equal standing to those passed in Westminster, as do judgments of the Court of Justice of the European Union (often called simply 'the European courts').

In addition, the European Convention of Human Rights (ECHR) – drafted by the Council of Europe (not an EU body, although easily confused with the Council of the European Union) and signed by the UK in 1950 – gives British individuals a right to take their case to the European Court of Human Rights in Strasbourg if they believe that the state has breached one of their fundamental freedoms.

While some see these bodies of European (statutory and case) law as undermining the constitution and national sovereignty, others regard them as adding to the freedoms and rights of individuals.

The ECHR was given further effect in the UK with the Human Rights Act 1998. Despite its frequent disparagement in recent years by home secretaries keen to act independently, the Act is recognised as a last defence for ordinary citizens against state power. Proposals to amend the Act would consequently need to be very carefully considered – not least because the Act is incorporated into the Scottish devolution settlement and the Good Friday Agreement with Northern Ireland.

The national 'rulebook'

The thing that generally guarantees people's freedoms as citizens is a constitution, a sort of national 'rulebook' that outlines how the country should be governed. Without a legal framework within which they must work, egocentric politicians have an alarming tendency to become despotic; a constitution keeps them on the straight and narrow. Most democratic countries have a written constitution – a single document to which everyone can refer – and it usually:

■ curtails the power of those at the top by setting limits on what they can do;
■ keeps the courts separate from the executive (politicians);
■ sets out who does what – that is, the powers of different branches of government, including Cabinet, Parliament and monarch – and ensures that if one branch overreaches its powers, the courts can be called on to slap it down; and

As well as applying the law – both criminal and civil – the courts play a huge role in protecting British citizens from potential abuses by the state. Without the law to settle disputes, the strong would most likely triumph over everyone else. Judges are also selected to preside over lengthy public inquiries because of their experience in dealing with disputes and witnesses.

ENGLAND and WALES

CRIMINAL LAW

- Offences against citizens and society, such as burglary, car theft or violence against another person.
- The Crown (ie the state) brings charges, rather than the person wronged, eg *R v. Smith* (where 'R' is the Latin *Rex*, meaning King, or *Regina*, Queen).
- The standard of proof at criminal trial is 'beyond all reasonable doubt'.

CIVIL LAW

- Disputes between people and organisations, in which one person or group sues another person or group, eg for negligence or breach of contract.
- Cases vary massively, from minor wrangles between neighbours over who owns a bit of garden, up to complex libel cases or disputes involving multinational corporations.
- Cases are named according to the claimant and defendant, eg *Rylands v. Fletcher*.
- The standard of proof in a civil case is 'on the balance of probabilities'.

GOING TO COURT

Magistrates' courts

- Over 90% of all prosecuted cases are tried here, mostly less serious crimes such as shoplifting.
- Cases are presided over by justices of the peace (JPs), members of the public with no legal training, but with backup from district judges.
- This is also the starting point for most serious cases, such as murder, with the defendant making a brief appearance before being committed to stand trial before a higher court.
- The magistrate may order the defendant to be held on remand in prison until the case can be heard, or allow release on bail.

County court

- This is the lowest rung at which cases of a financial value up to £50,000 are heard.
- The small claims court can fast-track disputes involving up to £5,000.
- The vast majority of cases (such as personal injury claims, landlord–tenant disputes and debt recovery cases) are heard at this level.

Crown court

- The worst crimes (eg murder, rape, robbery with violence), in which there may be a custodial sentence, are presided over by circuit judges or legally trained 'recorders', but the most grave cases are tried by a high court judge.
- Defendants are entitled to trial by jury, with (usually 12) jurors selected at random from the electoral roll. (Jury service is mandatory.)
- The most famous crown court is the Central Criminal Court at the Old Bailey in London.

High Court

- More complex cases, including most libel cases, are heard here.
- It has three divisions: the Queen's Bench Division (QBD); the Chancery Division (Ch); and the Family Division (Fam).
- The Queen's Bench Division deals largely with contract and personal injury/negligence cases.
- The Chancery Division deals with land law and insolvency, among other things.
- The Family Division deals with matters such as high-profile divorce cases and disputes about medical treatment.

Court of Appeal

Appeals to Crown court sentences are heard here, but not every case can be appealed – a compelling reason must exist, such as a flaw discovered in the evidence. Interestingly, people found guilty of a crime can be acquitted by the monarch who, on the advice of the Home Secretary, can grant a pardon (sometimes coming a little late when granted posthumously!).

The Civil Division deals with appeals from lower courts. But the appeals process is long and expensive, with the losing side sometimes forced to pay the winner's enormous legal costs.

Three judges normally hear appeals, with verdicts reached by a majority.

UK Supreme Court

The highest court in the land hears appeals for criminal and civil cases for the whole UK barring Scottish criminal cases (see below).

Decisions reached here are binding on all lower courts and also set future legal precedent.

SCOTTISH courts

CRIMINAL LAW

- Minor criminal cases are heard in **Sheriff courts**.
- More serious cases go to the **High Court of the Justiciary**, which also handles appeals.

CIVIL LAW

- Most civil cases are also tried in **Sheriff courts**, regardless of likely financial value.
- In civil cases, the losing party has a right of appeal to the **UK Supreme Court**.

EUROPEAN courts

Laws made by European courts apply in all member states. The two main courts are:

- the **European Court of Justice (ECJ)**, which passes judgments relating to EU legislation; and
- the **European Court of Human Rights (ECtHR)**, which decides on matters related to the European Convention on Human Rights (ECHR).

The Human Rights Act 1998 provides that UK courts can initially decide the matter should a British citizen feel that his or her Convention rights have been breached, with appeal lying ultimately to the ECtHR.

guarantees the freedoms and rights of individual citizens, such as freedom of speech, the right to vote and the right to not be convicted without fair trial.

Any constitution needs to be flexible enough to adapt over time, jettisoning outdated laws in favour of more up-to-date ones. But it also needs to be rigid enough to restrain potentially dictatorial or deranged prime ministers. Constitutional change should therefore be effected only with a reasonable degree of difficulty, to protect the rights of the individual in the face of short-term political objectives.

WRITTEN OR NOT?
The United States sets great store by its written Constitution, regarding it with the sort of reverence normally reserved for holy scripture. Many US citizens can reel off quotes from their Bill of Rights, such as the infamous right of US citizens to bear firearms. But the United States operates a federal system of government, with less power held centrally and central government in Washington unable to overrule local state laws; Britain has an unwritten, 'unitary' constitution, with the majority of ultimate power residing in central government at Westminster. Unwritten constitutions are generally more flexible than written ones.

THE BRITISH CONSTITUTION
Cynics say that the UK is a country famous for making up its constitution as it goes along – but it's a mistake to imagine its unusual unwritten constitution as some sort of flexible fairy tale. In fact, the UK does have a 'rulebook': rather than a single document, it comprises a web of interwoven laws and traditions, which enshrine our rights and obligations as British citizens, able to express ourselves without fear of some unhinged dictator unleashing their secret police. No single person has the power to change the UK constitution – not even the prime minister: changes can be made only by majority vote in Parliament.

In addition to the statutory law passed by Parliament (which are its most important pillar because statute law outranks everything else), the British constitution comprises case law and convention.

- **Case law** Judgments in certain cases establish legal precedent – that is, the judge's decision in one case becomes binding on judges in subsequent similar cases. If a government doesn't like the precedent set, it can trump it by enacting a new statute, which the courts will then be bound to interpret and enforce.
- **Convention** By 'convention', we mean essentially tradition. It is, for example, established by convention that if a government loses a vote of 'no confidence' in the House of Commons, it will immediately call a general election. No law decrees these conventions; politicians simply accept that certain actions must follow certain events, to check those in power.

Strengths
- **Flexibility** The British constitution evolves over time, allowing it to adapt as times change.
- **Judicial supremacy** The independent courts system holds everything together. Everyone is subject to and equal under the law, no matter how rich, famous, or powerful (although money can buy the best legal counsel).

THE AXIS OF EVIL

To keep the democratic machine running smoothly, it's essential that all of the big sources of power in the country are kept separate and independent – safely tucked away in their respective boxes. This doesn't relate only to the usual suspects – Parliament, Number 10 and the judiciary (whose duty it is to enforce the laws); for a start, the military wields enormous might. But perhaps the power to which we're most exposed day in, day out, is the power of markets and big business – and we ought not to forget the potential power of the Church, something that we tend to disregard in the modern age.

So what would happen if ever the twain were to meet and different power centres form alliances? The rather worrying answer is that we'd soon be waving goodbye to those rights and freedoms that we have as honest British citizens. This is why shudders tend to creep up our spines at the thought of theocracy (religious and political power allied), or military juntas (military and political power combined).

And it's no less important to keep economic and political power apart – lest we wind up, at best, with corrupt 'crony capitalism' (rule by bankers) or, at worst, communism or fascism. Should those who control big business be allowed also to control the state (or vice versa), history shows that the public will regret it. So we need to be vigilant for any apparently well-meaning politician attempting to tamper with our constitution, perhaps citing the benefits of free markets and deregulation to justify setting irrevocable changes in motion…

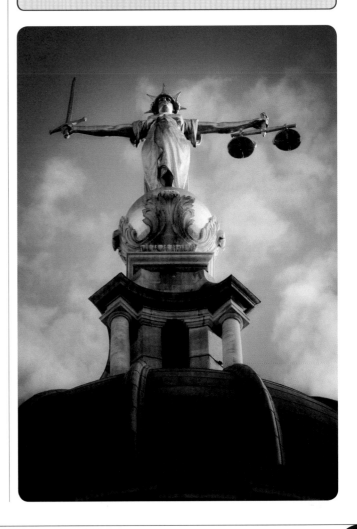

Weaknesses

- **Old and unreliable** Some argue that the unwritten constitution, with its higgledy piggledy reliance on old laws and traditions, is long past its sell-by date. With a written constitution, everyone knows where they stand.
- **Too much centralised power** In a majority government, the prime minister and his or her party can push through change as they please, so the constitution is effectively at their mercy. Westminster politicians are also seen to be increasingly out-of-touch with the rest of the country – and it's even argued that this tiny 'anointed' elite run things mainly for their own benefit and that of their chums.
- **Risk to civil liberties** In the same way, a majority party can pass laws that restrict citizens' liberties. In 2007, for example, the government proposed detaining suspects for an astonishing 120 days without charge – which proposal was (thankfully) rejected.
- **Rules that are too vague** The conventions that underpin the constitution are too easily moulded over time: while ministers would once have been expected to resign if their senior advisers were proven to have lied in public or to be incompetent, today the minister simply sacks the adviser and carries on regardless.
- **Not democratic enough** Parties frequently promise one thing in their manifestos, but fail to deliver once in government, without their members batting an eyelid. Increasingly, too, people in senior governmental positions haven't been elected by the people, being instead 'special advisers' (or unelected peers in the House of Lords).
- **It's unrepresentative** The constitution enshrines the first past the post (FPTP) voting system, which ignores millions of votes (see Chapter 7).

KEEPING THEM HONEST

In the UK system, enormous power is concentrated in the hands of people at the top, especially the prime minister and MPs. This power is limited by the following.

- **Elections** Every five years, we get a chance to vote the buggers out of office if we're unhappy with their performance.
- **The party system** Even the most powerful prime ministers ultimately depend on the support of their MPs, who in turn rely on public support, so pushing through unpopular new laws could spark a revolt.
- **Media scrutiny** Dodgy dealings can't easily be kept secret. Efforts to change the constitution are immediately reported, as are the views of opponents.
- **Devolution** Since the 2014 Scottish independence referendum, even more power has been devolved away from the centre in Westminster to home nations and regions.
- **The courts** Judges have the power to review allegations that ministers or government officials have acted illegally, exceeding their powers (although the courts can't directly override statute law passed by Parliament).
- **EU membership** Since the legislation passed by the European Commission has precedence over Acts of Parliament, depending on your views this either undermines UK sovereignty or is a check on power.

Clinging on to power

Like FIFA being dragged kicking and screaming into the 21st century, the political classes resist change. More decisions and functions of government are centralised in Britain than in any other European country, and the politician isn't generally the sort of animal that relishes giving up power. One of the paradoxes of the British system is that we've been skilled at constructing federal constitutions for other countries: 'British blood flowed through the veins of the American founding fathers, who wrote the US Constitution; when Australia and Canada became independent, they did so as federal states; and after the Second World War, the Allies – Brits to the fore – devised a federal constitution for Germany that has served that country extremely well' *(Andrew Rawnsley)*. Regional governments in Germany have substantial powers and central government can't ride roughshod over them; indeed, regional support for local businesses has been a major factor in the success of German industry.

Devolution

The biggest constitutional change in the UK since the war came in 1999, with the devolving of powers from Westminster to the Scottish Parliament, the Welsh Assembly and the Northern Ireland Assembly. But the 2014 Scottish independence referendum set in train major changes to the future governance of Britain, sparking desire for a less centralised, more federal model for *all* of the UK, including the English regions. Opinion polls show that the public largely supports a devolved *English* parliament. It's suggested that this might be more representative if it were to be situated away from the Westminster bubble, following the lead of the BBC and its creation of 'Media City' in Salford. One proposed location for a new parliament is the ancient – geographically central – town of Lichfield in Staffordshire.

SCOTTISH PARLIAMENT

The Scottish Parliament at Holyrood, Edinburgh, has substantial powers over areas including health, education, agriculture, policing and justice, transport, environment and tourism. Some key 'reserved powers' remain in Westminster's hands, such as defence and national security, and foreign affairs; crucially too, because Scotland uses the pound sterling, the power to set Bank Rate remains with the Bank of England in London. Tax policy is being further devolved in light of the close referendum result, including full control over income tax rates and bands (but not the levels of personal allowance), freeing Holyrood to spend the money raised as it wishes. (Cannily, the SNP chose not to use its pre-existing freedom to raise or cut taxes by up to 3p in the pound ahead of the independence referendum.) Control over important welfare powers has also been devolved.

Like Westminster, the biggest party with the most votes forms the Scottish government, headed by the 'first minister', who appoints a Cabinet drawn from 129 MSPs, who represent Scotland's six million inhabitants. It's the job of Parliament to scrutinise the actions of the executive – the Scottish government.

WELSH ASSEMBLY

Over in Cardiff, the National Assembly for Wales has more limited powers than the Scots. Although it can make laws ('Assembly Measures'), the Secretary of State for Wales (in Westminster) has the power to veto them. The legal system is the same as in England. There are 60 elected members of the Welsh Assembly, who govern

The Scottish Parliament in Holyrood, Edinburgh. Less adversarial seating arrangements help discourage 'ya-boo' politics.

in coalition. As in Scotland, fortunate Welsh citizens benefit from free NHS prescriptions, lower tuition fees for students and discounted care home fees for the elderly.

NORTHERN IRELAND ASSEMBLY

The Northern Ireland Assembly has more limited powers than those of Scotland and Wales. Given the long history of the Troubles, the 'power-sharing' system is designed to promote cooperation between former bitter enemies. Seats in Cabinet and top jobs are divided fairly in relation to each party's share of the vote and its seats in the Assembly. The two most important posts are the first minister and deputy first minister, which the leaders of the two most popular parties share.

Federalism in the UK

Politicians have long been fond of voicing vague ideologies such as 'localism', which sounds cosy and comforting; in practice, the closure of local post offices, pubs, libraries, village shops, cottage hospitals and bus routes stands in stark contrast to politicians' warm words about 'Big Society'.

Nonetheless, all parties now declare themselves committed to greater devolution of power within the protective UK umbrella – but the question is: how best to implement it?

As Andrew Rawnsley of *The Observer* points out, if Scotland, Wales and Northern Ireland were all there is to it, it wouldn't be hard to construct a federal model for the UK. There's little resistance at Westminster for more self-government in Cardiff and Belfast. The difficulty is England. Being so much bigger, with 85% of the UK population, it's harder to construct a balanced model of English federalism, and in the past poorly thought-out initiatives for devolution to 'regional assemblies' have garnered only lukewarm support.

Unlike the United States, France and Germany, England doesn't have a history of strong, independently minded regions commanding robust loyalties. So when it comes to handing back real powers, the sensible way forward is probably to go with the grain of the existing structures: money and powers might be devolved to familiar metropolitan areas and counties. But this process would need to be managed intelligently, with quality controls applied to bring badly run councils up to par.

In countries such as Germany, major regional cities drive the national economy, thanks to their delegated powers to shape local industries and communities. There are nine German cities in the league table of Europe's 'Top 50' cities (by wealth per capita), but only two English cities (London and Bristol).

As part of the devolution agenda, all of Britain's great cities and towns could follow the proven German model, with greater autonomy to build strong local economies. Enhanced revenue-raising powers could allow local governments to sell bonds, with sensible levels of borrowing permitted to build new homes and factories.

WHO GETS TO VOTE ON ENGLISH LAWS?

Since devolution, Scotland, Wales and Northern Ireland have had their own parliaments or assemblies, the members of which only the Scots, Welsh and Northern Irish can elect – and yet they also get to elect members to the UK Parliament in Westminster. This means that Scottish domestic matters are the exclusive domain of the Scottish Parliament and its members, while a Westminster MP who hails from a Scottish constituency (say, the county of West Lothian) has the right to vote in the UK House of Commons on proposed new laws that affect only England. This raises a bit of a conundrum, commonly known as the 'West Lothian question'.

Most matters before the House of Commons are 'British' in their scope, presenting no problem; when it comes to voting on legislation that affects only England, it should be a simple matter for Scottish MPs to abstain. The complication is that any change will create winners and losers: unlike the Tories, which command a majority of English MPs, Labour has larger numbers of MPs with seats north of the border – and without those votes, a Labour prime minister could find himself or herself powerless to win parliamentary votes on matters affecting only England, such as the NHS.

Monarchy

Unlike most other Western countries, Britain didn't rid itself of monarchy, but instead transformed it into a 'constitutional monarchy'. Despite being head of state, the monarch is constrained by a straightjacket that limits her role largely to rubber-stamping what goes on in Parliament, along with ceremonial duties such as formally appointing the prime minister, Church of England bishops and members of the House of Lords. The monarch also attends the annual state opening of Parliament, usually in June, and has to read out the government's legislative programme (no matter how abhorrent) as if it were her own agenda.

The crucial restriction on the power of the monarch is that she must always act 'with the advice of ministers' – a nice way of saying that she must do what she's told by the government, for example dissolving Parliament only when the prime minister asks her to do so. The personal political views of the monarch must never be voiced and she has no choice over whom she confirms as prime minister. (It was widely rumoured the Queen was no great admirer of either Thatcher or Blair, yet had the painful duty of appointing them three times each!)

So what would happen if the monarch were to disobey ministers? In this case, a majority of MPs in Parliament could vote to ask the monarch to abdicate, or even vote to abolish the monarchy altogether. This would make interesting TV viewing, since the monarch is commander-in-chief of the British armed forces, to whom the military swear allegiance.

One curious anomaly is that, under the UK constitution, the monarch is theoretically allowed to make laws, as was the case in the 'old days' of rule by royal whim. But this power is never exercised, because the monarch is bound by the 17th-century convention that Parliament is the UK's law-making body.

Outside the UK, however, the palace still exercises a significant power: the Privy Council (a group of former politicians who act as advisers to the sovereign) acts as Court of Appeal for some small Commonwealth countries – and sometimes passes judgment in cases in which defendants face the death penalty.

Honours

The granting of honours involves the elaborate deception that those to be honoured are chosen by the Queen; in fact, she has little power to select the honours given in her name. Interestingly, some years

ago, the Queen suggested changing references to the old 'British Empire' in honours such as Member of the Most Excellent Order of the British Empire (MBE) and Officer of the British Empire (OBE) to something more relevant, but she was overruled by politicians.

Royalist or republican?

James Bond operates 'On Her Majesty's Service' – but he's not the only one. From HM Prison Service and HM Armed Forces, to Royal Mail and HM Revenue and Customs (HMRC), the word 'royal' and the appearance of the royal coat of arms convey a noble sense of duty. They speak of British identity, of a unifying sense of patriotism, authority and public service – of a higher calling than simply short-term profiteering. A great many bodies gain legitimacy and prestige from royal charter, including the Royal Air Force (RAF), the Royal Navy (RN), the Royal Institute of British Architects (RIBA) and the Royal Shakespeare Company (RSC), to name but a few (section 'R' in the phone book is remarkably well populated).

Republicans may despise pomp and circumstance, but no other country can compete when it comes to putting on a national show or hosting state visits, with foreign presidents wafted through London in gilded coaches. This regal fairy tale may be manipulated behind the scenes by artful politicians, but the Queen still represents the spirit and unity of the nation, whilst remaining above the political fray.

On the one hand, the appeal of monarchy has always depended on it being remote from ordinary people, on not allowing too much daylight in to shatter our illusions. No one knows the monarch's

Table 8.1   The cases for and against the British monarchy

Royalists	Republicans
☐ Enjoys widespread popular support	☐ Has no real power, so what's the point?
☐ Works hard to promote Britain around the world	☐ Elitist and not democratic, ascending to the throne via heredity
☐ Is a unifying symbol of British national identity	
☐ Is above petty party politics	☐ Too costly: royal family receives payment from the Civil List – which is funded through taxation
☐ Provides welcome continuity in a fast-changing world	
☐ Attracts hundreds of thousands of high-spending tourists	☐ Not as popular as it once was and minor royals can behave badly, plus there are too many hangers-on
☐ Gives the papers something colourful about which to write	☐ Costly to heat all those palaces!

THE PROFESSIONALS

Traditionally, the royal family is closely linked with the armed forces – the army, navy and RAF. As a nation, we generally trust our military leaders more than we do those in other professions. The British military has enhanced its reputation at a time when other traditional institutions, such as Westminster and the Church of England, have been the authors of their own decline. Unlike the British banks and other corporations with uncertain loyalties to British interests, the military remains emphatically British, even when fighting alongside NATO countries.

While the armed forces are under the control of the Ministry of Defence (MoD) and the MoD is under the control of Number 10, the need for secrecy protects it from parliamentary intervention, which separation is justified as essential to the security of the state. Critics claim that the MoD today, like many government departments, suffers from short-term thinking, fighting skirmishes over budgets and leaving little time for long-term strategy. Moreover, many defence companies, including foreign multinationals, number ex-ministers among their directors – presumably to facilitate access to MoD decision makers.

Over the years, the army has been deployed to rescue politicians who've got themselves into domestic crises – most famously standing in for botched outsourced security at the London Olympics, but also helping to tackle the foot-and-mouth crisis and supplying cover during fire services strikes.

But while concerns remain about excessive perks, such as grand houses for senior officers, the military is seen to have upheld high standards of professional pride and tradition, resisting political upheavals affecting the MoD. In defiance of today's 'neoliberal' values of personal ambition and individualism, the military is motivated not so much by making money, but by traditional values of public service and collective ideals. The military is, of course, naturally collectivist: to win battles, it has to be.

HP SAUCE

The image on bottles of HP Sauce is one of the most iconic images of Britain, figuring prominently on every tourist's itinerary. Better known as the 'Houses of Parliament' (hence 'HP'), the Palace of Westminster – a masterpiece of the Victorian Gothic Revival – contains 100 staircases, 1,100 rooms, 5 km of corridors and, of course, hundreds of MPs and peers responsible for governing the lives of some 65 million Brits. Each MP has his or her own office space, with access to a small army of staff providing administration and security. Like a giant ocean liner with open terraces stretching down the river, the building boasts restaurants, bars, post offices and even a gym. The annual cost of running Parliament comes to around £500 million, including MPs' salaries and pensions. In addition, ministries down the road in Whitehall house thousands of civil servants.

Some would say that the architectural grandeur of Westminster promotes among MPs feelings of self-importance and detachment from voters. Today, the Houses of Parliament are a fortress, crawling with security personnel on high alert and buttressed with anti-terror concrete blocks to deter car bombs.

Thanks to the government's relaxed takeover rules, this most iconic of British brands is now US-owned and produced in Holland.

© g-pics / Shutterstock.com

---

personal opinions and she does not give interviews. On the other hand, many appreciate the Queen as a working mother with a demanding job, a dysfunctional family and tiresome relations. Crowds in their millions turn out to commemorate royal weddings, jubilees and funerals.

Defying the pressure of publicity, the Queen remains dignified – despite the media's desire to boost circulation by emblazoning royal scandals across front pages. In the years since the lowest point – the infamous *annus horribilis* of 1992 – the royals have quietly turned their attention to helping the dispossessed and disadvantaged, for example by means of the Princes Trust and Duke of Edinburgh awards, filling a 'gaping hole in the political system'.

A large majority of British people are in the pro-royalty camp, although many feel that the minor royals should be more self-sufficient. Some say that only the monarch and her heir should receive public money, and that they should have to pay tax on their vast wealth (the Queen actually pays a sum equivalent to income tax on her private income and the 'Privy Purse'). To quote Sir Anthony Jay: 'The strength of the monarchy does not lie in the power that it has, but the power it denies others.' Perhaps the most persuasive argument in favour of retaining the monarchy lies in a simple test: take the word 'president' and then add the name of any recent prime minister…

Parliament

The Houses of Parliament comprise the House of Commons, known as the 'Lower House', and the House of Lords, known as the 'Upper House' (because the Lords were originally aristocrats of high birth). The Commons is the real centre of power, where the party with the biggest number of seats forms the government. Although members of both Houses can propose new legislation, without the support of MPs in the Commons there's zero chance of it becoming law.

Watching the BBC Parliament live on TV isn't exactly enthralling, so it's little wonder that many of us find sport and drama more appealing than day-to-day politics. In times of crisis, however, Parliament is suddenly invigorated and important: like a lazy lion, it reacts only when sensing danger, prodded by public anger and popular protest, or a threat of war.

Loss of power

In theory, the House of Commons is omnipotent, having inherited the powers that once belonged to the monarch. But, in recent decades, much of this power has seeped away. The role of political debating has largely been played out on TV, radio and social media. Devolution of power to the home nations has been successful and the process is set to continue. And without a written constitution to pin things down, the fate of the British people is increasingly being shaped by forces not only beyond Parliament, but also beyond our island itself: agriculture and trade is heavily influenced by Brussels; human rights law is ultimately settled in Strasbourg; much of Britain's defence, security and foreign policy is effectively formulated in Washington DC; investments of people's savings and pensions are determined by unaccountable 'wolves of Wall Street'; and jobs are affected by the decisions of overseas multinationals, with workers finding themselves competing with global labour markets in India and the Philippines.

The House of Commons

The House of Commons comprises some 650 MPs (at last count), each of whom represents a different constituency. The nation's major law-making body, what happens in the Commons affects us all. This is where our rights and liberties are determined, plus, of course, the Budget set, dictating tax rates and the price of things such as alcohol and petrol.

The House of Lords

In total, the House of Lords comprises nearly 800 lords and ladies (known as 'peers'). Only around 92 are 'hereditaries' – traditional peers who've inherited their titles ('Duke/Duchess', 'Marquess/ Marchioness', 'Earl/Countess', 'Viscount/Viscountess', or 'Baron/ Baroness'). Numbered among these are also Anglican bishops known as the 'Lords Spiritual' (as distinct from their less God-fearing brethren, the 'Lords Temporal'). The vast majority of peers are, however, now commoners 'enobled' on the recommendation of grateful prime ministers.

The Lords is a delightfully quirky institution: peers still delight in addressing each other as 'my noble friend' and one of the more curious enduring traditions is the special row of seats reserved for unmarried daughters of peers – a sort of aristocratic marriage-broking agency!

The rather more serious role of the Lords is to:

- introduce new laws for debate;
- debate proposed new legislation drawn up in the Commons and vote on whether to accept or reject it; and
- propose amendments to new legislation.

But the Lords is essentially toothless – no ageist slur intended – because the House has no power to kill the Bills. If the peers don't like the legislation sent by the Commons, all that they can do is propose amendments and send it back, basically playing an advisory role to the Lower House.

Nonetheless, the House of Lords remains the best thing that we have when it comes to holding big-headed bombasts in the Lower House to account. Governments are quite capable of 'fooling all of the people some of the time' – perhaps long enough to get some draconian new law enacted (such as detention without trial after the Iraq War) – and while we, as voters, can then hold the Commons to account at election, we can do so only once every five years. The nation needs an institution that can keep the Commons in check on a day-to-day basis and in the past, in times of serious crisis, the Lords has proven itself able to do just that, speaking independently and with wisdom. Some peers can bring to bear a lifetime's specialist knowledge and some are formidable minds, with rare expertise on legal, military, or foreign policy questions; the problem is that only a handful take the role seriously enough to turn up regularly.

NOMINATING PEERS

Most peers bedecked in 'ermine' robes (actually made of rabbit fur) have arrived in the Upper House having been nominated by prime ministers and opposition leaders past and present. All former Cabinet ministers are entitled to peerages – rewards for

WHAT DO MPs ACTUALLY DO?

- **Attend meetings** Most of the work of Parliament takes place in committees, which scrutinise proposed new laws and can hold government departments to account.
- **Vote on proposed new laws** While MPs are, in theory, responsible for representing their constituencies in relation to new legislation, in practice they're instructed by 'whips' when to turn up and how to vote, so it's rare that an MP will vote against his or her party line.
- **Propose changes to existing laws** The chances of success are, however, minimal.
- **Look after the locals** Each MP has a local office where he or she is expected to hold a weekly 'surgery' at which their constituents can discuss local problems. Sometimes this means redirecting the constituent towards someone else who can help, but occasionally a decent MP will take up a case, such as when MP Tom Watson battled to expose serious abuses by powerful multinational media interests, including illegal phone hacking. It should be said that many MPs are deeply committed to the welfare of their constituents – a cross between the Citizens Advice Bureau and a social worker.

It's not all hard graft though; there may also be the opportunity to engage in media interviews and brief journalists. They get to hold receptions at Westminster for important constituent and pressure groups, and some even enjoy foreign travel.

loyalty and a final accolade in their careers. As well as defunct politicians, there's a sprinkling of businessmen, media people and even ageing trade unionists, most of whom defend their privileges as stubbornly as any aristocrat. Today party donors, fundraisers, legal advisers and lobbyists seem to do particularly well, along with former public relations advisers such as the Freuds, Saatchis and Bells of this world.

The prime minister has the power to nominate new peers to sit in the Lords. The convention is, however, that the prime minister will invite the leaders of the two main opposition parties also to submit names (ensuring, of course, that he or she takes the lion's share and secures a majority of supporters in the Lords). The list of nominees is then sent to the monarch, who might feel faint at the sight of some of the names, yet has no option but to approve them. These nominees then become 'life peers', which means that their children don't inherit the right, unlike the offspring of the hereditary peers.

Unlike MPs, members of the Lords don't have a constituency. So although a title may refer to a particular part of the country (for example former Labour MP 'Lord Robertson of Port Ellen'), the association is purely ceremonial.

REFORM OF THE LORDS

Critics say that the peerage nomination system wouldn't look out of place in a 'Third World dictatorship'. It's certainly rather worrying that prime ministers can populate the Lords with dozens of their mates without being accountable to anyone. Love them or loathe them, many of the old hereditary peers were deeply rooted in the regions and rural areas, and provided a voice from the north and Midlands, whereas most new life peers are based in the capital and the affluent south-east.

The process of *buying* peerages remains discreet, but the rich are sometimes prepared to contribute large sums to political parties and to weather accusations that they've 'donated' their way on to the red leather benches. And while many ambitious people want to be peers, few of these actually want to participate in the demanding process of legislating or even voting. Only a minority are motivated or qualified for the time-consuming process of combing through Bills and listening to long debates. Voting records are unimpressive: even the most famous peers voted only rarely (Lady Thatcher voted four times and Lord Lloyd-Webber, three times to date). Most peers do not take the position seriously as a political activity, but still pick up generous fees for the briefest of appearances. Worse still, the tabloids have had a field day exposing greedy peers willing to take envelopes stuffed with notes in exchange for promoting dubious international business interests.

In its present form, it would be hard to devise a less efficient system for scrutinising new laws. More worryingly, the blatantly undemocratic system used to nominate peers might appear to border on the corrupt. Some would say that, as things stand, it's an expensive national disgrace. One suggested reform is therefore that the Lords might be reinvented as an elected senate, representing the home nations, city regions, towns and counties across the UK. Additionally, perhaps, it might be situated in the 'real world' away from Westminster, for example in York or Derby.

Inside Parliament

Most parliaments around the globe have generously sized debating chambers in which members sit in rows of semi-circles, as in the Scottish Parliament. This is a less adversarial layout than that in the Commons, in which MPs famously sit on green leather benches facing each other, eyeball to eyeball, with the Speaker planted

- **The Speaker** Sitting between the warring tribes of government and opposition is the Speaker of the House of Commons, an ancient role dating back to 1376. His or her main jobs are to manage debates by inviting individual MPs to speak one at a time and disciplining MPs who don't behave (by 'suspending their privileges'). The Speaker is supposed to be independent, despite being an MP and belonging to one party, and isn't allowed to participate in voting (except in the unlikely event of a tie).
- **Leader of the House** The Leader is a government minister whose job is to decide which Bills and debates will be presented before Parliament, within the limited time available.
- **Parliamentary Ombudsman** More formally the 'Parliamentary and Health Service Ombudsman', this is an independent body that investigates cases of maladministration by the government, headed by the Ombudsman herself.
- **Serjeant at Arms** As head of security in the Commons, this job, dating back to 1415, occasionally involves escorting out of the chamber MPs whom the Speaker has told to leave.
- **Black Rod** Chief bouncer and head of security in the Lords, the Black Rod accompanies the monarch at the state opening, traditionally striking the door to the Commons three times with the ebony stick (staff) topped with a golden lion from which his or her title (dating back to 1350) derives.

between them like a referee. (Seating in the Lords is similar, except that its benches are red.)

The party in government sits to the Speaker's right and the opposition parties, to his or her left. The prime minister and Cabinet ministers sit on the front bench, mirrored by their opposite numbers. The largest of the opposition parties sits nearest to the Speaker. Quirkiest of all, the opposing front benches are separated by a red line drawn on the carpet roughly two sword lengths apart, which members are traditionally not allowed to cross during debates.

The Commons presumably pioneered the concept of 'hot desking', since it can seat only 427 MPs at any one time (which is why you see gaggles of excitable MPs standing around on the rare, but important, occasions on which they all bother to turn up, such as to vote on the Iraq War).

DEBATING

When speaking in the Commons, MPs must refer to each other either as 'my honourable friend' for their party colleagues, or 'the honourable member' for the opposition (a custom that dates back to a time when MPs were unquestionably considered to be deserving of respect). The Speaker acts as master of ceremonies, umpiring debates, and individual MPs can't speak without first being 'called'. After sufficient debating time has elapsed (which could be anything from minutes to several days), the Speaker brings proceedings to an end and may call on MPs to cast their votes.

As well as hosting debates about new legislation and entertaining us with Prime Minister's Questions (PMQs) each week, parliamentary time is sometimes reserved for special 'opposition days' on which the main opposition party debates government policy – often with the aim of highlighting alleged incompetence or corruption, so as to cause maximum embarrassment.

Many MPs work very long hours. But for those of a wayward bent, the system is a skivers' charter.

Occasionally, you might hear an MP whinging about the long school holidays of the teaching profession; it turns out that MPs do just as well, enjoying a total of 12 weeks' leave in a typical year – at Christmas, Whitsun, summer and autumn. Particularly generous is the six-week summer recess (originally scheduled so that MPs might escape the foul stench of a filthy Thames warmed by the summer sun). Sometimes, recess will even start early if the debating schedule is done and dusted. The parliamentary term generally begins in November, with the state opening of the House of Commons, and closes the following November, with 'prorogation'. The Lords have even longer holidays.

During recesses, more diligent MPs may choose to spend time in their constituencies, attending local events or holding advice sessions in surgery. (The Lords, of course, don't have constituencies, so are free to do what they please.) At these and other times of the year, some MPs and peers manage to squeeze in additional well-paid jobs, drawing substantial earnings from directorships and other lucrative positions – but if those outside business interests stand to benefit from decisions made by the same 'honourable member' wearing a different hat in government, conflicts of interest can clearly arise. What's more, this means that some MPs effectively work in Parliament only part-time, while drawing a full-time salary.

The basic annual salary for an MP at the time of writing is £74,000, plus generous expenses for running an office with staff, a 'second home' allowance (for somewhere to live in London when away from the constituency) and travel costs. Moreover, MPs benefit from a 'gold-plated' pension scheme that is extraordinarily generous. Cabinet ministers are paid an additional salary – probably because while most MPs nip off back to their constituencies early on Thursday evenings, Cabinet ministers must take with them a deep, red box filled with paperwork through which they must plough by Monday morning.

DISHONOURABLE BEHAVIOUR

Tradition dictates that MPs maintain a veneer of politeness towards one another. They may think an opposition member is telling porkies, but MPs are strictly forbidden from suggesting any dishonesty or calling another a liar outright; if they intimate as much, the Speaker will swing into action, pronouncing them 'out of order'. Even mild personal insults are not tolerated: words such as 'traitor', 'sod', 'shite', 'slime' and 'git' have all been decreed as beyond the pale. Referring to a member as being 'under the influence' of drink or drugs is also out of order; the only person allowed to drink alcohol in the chamber is the chancellor, during the Budget Speech. The Speaker will ask miscreants to withdraw outrageous accusations on pain of being suspended from sitting in the House.

How strange it is, then, that MPs and Lords enjoy 'parliamentary privilege', which means that they're allowed to say anything that they want in the debating chamber without being sued for slander or defamation… Even more bizarrely, MPs are free from arrest within the Palace of Westminster (although only for civil matters, not criminal offences). Clearly, some are more equal in the eyes of the law than others!

DOWN TO WORK

Much of the work of Parliament is done by MPs in various committees. These meetings are sometimes televised, with snippets of cross-examinations sometimes featuring on news bulletins, and experts are sometimes called in to advise.

There are two main types of committee.

- **Standing committees** These are temporary groups, formed to examine a particular Bill before Parliament and come up with any necessary amendments. After a few weeks, once their work is done, they're disbanded. Committees typically comprise anything from 14 to 50 people, the membership in proportion to the number of seats of the parties in Parliament. A big majority usually means fewer (unwelcome) amendments to the Bill.
- **Select committees** These are permanent groups, tasked with assessing how well government departments are performing (known as 'departmental select committees') or scrutinising how well broader government is working. Membership is proportional to a party's seats in the Commons.

There are some 20 departmental select committees, covering departments such as defence, health and foreign affairs. Membership of the most important committees, such as the Treasury Committee, is prized by MPs as a status symbol.

Two well-known non-departmental select committees include the Standards and Privileges Committee, which monitors the behaviour of MPs (not a pretty sight), and the Public Accounts Committee (PAC), which examines government spending, highlighting waste and pointing a fearless finger at tax-dodging corporations and incompetent bankers, etc. Margaret Hodge has forged a distinguished career as PAC chair, shining the light of truth into murky corners.

Committees meet about once a week, but their powers are limited: ministers and civil servants who want to keep dodgy dealings secret can cite 'national security' (as was the case with the Foreign Affairs Committee's inquiry into the Iraq War).

Making law

Identifying areas for new legislation

Before the government proposes new laws, it first publishes a consultation paper – known as a 'Green Paper' – setting out the idea behind the proposal. It calls for interested parties to voice their views.

With these views taken on board, the proposed new law is amended before reappearing in the form of a 'White Paper'. This is duly discussed by the relevant minister in Cabinet, before civil servants draft the resulting Bill (a proposed new Act of Parliament).

Proposing new legislation

The Bills that are thrown into the lions' den for debate might be designed to fulfil pledges that the party made before the election. Or perhaps their purpose is to address some new emerging problem in need of a legal solution. Another possibility is a 'Finance Bill', an essential piece of legislation to allow the Budget to be legally implemented and taxes collected (subject to a special process).

There are two main types of Bill:

- **Public Bills** Public Bills are put forward ('sponsored') by the government minister responsible for the area that the new law will affect: a hospitals Bill, for example, would be introduced into the Commons by the Secretary of State for Health. These types of Bill nearly always make it through to become law, even when other parties are opposed, because a majority of MPs will toe the party line and vote for them as instructed. Most public Bills take a few months to move through the process of enactment (see below), although in an emergency, such as war or epidemic, it's possible to pass laws in a matter of days – or even hours.
- **Private members' Bills (PMBs)** These are Bills sponsored by individual backbench MPs of any party in the Commons or the Lords. Most fail to make it to law: only about one in ten succeeds, and it has no chance if the majority party opposes it or if the member runs out of time to debate it. So, with such a slim chance of success, what's the point? The main reason is that introducing a PMB raises the profile of the cause – and of the MP introducing it.

Limited debating time in each parliamentary term ('session') means that the government needs to prioritise the public Bills that it really wants to see passed into law. The amount of time set aside for debating and voting on PMBs is even more limited (only a Friday, after most MPs have left for the weekend), so time is the enemy and such Bills are easily sabotaged. One of the many stupidities of the system is that it allows rogue MPs routinely to kill off proposals by filling the time allocated with childish non-stop gabbling – 'talking out' Bills to which they are opposed.

Effecting new legislation

Bills have to pass a number of hurdles before they can become law – even public Bills.

- **First reading in the Commons** During this first stage, the new Bill is launched and MPs vote on whether it should progress further. (If debating time is short, the first reading can be heard in the Lords.)
- **Second reading** The result of a successful second reading is that the Bill proceeds to the committee stage (although certain Bills, such as Finance Bills, can be fast-tracked directly to the third reading).
- **Committee stage** A standing committee examines the Bill carefully, proposing amendments, which results in publication of a revised version of the Bill.
- **Report stage** The revised Bill is debated and further amendments may be made.
- **Third reading** At this final vote in the Commons, no further amendment may be made and MPs must decide only whether the Bill may be passed to the Lords.

When sent to the House of Lords, a Bill goes through a similar process of three further readings at which the peers can propose amendments, which the Commons can choose to accept or not. If it accepts and makes the amendments, the Commons must send the Bill back to the Lords for further consideration – and so begins the game of 'ping pong'. If the Commons rejects the amendment to the Bill, the worst that the Lords can do is 'vote it down', which simply delays it for a year.

Finally, the monarch must give the Bill 'royal assent' before it can be enacted – often said to be merely a formality (given that the last withholding of assent occurred in 1707). And MPs are always on about cutting red tape!

Local government

For most of us, the actions taken by local government have more effect on our day-to-day lives than those of the Westminster windbags. People often say that councils simply 'empty our bins', but there's a lot of important stuff going on at county hall – involving refuse collections, recycling and council dumps, certainly, but also:

- oversight of state schools;
- provision of social services (care for the disadvantaged and elderly, etc);
- planning and property development decisions;
- building control (safe construction);
- environmental health (including hygienic food, safe accommodation and a clean environment);
- maintenance of roads and some local public transport;
- management of local amenities, such as leisure centres, pools, parks and libraries;
- oversight of local police and fire services; and
- provision and management of some social housing.

Totting up all of these activities goes some way toward explaining why local government is one of the country's biggest employers (along with the NHS). And it's interesting to take a moment to assess the comparative worth of local and national government, perhaps by considering what would happen if Westminster politicians were to go on strike… Would anyone really notice? In contrast, we know from local government strikes during the 1978–79 'Winter of Discontent' just how quickly chaos resulted – which was a major factor in bringing down Callaghan's Labour government.

Who pays?

The UK is the most centralised state in the Western world. Most of the money spent by councils in the UK actually comes from central government, paid out of national tax revenues. Among countries that are members of the Organisation for Economic Co-operation and Development (OECD), an average of 55% of local and regional government expenditure is financed from local taxes; in the UK, it is only 17%. Because central government keeps its paws firmly glued to the purse strings, it retains real power over local councils – and this can sometimes lead to accusations of fiscal favouritism where the party in power at the local council is of a different hue to that governing nationally.

The balance (the 17%) is funded by means of Council Tax in combination with business rates, plus other sources of income such as various licences, parking fines, congestion charges and rental income. Council Tax is based on comparative property values (dating back to 1991), with each home banded A–G, the latter being highest value. One criticism is that the bands are too few, with band G covering a hugely disparate range of properties from, say, large detached through to the multimillion-pound palaces of the super-rich.

How councils are structured

The way in which local government is structured is a complex patchwork varying across the country. 'Principal authorities' are the main bodies, in some areas comprising 'county councils' with powers split with smaller 'local district councils'. In other parts of the country, and larger towns and cities, there's often a single unitary authority that combines both functions. Scottish and Welsh local government is divided into unitary authorities (32 and 22, respectively). London, and big metropolitan areas such as Manchester, Leeds and Liverpool, have their own city councils, with separate boroughs delivering the services. In London, the Greater London Authority (GLA) oversees the 32 London boroughs. Elsewhere, there may be smaller parish and town councils known as 'community authorities'.

MAYORS AND COUNCILLORS

Regardless of what councils call themselves, at local elections residents get the chance to vote for their councillors, the people who make the big decisions. Once elected, up to ten of them will typically form a cabinet, nominating one of their number as council leader.

There are 12 elected mayors across England, although almost all towns and cities in the UK have a (non-elected) ceremonial mayor who turns up at civic and other public events sporting heavy-duty chest bling, sometimes accompanied by a town crier, tastefully dressed in 18th-century frills, vigorously ringing hand bells and bellowing 'Oyez! Oyez!' – and terrifying the children.

Chapter 9

OUTSIDE INFLUENCES

Democracy doesn't always do what it says on the tin. The voters of ancient Athens may have enjoyed a direct relationship with their elected bigwigs, but when was the last time you had an opportunity to heckle your local MP in the flesh?

Modern politics is thronging with middlemen. Coming between politicians and the people are the media – so familiar that we hardly notice them; yet this is the window through which the world of politics is glimpsed. Depending on your viewpoint, the media are either a blessing or a curse: a force for good, shining light into murky corners; or a lens that wickedly distorts the truth.

More worryingly, the essence of democracy – the famous 'government for the people' – is constantly under threat, with national treasures at risk of being siphoned off into well-upholstered pockets. Honest citizens therefore need to be vigilant. Open just about any newspaper and you'll spot the usual suspects – the super-rich 'fat cats' presiding over privatised utilities, City bankers, multinational corporations and foreign oligarchs, many of whom choose to conduct their operations clandestinely via professional lobbyists. If all else fails, we can always blame the French.

The media

The media exert an overwhelming influence on politics. No one can expect to be prime minister without mastering the TV screen. Yet most political news seems to revolve around scandal, sleaze and petty inter-party bickering, or brain-numbingly dull political drones spouting endless public relations guff, pumped out by unquestioning newsrooms. But a healthy democracy depends on the existence of a 'free press' to root out lies and corruption – and that's why the subject 'controlling the media' appears on page 1 of any dictators' handbook.

So is the media a force for good or ill?

Uneasy relationship

Politicians and journalists are locked in a love–hate relationship. Politicians need the media to get their message across, but they don't like answering awkward questions or too much delving into their personal foibles. In elections, favourable coverage in the press (both national and local), and on TV and radio news channels, can be crucial in swinging votes.

Conversely, the media need access to people in power as a prime source of stories and juicy gossip. Politicians like to sweet-talk editors and tip off prominent journalists, who are always looking out for a sensational story.

Not so long ago, politicians were treated with great deference by the media – perhaps back in the day MPs were more deserving. But society has changed: MPs are now expected to be permanently 'on message', collectively parroting the same lines as their leader. Any slip-ups in speeches or interviews are broadcast mercilessly. The more serious media adopt a searching, and sometimes aggressive, approach to robotic politicians refusing to answer straight questions. Interviewers from the Paxman school of interrogation skilfully skewer differences of opinion between MPs from the same party, or lay bare personal greed and corruption.

Governments have responded to media pressure by commissioning experts to tutor MPs in how to turn questions around to score points and sell policies, never giving a simple 'yes'/'no' answer. But media training has resulted in bland, manufactured sound bites ('Let me be *very clear*…'), the insincerity of which is obvious, turning off voters.

What the papers say

The newspaper world is divided into three tiers. In decreasing order of levity and increasing order of popularity (and scandal, lurid gossip, sex and celebs), these are:

- the 'qualities' (*The Times*, *The Guardian*, *The Telegraph*, *Financial Times*, *The Independent*);
- the 'mid-markets' (*The Mail* and the *Daily Express*); and
- the 'red tops', or tabloids (*The Sun*, the *Daily Mirror* and the *Daily Star*).

Scotland has its own papers: *The Scotsman*, *The Herald*, the *Daily Record* and the *Scottish Sun*.

Newspaper readership is one pointer toward social class, with the qualities drawing readers from among management and professional groups, while the mid-markets draw their readership from among these, as well as middle management, with the tabloids largely read by (what used to be called) 'blue collar' workers.

Print circulations may be shrinking as people get their news online, but the press remains enormously influential in forming opinions: a big story can fuel conversation in homes, offices and factories around the country. They are the most dominant media force when it comes to setting the political agenda. At their best, they provide democratic opposition to the worst tendencies of government; yet that role is essentially negative – the press will rarely offer alternative policies. Moreover, journalists aren't elected representatives of the people, and polls show that tabloid journalists are as distrusted as politicians. They are largely unaccountable and depend on commercial masters frequently accused of being more interested in profits than public service, under pressure to boost circulation or ratings.

SPEAKING TRUTH TO POWER

In recent years, some of the biggest triumphs in journalism have come from *The Guardian* (in relation to phone hacking, state surveillance, etc) and *The Telegraph* (MPs' expenses). Even the much-maligned tabloids have done sterling work proffering bags of cash incognito to expose dim MPs and venal Lords happy to abuse their positions of trust. But it was the MPs' expenses scandal that revealed extraordinary levels of deceit and corruption in the Commons, culminating in a host of resignations and public revulsion.

There is one publication that is head and shoulders above the rest when it comes to exposing wrongdoing, corruption and hypocrisy in – and poking fun at – government: *Private Eye*. The mainstream media sometimes picks up and pursues a story that was first run in *Private Eye* – usually several months, or even years, after its publication. British democracy owes a debt to Ian Hislop and his team – veteran defendants in innumerable libel cases brought by the rich and powerful.

WHO PULLS THE STRINGS?

Governments seem to fear newspaper editors and owners more than their parliamentary opposition and wider public opinion. 'Press baron' proprietors tend to choose editors who share their views. Politicians know that the newspapers' agenda can quickly become the national agenda, inviting the public to share the paper's opinions. This symbiotic relationship was brought into sharp focus after the 1992 general election, during which top-selling tabloid *The Sun* had vigorously campaigned against Neil Kinnock's Labour: a Conservative win saw *The Sun* boasting 'It's *The Sun* Wot Won It'.

More recently, the phone hacking trial has revealed how prime ministers of both main parties have curried favour with one news

organisation above all: Rupert Murdoch's News International (now renamed News UK), publisher of both *The Sun* and *The Times*. To gauge the reaction of the press, prime ministers such as Blair and Cameron were known to brief editors of major national newspapers such as *The Mail*, *The Sun* and the *News of the World* before announcing major policy decisions publicly. The support of the press is seen as crucial in convincing the public to support a particular new law or policy – but this is hardly a resounding accolade for democratic government.

Not being bound to the sort of 'impartiality' regulations that restrict TV channels, the print media are free to sprinkle stories with political bias and even to pursue vendettas against people or parties. Yet newspaper proprietors appear largely protected from publicity themselves.

There is nothing new about press barons, of course, but much of the British media are now offshoots of multinational empires. Some three-quarters of UK newspapers are owned by a handful of non-native corporations or billionaires, whose agendas may not be particularly pro-British or even work in the interests of the British people. These owners, based overseas (some in tax havens), have relatively little democratic accountability despite wielding enormous political power and financial influence.

LEVESON LIFTS THE LID

Desperate to attract readers, some tabloid newspapers came to regard themselves as above the law, resorting to illegal methods such as phone hacking and paying criminals or police for 'scoops'. In extreme cases, entire stories were simply fabricated, resulting in unwarranted intrusion into private lives and harassment of innocent people. But with powerful friends in Number 10, what could stop them? Both Cameron and Blair were in thrall to *News of the World* editor Rebekah Brooks, exchanging chirpy text messages and spending leisure time with her. Another former tabloid editor, Andy Coulson, was appointed as David Cameron's chief press secretary, later to be sentenced to 18 months in jail for conspiring to hack mobile phones.

The challenge facing the subsequent Leveson Inquiry was to come up with a system of rules that would prevent such abuse, whilst permitting genuine investigative journalism in the public interest. It's not easy to strike a balance between the unregulated

bullying of innocent people and a state-regulated press that blocks exposés of corruption and abuse. A regulatory system should protect free speech *and* protect against the excesses of a 'free' (permissive) press. As a consequence, we might question whether state regulation is the answer, with the media told what to do by politicians? On the other hand, TV broadcasters have to comply with government regulations and yet are able to break big stories (such as Saville) – so why not the press?

The solution may simply be to enforce the laws that we already have – against harassment, libel, bribery, etc – in the context of such invasions of privacy as phone hacking. The problem is that the press can exert enormous power over the government and the police. While the attorney general, the government's chief lawyer, has the power to prosecute rogue editors, if the prime minister has close links with that editor, can the attorney general act independently? At the very least, then, the regulator itself should be independent of the press or the politicians whom the press are investigating. As *Private Eye* editor Ian Hislop points out: 'In so many of the appalling cases that have turned the public mood against the press it seems to me there is a failing not only by the press but by the police and the legal establishment.'

Table 9.1 Who owns the national papers?

Newspaper*	Owner	Owner's country of residence
The Sun/Sunday Sun	Rupert Murdoch/News UK	United States
Daily Mail/Sunday Mail	Lord Rothermere	France
The Mirror	Trinity Mirror plc	UK
The Times/Sunday Times	Rupert Murdoch/News UK	United States
The Telegraph/Sunday Telegraph	David and Frederick Barclay	Channel Islands
The Guardian/The Observer	The Scott Trust Ltd	UK
The Independent	Russian billionaires Alexander and Evgeny Lebedev	Russia/UK
Daily Express	Richard Desmond	UK
Financial Times	Pearson plc	UK

* Listed in order of print circulation, high to low

This is the BBC

The British Broadcasting Corporation (BBC) is the biggest public service broadcaster in the world and probably the most influential. Funding comes from the TV licence fee that everyone in the UK who owns a TV (apparently 99% of the population) pays. Because it relies on government to support the licence fee, the BBC is always potentially vulnerable to political influence, although it doesn't have to pander to corporate influence or defend itself against takeover by a multinational media giant. Foreign observers are generally impressed by its impartiality and prestige, and the fact that, as a publicly funded broadcaster, the BBC can be fiercely independent of government at times of crisis. It's seen as a purveyor of truth, countering misleading government statements and sometimes even acting as a substitute for effective political opposition. And on the whole, it gets the balance about right.

Unlike the press, the BBC is bound by its charter to take an impartial approach, adhering to strict journalistic guidelines. It mustn't be seen to be favouring one party over another, so when one politician makes an accusation about an opponent, the BBC has to give the accused a right of reply. In the run-up to a general election, all main parties are given equal air time.

Politicians like to appear on TV and radio because of its huge reach and the fact that its interviews tend to drive stories for other media outlets. BBC current affairs programme *Question Time* attracts around 2.7 million viewers, *BBC News at Ten*, some 5 million, and BBC Radio 4 *Today*, up to 7 million listeners. But that doesn't stop politicians on all sides from routinely pointing fingers: the Blair administration famously accused the BBC of bias in the run-up to the Iraq War, when it alleged that the government had spun evidence with 'dodgy dossiers' to justify its case.

The BBC's failings are common to many British institutions: it's said that bloated, unaccountable and overstaffed management award themselves huge salaries despite making poor decisions, such as to shelve the *Newsnight* Jimmy Savile abuse investigation in 2011. Another inglorious episode involved the executive responsible for the inept coverage of the 2012 Queen's Diamond Jubilee being promoted to director-general (only to resign shortly afterwards trousering a stupendous pay-off).

Nonetheless, despite such high-profile mishaps, many would agree with the *New York Times* when it described the BBC as 'more trusted than the government, more respected than the monarchy and more relevant than the church'.

24/7 news channels, websites and blogs

In recent years, broadcast and online media sources have exploded in number, with hundreds of TV stations and two leading 24-hour news stations – Sky News and BBC News 24. National and local radio stations also bombard listeners with news bulletins and talk shows. Added to this is a proliferation of blogs, social media and political websites, which have enormously boosted awareness of politics. And yet viewing figures for current affairs programmes remain comparatively small, except in times of crises and when big political stories break.

Blogs, by their nature, tend to be biased opinion, some bloggers even resorting to libellous untruths and gossip to gather audience (a phenomenon that's not entirely alien to mainstream media). Many politicians have their own blogs, allowing them to 'control

SPINS AND SPADS

Great leaders such as Churchill and Attlee didn't much care for spin. Labour Prime Minister Harold Wilson called public relations 'a most degrading profession'. Today, politics has become an incestuous cat-and-mouse game in which politicians and the media are obsessively engrossed. It was New Labour that showed how the media could be mastered by teams of advisers, schmoozing with press contacts to secure coverage, intervening to correct 'damaging' articles, and manufacturing sound bites and slogans. Teams of writers in Number 10 penned hundreds of articles signed by Tony Blair.

This focus on news management has overwhelmed the state machine. When the Cameron government was criticised for economic 'short-termism', the simplistic solution was coaching MPs to emphasise the phrase 'long-term economic strategy' in every media interview.

Media demand for rapidly changing stories is such that they have become increasingly dependent on government sources. News channels requiring headlines every hour have offered greater scope for the government spin machine to churn out chaff, from among which the media has little time to verify the wheat. Desperate for 'leaks', with short-term horizons and watered-down critical faculties, key parts of the media have become easy prey for spin doctors and lobbyists trained to tempt them with tit-bits. Even policy announcements are increasingly aimed at the 24/7 news cycle and grabbing favourable headlines rather than driving forward coherent change in the real world.

Many top politicians now employ 'special advisers' ('spads'), who act as hard-nosed gatekeepers, vetting journalists and channelling their political masters toward 'soft' sympathetic media. Probably the best-known among these was Blair's right-hand man, Alastair Campbell, parodied in the hit TV series *In the Thick of It* as a foul-mouthed, aggressive enforcer, renowned for giving senior ministers a dressing down.

the message' by 'going direct'. Indeed, the public relations machine at Downing Street runs a blog ostensibly written by the prime minister, featuring nice family photos and gushing self-applause. But new media can backfire – former Prime Minister Gordon Brown's risible broadcast on YouTube attracted much mirth – and can even embarrass entire regimes by exposing state activities and human rights abuses (hence countries such as China, Iran and Israel periodically block access to Twitter or Facebook).

BROADCASTERS

Regional television dwindled after the Broadcasting Act 1993, and although local radio has since blossomed and regional TV news survives, today we may have more channels, but are subjected to greater conformity.

Most countries place a high value on their indigenous culture and are understandably wary of handing the power of national broadcasters to rootless global corporations. The UK, however, sets few obstacles to overseas ownership and, despite the enormous success in recent years of British TV dramas both at home and abroad, a plethora of recent deals threaten to turn British TV – notably Channel 5 and ITV – into a satellite of the US media. Few politicians have the 'cajones' to stand up to these powerful media mega-corporations, and the suspicion is that, in return for short-term political support, obstacles may magically vanish from the path of long-term corporate interests.

Pressure groups

A pressure group comprises a gaggle of like-minded people aiming to influence government policy, usually on a specific subject (hence they're also known as 'special interest' groups). There are myriad pressure groups – from the very small, perhaps concerned with a single issue such as keeping a local hospital open, to respected professional bodies representing a particular occupation, such as doctors or architects. Pressure groups can give a voice to 'forgotten' parts of society and allow minorities to be heard more effectively. Those representing ordinary people can help to keep politicians grounded and can inform political debate, while professional groups can provide valuable expertise if they're consulted when new policies are formed.

The real concern is that some pressure groups are enormously powerful, drowning out other professional bodies and the general public, with a detrimental impact on democracy. Most controversial of all are multinational corporate lobbyists, representing the tobacco, alcohol, oil and defence industries, which can bring enormous pressure to bear on ministers behind closed doors.

Types of pressure group

- **Professional bodies** These groups promote the interests of their members: the Law Society represents British lawyers; the British Medical Association (BMA), doctors; the British Dental Association (BDA), dentists; and the Association of Chief Police Officers (ACPO) – well, you've got the idea. If new government policies are launched after consultation with the relevant groups, they're likely to be better received.
- **Business bodies** The Confederation of British Industry (CBI) and the British Chambers of Commerce (BCC) are frequently consulted by government.
- **Trade unions** These aim to promote their members' interests to government, to improve pay and conditions, and to promote social justice. Nearly 7 million people subscribe to a union in the UK and the Labour Party still draws significant funding from the unions.
- **Charities** Many well-known charities, such as the Royal Society for the Prevention of Cruelty to Animals (RSPCA), the National Society for the Prevention of Cruelty to Children (NSPCC) and Age Concern, keep an ear to the political ground and may be consulted by government.
- **Cause related groups** These are groups of people concerned with a particular social or ethical issue, such as protecting the environment. The group campaigning against the high-speed rail link (HS2) was highly organised and staffed largely by passionate volunteers.
- **Human rights and environmental groups** Professionally run, well-funded groups such as Greenpeace and Amnesty fight for environmental causes and human rights. Charities such as Liberty campaigned for the repeal of draconian anti-terror laws that threatened once-guaranteed constitutional rights; they also helped to expose the complicity of UK secret services in US forces' use of torture.
- **Corporates** Powerful corporate lobbyists appoint specialist public relations agencies and lobbying firms, sometimes employing hundreds of people. The British Bankers Association (BBA) lobbies for deregulation and lower taxes for its members, for example, as does the Scotch Whisky Association (SWA).

Another way of defining pressure groups is whether they're 'in' or 'out'.

- **Insiders** Some groups have the ear of government, because their objectives are seen as broadly desirable and reasonable. Indeed, government may even need their support to implement its policies, or may want to take advantage of members' skills and expertise by consulting them when forming policy (albeit that Cameron's hugely controversial NHS reforms were driven through in the face of opposition from nurses' and doctors' bodies). To be on the 'inside', it also helps if a group has broad public support and uses peaceful methods.
- **Outsiders** Government is unlikely to engage with groups whose aims it doesn't consider desirable, or whose members are considered too extreme to consult, perhaps employing 'direct action' or other illegal methods, as does the Animal Liberation Front (ALF) in its fight against vivisection. Outsider groups may appeal to only limited numbers of people.

For some groups, of course, being 'in' or 'out' may simply depend on which party is in power: trade unions were firmly 'out' as far as the Thatcher government was concerned.

Exerting influence

There are six main tactics that pressure groups can use, as follows.

- **Employ professional lobbyists** Professional lobbying has grown massively in recent years and is now a multimillion-pound business, generally conducted behind closed doors.
- **Motivate membership to contact local MPs** If enough people write to their MPs, it can sometimes have an effect – particularly for big local issues. Politicians know that ignoring or angering their constituents won't get them re-elected.
- **Directly target MPs** Big pressure groups have offices close to government in Westminster, and also in Brussels or Strasbourg close to the European Parliament. Laws made by the European Commission have the same weight as those made by the British Parliament, so any group wanting to see a change in the law might want to gain influence in the European Union. Pressure groups can also seek to influence the views of backbench MPs, who, despite having limited power, can usefully introduce draft legislation to be debated in Parliament.
- **Get 'hotline' access as an expert** Once a pressure group can grab the ear of ministers or senior civil servants, it can effectively 'get inside' the workings of government and have its views heard. This is a two-way street: government will call upon the group's specialist knowledge, mindful of getting its support for future policies.
- **Court public opinion** Appealing to the public directly – effectively over the heads of the politicians – is another way in which pressure groups try to change government policy. Most will try to secure positive stories in the media; some will take out adverts in the press to promote their messages; others will pull media stunts – such as Fathers 4 Justice staging rooftop protests dressed as superheroes.

■ **Stand for election** On occasion, members of pressure groups have decided to influence things directly by standing for election themselves. In 2001, retired doctor Richard Taylor stood as an independent candidate for Kidderminster Hospital and Health Concern in a bid to prevent closure – and won by a landslide!

DIRECT ACTION

Another common tactic of pressure groups is to 'take it to the streets'. People have a legal right to gather and express their views, and thousands of peaceful demonstrations, marches and rallies take place across the UK each year. If the group's views attract media interest and strike a chord with the public, this can sometimes have a very real effect on government. At other times, even a 'million-person march' – such as that protesting the Iraq War in February 2003 – can fail to influence a government hell-bent on military action.

Direct action can involve peaceful strikes and sit-ins – or it can involve targeting key 'assets' or personnel, which takes it into illegal territory. Greenpeace has famously made headlines by sabotaging rogue Japanese and Norwegian whaling ships.

SIZE MATTERS

A golden league of pressure groups doesn't necessarily dictate government policy, but certainly has influence in the corridors of Whitehall. The members of bodies such as the National Farmers' Union (NFU) employ millions of people nationwide and what their leaders say tends to attract media coverage. So the CBI, for example, doesn't need to organise marches to get its message across; what it says already carries weight in government, because its members represent business and wealth, and what they suggest tends to be thought good for the economy (and hence for the government's chances of getting re-elected).

Powerful pressure groups that strongly disagree with government policy sometimes challenge its legality in the courts. Their lawyers may argue that a minister has exceeded his or her legal powers, or that a policy is discriminatory to a certain group, or breaches European human rights. The worry is that this option gives wealthy multinationals disproportionate influence, because they can easily fund the costs of litigation.

Big-money lobbying

Lobbying is a massive multimillion-pound business in the UK – plus there are some 15,000 lobbyists working in Brussels. Big money spent secretly schmoozing elected politicians is a recipe for corruption. While MPs have to declare any gifts that they receive (subject to a fairly hefty £1,500 lower threshold) in the public 'register of members' interests', some MPs continue to enjoy generous corporate freebies, and plenty of wining and dining, and there are cases on record of politicians subsequently looking favourably on the interests of lobbying firms' clients.

Of course, persuasion can take many forms, not necessarily involving gifts; there may be a promise of a lucrative job further down the line, or indirect assistance for family members. And another way of influencing MPs, as we've already seen, is to make hefty donations to their election campaign (see Chapter 7).

Some hugely powerful bodies – foreign multinational corporations, oligarchs and dictators – devote huge sums to lobbying in the hope of manipulating MPs, potentially acting against British interests. For example, the oil industry can cumulatively mount enormous pressure on ministers whom they hope will ignore objections from local residents over, say, drilling

ONE-WOMAN VICTORY

In 2009, TV actress Joanna Lumley used her high profile and popularity to campaign for the right of Gurkhas (Nepalese soldiers renowned for bravely fighting and serving in the British Army) to settle in Britain. Ms Lumley made powerful speeches, organised rallies and ran rings round the hapless government minister, confronting him on camera. After trying to placate her with platitudes, eventually the government relented – doing the right thing as a result of public pressure.

or fracking. When multimillion-pound contracts are at stake, is it right that the wheels can be oiled in this way? And what of the disturbing fact that senior members of multinational corporations are sometimes invited to draft government policy despite obvious conflicts of interest?

The UK, regrettably, has a tendency to unquestioningly imitate the United States, where powerful corporations and the lobbyists whom they employ can exert huge influence on politicians – not least by generously funding not one, but *both* of the main parties. This is why, for example, US environmental policymakers have been reluctant to accept the existence of and address climate change, responding to pressure from the massive US oil and automotive industries.

What exactly is 'lobbying'? The official definition talks about 'attempting to influence government' and 'advising in a professional capacity', both of which sound reasonable. Surely we'd want our government to be well advised, and perhaps influenced, by experts in relevant fields?

Take the trouble to look a little closer and you might be able to spot something scary lurking in the background: a real danger that those blessed with powerful financial resources will easily gain undue influence over elected representatives sitting at the national control panel. This isn't just because professional lobbyists (people who are paid to influence government policy) might resort to flagrant bribery – always a possibility – but because, like everyone, our political leaders tend to listen to the case that is put most loudly and most effectively. It follows that those who can afford the most persuasive lobbyists will be those who can influence government policy most strongly, even if all politicians are scrupulously honest.

Is there a market solution?

There are some things that the 'free market', if left to its own devices, can remedy. Countering the undue influence that might be brokered by lobbying isn't one of them.

Suppose that our friend Moriarty has come up with a strategy by means of which, if the government changes its policy, he stands to gain £65 million, but which change will cost every individual in the UK £2. Moriarty can afford to spend a substantial amount of financial muscle on lobbying, let's say £40 million, to get the policy change that he needs and still pocket a cool £25 million. That leaves only one big decision: who should Moriarty employ as a lobbyist to put his case to government? In many cases, it might be an ex-politician or civil servant – someone with 'contacts'.

So let's suppose that everyone in Britain wises up to Moriarty's scheme and tries to lobby against the change in policy. To raise the required money to outbid Moriarty, everyone else is going to have to pull together – and it's almost impossible to coordinate the whole of British public to fight change. Would you be prepared to become involved in a protracted political lobbying campaign simply to save £2? And even if we were all motivated to fight, there'd be nothing to stop Moriarty from having another go next year… Isn't it simpler to let Moriarty have the £2 and get on with our own lives?

The essence of the lobbying problem is that the logistics mean

The phrase 'lobbying' comes from the gathering of MPs in the hallways (or lobbies) of the Houses of Parliament before and after debates.

that Moriarty can coordinate his efforts, while the rest of us can't. Yes, the country as a whole loses – but the loss is so widespread that few individuals consider it worth their while to protest. So, under the system of lobbying, we can expect Moriarty – and thousands like him – to exercise more influence through lobbying than can you or I.

What's more, to add insult to injury, as Moriarty pockets his £25 million, he'll probably be promoted in the local paper as an entrepreneur and wealth creator. The paper might even declare that we need more like Moriarty if Britain's to be competitive on the world stage.

So what to do?

The size of the lobbying industry in the UK is estimated to be in the order of £2 billion; the finance industry alone spent over £90 million on lobbying in 2011. And not all lobbying is done by big business: charities and special interest groups want a slice of the pie too. For example, lobbying from local authorities for new HS2 links and changes to the route, aiming to keep voters on side, are likely to add around £30 billion to the overall costs of the project (see **Part 3**).

The problem with any corporate or special interest lobby group is that they circumvent public debate: why bother spending money on convincing the public when you can get a one-to-one meeting with a politician via a lobbyist? This is the pull of professional lobbying: for a fraction of the costs of wider campaigns, a group can employ a third party to grant it direct access to and influence over the decision maker.

It would, of course, be impossible to eliminate lobbying altogether: every time local residents visit their MP, in effect they're lobbying. In Britain, freedom of speech gives the absolute right to any individual to present his or her case to a local MP or to government more generally. With regards to corporate lobbying, we voters have no idea who is saying what to whom (and how much it's costing them/us to say it), muddying the waters in which any objection to lobbying would have to swim.

One possible solution would be to set up a register of lobbying activity (as has indeed been proposed by the House of Commons' Public Administration Committee). This register would be independently managed and enforced, and would provide information on:

- lobbyists and the names of their clients;
- the past and current links between politicians, lobbying firms and their clients; and
- a list of those politicians being lobbied.

This would help to make the powerful and secretive lobbying industry more democratically accountable. In addition, it would surely make sense to prohibit former politicians and civil servants from becoming professional lobbyists – and vice versa. Further, if the industry is to be transparent, we also require public access to cost–benefit analyses of any decisions that have been influenced by professional lobbyists. This is particularly important when, as we'll see later in the chapter, government is in the business of privatisation and marketisation – subcontracting millions of pounds' worth of public services to the private sector.

But it's unlikely that these proposals will be implemented any time soon.

In fact, it seems reasonable to suppose that lobbyists are lobbying hard to ensure that these very proposals to regulate the profession will never come before Parliament.

Think tanks

A think tank is a group that commissions research and then develops policy ideas that government may (or may not) adopt. Hundreds of think tanks exist in the UK and most have a particular right or left leaning. Nearly every aspect of public policy, from housing to crime, is informed and reviewed by at least one such body. Respected think tanks frequently field experts for TV and radio news shows, although waters become muddied where big corporates (such as tobacco, gambling, or alcohol) fund research that – surprise, surprise – turns out to support their own agenda. The BBC has, on occasion, been accused of not making this funding clear, thereby giving the impression that the spokesperson is impartial. (The first question to ask when considering research is always: who's funding it?)

Some well-known think tanks include:

- the Joseph Rowntree Foundation, which researches and puts forward solutions as to how best to alleviate poverty;
- the Kings Fund, which monitors provision of health care in the UK;
- the Adam Smith Institute, which proposes free-market solutions to economic problems ('We propose things which people regard as being on the edge of lunacy. The next thing you know, they're on the edge of policy', said its former president, Madsen Pirie);
- the Institute for Fiscal Studies (IFS), which assesses how well government finances are being run and the nation's economic prospects; and
- the Centre for Policy Studies, a right-leaning group that proposes how public services might be reformed and privatised, and government downsized.

Privatised services

There is another very powerful outside influence bearing down on government. When essential services such as water and power are controlled and operated by third parties, the threat of the lights going out, or – heaven forbid – of drinking water being contaminated and raw sewage floating in the streets, concentrates political minds with precision. It's worth recalling the 'Great Stink' of 1858, when the stench of untreated human effluent in the Thames outside Parliament prompted politicians to fund massive public work programmes of sewer construction. Today, all parties are conscious that their hopes of being re-elected are likely to be crippled if their term in power is chequered with power cuts – or worse. The providers of essential public services therefore enjoy a certain amount of leverage over government, so it's worth taking a look at how the current state of affairs came to pass – and what the future might hold.

Changes

Until the 1980s, Britain's essential services were in public ownership: the state owned and operated all of the utilities (water, gas and electricity), the railways, council housing, education and the criminal justice system. This isn't to say that there was no private sector involvement: most doctors' practices were (and still are) private partnerships, which are paid fees by the government; likewise, many lawyers in the criminal courts are private contractors paid on a fee basis. However, private sector involvement was limited to individuals and a handful of small local companies.

Over the last 35 years, British people have witnessed a revolution, with the private sector dominating services traditionally run on a 'not for profit'

BRIBERY AND CORRUPTION

HON. MEMBER (on Terrace of Parliament Palace): "O, you horrid, dirty old river!"
FATHER THAMES: "Don't *you* talk, Mister Whatsyername! Which of us has the cleaner hands, I wonder?"

basis. Some of these 'privatisations' are easier to justify than others. The least plausible are natural monopolies, such as utility companies, within which the market lacks the mechanisms to create effective competition. The big risk with thus creating a privately owned monopoly is that it effectively grants the corporation a licence to print money.

Pure privatisation involves transferring ownership of a state-owned asset (such as Thames Water) to the private sector – selling the whole thing off, lock, stock and two smoking barrels. However, there are other schemes whereby the private sector gets involved, such as private finance initiatives (PFIs), franchising or subcontracting (also known as 'marketisation' or 'market testing'). It's easy to confuse privatisation – the outright disposal of an asset – with alternatives such as subcontracting or outsourcing to private contractors public services ranging from emptying the bins to the running of an entire NHS hospital or HM prison.

The pros and cons of privatisation

Privatisation is often said to improve the efficiency of a service (although how this 'improvement' is measured is debatable). At heart, however, private and public sectors are very different animals, with differing motivations governing the supply of services to the public – and the price. Perhaps the most obvious difference is the need for privateers to carve out healthy profits; on the other side of the equation, there's the notion of 'public service' as motivating the public sector workforce alongside pay.

In practice, the need to maximise profits when running public services raises some interesting questions: might the public be persuaded, for example, to accept a profit-maximising level of power cuts? This is why privatised corporations supplying essential services such as water need to be heavily regulated (at public expense) to try to align the corporate's pursuit of profit with the public's expectations of service. For example, the Water Services Regulation Authority (Ofwat) and the Office of Gas and Electricity Markets (Ofgem) attempt to regulate utility markets – to keep provision secure and affordable for the public. Critics argue that regulation by a large state bureaucracy inevitably dilutes the efficiencies gained from private ownership; others cite 'regulator capture' – the emasculation of the bureaucratic 'gamekeepers', reduced to issuing vague, unenforceable threats to which providers may respond with threats of their own – raising the spectre of cuts in supply and slashed forward investment.

A further justification of privatisation often proffered is that 'the private sector is more innovative than the public sector'. If anything, however, the evidence suggests that the opposite tends to be true. The new owners of privatised utilities were arguably more interested in doing financial deals than supervising sewer replacement.

As with all government policies, there are winners and losers. With the benefit of some 40 years' hindsight, analysis indicates the following results of privatisation.

- **Consumers have lost out** In general, when public corporations were privatised, prices increased more quickly than wages and the quality of the service provided deteriorated. In some cases, the ethos of public service and technical excellence has been sacrificed in the quest for profit, with higher customer charges and rocketing levels of consumer complaints.
- **Investors have done well** Because many of these newly private companies' stocks are owned by overseas hedge funds, foreign investors in particular have benefited from privatisation.
- **Jobs have been lost** Employees of former public companies have seen 170,000 jobs slashed since privatisation, and those who kept their jobs have seen their pay and conditions deteriorate. Such disruption in the labour market has had knock-on effects in terms and conditions of employment elsewhere in the economy.
- **Executive salaries have risen** Executives have benefited from salaries sky rocketing to a total annual bill of many millions of pounds.
- **Taxpayers are left unsure whether they're better off or not** Privatisation raised billions of pounds in the short term. In some cases, government also appeared to benefit, with loss making corporations removed from the balance sheet. But, in other cases, public assets were undersold – that is, the price achieved was significantly lower than the true market value of the business (Royal Mail). Ironically, some privatised companies, rather than relieving HM Treasury of a financial burden, have required substantial subsidies, funded by the taxpayer – the worst of both worlds.

Outsourcing (marketisation)

Governments and some local councils have been keen to contract out responsibility for providing certain services to private firms. But how effective has this 'outsourcing' actually been? The task of aligning the corporate pursuit of profit with the efficient provision of public services isn't easy, as recent scandals involving firms such as G4S, Serco and A4E indicate. According to government auditors,

OLYMPIC-SIZED DISASTERS

You may recall that the security company G4S came close to scuppering the otherwise hugely successful London 2012 Olympics. Thanks to botched security, the government was forced to draft in army personnel at the last minute, some of whom had just returned on leave from battle zones in Afghanistan. It is perhaps less well known that the same contractor was caught fraudulently overcharging taxpayers for tagging 3,000 non-existent criminals. Amazingly, it took eight years before this fraud came to light, because no one in government had apparently bothered to check up on G4S. In November 2013, the Serious Fraud Office launched a criminal investigation into the claims. In some cases, it was found that charges continued to be levied for years after tagging had stopped – even after the taggee's death! Even more astonishing is the fact that, after a short respite, G4S was subsequently awarded contracts to run services for HM Revenue and Customs (HMRC) and the government's Help to Work scheme.

Committees of MPs have consequently described the recipients of lucrative government contracts, such as Serco, Atos, A4E and G4S, as a handful of 'privately owned public monopolies'. With more such contracts being signed regularly, such as the outsourcing of probation services, it's worrying to note a new trend toward draconian termination clauses. Should a future government seek to terminate these contracts it will need to pay a termination fee equivalent to the money that the company would have made over the remainder of the ten-year term – making cancellation all but impossible.

an estimated £40 billion of outsourced contracts has left taxpayers exposed to a risk of widespread fraud and overcharging.

In addition, while the intention of outsourcing is to drive down costs and drive up innovation through competition, in most cases only a few very large corporations dominate the market. The consistency with which such firms win contracts, even in areas seemingly unrelated to their core competencies (and despite past evidence of gross incompetence or even corruption), suggests that the theoretical gains might not be realised.

Based on the evidence, it seems reasonable to conclude that the risks associated with outsourcing are sufficiently great that the onus should be on the private sector to prove itself genuinely more efficient in terms of both quality and cost. In other words, unless it can clearly be shown that private provision is better, voters would be wise to insist on maintaining – or even reverting to – public ownership. This is particularly true where outcomes are complex and not easily measured – where it isn't clear whether the corporate sector is delivering value for money.

Private finance initiatives (PFIs)

Private finance initiative (PFI) schemes are similar to outsourcing, but also allow the government to perform an accounting trick: it can 'disappear' all of the debt that it would otherwise accumulate when building and operating services.

Suppose, for example, that the government wants to build a new hospital, but has committed itself to no more borrowing (or at least to no more obvious borrowing) because it wants to impress global markets by (apparently) behaving 'prudently'. The problem is that the cash-strapped politicians still have their eye on the prize. Like a benign fairy godmother, PFI allows the government to contract out the building of the hospital to the private sector, which – hey presto! – comes up with all of the funding. The government has no upfront borrowing costs, so there's no red ink showing up on the books; what would otherwise have appeared as current government debt instead appears as a contract to make a series of payments over a period of years – as some sort of monster mortgage.

Most PFI contracts are to 'design, build and operate'. The private firm will not only build the hospital, but also manage maintenance and support services (such as cleaning) for the life of the contract. Thus PFI generally involves a component of outsourcing – and there are usually a number of additional charges hidden in the small print, imposed for services not included in the contract.

The big catch with PFI from the point of view of the taxpayer is that the full cost works out to be massively more than it would have been had the government simply borrowed the money in the first place. In practice, the adoption of PFI has been estimated to increase taxpayer costs on a typical project by 2.25% per year compared to 'traditional' public procurement. Over the lifetime of a project, such additional costs begin to add up: Hexham General Hospital in Northumberland was built in 2004 for £51 million; under the terms of the PFI contract – which included maintenance over 32 years – the cost to taxpayers was to total £249.1 million by the time the 'mortgage' expired in 2033. (In 2014, the local county council and NHS trust 'bought out' the contract, saving the government an estimated £3.5 million annually.)

Independent sources suggest that PFI contracts will ultimately cost British taxpayers over £300 billion on assets worth less than £55 billion. The cost of PFI for 2014 alone was approximately £9 billion. Compare that with an annual shortfall in the NHS in England estimated at approximately £2 billion and it's difficult to avoid the conclusion that PFI money might have been better spent on front-line health care services.

Although there's nothing wrong with PFI in theory, because of the way in which the contracts obscure the levels of debt and the future obligations that governments accrue, there is significant potential for inefficiency in practice. One way in which we might ensure that PFI contracts really do provide good value for taxpayers would be to require the present (expected) value of all PFI contracts into which the government enters to be clearly shown as current government debt on its balance sheet, and require it to be compared with the costs of traditional public debt financing.

Public funds and private profit

In 1999, Margaret Thatcher's favourite free market economist Milton Friedman astutely observed:

As a believer in the pursuit of self-interest in a competitive capitalist system, I can't blame a businessman who goes to Washington DC and tries to get special privileges for his company. He has been hired by the stockholders to make as much money for them as he can within the rules of the game. And if the rules of the game are that you go to Washington to get a special privilege, I can't blame him for doing that. Blame the rest of us for being so foolish as to let him get away with it.

Similarly, neither can taxpayers blame the corporate sector for descending on Westminster to negotiate deals to boost their profits. However, it's the job of our elected politicians to ensure that such deals are of as much benefit to the British public – the voters who elected them – as they are to the corporate sector.

IS THE TIDE TURNING?

Bringing outsourced essential services back into public ownership is a popular idea: polls show that two-thirds of respondents are in favour (including a majority of Tory voters). Evidence from a handful of remaining publicly owned utilities, such as Scottish Water, indicates that not-for-profit business provides a better service at lower cost, while the East Coast Main Line service actually delivered a whopping £800 million surplus to state coffers when operated under public ownership.

In other parts of the world, a quiet process of 'remunicipalisation' has been taking place, steadily bringing privatised public services, utilities and resources back into public ownership. In the past decade, 86 cities around the world have resumed responsibility for their water supplies. In Germany, the majority of energy distribution networks have now been returned to public ownership. Even in the United States, a fifth of all previously outsourced services have been brought back in-house.

In Britain, more than half of local councils have decided that their stretched resources are better spent bringing services back in-house – but central government has little in the way of spare money. Should a German-style reclaiming of services be consigned to the bin labelled 'nice idea, but unrealistic'? Not necessarily…

It's claimed that transferring ownership need not incur a net cost to the public purse. Payment of 'full market compensation' could be made in the form of a 'government bonds for shares' swap, with interest paid on the bonds funded from substantial future revenues and from savings made by trimming the fat from regulatory watchdogs. At the very least, we might demand that our elected representatives put forward a 'public service users' Bill' that requires the government to give us a say in whether essential services (and the NHS) should be privatised in future – something for which the 'We Own It' campaign is presently lobbying.

Source material: Seumas Milne, Anne Karpf and BBC

Since privatisation Royal Mail have questioned whether 'universal delivery' to the Highlands and Islands can be maintained.

Chapter 10

THE WIDER WORLD

Britain has some major advantages in the wider world thanks to the English language and historic ties with former colonies. Some would also say that Britain benefits from a 'special relationship' with the United States and from its membership of the European Union. But there's one factor above all that determines a nation's status and power on the world stage: the success of its economy.

A trading nation

Britain grew rich from international trade, exporting globally when other countries were barely out of nappies. Today, the United Kingdom has the sixth largest national economy in the world, as measured by gross domestic product (GDP), behind the United States, China, Japan, Germany and France, and followed by Brazil, Italy, Russia and India. In Europe, we're the third largest economy, with Italy a close fourth. The British economy is dominated by the service sector – especially financial services – but major strengths remain in a handful of industries such as pharmaceuticals, aerospace, and oil and gas production.

Nation states vs global problems

A political party can be in government, but not in power. We live in a world of increasingly global problems that nation states acting alone struggle to resolve. The result of this, among other things, is disillusionment with politics: why care about pretentious politicians when they're effectively powerless? Some argue that, in the face of global forces, national sovereignty has become a myth.

It is, however, more important than ever for Britain to have a

strong voice on the international stage. Acting alone, a government can be hoodwinked by multinationals, which play on the loopholes and differences between national legislations to avoid paying tax anywhere. The case for shared action is also clear when it comes to matters such as cybercrime, which disrespects frontiers as readily as do air and sea pollution. Defence too is increasingly a shared responsibility. But above all, without joint action on climate change, we may well be heading for extreme weather conditions that could cataclysmically undermine our prosperity.

Foreign policy

When it comes to foreign policy, trade usually trumps ethics. *Realpolitik* often means having to settle for the lesser of several evils. Nonetheless, everyone agrees that foreign policy should have what late Labour Foreign Minister Robin Cook called 'an ethical dimension'. Unfortunately, this can be a hard circle to square, since one of the British economy's few export success stories happens to be in defence, the UK ranking second only to the United States in terms of arms exports worth more than £5 billion per year. Defence exports provide employment for 150,000 people in the UK. This can have other implications, too: it's not entirely coincidental that Britain sometimes hesitates to openly criticise nations such as Saudi Arabia and Qatar, to whom we sell millions of pounds' worth of weaponry. After all, antagonising customers is bad for business. Foreign sovereign wealth funds also own vast amounts of UK property, with stakes in many British businesses, and we're increasingly dependent on the Chinese for investment and construction of nuclear power plants and high-speed rail. So if Beijing isn't over the moon about the idea of the British prime minister meeting the Dalai Lama, for example, there's a good chance that economic muscle may ultimately dictate political outcomes.

Diplomats

The grandeur of the Foreign Office building in Whitehall and the splendour of our imperial embassies around the globe, staffed with erudite diplomats, evokes a long-vanished imperial age, in stark contrast to today's shrunken economic state. Yet the expertise of the Foreign Office, with its deep knowledge of cultures and exotic languages, is essential to maintaining good relations with governments around the world and for successful bureaucratic negotiations in Brussels. However, diplomats today are increasingly interlocked with big business, with ambassadors asked to 'open doors' overseas to help the UK to land big contracts. And when it comes to the developing world, the Foreign Secretary has a rival in the Department for International Development (DfID), responsible for administering overseas aid.

The security services

Not only is the Home Office responsible for the police force in England and Wales, but it also has a more secretive arm: the 'political

---

WAR BY OTHER MEANS

Invading other countries is *so* last century. In today's globalised world, the credit card is mightier than the cluster bomb. So it's interesting to speculate whether it would be possible for one country to utilise its financial muscle to gain control of another, without the need for all that messy military stuff – tanks, bullets and bombs.

It's no secret that 'soft power' – money and diplomacy – can buy enormous influence. Poorer developing nations are no strangers to wealthier nations pulling the financial strings behind the scenes to influence military and political agendas. But would it be possible, in effect, simply to 'buy' a relatively prosperous democratic nation, starting with vast swathes of land and property – the ultimate in imperial consumerism?

Britain makes no bones about being 'open for business' and many of today's giant corporations are far wealthier than some medium-sized states. Inviting foreign investment is a good thing, up to a point – but being overly keen on incoming money, no questions asked, can sometimes smack of desperation. When does 'open' become 'wide open'? Countries such as the United States and Canada, for example, don't hesitate to draw lines in the sand when it comes to some foreign takeovers. France tends to adopt a protective approach to preserving its national champions from acquisition by overseas predators. And governments in China and the United States tend to regard their global technology companies as tentacles of state power. When push comes to shove, they know whose side they're on – and it isn't ours.

Such surreptitious seizing of control might involve:

- funding political parties to gain influence, imposing puppet candidates and ministers;
- funding lobbying of politicians to facilitate investment in strategic assets and, ultimately, imposing changes to the education curriculum;

- funding lobbying of strategic pressure groups to ease the path to controlling stakes and the appointment of key personnel;
- embarking upon an extensive programme of land and property purchases;
- taking over major companies or acquiring controlling stakes in key industries – ideally those with access to cutting-edge technologies such as aerospace, defence, IT and medicine;
- acquiring strategic rights to national oil, gas and mineral reserves – as China has done in much of Africa;
- acquiring controlling stakes in key assets such as the National Grid, and energy and water companies, with a view to using threats of blackouts and supply cuts as leverage over government;
- gaining control over major infrastructure, such as nuclear power, ports and rail;
- commencing a programme to acquire controlling stakes in key media; and
- diluting traditional communities and weakening national pride (for example Chinese state-sponsored migration to 'balance' the Tibetan national population).

Individually, all of these actions have, at one time or another, been officially sanctioned or successfully implemented. The more sensitive acquisitions might be made by stealth, anonymously through complex networks of third parties and holding companies, registered wherever necessary. Certainly, there is no shortage of ultra-sophisticated clandestine financial assistance.

So the tantalising question is: could such action be coordinated by a single major power, or do such notions belong purely in the realm of James Bond? *Should we be worried?*

police', better known as the internal Security Service, or 'MI5'. International security and espionage is the domain of the Secret Intelligence Service (SIS), better known as 'MI6', famously ensconced in its showy headquarters by the Thames. But there's more to MI6 than spooks and 007-inspired fantasies; its local knowledge and

FOREIGN BASES

Is there a case in the 21st century for maintaining foreign military bases on British soil? It's not widely known that there are nearly 10,000 US military personnel still stationed in Britain some 70 years after the Second World War ended. These forces are located in a number of major military installations under American control, misleadingly prefixed with 'RAF'. Even Britain's own colonial-era overseas bases, such as Diego Garcia, have long been handed over to the US military. This raises questions about whether Britain's security and independence is compromised by the presence of a foreign power.

There is one US military site above all that has aroused particular interest. Critics say that the UK government has little idea what happens at Menwith Hill, near Harrogate, which has been run by the US National Security Agency (NSA) since 1966. This base is shrouded in secrecy, but is known to be a key link in the missile defence shield that alerts the United States to the launch of ballistic missiles. It's also involved in drone programmes and forms part of the US eavesdropping system that intercepts communications from around the world.

One key question is whether this heightens the risk of a pre-emptive attack on the UK, as a means of disabling America's missile-detection system. And if the position were reversed, would the United States welcome a secret RAF airbase in Colorado?

Source material: Richard Norton-Taylor.

contacts can help to circumvent obstacles for UK companies looking to secure key overseas contracts. Human intelligence is, however, increasingly being supplemented by signals intelligence from Government Communications Headquarters (GCHQ), the massive electronic eavesdropping system in Cheltenham, which depends heavily on US cooperation for its success.

The Joint Intelligence Committee (JIC) coordinates all of the various intelligence agencies and is the link with government. But the value of the security services to the nation depends on their ability to supply information untainted by the desire to please politicians. Too close a link can mean pressure to come up with the answers that politicians want to hear, as was the case with Soviet intelligence. The Hutton Inquiry illustrated how, in the build-up to the Iraq War, 'relentless pressure' was applied by 'a small group at Number 10 who were determined to execute their own prearranged policy for war'.

Military power

Britain ranks as a leading military player because of its proud history, highly professional armed forces and the fact that it packs enormous destructive capability in the form of nuclear missiles, in a fleet of hi-tech submarines. The need for nuclear capability stems from the Second World War and the subsequent cold war; times have changed and the threat today is more likely to rise among radical terror groups. Yet Britain retains nuclear capability, alongside the United States, Russia, China, France, India, Israel, North Korea and, most recently, Pakistan – some of which are hardly known for their political stability. The expense is enormous and, although deemed 'independent', the UK nuclear arsenal is American in origin; in effect, it would never be fired without prior consent from the White House.

Sitting at the top table

In a globalised world, smaller countries such as the UK can exert influence on world events and derive huge status from membership of important international 'clubs'.

The United Nations (UN)

The United Nations (UN) is the nearest thing that there is to a world government, with 192 member nations. Headquartered in New York, the UN aims to reconcile differences and to facilitate peace between nations, through military intervention if necessary. It also provides assistance to communities devastated by war, famine, or disease. Member states provide support with money and staff, and also supply troops for UN peacekeeping duties, their vehicles famously painted white. The UN carries serious moral weight, and any government that stands against UN resolutions risks having trading sanctions imposed, which exert enormous economic pressure.

THE UN SECURITY COUNCIL (UNSC)

Owing to its status at the end of the Second World War as one of the victorious Allied powers, the UK has a place on the UN Security Council (UNSC). Membership gives Britain considerable clout on the international stage. There are 15 member states, but only the five permanent members have the individual power of veto to block decisions (the United States, the UK, Russia, China and France). So the UNSC can decide on a course of action only if all five members agree. Interestingly, since 1947, the UK has vetoed only 32 out of 2,000 resolutions, while the United States has vetoed 82 (often in support of Israel) and Russia, 123.

UN BODIES

Much of the work of the UN is done by its 17 agencies, including the World Health Organization (WHO), the World Food Programme (WFP), the United Nations Development Programme (UNDP) and the United Nations Scientific and Cultural Organization (UNESCO). In addition, the World Bank and the International Monetary Fund (IMF) are the international financial arms of the UN.

The International Monetary Fund (IMF), based in Washington DC, works to foster global growth and economic stability. It has 188 member countries, whose economic and financial policies it monitors. It also works with developing nations, which have limited access to funding via private international capital markets. The IMF can provide emergency bailouts to member states in economic difficulties, subject to their agreeing to take its prescribed economic medicine. Britain harbours painful memories of Chancellor Denis Healey being forced to go 'cap in hand' to the IMF in 1976 for a £2.3 billion bailout when unemployment and inflation spiralled.

THE UN COURT

The UN has its own court, the International Court of Justice (ICJ). Located in The Hague, Netherlands, the ICJ hears disputes between states over various matters, including violations of treaties and of state boundaries, and grants 'advisory opinions' to states seeking clarification of other matters of international law.

The G8 and G20

The 'Group of 8' (G8) is made up of eight of the largest world economies, and was originally formed to encourage economic cooperation and to promote growth among member states. (It was formerly the 'G6' and the 'G7' before Canada and Russia, respectively, were invited to join.) Leaders of the G8 nations meet once a year to discuss topics ranging from global warming to debt relief.

The Group of 20 (G20) is a more recent incarnation, incorporating major players such as China and Germany (who, rather oddly, aren't part of the G8), granting them a voice among the finance ministers of the 20 biggest global economies.

In recent years, high-profile G8 and G20 summit meetings have been accompanied by violent protests from anti-globalisation and environmental groups, who regard these powerful groups as self-serving clubs of the wealthy.

The largest world economies also hold an annual winter bash in Davos in Switzerland. The World Economic Forum attracts an unholy alliance of super-rich tycoons, top economists and big-name politicians, plus armies of media and lobbyists. Some take the view that sinister *Goldfinger* figures use the occasion to hatch insidious plans for world domination in mountain lairs; others, that it's an overhyped mutual preening shindig for those afflicted by too much money.

The Organisation for Economic Co-operation and Development (OECD)

The Organisation for Economic Co-operation and Development (OECD) is an international economic body comprising 44 nations representing more than 90% of the world's economy. Its mission is to stimulate economic progress and world trade. The OECD is supported by the G20 in its efforts to crack down on tax avoidance by multinational companies.

The World Trade Organization (WTO)

The WTO promotes free movement of goods and services around the globe, without tariffs or trade barriers on imports. It has 151 member states and tries to level the playing field by discouraging countries from subsidising their own industries. It also hears trade disputes, negotiations over which can drag on for years.

The North Atlantic Treaty Organization (NATO)

The North Atlantic Treaty Organization (NATO) is a military alliance originally designed as a safeguard against the post-war threat from the Soviet Union. The United States supplies most of the troops and funding, followed by the UK. It's based on the understanding that an attack on one NATO member is an attack on all. Since the end of the cold war, NATO has expanded its membership to include several former Soviet bloc countries, such as Poland, and has controversially been involved in US-led conflicts in places such as Afghanistan.

The European Union: A vexed question

The European Union started life as a group of six countries that banded together in 1951 to form the 'European Coal and Steel Community' (ECSC), the key objective of which was to prevent future war between France and Germany by integrating heavy industries. Subsequently, other western European states joined, with the main aim of cooperating economically. Britain has been a member since 1973.

Zoom forward to today and this cosy alliance has morphed into a 'super-state' comprising 28 member states and some 500 million people. Four western European nations are not members – Norway, Switzerland, Iceland and tiny Liechtenstein, which together form the European Free Trade Association (EFTA) – but they have trade and border agreements with the Union, and all bar Switzerland combine with it to form the European Economic Area (EEA).

Some of the main EU objectives are:

- free trade between member states, and free movement of people, capital, services and goods;
- preventing any member state from gaining 'unfair advantage', for example from its government subsidising domestic industries;

- the harmonisation of national laws (such as business and consumer law);
- protecting EU businesses from unfair competition from non-EU countries; and
- 'an ever closer union among the peoples of Europe'.

Encroaching on our turf

The growing power of the European Union is causing big waves in British politics. In 1985, the UK Parliament ratified the Single European Act (SEA). This didn't cause much of a stir at the time, but turned out to be hugely significant, changing the legal landscape in Britain: for the first time, laws drawn up by EU legislators had equal power to those drawn up by the UK Parliament. Today, experts estimate that nearly two-thirds of new laws affecting the lives of British people result from EU legislation.

The European Union comprises a Parliament, a Commission and a Council of Ministers, plus a massive civil service (Secretariat) funded by member states. It has its own flag and a currency – the euro (€) – adopted by 18 of the member states (the 'euro area', or 'eurozone'). What's more, regulations and directives of the European Commission – EU law – apply in all member countries. Although we're able to vote for members of the European Parliament (MEPs), voter apathy is high and, rightly or wrongly, most people regard European elections as pretty meaningless.

Paying for it

Each EU member state pays a subscription roughly proportionate to the size of its economy. As well as funding the EU Parliament, Secretariat and MEPs' pay and expenses, this money goes towards the Common Agricultural Policy (CAP) and other funds targeted toward poorer member states to support infrastructure projects and to alleviate economic hardship.

Naturally, arguments rage about who pays what towards the EU Budget. The Germans contribute most, but get back only half of this in grants and CAP payments. Conversely, poorer member states might get back four or five times the amount that they contribute – one reason why membership is so popular in the newer member states. Nearly half of all of the money that the European Union spends goes towards the CAP, which guarantees farmers a minimum price for crops and helps to preserve rural heritage. The CAP became notorious in the 1980s for blindly subsidising farmers in mainland Europe to overproduce, resulting in giant 'wine lakes' and 'butter mountains'; in recent years, it has been partially reformed.

As one of the biggest economies, the UK stumps up billions of pounds in contributions, but because we have a relatively small agricultural sector, we receive limited sums in CAP payments in return. To redress the balance, the UK benefits from a rebate – granted only after bitterly contested negotiations by the Tory government in the 1980s.

Economic and monetary union

The common currency, the euro, is used by 18 of the 28 member states, including all of the big nations except for the UK. The euro has resulted in unsustainable trade imbalances, particularly amongst the southern member states. The chief beneficiary has been Germany, with booming export industries, thanks to a relatively low exchange rate. Some economists say that monetary union is now basically dysfunctional. Prime Minister Gordon Brown may not have covered himself in glory by selling off British gold reserves at rock-bottom prices (395 tonnes of gold were sold between 1999 and 2002 – about

Increasing numbers of Eurosceptics within UK politics want to see Britain leave the European Union – or at least see the return of its sovereign powers. Many other people believe that EU membership has been good for Britain. So what are the arguments for and against staying in?

FOR

- The European Union is a major export market for Britain (although we import more than we sell), so why put it at risk?
- Britain has few native world-class industries remaining, being instead dependent on the presence of foreign manufacturers (Airbus, Nissan, Honda, Siemens), some of which may threaten to 'disinvest' – to move production elsewhere. (Perhaps the government might consider acquiring stakes in major employers to gain some leverage, for example via a UK sovereign wealth fund?)
- Government doesn't have any coherent 'exit strategy' should it decide to leave the Union. Drifting out to sea as an independent island would demand a powerful motor – a strategy to steady the economic waves, lest we sink beneath them. As things stand, the latter seems more plausible.
- Norway and Switzerland still have to abide by some EU rules, even though they have no influence over how they are formed. It's surely better to retain influence and help to shape the Union to suit ourselves?
- Scottish voters might demand a new referendum if the Scots overwhelmingly wanted to stay and the rest of the UK voted to exit.

AGAINST

- The EU super-state, the European Commission and the Parliament are sometimes perceived as corrupt, and the CAP is wasteful, undemocratic and a waste of resources.
- We have to contribute to the EU Budget far more than we get back. In 2013, we paid €14.5 billion and directly received only €6.3 billion – half of which was paid to UK farmers to subsidise food production – plus another €1.1 billion in research grants.
- The European Union has been enlarged to the extent that our voting power has been all but stripped bare.
- Britain could negotiate an amicable divorce, but retain strong trading links with EU member states on the basis that BMW, for example, wouldn't want to stop selling cars to an independent Britain. Moreover, the European Union has a UK trade deficit of some £56 billion, so Europe has more to lose than does the UK.
- Membership of the European Union means that the UK's judges must comply with European law, which some see as a threat to legal autonomy and author of some apparently unjust outcomes.
- Norway and Switzerland have thrived outside the Union. Both countries have access to the single market (as part of EFTA), but are not bound by EU laws on agriculture, fisheries, justice and home affairs, and can set limits on the free movement of people (that is, immigration).

58% of the nation's total reserves), but his resistance to joining the common currency proved to be the right decision for the UK, helping us retain more flexibility and control over our economy. The pros and cons of EMU are discussed in more detail in Part 1.

Enlargement

In a move that it might now regret, the British government pushed for massive expansion ('enlargement') of the European Union in 2004, supporting the entry of poorer countries from eastern Europe and greater powers for the European Parliament. This radically changed the balance among member states: newer members gained voting rights that diluted the power of the bigger countries, such as France, Germany and the UK; and with most of the newer members relatively poor, budgets for agriculture and development were strained. But perhaps the biggest bone of contention has been the migration of people from poorer countries to richer states, leading to accusations of incomers 'stealing our jobs'.

Eurosceptics

The UK isn't alone in facing public outcry against EU membership, with concerns voiced widely about the dangers of a 'United States of Europe' (a 'federalist agenda'), in which nation states become subservient to a centralised pan-European government. Over the years, the tabloids have also poked fun at 'ridiculous' rulings emerging from Europe.

Sometimes, Brussels has indeed proved to be oddly intrusive, ruling on the minutiae of everyday life – most infamously, the straightness of cucumbers and the bendiness of bananas (since repealed). At other times and in more important areas, such as financial regulation and clamping down on tax havens, it has appeared impotent. The outcome of the 2014 MEP elections pointed toward a British public yearning for simple, nationalist solutions, nostalgic for national certainties – a battle cry against the emerging 'super-state'.

Those who bristle against Brussels argue that they're driven to do so not by a dislike of foreigners, but by a desire for more localised democracy and more sovereign autonomy – the return of 'the nation'. Yet continuing economic woes – austerity measures – across Europe are proving fertile ground for more extreme parties, with European elections seeing swathes of nationalists elected to the European Parliament. So it's worth reminding ourselves of the crowning glory of the European project: today, Germany exports luxury cars – not flying bombs and stormtroopers – competition through market forces rather than armed forces.

The Commonwealth

Britain may have lost an empire, but it's gained a 'commonwealth of nations'. Comprising former members of the British Empire, the aim is to promote peace, economic growth, human rights and cultural cooperation among them. Many nations share traditions dating from their colonial history, such as driving on the left, playing cricket and rugby, and a shared system of common law, democracy and language.

There are 54 Commonwealth nations in total – around a quarter of all countries in the world. It's a valuable club, particularly for smaller nations that otherwise rarely appear on the world stage. Conferences are held in one member state every two years. The head of the Commonwealth is the British monarch. Although a purely ceremonial role, the Queen is actually head of state for 16 of the member nations, including Australia and New Zealand. There's also a Commonwealth secretary-general, elected every four years by the heads of government.

One of the most prominent, and entertaining, events in the calendar is the Commonwealth Games – a mini Olympics, the last held to great acclaim in Glasgow in 2014.

British overseas territories (BOTs)

It's not widely known that the British Empire still exists in the 21st century, but it's bonsai-sized. Some 16 'British overseas territories' (BOTs) are still run by the UK – mainly comprising exotic destinations in warmer climes, including Saint Helena, the Turks and Caicos Islands, Anguilla, Bermuda, British Antarctic Territory (BAT) and the familiar Falklands, plus (closer to home) Gibraltar.

Britain has retained these interests in accordance with the wishes of the local populations: many BOTs are so small that they benefit from a bigger partner, and in some cases British military bases continue to provide valuable employment. Interestingly, people from BOTs benefit from entitlement to full British citizenship, which means that they're allowed to work anywhere within the European Union.

The 'special relationship'

The United States is still the world's premier economy and leading military superpower, and it exercises enormous influence over Britain. We like to think that our two nations share a 'special relationship' – a phrase first coined by Churchill, stemming from our role as allies in the Second World War and subsequent major conflicts, such as the

---

HOW TO BECOME TOP DOG

You've got to hand it to the Americans: they know how to top the charts. So what's the secret of their phenomenal success – and could the UK emulate it?

- **Economic power** Many world-leading US corporations are enormously successful, employing millions around the world and aggressively marketing their wares on a global scale, from Coke, Pepsi and McDonalds, to Boeing, Microsoft, Apple and Google.
- **Military might** Economic success has allowed the United States to invest in a massively powerful military.
- **Technological leadership** The United States has a lot of world-class specialist universities that have helped to generate numerous key technological advances. Military and private sector research is also lavishly funded, giving the United States a lead when designing new products to sell globally.
- **Cultural output** US cinema and music dominates the planet – not least the UK, because of our shared language. British TV and news channels increasingly buy US product.
- **The mighty dollar** After the Second World War, the United States flexed its economic muscle and the dollar replaced the pound sterling as the world's 'reserve currency'. This means that most world trade is carried out in dollars, including sales of oil and gold, and many countries hold large reserves of the currency. But the mighty dollar isn't as powerful as it was before the 2008–09 global financial crisis, which triggered a massive expansion of US government debt.

Korean War. Yet we're not the only country to jealously guard close bonds with the big kid on the block; like a polygamous marriage, numerous others proudly brag of their 'special relationship' with the States – from Israel and Japan, to Canada and Mexico. The UK can, however, lay claim to a shared history when it comes to former subjects of the Crown colonising the New World. It's widely known that the Pilgrim Fathers, pioneers from the British Isles who founded much of modern North America, set sail from Plymouth, and that George Washington originally served as a lieutenant colonel in the British Army. Less familiar are some of the more awkward moments, such as the enforcement of crippling debts owed by Britain to the United States after the Second World War, and the fact that, in 1930, the Americans actually approved plans (known as 'War Plan Red') for a naval war with Canada and Britain.

Today, it's often said that the UK sets too much store by its links to its powerful transatlantic partner and that the relationship is a one-way street. While there is indeed much to celebrate, especially in the world of music and the visual arts, UK pop culture is largely dominated by American output. Other critics complain that, today, the UK is effectively the '51st state', with poodle politicians glued to the heel of US defence and foreign policy – those who loudly declaim European influence tend to be mute in the face of subservience to the States. Indeed, when Labour Prime Minister Harold Wilson kept Britain out of the Vietnam War in the 1960s, he demonstrated rare grit in the face of US financial and political pressure.

In terms of the military, UK security services share a lot of information with those of the United States, as well as control of some British air bases and nuclear weaponry. This increasingly close relationship, which sees opposite numbers in Washington and Westminster sharing ideas and advisers, led politicians in Westminster to portray the 9/11 terror attacks on the United States as direct attacks on Britain. What's more, that 'special relationship' means that, today, we readily forgive transgressions within living memory, such as the fact that financial donations from US-based 'Noraid' helped to fund IRA bomb attacks on London just 20 years ago. Shared blood, it seems, is thicker than Semtex.

One current bone of particular contention is the extradition treaty with the United States, which was rushed into law to assist in the 'war on terror'. The concern is that it's now far easier to extradite a British citizen to the United States – based on nothing more than 'reasonable suspicion' – than it is a US citizen to Britain. This disparity has seen UK citizens dragged into disputes over work expenses or computer hacking suffering significant distress in cases that, critics say, would be more effectively tried in the UK.

The rise of China

Today's China is said to be the 'workshop of the world' – a position that Britain held in the 19th century. Just as British wealth was built on manufacturing, exports and trade, so now has China amassed enormous financial reserves. It already owns increasing numbers of UK businesses; land and natural resources too are sought-after.

China enjoys massive trade surpluses, and large amounts of this money have been loaned back to the US and UK governments in the form of buying national debt, giving the Chinese significant power.

Scotch whisky is probably our biggest export to China, but overall UK exports remain weak, whilst imports have boomed. Our future fortunes will be tied to how well we can boost exports to growing economies such as China and India (as long as we stop borrowing off them).

China – the new 'workshop of the world' – enjoys massive trade surpluses with the UK.

In a global world, should governments set guidelines for their country's population level? Is there an optimum density beyond which citizens start to feel uncomfortable, with implications for social unrest or mental health? How many people can the British Isles comfortably accommodate?

In the early 1960s, Poet Laureate John Betjeman spoke about 'this overcrowded island' with its 'hellish road conditions', predicting that 'traffic would triple in 10 years'. Fifty years later, Betjeman's 7 million cars have rocketed to 30 million – a figure expected to hit 40 million by 2020. Gridlock beckons – but it can't all be blamed on the BBC's *Top Gear*. In the intervening years, consumers have become wealthier, roads have improved and the railways have been prematurely pruned.

But rising traffic congestion also reflects population growth. Since 1964, the population of the UK has grown by about a fifth (by 11 million people, from 54 million to 65 million), climbing sharply in recent years, with high levels of net inward migration since 2001. Birth rates too have leapt 18% in a decade to an average of 1.9 births per woman in Britain – compared to 2.0 for the French, 1.88 in the United States and a very constrained 1.38 in Germany (but then Germans don't drink that well known aid to fertility, Guinness!)

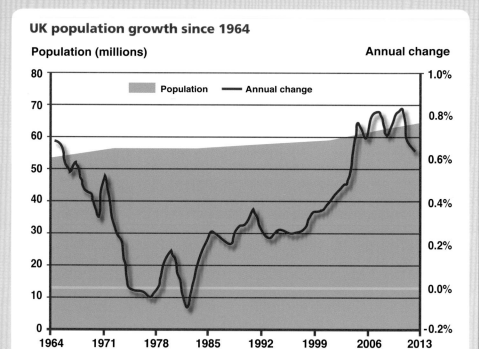

UK population growth since 1964

Population (millions) — Annual change

Population density

It's interesting to compare which countries have the most room to accommodate growing populations. Not surprisingly, the United States comes in at a relaxed 35 people per km². Happily, the country's wide open plains should be able to accommodate the 'tired... poor... huddled masses yearning to breathe free' for many years to come.

Back in Europe, France has a pretty laidback 121 persons per km². The UK population density overall is 265, rising to 395 in England, comparable with the Netherlands, which has traditionally been the most crowded nation on the continent (excluding island and city states such as Malta and Monaco). This means that the population density in England is almost double the level in Germany and more than three times that in France. But in south-east England it jumps to 450 residents per km². The population density in the whole of England is projected to exceed this by 2031, rising to 464 people for every km² – and there are only so many extra runways and new towns that you can cram on to a small island.

Germany and the UK compared

Germany has the opposite problem to that of the UK (and not only in terms of Germany's phenomenal economic prowess). Its population is currently estimated at around 82.6 million – little changed over the last 20 years, during which time the UK population has risen by around 7 million (about 12%). Germany is the largest country in the European Union, comfortably accommodating the 16th largest population in the world. Even with a high percentage of immigrant population, mostly from other European countries – just under 10 million people were born outside the country (like Britain, about 12% of the population) – its birth rate is one of the lowest in the world; if current trends continue, the population could drop to less than 70 million over the next 50 years, with dire consequences for succession planning and pensions funding.

Projections in the UK

The UK population is projected to grow by over 9 million over the next 25 years, increasing to around 74 million. One would hope that politicians are busy planning ahead to provide decent housing, jobs, schools, health care and services for 9 million extra people – the equivalent of the current population of London, or (if you want to be dramatic) the combined population of ten of the UK's largest cities, including Birmingham, Leeds, Manchester, Edinburgh, Liverpool, Bristol, Cardiff and Newcastle.

Alternatively, to limit the population of the UK to sustainable levels – say, below 70 million – net migration (the difference between the loss of Brits to other countries and the gain of new blood from elsewhere) would need to stay below around 40,000 a year, which is significantly below net current levels of more than 240,000.

Tricky one!

Chapter 11

WELCOME TO THE MACHINE

Political parties are weird and complex organisations. Under constant scrutiny from the media and crammed with giant egos shamelessly jostling for power, unless managed professionally they have a tendency to savagely tear themselves apart. So here we look at how the party machinery works in government, what happens when it goes wrong and what it means for the rest of us.

Party operations

Party leaders are national figureheads – celebrities with real power. But they stand at the summit of a huge human pyramid that, more often than not, is seething with discontent.

RECALL LAW

What happens if an MP turns out to be a corrupt waste of space? Support grew for a 'recall law' after the expenses scandals of 2009, when numerous MPs were found to have taken advantage of ill-defined rules, making dodgy expenses claims for odd, unrelated items (remember the floating duck house?) and expensive mortgages on second homes. Likewise for elected public officials, the Rotherham child abuse scandal exposed a shocking lack of accountability when it emerged that no one had authority to dismiss Police and Crime Commissioner Shaun Wright, former head of Children's Services.

A recall law would allow local voters to hold rogue MPs to account. To force a by-election, angry voters would have to collect the signatures of 10% of constituents (a tall order given that only 50% may have voted even in the general election). After the expenses scandal, politicians made all sorts of promises to 'clean up politics' in this way – but the net result was a limp law whereby recall can be triggered only for MPs convicted and sentenced to jail, or if MPs in the House of Commons resolve that their colleague has engaged in 'serious wrongdoing'. In other words, any recall remains subject to parliamentary veto – and if MPs agree to a recall of one among their number, who's to say who'll be next? It seems they still don't get it.

Members of Parliament

At the last count, there were 650 MPs elected to the House of Commons, courtesy of voters in their local constituencies. Most are ordinary 'backbenchers' unattached to any particular department – and as power has become more concentrated at the top, these regular MPs have found that they've got less influence over what's going on. There are myriad reasons for this loss of power and status, the following among them.

- **Public disgust** Many MPs today aren't as 'Right Honourable' as their official titles might suggest, as we know from expenses scandals, undeserved pay rises and childish behaviour in the Commons.
- **Public disinterest** Most MPs simply parrot the party line, kept on a tight and tedious leash – one bore blurring into another.
- **Media apathy** The prime minister's and other MPs' speeches are no longer widely reported, the media focusing more on carefully constructed communications passed down by the spin machine at Number 10.
- **Low profiles** Lack of parliamentary time means that MPs find it almost impossible to get their own Bills enacted – one of the main ways in which a backbencher can raise his or her public profile.

Control freakery

The old maxim 'united we stand, divided we fall' applies in spades to politics. If politicians from the same party start hotly disagreeing in public, they may as well simply sign the party's death warrant. So parties are professionally organised, like businesses, with chains of command and disciplinary procedures for those who transgress. Once something becomes policy, all members must stick to the script – and stay 'on message', personal views be damned. If someone breaks rank, his or her days are numbered. And as a consequence much media time is spent trying to tease out the tiniest hint of trouble – a silly game of cat and mouse that many voters find really rather tedious.

This may sound like control freakery, but voters also tend to disapprove when parties are divided: if MPs are bickering amongst themselves, how will they ever get things done in government? The downside of course is that politicians end up sounding like droning automatons, which completely turns people off from voting. In truth, most party members don't have to be straightjacketed – they may genuinely believe in what the party stands for (even if they privately disagree with some of the detail), or career goals may dampen down their dissent – but if necessary, discipline can be maintained by the following means.

■ **Promise of promotion** An MP's career prospects depend on his or her keeping in with the right people. Senior party figures decide who moves up the ranks and the prime minister chooses who sits in the central cabal – the Cabinet. So any MP who gathers a reputation as a troublemaker is unlikely to be granted a seat at the top table.

■ **Withdrawing the whip** In this context, the 'whip' means party membership. An outspoken MP risks having the whip 'withdrawn' – that is, being suspended from the party and deselected as a candidate, so that he or she can't stand for election and is cast out into the political wilderness. Sometimes, however, this might be only a temporary measure: if the MP plays nice and gets back into the good books, the whip may be restored.

MR WHIPPY

There's a slightly unsavoury fixation with whipping in politics – speculation about which is probably best left to the tabloids. The leadership seems to see itself as some sort of Victorian lion tamer, whipping MPs into line (and teasing them with scraps from the top table).

In each of the major parties, one or two MPs will be designated 'whips', charged with ensuring that members toe the party line. Not known for their niceties and rarely recognising that a carrot can achieve more than a stick, these whips have an armoury of threats poised for deployment against any MP bold enough to follow his or her conscience. The reason is straightforward: if too many members fail to vote in line with leadership, a government Bill could fail – and once a government starts losing votes in the Commons, it will quickly be condemned by the media as weak and ineffective, damaging the party's chances of ever getting re-elected.

There are three levels of imperative with which whips demand obedience, as follows.

■ **Three-line whip** Attending and voting in line with the leader is absolutely essential. Ignore this instruction at your peril.
■ **Two-line whip** Attendance is expected, but MPs can 'pair off' – which means that an MP intending to vote one way, but unable to attend, officially agrees with an opposition member intending to vote in the opposite way that neither will turn up. So the two votes cancel each other out and the result is unaffected by the MPs' absence. (imagine the consequences if such lazy practices should spread to society at large!)
■ **One-line whip** Finally, at the lowest level of imperative, MPs are asked to turn up, but it's not a big deal if they have more pressing matters to which they must attend.

PARTY BIGWIGS

■ **The party chair** plays the role of a bridge between ordinary 'grass roots' members and the top dogs. He or she can play a dual role, advising the leadership on popular feeling among members (but don't shoot the messenger!) while also galvanising support.
■ **The party treasurer** is in charge of fundraising – of wooing big donors, so that there's enough in the war chest to fund election battles.
■ **The head of communications** is responsible for media strategy, ensuring that the media – and thus the public – perceive the party as positively as possible. Often, he or she isn't a party member, but a thick-skinned former Fleet Street journalist.

Some votes on new legislation are considered a matter of conscience – including issues with a strong moral dimension, such as the death penalty – and this means that the leadership stays neutral and issues no imperative at all. This type of vote is known as a 'free vote'.

Party conferences

OMG - it's Party conference season again. Showbiz for the terminally dull… Suddenly, the centre of a town is beset by swarms of police and security staff in hi-vis jackets. But beneath the veneer of spin, soundbites and seaside hotel naffness, the aroma of raw power and big money can sometimes be detected. Leaders regard these autumnal parades of artifice much as many corporations regard the obligatory annual general meeting: as a duty that must be endured, at risk of political embarrassment when rubbing shoulders with real people.

As well as being a chance for dwindling numbers of ordinary party members to mingle with the political elite, the main function of party conferences is:

- as a platform to attract massive media coverage, carefully choreographed to project the party and the leader in the best light possible;
- to raise funds from donors and members;
- to announce new policies, but outside of the parliamentary context, making for ready damage limitation; and
- to hold 'fringe meetings' at which new ideas can be hotly debated at a safe distance from the main stage.

In the not-too-distant past, annual party conferences were dramatic occasions, at which passionate rows would erupt between politicians. At a time when party policy was voted for democratically, what happened at the conference *mattered*. But such animated antics, fireworks and public washing of dirty laundry have been deemed distasteful in these days of 24/7 media coverage. So while policy is still discussed in vague 'feel-good' terms, the leadership no longer pays much attention to what conference delegates decide. Today, like so much else, the season is stage managed, with politicians delivering carefully choreographed speeches to well-rehearsed, delirious standing ovations.

" IF YOU HAVE BEEN AFFECTED BY THE ISSUES DODGED DURING THIS CONFERENCE ... "

Given government's overwhelming obsession with centralised control, one of the great paradoxes of modern politics is why, in certain circumstances, it's so keen to give power away, contracting out services and selling off state assets (see Chapter 9). One possible explanation is familiar, old-fashioned laziness: for some MPs, the job would ideally involve generous remuneration and perks, with plenty of foreign travel and grandstanding on the world stage, but not too much tiresome responsibility.

Between outright privatisation and retaining state ownership, however, lies a third option: the 'quango'. Sounding like a cross between an unhealthy fizzy drink and a high-energy dance routine, the 'Quasi Non-Governmental Organisation' is actually an executive agency that manages public services on behalf of a government department. Estimates vary, but some reckon that there are well over 1,000 quangos, including the Environment Agency, the Welsh Development Agency, the Highways Agency and the Benefits Agency, many of which are criticised as 'too powerful' on the basis of their big budgets and well-paid directors.

Most worryingly, unlike elected officials, the accountability of the quango is limited. Sometimes, when things go wrong – such as when people needing passports in 2014 faced headline-grabbing delays – the agency will be brought back in-house; hence the Passport Office has been brought back into the Home Office. Such failures are, of course, more difficult to remedy where services have been outsourced or sold off completely – leaving cheeks not so much orange as bright red.

Power at the top

As we saw in Chapter 7, the party with the highest number of MPs following a general election forms the government, with the party leader stepping triumphantly into the role of prime minister.

Number 10

Dictators and presidents tend to reside in grand buildings; as a rule, the less democratic the regime, the more palatial the abode. One of the charms of the British system is that our glorious leader appears to live and work in a terraced townhouse (albeit a Georgian terraced townhouse). But all is not as it seems: like the Tardis, it's bigger on the inside – a cavernous operations centre churning out press releases and statements to the media. Moreover, it is linked via mazes of corridors to the Cabinet Office round the corner in Whitehall, meaning that ministers can choose to meet secretly without anyone noticing their comings and goings. The prime minister also enjoys the perk of Chequers, a 16th-century country retreat in Buckinghamshire, where visiting world leaders will be wined and dined, and dissent quelled amongst rebellious MPs.

The top job: prime minister

The British like a strong prime minister who looks and sounds the part. We want leaders who can communicate properly and who can lift our spirits with a genuine vision. We want photogenic leaders who don't fade into the background when stood next to the president of the United States. This points towards a prime minister who's little more than a talented actor, skilled in the art of sounding sincere on TV – but is this what the nation really needs?

Prime ministers have enormous power at their fingertips. In recent years, power has increasingly been centred on Number 10 and so dominant has the prime minister become in British politics that many forget that our head of state is actually the monarch. This power stems from the authority to make or break the careers of just about all the other big party players. The prime minister decides who gets what jobs (including the top bananas sitting in Cabinet and the Lords), as well as having the final word on government policy and new laws. Plus there are some other highly potent powers, including:

- establishing or abolishing entire government departments;
- chairing meetings of the 'inner circle' (the Cabinet), and periodically hiring and firing ministers in 'reshuffles' (see later in the chapter);
- representing the country overseas;
- driving the country into war and making key military decisions; and
- withdrawing the whip from badly behaving MPs and dictating who can stand as a candidate.

HOW TO BECOME PRIME MINISTER

Prime minister is the ultimate prize for party leaders. To create a vacancy, the incumbent often has to be physically prised out of the hot seat. It's a mighty long way to Number 10. To get your hands on the keys, you first need to be elected to Parliament, having served your (long, long) time climbing the political ladder, whispering all the right things in all the right ears. Next, you need party members to elect you as their leader (which, for Labour, involves an elaborate 'electoral college' system comprising MPs, MEPs, ordinary party members and trade unions). Then there's the small matter of leading those trusting party members to success in a general election. The last part is easy: riding in the back of a limo to Buckingham Palace to receive the royal seal of approval.

LIMITING POWER

The great thing about democracy is that power runs both ways. However some prime ministers are well known to have preferred the idea of a one-way system and a perpetual life presidency – but the gods of politics won't stand for such shenanigans, shunting off those who develop delusions of regal grandeur, before they entirely lose touch with reality.

The obvious way in which poorly performing prime ministers are seen off the premises is a loss at a general election: the leader has no choice but to bow to the will of the people and step down. The danger seems to arise on those rare occasions when power-hungry prime ministers are elected for a third term, and start to behave like dictators who can't be challenged.

Fortunately, all parties have other devices for deposing leaders who've become liabilities. This can involve a vote of 'no confidence' when a prime minister has pursued policies so unpopular that they've devastated the party's chances of success at the next general election; alternatively, with enough internal support, an ambitious MP might mount a leadership challenge. In some instances, MPs might simply want to fire a warning shot across the leader's bows by nominating a 'stalking horse' candidate – someone who's not really a serious contender – much to the delight of the media who like nothing more than rumours of plots and coups (all of which rather gets in the way of running the country).

THE MYTH OF THE STRONG LEADER

As a nation, we like a strong figurehead in the top job, although not necessarily one in the Vladimir Putin mould. Good leadership isn't about 'flamethrower' displays of strength. Vigorous, chest-beating, 'alpha male' characteristics might make for entertaining *Apprentice*-style TV, but they don't generally make for successful organisations. So it's important not to confuse the 'comic book' appearance of strength with professional leadership.

Many of the UK's problems in politics, business and even the NHS stem from perpetuation of the old idea that leadership means domination, not participation. Modern politics is increasingly 'top-down', resulting in poor decisions that clearly haven't been properly considered, perhaps because they were made without input from the Cabinet and the experienced Civil Service.

Informed decisions are made only in consultation with others, and they are successfully implemented by winning people over, not by barking orders. The danger is that if the leader is wholly responsible for appointing to the top jobs, then a culture of obsequious 'yes men' is inevitable. Stalin famously silenced his flatterers by ringing a bell; in Britain, both Thatcher and Blair knocked away their naysayers, only to become embroiled in messianic hubris that led to their downfall.

Japanese and German car companies with hugely productive factories in Britain transformed UK industrial relations. The strength of their inclusive management style couldn't be more different from British industry's traditional 'them and us' approach. Strength, for these companies, is defined as the ability to listen to other voices, particularly those who might have different experiences that might inform better judgements. Leadership is about empowering others in an organisation and harnessing their energy. More commonly, we find a 'Mid Staffs Hospital' culture wherein whistleblowers, who should be thanked for sounding early alarm bells, are bullied and threatened by a management too weak to cope with critical feedback.

Heather Rabbatts, director of the Football Association and pivotal former chief executive officer of formerly failing Lambeth Council, makes the point as follows: 'Great leaders have strong people around them. They're not worried about someone being brighter than they are – because they know that will help them make better informed decisions.'

So leadership is a collaborative responsibility. Football managers and their assistants often move together around different clubs. As the legendary Brian Clough found to his cost, the Number 2 is very important. So we should look for enlightened politicians, people who listen to others.

Evidence-based policy

One of the big changes over the last 20 years has been the advent of 'evidence-based' policymaking – which is obviously better than the traditional approach: making it up as you go along. The 1999 White Paper *Modernising Government* noted that government 'must produce policies that really deal with problems … and are shaped by evidence rather than a response to short-term pressures; that tackle causes not symptoms', all of which sounds eminently sensible. It doesn't mean that evidence automatically trumps all other influences on policymaking, but it is supposed to put an end to policies driven by supposition and hearsay. In practice, though, when evidence and political views conflict there's a good chance that the evidence will simply be stuffed down the back of the sofa. Allegations that a 'dodgy dossier' was used to justify the Iraq War are familiar. More recently, the state-owned East Coast Main Line service was re-privatised, despite its enormous success in returning more than £1 billion to the taxpayer and generating excellent customer and employee satisfaction ratings. And what of the sacking of government 'Drug Tzar' Professor David Nutt, whose evidence happened to conflict with the required message? *Plus ça change…*

QUESTION TIME: PRIME MINISTER'S QUESTIONS (PMQS)

The UK Parliament is famously adversarial (see Chapter 8). Each side tries to make its opponents look daft and incompetent, while trying itself to seem able to solve all of the nation's problems. This, at least, is the impression that you get when watching Prime Minister's Questions (PMQs) – a televised set piece that takes place in the Commons every Wednesday afternoon, during which the prime minister is quizzed for half an hour or so on what his or her government is up to. Those hoping to ask questions make themselves known at the outset and are called in random order. Even backbench MPs have a (limited) chance to ask questions, which means there's scope for genuine contention. Sycophantic government backbenchers often waste time fielding a 'helpful' (scripted) question that allows the prime minister to boast of recent successes; opposition MPs peck at the government, posing awkward questions – and sometimes knock the prime minister off his perch. Although PMQs has become geared to creating TV news soundbites, there's still scope for slip-ups and gaffes which can make it quite entertaining.

Cabinet

The Cabinet is a central group of top government ministers, appointed by the prime minister, meetings of which the prime minister chairs as though he or she were the nation's chief executive and the Cabinet, its board of directors.

Each member is the head of a government department, often known as a 'minister' (more formally, as 'secretary of state'). Cabinet meetings are held once a week, usually on Thursdays, and it's here that ministers decide what policies the government will pursue and monitor progress towards policy goals.

Not all ministers are appointed to sit in Cabinet, but the heads of some 30 of the biggest departments, such as the Secretary of State for Health and the Chancellor of the Exchequer may be included (with ministers in charge of some smaller departments invited to attend only when their particular area is under discussion).

In addition, the prime minister can choose to appoint to the Cabinet a 'Minister without Portfolio' – that is, as a minister with no department – any elected politician whose advice is especially valued.

THE SHADOWS

As in football, successful teams need to mark key players. Thus the leader of the opposition appoints members of a 'shadow Cabinet' to monitor the actions of top government ministers and to highlight failings in government policies. The shadow Cabinet sits on the front benches, facing the prime minister and its opposite numbers in government.

ONE-WAY TRAFFIC

Back in the day, Cabinet meetings were a forum in which new ideas would be thrashed out by a motivated team keen to generate new policies. More recently, prime ministers have tended to hog the limelight. Thatcher was criticised for ignoring her Cabinet entirely, and Blair, for 'sofa government' – for basing government policy on the advice of a few close advisers, some of whom weren't even elected. Cabinet meetings became shorter, focusing less on debating the political agenda and more on disparaging the opposition and dutifully reporting the progress of policies imposed top-down. In the words of former minister Claire Short, 'Cabinet government has collapsed and ministers have become zombies – the living dead of British politics'.

'Tomorrow … the world!' Blair and Brown plot the rise of New Labour.

Today, many big government decisions are not taken by full meetings, but by groups of only four or five ministers sitting as Cabinet committees (or 'kitchen Cabinets'), the argument being that these smaller groups can work more quickly, sometimes with eight or more committees operating at the same time. We might, however, draw other conclusions.

LACK OF TALENT

Cabinet has been weakened not only by bombastic prime ministers, but also by the declining quality of personnel. We have noted already that the qualities valued in MPs and ministers today relate more to presentation skills than to the ability to make and implement informed decisions. There seems to be a shortage of down-to-earth politicians who talk the language of voters; instead, multi-millionaire ministers surrounded by the privileges of office have scant contact with ordinary people. It's certainly apt, then, to echo the words of post-war Prime Minister Clement Attlee: 'You've got to have a certain number of solid people whom no one would think particularly brilliant but who, between conflicting opinions, can act as middlemen and give you the ordinary man's point of view.'

THE MINISTERIAL CODE

All leading figures in government are expected to adhere to the Ministerial Code, which sets minimum standards of behaviour for ministers. One of the key principles of government set out in the Code is 'collective responsibility', which effectively means that all members must speak with one voice, upholding the decisions of the Cabinet in public even if they may disagree with them in private.

Sometimes, the resulting crisis of conscience can be too tough to stomach: in 2003, Foreign Secretary Robin Cook resigned his post, unable to accept collective responsibility for the government's decision to invade Iraq. At other times, an unhappy minister will secretly 'brief against' another minister – asking an adviser to talk to the press, which will then report dissent based on an 'undisclosed source'.

RESIGNATIONS

In addition to collective responsibility, Cabinet ministers are responsible for their own departments. But taking 'personal responsibility' doesn't come easily. In years long gone by, this might have involved doing the honourable thing and resigning in the event of a department's failings or one of their senior civil servants made an unforgivable boob. Rather than one's actions bringing shame on others, a true gentleman might resort to the pearl-handled revolver and glass of whisky. These days however, ambitious ministers rarely do the decent thing. Resignations now come about only grudgingly under sustained media pressure following some blatant mistake with far-reaching consequences, or a profound scandal (involving rigging expenses, bribery, or criminal activity, for example). In most instances, the minister will simply try to sit tight until the media furore has abated. If finally forced to resign, he or she will often be heard to say that the resignation is 'for the good of the party' – avoiding any admission of culpability even while walking out of the door. Loyalty to party sometimes seems to come before loyalty to family, Queen or country (but not necessarily wallet).

Small wonder, then, that respect for politicians seems to be at an all-time low.

MUSICAL CHAIRS

Membership of Cabinet rarely stays the same for a full year, let alone throughout a government's entire term. Ministers come and go, riding the waves of fortune, favour and incompetence as the prime minister 'reshuffles' the cutlery, aiming to bring new blood into the Cabinet and promote loyalists. For those no longer considered to be up to the job, or those whose dissenting voices have been a little too loud, or those who are starting to be seen as future challengers for the top job, out come the long knives… But while the media thrives on the resulting gossip – who's hot and who's not – unless ministers are given the opportunity to get to grips with the role, they can be doomed to making poor decisions. And all this manoeuvring about can be hugely disruptive to government.

Unelected power

As we saw in Chapter 9, one of biggest changes in modern politics has been the rise of unelected special advisers ('spads'). Often former journalists or public relations gurus, spads have enormous influence behind the scenes on policy and its presentation to the media. A huge explosion in their number took place under New Labour, with Blair having more than 50 special advisers, compared to the eight of his predecessor, John Major. There are therefore serious concerns that spads have become far too big for their boots – unelected henchmen wielding bias behind the scenes, in lieu of impartial civil servants.

When self-styled 'adviser' and Defence Secretary Liam Fox's former flatmate, who was not a government employee and had no clearance, was allowed to attend confidential meetings over a period of several months (perhaps, as some have suggested, to gain information for his own benefit) the breach of national security was such that few would swallow the plot line even in pulp spy fiction.

The judiciary

Respect for the judiciary depends on their maintaining professional integrity and resisting pressure from Number 10. There are, however, two key appointments that regularly interface with government.

- **Lord Chancellor** The Lord Chancellor is a member of the Cabinet and responsible for the independence of the courts system. Formerly the head of the judiciary – effectively the top judge in the land – this function was removed in 2005 to salve concerns about the separation of powers (see Chapter 8). The principle behind the separation of powers is one of 'checks and balances': it's essential to democracy that judges are independent and have no inhibitions about defying government, lest the dragon of 'elected dictatorship' rear its fearsome head.
- **Attorney General** Chief legal adviser to government, the gravest role of the Attorney General is to confirm the legality of war. The first non-MP appointed to the job (under the Blair administration) was a Queen's Counsel (QC).

Yes, Minister

The popular 1980s TV show *Yes, Minister* shone a humorous spotlight on the world of civil servants working behind the scenes to keep the machinery of government moving. Sir Humphrey and his colleagues deployed wit and judgement to keep hapless ministers out of trouble. Civil servants aren't elected like politicians and not all public sector workers are civil servants (consider armed forces, police, NHS and council staff, etc). Despite cutbacks over recent years, the Civil Service continues to employ more than 400,000 across the UK, only about a fifth of whom are based in London; without these valuable folk, the workings of government would quickly grind to a halt.

Government departments

The work of government is carried out in various ministries, such as the Department of Health (DoH) or the Department of Transport (DoT). Towering above all other government departments is HM Treasury, which is responsible for controlling public spending and shaping the nation's economic policy. The enormous power of these 'money men' can frustrate even prime ministers, leading Harold Wilson famously to quip: 'Whichever party's in office, the Treasury's still in power.'

Although the prime minister (and Cabinet) makes the decisions about which policies to pursue, it's the government departments that are responsible for making sure that those policies are implemented. This means that most day-to-day decisions are made by civil servants. An impartial Civil Service can offer advice on how best to transform policy into workable law, and then administer it – if necessary, proposing new laws. At least, this is how things used to work: ministers and civil servants interacting. Today, ministers are more likely to turn to their own inner circle of advisers, whose main concern is tomorrow's headlines and whose loud voices may drown out the wise words of experience. In recent years, civil servants have sometimes found themselves co-opted into this daily flow of 'initiatives' aimed only at the news agenda, while the MPs appointed as their ministers may be in post for only a few months. Even in HM Treasury, as in much of government, the emphasis is increasingly on the short term, with an inward focus on departmental budgets rather than on serious long-term policy. Maybe this explains why government policies so often seem to be amateurish and poorly thought-through?

The link

At the top of the Civil Service is the Permanent Secretary at the Cabinet Office, the crucial link to the prime minister and senior politicians. Government is a massive organisation, so to ensure that ministries don't step on each other's toes, the Cabinet Office coordinates them on a day-to-day basis, with the aim of achieving 'joined-up government'. The Cabinet Office is therefore at the centre of the Whitehall web and the 'Cabinet Secretary' is appointed by the prime minister from among the upper ranks of the Civil Service.

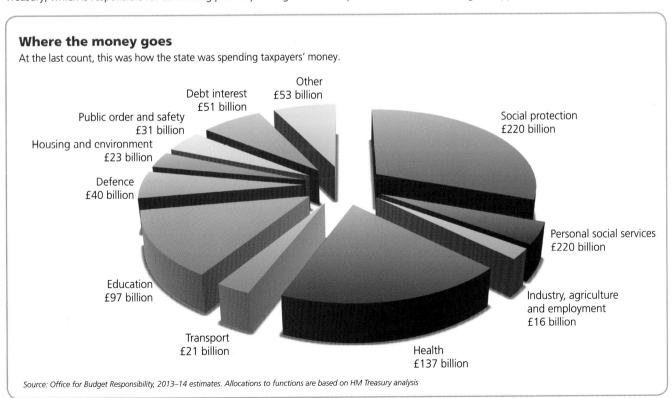

Where the money goes

At the last count, this was how the state was spending taxpayers' money.

- Other £53 billion
- Debt interest £51 billion
- Public order and safety £31 billion
- Housing and environment £23 billion
- Defence £40 billion
- Education £97 billion
- Transport £21 billion
- Health £137 billion
- Social protection £220 billion
- Personal social services £220 billion
- Industry, agriculture and employment £16 billion

Source: Office for Budget Responsibility, 2013–14 estimates. Allocations to functions are based on HM Treasury analysis

The job

Civil servants have two key jobs: helping ministers with research and advice; and implementing government policies, so that they work in the real world. For example, a civil servant might be asked to research the impact of new airports or to monitor the cost of a major construction project. Other branches include advising people looking for work at job centres.

A career in the Civil Service is the archetypal well-paid 'job for life' – and it needs to be if it's to encourage people with valuable experience to stay for the long haul. But the rewards are not confined to salary, perks and gold-plated pensions; those in the upper echelons can also expect an honour recognising long-standing service to the state — hence *Sir* Humphrey. Perhaps surprisingly, in this era of 'free market' thinking, the 'public service' ethic is still a powerful motivator and the belief that a civil servant can 'make a difference' remains a key recruitment draw.

The Civil Service provides a stable counterbalance to the short-term wheezes of transient ministers. The permanent denizens of Whitehall have seen many mad schemes and political masters come and go. And with politicians expecting civil servants to achieve the impossible, combining loyalty with independent judgement when implementing rash promises, there's always a chance that the two sides might cross swords – or at least exchange cross words.

MERITOCRACY

Once upon a time, any twit with a surplus of money could buy a top rank in the army or Civil Service. But being rich and knowing the right people aren't necessarily the best qualifications to guarantee good work. Indeed, things had become so hopeless in the early Victorian era that radical change was required and, in 1854, the Northcote–Trevelyan Report set out its blueprint for a British system of 'meritocracy' – a novel concept at the time. The Civil Service now

had to operate on the basis of genuine ability and talent rather than on how rich your father was or whether you had a mate on the inside who could pull a few strings. Corruption, nepotism and favouritism were consigned to the dustbin of history. Professional civil servants were now expected to resist commercial pressures and corruption from business interests which encircled government – companies and lobbyists pitching for lucrative state contracts. The result was dramatic improvements in efficiency.

Today, it's mildly reassuring to know that interviews and aptitude tests still apply at every rung of the Civil Service ladder (tests that might be well applied to some MPs). So it can be a long, hard climb to the top. It's rather less reassuring to realise that the influence of these carefully selected civil servants has sharply declined in the face of the highly paid management consultants whom ministers parachute in simply to tell them (so cynics say) what they want to hear. These days, few senior politicians welcome advice or statistics which dare to point in a different direction.

ACCOUNTABILITY

Back in the days of Empire, the British Civil Service competently administered the affairs of more than a quarter of the world's population. Today after years of cutbacks, it seems they sometimes seem hard pushed to pick up the phone. Yet most try hard to live up to past standards, and cases of unethical or corrupt conduct are extremely rare. At the top, the 'Sir Humphreys' (parliamentary under-secretaries) are accountable to the Cabinet Office and may occasionally make an appearance before a parliamentary committee to justify the running of their departments. As a further safeguard, they're also accountable to the Civil Service Commission, an independent body that ensures recruitment remains purely on the basis of professional merit.

CODE OF BEHAVIOUR

Two qualities that aren't generally associated with politicians are integrity and keeping a low profile. But since someone has to take a grown-up approach to running the country, civil servants adopt a strict code of behaviour. Talking to the press is banned, because breaking confidentiality could cause the government serious embarrassment; in return, as part of an unwritten bargain, ministers are supposed to take the flak for mistakes made further down the line.

The Whitehall Code of Behaviour is based on the following three key principles.

- **Stay politically neutral** Civil servants are barred from standing for election. Even if they hold a different personal view and disagree with policy, they're still expected to carry out the instructions of ministers.
- **Maintain a low profile** Politicians love basking in the limelight; civil servants are supposed to stay firmly in the shadows.
- **Stay for the long haul** Quixotic politicians come and go, but it's important for the continuity of government that civil servants develop valuable knowledge and experience over many years.

PROJECT MANAGEMENT

The Civil Service has a somewhat chequered history when it comes to making things work in the real world. Former Cabinet Secretary Gus O'Donnell put his finger on the problem when he said: 'We don't do project management.'

Some years ago, HM Treasury recognised the difficulties of supervising massive nationalised industries such as British Rail; unlike the French Civil Service, which successfully extended its high-speed rail network, Westminster lacked an 'entrepreneurial tradition'. Privatisation was meant to resolve the problem by ridding the Civil Service of the responsibility. But the same lack of commercial nous resulted in some spectacular failures in managing the tendering and contracting-out of major projects. Many were surprised at the Treasury's naivety in the face of unscrupulous salesmen, whose chief objective seemed to be taking the state for a ride, not improving public services. And as disastrous experiences such as Railtrack and National Air Traffic Services (NATS) unfolded, government discovered that accountability for public services is very difficult to evade.

Reform

Every new government proudly announces its plans to cut waste by 'de-privileging' staff and reducing head counts in Whitehall. But, in some cases, this has proven counter-productive, such as slashing staff at HM Revenue and Customs (HMRC) to the extent that many taxpayers now find it almost impossible even to get a call answered (and poor communication leads to expensive mistakes).

Some past recommendations for reform have been sensible, such as giving greater autonomy to civil servants and setting clear goals to improve value for money (*ie* proper management). But hefty cutbacks risk demotivation and low morale – not least while

governments have been uncritical of the performance of the bloated corporations to which they have outsourced services.

Despite being subject to such undignified onslaughts, the Civil Service today is still very much the backbone of government – an important force, whose value and significance tends to be underplayed.

OUTSOURCING AND THE PRIVATE FINANCE INITIATIVE (PFI)

As we saw in Chapter 9, by adopting a 'build now, pay later' ethos, politicians found that they could crow about the benefits of new schools and hospitals on their watch, whilst the costs become somebody else's future problem.

Public services have therefore increasingly been subcontracted to private companies under private finance initiatives (PFIs) or public–private partnerships (PPP). Yet many such schemes have failed spectacularly, such as the privatisation of London Underground, which had to be brought back under state control. Government departments also seem particularly easily bamboozled by IT contracts worth billions.

Theoretically, the public interest is protected by the National Audit Office (NAO), which has produced scathing reports on disastrous projects with soaring costs and overruns, such as the Millennium Dome and British Library – but the NAO's scope is limited. With PFI/PPP it therefore seems that government is increasingly interlocked

Disasterous cost overruns and poor project management are not uncommon – construction of the millenium dome came in at a cool £204 million over budget.

The Civil Service does pretty well out of the honours system (see Chapter 8). The Cabinet Secretary automatically receives a knighthood on assuming the job and also puts forward names of deserving civil servants for honours.

The UK honours system is meant to recognise outstanding contributions to society, culture and government. Twice-yearly (at New Year and on the monarch's official birthday), a list of some 1,350 'deserving' people is drawn up. The prime minister effectively decides who to honour and the monarch does her ceremonial duty – bestowing everything from knighthoods to peerages.

The system was devalued in the 1920s, when Prime Minister David Lloyd George allowed the government of the day to sell such honours for cash donations. At the time, this wasn't illegal because no one had ever imagined that a prime minister would stoop so low; it was outlawed in 1925. Fast forward to 2007 and senior fundraisers in government were accused of handing out honours to party donors: police interviewed Blair in person, but no charges were ever brought and the case was dropped.

It is prime ministers who must take most blame for debasing the system for their political ends with honours conferred on tax dodgers, casino bankers, public relations consultants and retired politicians, amongst others. Meanwhile, the list of refuseniks who've declined knighthoods or peerages on ethical grounds includes famous names such as Stephen Hawking, Alan Bennett, Harold Pinter, David Hockney and LS Lowry.

with the ambitions of profit-hungry business, which it sometimes seems to forget are its duty to control.

REVOLVING DOORS

Up until the 1960s, strict rules were in place to delay the transition of public staff into the private sector. The rules have since been relaxed and, today, there are well-worn paths between Whitehall and lucrative jobs on boards of major defence contractors, for example. Former civil servants increasingly move in and out of investment banks and multinational corporations, whose national allegiances are unknown. It's now less clear than ever who are the gamekeepers and who are the poachers.

Want to get involved?

God knows, politics in this country needs reviving – and perhaps you might be just the person to inject some fresh blood? … But how to get to Parliament?

If you hail from a humble background, don't be dismayed: several leaders of the Labour Party, and even former Tory leaders John Major and Margaret Thatcher, all came up the hard way. The first step towards Parliament is either to join a political party or to stand for election as a local councillor. Many of today's leading politicians even started out by volunteering, leafleting and canvassing door-to-door or fundraising, in support of other candidates.

Having joined the party of your choice, you need to convince your fellow members that you're the right person to be selected as a prospective candidate (with a decent chance of winning). All parties have procedures for approval, but it helps if you raise your

Conservative MP John Major made it to the top from a humble background.

© David Fowler / Shutterstock.com

Alan 'Howling Laud' Hope, leader of the Monster Raving Loony Party.

profile by demonstrating that you're committed to the cause. (A young Tony Blair famously wrote to then Labour leader Michael Foot claiming that he found the works of Karl Marx 'illuminating in so many ways'.) Even then, it's not unusual for candidates to lose a couple of elections before eventually securing a more winnable seat. Alternatively, you might stand as an 'independent', campaigning on a big local issue. Former broadcast war reporter Martin Bell famously stole the safe Conservative seat at Tatton with an 11,000 majority in 1997, running on an independent, anti-corruption ticket.

Of course, you might decide that you don't want to stand for election. In that case, you might try writing a political blog or joining a pressure group, or penning a column for a paper, which can eventually lead to party success via the 'back door', perhaps as a special adviser.

Who can stand for election?

Anyone can stand for election to Parliament (or a local council) on condition that they are:
- at least 18 years old;
- a British citizen (or a Commonwealth citizen with indefinite leave to stay in the UK); and
- a local resident for at least a year prior to the election.

You're not allowed to stand if you:
- are a civil servant;
- are a member of the clergy, police, or armed forces;
- are a resident of HM Prisons (serving more than a year);
- are an undischarged bankrupt; or
- have been previously found guilty of electoral fraud.

Battle plan

To improve your chances of winning, it will help if you can raise your profile locally well ahead of the election. As a first step, you should certainly make the acquaintance of the editor of your local paper.

There are three further practical steps that you must then take if you intend to stand.

- **Submit your nomination** First, fill out a form (available from your local council), confirming your wish to stand. This must be countersigned by no fewer than ten voters and you must hand it in to the organisers in person.
- **Pay your deposit** Next, pay a deposit of £500, or £5,000 for European elections (with no deposit needed for local council elections). This deposit is refunded if you get more than 5% of the votes cast; otherwise, you lose it.
- **Appoint an agent** Every parliamentary candidate must have an election agent, to ensure that his or her campaign is professionally coordinated.

All candidates are entitled to free delivery of one small leaflet to every house in the constituency, but the content mustn't be 'offensive' – which is, of course, a matter of personal opinion!

The final furlong

Once elected, MPs have to work their way up. Only a small number of MPs ever rise up the ranks, climbing the departmental ladder to Cabinet offices such as Foreign Secretary. Ministers are appointed by the prime minister, so ambitious MPs need to be adept at adhering to diktats from Number 10.

Good politics

Good politics will revive if enough people are inspired by fresh leadership and new ideas at the top. As the Scottish National Party (SNP) has shown, people will willingly work together to raise the national game, given the right motivation and a sense of belief. First, though, we need to rid ourselves of the pervasive parasitic culture of spin and hypocrisy. Politics should be about hope, about satisfying people's needs and aspirations. Politicians often say the right words – speaking of 'fairness', 'the march of the makers', etc – but rarely are their warm words put into practice or backed up by serious money. Might we rediscover the spirit of post-war Britain, when an innovative, outward-looking country earned its way in the world, generating secure jobs and affordable homes, and citizens were benefited by honest public services and utilities?

The ghost of *Glasnost* might even appear, fostering a new commitment to fairness and transparency, combined with the entrepreneurial genius of capitalist markets, driving us forward by getting the best out of people. We need to work with the market, not be controlled by it.

With the electorate so disenchanted with the political class, Darwinism prescribes its evolution: politicians must adapt to the new environment or risk extinction. The following are a few suggestions for change.

■ **Believe in better** With most voters hard-pressed to say what their local MP actually stands *for*, imagine the thrill of voting for someone genuinely committed to improving their living standards?

■ **Ban career politicians** All who stand for election should have worked at least one 'proper job' (preferably the hard physical variety) – and public relations and media positions don't count.

■ **Don't parachute in politicians** No one should stand for election in a place to which they have no connection, for example ambitious Londoners standing in safe seats in the north of England.

■ **Learn to 'talk proper'** The terrible fear that politicians have of actually 'saying something' results in meaningless soundbites and verbless slogans, such as '*Hardworking Britain Better Off*' – (sounds like a brainstorming session was abandoned when the fire alarm went off).

■ **Speak the truth** It's time to stop pretending that bankers and powerful corporations will meekly 'self-regulate', and that skewed market processes will automatically self-adjust to serve consumers.

■ **Ditch the media training** It looks insincere and creepy – and can be spotted a mile off.

■ **Get more done** MPs could be more productive if they had shorter (*ie* standard) holidays and worked a full-time five-day week.

■ **Get strict with salaries** A full five-day week would also do away with part-timers with second jobs taking home full-time pay, plus there need to be strictly maintained controls on expenses and perks.

■ **Streamline processes** Let's see a streamlined law-making process introduced into Parliament, with less of that old relic, 'red tape'.

Based on an original article by Suzanne Moore

Before HMS Westminster finally keels over and sinks beneath the waters of apathy – here's a brief summary of some of the key issues and some recommended reforms:

Loss of control

Political parties depend financially on a few rich men who increasingly expect to influence policy decisions. The major parties are haemorrhaging members, whilst financial demands open the floodgates to secretive lobbyists and wealthy corporations. We need to foster a culture of openness and financial independence – and this will undoubtedly mean regulating party funding.

Loss of trust

The public has lost trust not only in government, but also in financial elites beyond the control of shareholders.

Not one of the big political parties is engaging honestly with the loud warnings of economists – about a poorly funded NHS and social care, and the dangers of inequality, with permanently stagnant low pay – fearful of the consequences of confronting voters with the hard truth that there is no free lunch: you get the services that you pay for. If our very social fabric is to be saved, some taxes will need to rise.

In the City, the auditors and fund managers who are supposed to protect small investors and shareholders often appear to act in the interests of corporate directors, who are effectively unaccountable. The big beneficiaries of privatisations such as the Royal Mail have been small groups of global investment banks that dominate capital markets.

Lack of policies

None of the parties seems to have any long-term strategy for the country (other than to repeat the hollow words that they 'have strategy'). It's time to make the case for *good* capitalism in a decent society that embraces opportunity and innovation. The country needs a clear plan to rebuild British industry into an export success story. New wealth-generating industries need nurturing and a strong coordinated support. And tax revenues can be boosted by clamping down on unreasonable evasion and avoidance, wherever it might lodge.

Loss of influence

While we are sometimes eager to condemn the 'incoming tide' of EU laws and directives affecting agriculture, fisheries, trade and the movement of people, fewer bemoan the influence of the United States. While politicians are naturally drawn towards US money, power and influence, spurred on by a common language, the City is increasingly being subsumed within Wall Street. And yet politicians feel obliged to avoid criticism of US policy even when it discriminates against British interests.

Wasted votes

Most votes are wasted: the same two big parties still dominate, despite being more unpopular than ever. The voting system needs to be brought into the 21st century and consideration given to forms of proportional representation that have been proven elsewhere.

Out of touch

Politicians live in a Westminster bubble, propped up by a lazy media, engrossed in their own love–hate relationships. Amidst leaks, spin and counter-spin, they've lost sight of the real deal: the public interest. A Westminster administration might spend four years of its five-year term ignoring voters in favour of self-interest and corporate vested interests, switching to a 'people-friendly' track only in the run up to an election trail. But voters increasingly see through this.

Source material: BBC and Suzanne Moore

SOCIETY

Chapter 12

VISIONS OF SOCIETY

What is this thing called 'society'?

Let's be honest: we humans aren't the most harmonious of species. Much of our history has been devoted to enthusiastically slashing at each other's throats, plundering, invading and generally terrorising our neighbours. And when not busily engaged in violent tribal warfare, we have an unrivalled ability to mess up our environment – pooing in the proverbial nest. The icing on the cake is our unlovely tendency to conceal cruelty, barbarism and blatant greed beneath a cloak of breathtaking hypocrisy, ascribing higher motives to our evil deeds and citing holy scripture as justification – or, at the very least, a half-decent economist.

So devising systems to keep us on the straight and narrow, safely contained within manageable national boundaries, makes herding cats look easy. Fortunately, on those occasions when we get this right, we prove ourselves able to rise above our animal instincts – able to cooperate for the common good. Sometimes, we even go to extraordinary lengths of self-sacrifice, kindness and decency. So what sort of society do we need to bring out the best in us?

Lone wolves or pack animals?

At the heart of human nature, there is something rather puzzling – a conundrum of epic proportions. As individuals, we generally do better when we live and work side by side, coexisting peacefully in a stable society. Yet there is another side to our Dr Jekyll/Mr Hyde natures, and this darker persona also needs to be accommodated. Self-interest dictates that we take actions to increase our own 'stash', even if it sometimes comes at the expense of others. And if our Mr Hyde side is allowed free rein and gets out of hand, the result can be social breakdown, violence and war. But for us there is no magic

potion to solve this problem – we have to learn how to reconcile these apparently conflicting impulses – both individually and as members of a decent society.

Match of the Day may not be the obvious answer to humanity's problems, but team sports combine the perfect mix: players working together as a single unit, yet in competition with each other for a shot at glory. Within each team, individual star talent can shine – to huge acclaim – whilst competing as a team against rival 'tribes'. All sport is underpinned by the concept of fairness: both sides must have an equal opportunity to win, even to the extent of swapping ends of the pitch at half-time. There are lessons for society here. Players need clear rules otherwise they will be tempted to take advantage, seeking to win by foul means and dirty antics. Referees are there for a purpose – 'regulators' who enforce fair play, to enable the game to function smoothly, lest blatant cheating leads the game to break down – as hostility engulfs the pitch and aggrieved fans descend into violence. Even solo sporting heroes, such as Andy Murray and Lewis Hamilton, depend on the cooperation of complex support networks.

Sport, at its best, is a model for society. But managing teams of 11 or 15 (plus subs) is a doddle compared to coordinating a nation of some 65 million people. So how might we ensure that society hits the right balance between 'team' cooperation and 'star quality' individualism, and between 'give' and 'take' – our rights and responsibilities as citizens?

The first problem is in defining exactly what 'society' is. What we can say is that society comprises groups of individuals who have certain things in common.

- **Behaviour** We know how we're supposed to behave in different situations, for example 'social norms' dictate when we ought to shake hands or when we ought to kiss.
- **Culture** We share a common language, as well as common values and beliefs.

- **Aspirations** We have common goals – things that we want to achieve, as individuals and as part of a group.
- **Institutions** We belong to certain institutions, both formal ones such as the gym, church, or a sports club, and informal ones such as families.

To make things more complex, as individuals we play a number of different social roles all at the same time, for example 'wife/mother/lover/manager/employee/One Direction fan/local tennis champ'. We might also participate in a number of different social institutions that overlap – more than one sports club or a wider family network, for example. The accepted behaviour of these different groups may vary: you wouldn't necessarily sing bawdy rugby songs at your nan's golden wedding celebration (although your grandad might?).

Over the centuries, scholars have devoted enormous time and energy to trying to figure out what makes society tick. In medieval times, things were generally structured along religious lines as well as feudal – *ie* peasants and lord of the manor; Enlightenment thinkers applied rational scientific ideas. Today, society is seen as something of a 'shape shifter' – in a constant state of flux and not easily pinned down. Traditionally, societies had strong geographical identities – a country, a county, a town or a village – however, in the modern age geography is less important. Today it's not uncommon to have few ties to the neighbourhood in which we live. We might work on the other side of town or travel to the city centre for evening entertainment. We might identify strongly with a sporting club or an online virtual community we are part of, the MGB Owners'

THE RULES OF THE GAME

As all true fans will know, not all of the rules of football are official. Tempting though it might be to look the other way when one of our team's players secures a dodgy penalty by taking a dive, or by thumping a rival when the referee's not watching, we know that if all players were to behave in this way, the game would very quickly cease to be enjoyable as sport. Likewise, if a player is 'rubbish' because of a hangover or failure to train, he or she may not have broken any written rules, but the crowd will soon subject that player to some 'helpful words of advice'.

So sport comes with two sets of rules: the formal, written rules that have evolved over many years to improve the way in which the game functions; and the informal, unwritten rules of 'good sportsmanship'. Following the written rules isn't enough; a skilled player must also engage with the spirit of the game.

© Pinnacle Photography

The captains of Yeovil Town and Manchester United playing by the rules (January 2014).

Club, a synagogue we travel to in a different town or with other students who attend our university.

Naturally, once politicians and maverick economists get involved, the waters start to get a little muddied. Some aren't even prepared to admist to the existence of society. Others regard the 's' word as the work of the devil, impinging on the freedom of the individual. But more generally, it's accepted that our feelings of success as individuals, and our sense of freedom requires (at least the potential of) being able to interact with other people in society. If you don't believe this, consider Robinson Crusoe sitting in solitary confinement on his island. Or ask one of the richest men in the world, Warren Buffet, who observed:

'I personally think that society is responsible for a very significant percentage of what I've earned.'

Although we can't all be one of the richest men in the world, if we aspire to the Western dream of security, prosperity and peace, we need strong societies. But the benefits of society are not limited solely to material gains…

Motivating society: The social contract

When ancient seafarers discovered far-flung lands, with luck the indigenous people might have readily extend their hospitality to the hairy, unwashed nautical types staggering across their sands. But with zero knowledge of the native culture, it would be only too easy to make some dreadful faux pas – perhaps burping (or failing to burp) after a meal might inadvertently cause dire offence to the hosts, with potentially catastrophic consequences. Aliens landing on earth might face a similar dilemma, for the simple reason that it's not possible to play the game properly when you don't know the correct code of behaviour – the rules of society. This code has two sides – 'rights' and 'responsibilities' – what we expect of others and what others in return expect of us. In effect, there is a sort of contract between us and our fellows: a 'social contract'.

This is a debate that goes back a long way. Thomas Hobbes (who published *Leviathan* in 1651) had a pop at summarising the natural state of humanity. His view was that, without any form of governing power, life is a continual state of war – with every individual pitted against every other. A war of 'all against all'. The result of such unceasing and ruthless competition is that each person's life is 'solitary, poor, nasty, brutish and short'.

To rise above this warlike state there needs to be a trade-off between broader society and totally unfettered pursuit of individual goals (bankers please note).

John Rawls, in his 1971 book *A Theory of Justice*, argued that for a social contract to work, the basic principles need to be accepted as fair by people throughout society irrespective of their status, sex, age, religion and so on (Rawls has more to say on the topic of social justice – see Chapter 15.) Why is this important? Because when the social contract breaks down the results aren't pretty. Open up a newspaper on almost any day of the year and you will see the evidence of societal breakdown in one of the world's many trouble-spots in failed states.

MARY POPPINS VS J. CLARKSON

At heart, we are all libertarians: we love the idea of 'liberty' and 'freedom' – especially our own. The problem is everyone else!

Politicians tell us that too much regulation is inefficient and suffocating. Yet society insists we drive on the left-hand side of the road and limit our speed; it imposes driving rules, expects us to drive courteously and – worst of all – tax our vehicles. So why don't we rise up in revolt against all this oppressive state regulation? Because we instinctively see there's a 'social contract' at work here. If we can be assured that all other drivers will abide by the same rules that we're required to observe, ultimately we know it will work in our favour – we should enjoy a greater level of freedom than if everyone rejected the rules of Mary Poppin's 'nanny state'.

If everyone insisted on their right to drive however they wanted, wherever they wanted, and at whatever speed they wanted, the resulting mass pile-ups, casualties and violent disputes would mean *no one* would get very far. It follows that individual freedom may often best be promoted through the voluntarily limiting of our rights – on the condition that other members of society do the same.

Political visions

Most political leaders at some point get round to grandly pontificating about their 'vision' for society. Here we look briefly at what the three most radical prime ministers in recent British history have proposed.

No such thing as society?

In 1987, Margaret Thatcher gave one of her most famous and, arguably, least understood interviews, first asking 'Who is society?', then going on to declare: 'There is no such thing! There are individual men and women, and there are families.' On the face of it, Thatcher dismissed the long-established concept of society. However, the context in which she makes this statement is that of individuals 'casting their problems on society' and, by implication, abdicating their individual responsibility for themselves. She continued: 'The quality of our lives will depend upon how much each of us is prepared to take responsibility for ourselves and each of us prepared to turn round and help by our own efforts those who are unfortunate.'

Rather than a rejection of the existence of society, Thatcher was making the case for British citizens to take more responsibility for themselves and others less fortunate than themselves. More 'self help' and less reliance on the state for welfare. Thatcher suggests it is by the strength and vitality of this 'living tapestry' we might evaluate the effectiveness of our nation. However, it is by no means clear the economic policies adopted by her government strengthened this vital force of our nation; many argue that the adoption of naked free-market policies and the headlong pursuit of individualism contributed to an increase in inequality. Thatcher's economic policies probably did more to unravel than weave a living tapestry.

The Third Way

Since the French Revolution, politicians have commonly been caricatured as either 'left-wing' or 'right-wing' – the former focusing on people's responsibility to society and provision for the vulnerable, the latter more concerned with the freedom and rights of the individual. In the late 1990s, a path was proposed that might lie somewhere between the two: the so-called 'Third Way'. Supporters of the Third Way (for example US President Bill Clinton and British Prime Minister Tony Blair) believed in capitalism, but recognised that free markets tended to undermine social justice. They argued that the power of national government to manage the economy had been eroded by the power of global finance. The suggested solution was not to turn away from markets, but rather to shape and regulate them in such a way as to produce social justice as well as personal wealth – in effect, to harness the beast for the greater good.

The Third Way emphasised the role of communities in supporting individuals in need, but also argued that communities should hold those needy individuals to account. For left-wing politicians, a disadvantaged student's poor educational outcomes might be attributed to poverty or lack of funding; whereas right-wingers might emphasise that individual's poor choices. In contrast, the Third Way emphasised provision of high-quality education (with individual accountability by means of teacher performance targets) alongside insistence that parents support their children in school. Likewise, improvements in health were to be driven both by incentivising individuals to take greater care of themselves and by improved provision of hospital services (again, implemented by introducing targets).

Under the Third Way, employment was supposed to be the

'HOW CAN I TELL MY LEFT FROM MY RIGHT-ON ?'

major route out of poverty; hence policies such as the National Minimum Wage and Working Tax Credit were introduced to make work pay better. But this tended to marginalise people who made valuable contributions to society through unpaid work, such as by volunteering or by raising children.

While there is much to recommend in some of the Third Way policies, critics argue that it failed because it took no account of the moral dimension of society. Whereas policies based on classical economics promoted market forces as the most efficient way in which to create wealth, Third Way policies also presented market forces as the most efficient way in which to build society. In practice, the use of market incentives and sanctions to try to engineer social goals backfired. Financial targets imposed blindly from the top had the effect of undermining the 'invisible' human moral bonds that bind people together in society. They forgot that people matter. To function effectively, organisations rely on shared relationships, values and goals to motivate the staff who work there. At its worst, the obsession with meeting 'bottom line' targets was the root cause of tragedies such as the high mortality rates at Stafford Hospital in the late 2000s. In the end rather than being harnessed, the beast had the last laugh.

Big Society?

The Cameron government's 'Big Society' agenda was based on Thatcher's model of the 'living tapestry'. Realistically, however, it accepted that such a tapestry would neither weave itself, nor be magically woven by the invisible hand of market forces. At its heart, Big Society seeks to engage individuals with each other and with shared goals. Unlike the Third Way, Big Society also emphasises unpaid engagement with community projects. According to Cameron, it was all about 'giving people more power and control to improve their lives and communities' – but there was one thing lacking: money.

Those communities in which need is greatest are also those that lack the resources with which to meet those needs, but redistribution of funding was not a part of the Big Society agenda. Communities with ready access to resources (those that are 'doing all right, thank

' IT'S THE BEG SOCIETY '

K.J.Lamb

argues that: 'Public leadership is … about unlocking the capacity we all have to work collectively for the common good. … It's about relationships and reciprocity.' He suggests that a new relationship is required between public services and individuals. This 'relational state' approach recognises that relying on the market has not been a success, but it also accepts that we can't afford to return to previous levels of big spending on public services. Instead, Cruddas emphasises the importance of involving people from diverse backgrounds in policymaking and of seeking local solutions to local social problems. He suggests addressing social need by looking positively at what the vulnerable *can* do already, rather than at what they *can't* – which doesn't sound a million miles away from the ideology of both Big Society and Republica.

What everyone does seem to agree on is that localism is a big part of the solution – but talk is cheap: without clear direction and funding, this amounts to little more than hot air. Interestingly, however, in the light of the failure of the 'Third Way' politicians from all parties are beginning to realise markets cannot make society – rather the converse.

Social visions

However we like to frame it, we cannot deny that humans are gregarious, social animals. The fact is, we like to dwell in societies, rather than living as isolated hermits on the tops of mountains. Furthermore, the social contract is pivotal to the way in which we make choices as individuals. Psychologist Abraham Maslow famously

you very much') were consequently those most easily able to achieve more. So the Big Society agenda appears likely to widen the gaps, if anything making social and financial inequality worse.

Of course, few would dismiss the idea that we could all do more to look out for each other, but critics argue that Big Society has gone no further than many long-established charities and volunteering organisations have done for years, other than to re-badge their efforts as though they originated in government. Without sufficient resources, and with prolonged austerity, Big Society has struggled to fill the big shoes left by spending cuts to community services.

Contemporary visions

In this rapidly changing global age, traditional divisions between left- and right-wing politics are breaking down. One school of thought that attempts to make sense of the conflicts between localism and globalisation (see Chapters 2 and 16) originates with Phillip Blond, head of right-of-centre think tank Republica. In his 2010 book *Red Tory*, he rejects both a large welfare state *and* overreliance on markets to solve social problems, viewing the motives of big multinational corporations with suspicion and questioning the legacy of Thatcher. Instead, Blond emphasises traditional values and institutions – including the nuclear family, localism, the devolution of power from central government to local communities, small businesses and volunteering – as the mechanisms with which we might tackle social injustice.

There is also fresh thinking on the left of centre, moving beyond the traditional welfarist view of the relationship between the state and individuals in need. Labour MP John Cruddas

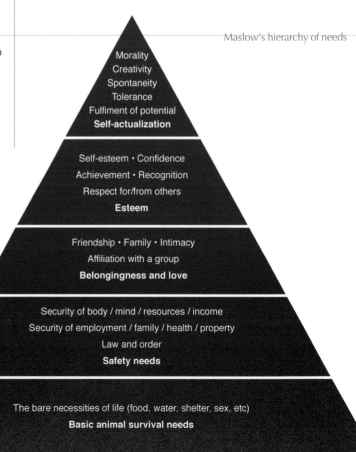

Maslow's hierarchy of needs

Morality
Creativity
Spontaneity
Tolerance
Fulfilment of potential
Self-actualization

Self-esteem • Confidence
Achievement • Recognition
Respect for/from others
Esteem

Friendship • Family • Intimacy
Affiliation with a group
Belongingness and love

Security of body / mind / resources / income
Security of employment / family / health / property
Law and order
Safety needs

The bare necessities of life (food, water, shelter, sex, etc)
Basic animal survival needs

recognised that there is considerably more to human behaviour than meeting material needs. Maslow's famous pyramid – the fascinating 'hierarchy of needs' – shows that once we achieve each level in life, we're motivated to climb to the next, seeking fulfilment of higher social needs. For example, once we've ticked off the basics like food, water and shelter we move up the pyramid, seeking deeper rewards, like friendship, jobs that are more gratifying, recognition, and self-fulfilment. So the better-off you are financially, the more motivated you tend to be by higher level stuff – like self-esteem and achievement, rather than supertanker-loads of cash (although enormous bonus payouts can be symbolic of recognition).

As we climb the pyramid, the path takes us beyond satisfying basic bodily needs, through mental stimulation and satisfaction, and ultimately into the realm of the 'higher self'.

Interestingly, some people find that they can fulfil their higher needs by reaching down to help those struggling to meet basic needs on the bottom rung, such as rough sleepers and refugees. Despite Richard Dawkins' assertions otherwise, this undoubtedly has some bearing on the way in which religion works in practice.

Nature's reward scheme

Scientists working with brain scan 'neuro-imaging' have demonstrated that we get a 'pay off' sensation in our brains when we make decisions resulting in monetary gain – part of our grey matter glows excitedly. And the more we earn, the brighter it glows (which perhaps explains the appeal of playing Monopoly). What's really interesting is that exactly the same (reward-processing) part of the brain is activated when we contemplate cooperative and altruistic actions – that is, doing good stuff makes us glow. We are, in effect, 'hard wired' to work together – to team up with others and abide by social norms. Rather more darkly, the same part of the brain is activated when we contemplate the punishment of those who've refused to cooperate, or taking revenge on those who've violated our rules and regulations (which makes sense from a 'survival of the tribe' perspective as pack animals – or indeed in sports where players need to work together to win by scoring, which is obviously likely to happen if fellow team members are fooling around).

Of course, we don't all sit down on our 18th birthdays and sign up to the social contract. Most of us learn about social norms in the same way as we learn to speak English: by observing how our parents and

people around us behave (perhaps including TV characters). Also we interact with our friends and fellows, all the while learning how to communicate and how relationships with other people work. If we grow up hearing French, we learn to speak French; if observing politeness, we learn to be polite; if we grow up observing littering or greed, we learn to litter, be greedy and so on. Our social norms and our mother tongue comprise a 'social language'; together they allow us to communicate and interact with each other. Although individuals have different accents and different outlooks on life, we have enough in common to communicate. In practice, a certain amount of difference in people's customs and dialects (so long as it does not amount to a completely different language) adds to the variety we enjoy in this country.

There are, however, some who might not learn the social language as children – perhaps because of deprivation or growing up in a different country – and thus may require instruction as adults if they are to interact constructively. Once immersed in a culture or society, however, most of us will pick up what's required of us, a bit like the way we learnt to speak, without a hard-and-fast set of rules – we simply *know* what seems 'right'.

Who do you think you are?

You might regard yourself as a pretty solid person – steadfast and not easily swayed. But research has demonstrated that, as we go through life, we modify the way that we behave. We unconsciously adapt to the standards of those whom we see around us and with whom we spend the most time, changing our outlook on life – and even the way we speak. As motivational speaker Jim Rohn once put it: 'We are the average of the five people we spend the most time with.'

For this reason, then, we should be concerned if politicians and business leaders appear to be 'out of touch' with the average person. Because they live in a bubble remote from ordinary people, the political class and the super-rich rarely share our concerns and values. Conversely, on the rare occasions when political and business leaders come up with solutions that appear to genuinely address our concerns, we feel they are 'speaking our language'.

It is not only the 'powers-that-be' who should take care not to lose touch. We all need to keep our feet on the ground because society, as well as sustaining the worth of our life, also provides the launchpad that allows us to achieve lift-off – the opportunity to satisfy our higher needs on Maslow's hierarchy. Although our nation is (generally) at ease with diversity, we should take care we do not become so diverse that we start to diverge. It is all too easy, as we see from the trouble spots of the world, for the natural human tendency to associate with those with whom we have most in common to lead to segregation; for segregation to lead to distrust; and distrust to lead to a dysfunctional society, breakdown and war.

So while few would think there's anything wrong with fellow citizens speaking a variety of languages, that is to say, people might be multilingual, there also needs to be a shared language which allows us to communicate. No 'living tapestry', no wholesome and sustainable society, can be woven without effective communication.

'I'M OK WITH THE SWEARING – BUT WHAT'S ALLEGIANCE?'

Chapter 13

THE TIES THAT BIND

The same mental programme inside our heads which influences our behaviour as part of the society of people in which we live, may also generate our desire to feel national loyalty and pride.

The 2014 Scottish independence referendum clearly showed that a nation is more than a group of individuals seeking their own selfish ends within a free market. Irrespective of whether people voted 'yes' or 'no', the issue of national identity – patriotism – was real and important. National allegiance is a very real sentiment. For those living in other parts of the UK, the prospect of the break-up of the union – the demise of Great Britain – also brought the subject of patriotism into focus.

Similarly, the success of the 2014 Commonwealth Games in Glasgow – and before that, the Olympics in London in 2012 – was built largely on the generosity and goodwill of the residents of those cities, who gave their time freely for no (monetary) reward – 'Big Society' without the politicians. This goodwill was given, at least in part, to demonstrate pride in those cities and the nation.

Pride and patriotism

'Patriotism' refers to a feeling of love for our country – of identification with and attachment to our nation, culture and fellow Brits. Their successes, somehow, become our successes, and we feel that our triumphs should be shared. Patriotism generally goes hand in glove with a sense of pride in our native land, and warm feelings of national loyalty. A spot of vigorous flag waving is often the simplest way to convey the patriotic urge. But although sometimes we find it hard to express, there's no doubt that it's a powerful sentiment. Patriotism can motivate us to build and sustain a better society, not just for our own personal good but to benefit us all: a country that's worthy of admiration. We might experience similar feelings towards our favourite football team, or a legendary guitar hero with whom we identify: when they win, we win – and that motivates us to share and cooperate, which appeals to our higher needs on Maslow's hierarchy (see Chapter 12). It simply *feels good*.

Drilling a little deeper, patriotic feelings don't arise simply because we're comfortable in Britain, or because we're better off here than we might be in another nation. If we attempt to attribute patriotism to a desire to increase our wealth, it ceases to be patriotism. We can no more ascribe love of our country to material reward than we can ascribe love of our family, neighbourliness or friendship to the fact they happen to ply us with irresistible chocolates every time we visit. It's a much deeper, more soulful sentiment than mere personal gain.

There is, however, a potential downside. Since the onset of the Global Financial Crisis in 2007–8, we have seen the rise of extremist and nationalistic political parties across Europe. Many of these cite patriotism as a means to gain political support, rather than a means of building a better society. There is a fine line between patriotism, jingoism and nationalism. A justifiable, shared pride in your country can potentially ratchet up into self-righteous intolerance and tribal aggression.

It's important to distinguish the legitimate pride we take in the achievements of our society from the denigration of other nations or peoples. It's perfectly possible for a UK citizen to hold that they would prefer to live in no other nation, while also recognising that citizens of other countries feel the same about where they live. A generous and inclusive patriotism – one that motivates us to maintain the society from which we all benefit – is a virtue; a mean-spirited and exclusive nationalism, seeking to create divisions between peoples, is a vice.

In Britain we have a lot to be proud of: the beauty of the countryside, our reputation as 'good sports' and for fair play, our tolerance, our general honesty and integrity as a nation, the NHS, the quality of our arts and literature, including the BBC. Britain, according to the film *Love Actually*, is: 'the country of Shakespeare, Churchill, the Beatles, Sean Connery, Harry Potter, David Beckham's right foot' (which dates it a bit!). We all have our favourites, worth celebrating, and worth preserving.

Amongst our other generous national traits is a healthy scepticism of patriotism itself. However, we should not be so afraid of the vice of nationalism that we turn away from the virtue of patriotism. Neither should we confuse a healthy scepticism with a negative cynicism.

The people of Britain, by and large, have a proud record of welcoming those born in different parts of the world to our shores. Although not perfect, compared with many other countries we can pat ourselves on the back for doing a decent job of kicking out racism, or at least tolerating differences. It probably helps that Britain has long been an outward-looking nation with strong trade and cultural links spanning the globe. But with the hot potato of immigration presently riding high on the political agenda (see page 150), it's worth taking a closer look.

The diversity debate

The most commonly cited touch paper for heated discussion is growing pressure on jobs, housing and health services, etc. But there's also passionate debate about the extent of 'multiculturalism' in Britain, and this is a subject that requires a thoughtful response rather than a kneejerk reaction (a sharp intake of breath or a hiss of 'Racist!'). At the heart of this issue lies a concern about social cohesion: that the introduction of too many varying cultures into British society may have diluted it to the point of disintegration. And when society disintegrates, that way violence lies.

Such concerns might sometimes confuse 'race' and 'culture', with some arguing that while we cannot choose our parentage or race, cultural orientation is largely a matter of choice. It may therefore be cultural differences, rather than ethnic differences that lie behind some of the worries about social cohesion. This raises the difficult question as to what extent a nation should absorb and celebrate cultural differences. National cultures need to evolve and adapt over time, but they also need to retain a core shared national identity - 'who we are'.

Celebrating diversity might involve embracing new foods, fashions, dance, music and traditions – which enrich our national identity. Consider, as an example, London's Notting Hill Carnival, which is now a vibrant part of the London scene.

One thing that can muddy the waters in this debate is the tendency to interpret the behaviour of a few extremists as representative of a culture as a whole. But we all know that at some point there are customs which cannot be accepted. For example, it has been suggested that an inability to distinguish between crimes and cultural traditions has led authorities to fail vulnerable young women and girls at risk of sexual exploitation. And few can be comfortable with our failure to prevent the radicalisation of some young British Muslims, furnishing 'IS' with many willing recruits. Yet there is nothing new in the phenomenon of young adults without much of a stake in society being seduced by the notion of doing something 'exciting and meaningful', enhanced by the lure of guns and violence.

WHEN IN ROME

In Barbados, it is considered rather poor form for men to wander around topless, unless on the beach. While the typical British male might think nothing of pulling off his shirt at the merest glimmer of sun, deliberately flouting Bajan sensibilities simply because it's OK at home would be disrespectful. Similarly, in Thailand, it's extremely impolite to show the soles of one's feet . As they say: 'When in Rome, do as the Romans do.'

In some ways, willingness to integrate is a basic courtesy to the host nation. But there's a 'critical mass' factor at work here: a few new arrivals will generally be eager to learn local ways and to speak the host language, of necessity; but when new arrivals settle in large, established, non-integrated communities – retired British ex-pats soaking up the Costa Brava sun, for example – the need tends to be less pressing. And

if the host nation has little sense of pride in its own unique identity (other than perhaps, in the UK's case, recognising its notoriety for binge drinking), then integration may not be such an appealing prospect.

A call for clarity

Let's look at some examples of instances in which multiculturalism has raised difficult questions for politicians and for society.

- BBC Radio 4 recently ran a story on the difficulties experienced by Ravi Bopara, the British-born England and Essex cricketer. Large numbers of cricket fans whose parents are similarly of Indian origin attend England–India matches at which – although UK citizens, born and raised in Britain – they fervently support India against their home nation. In Bopara's case, abuse is hurled vehemently – accusations that he's a traitor because 'he looks Indian' – leading the BBC to conclude that the famous 'Tebbit test' (the politician who called in 1990 for 'new Britons' to support the England team) seems to have fallen on deaf ears. Yet there are echoes here of traditional home nation rivalries within the UK, such as at Scotland-England matches.
- *The Telegraph* recently reported a speech by former Archbishop of Canterbury, George Carey, in which he asserted that Britain has a particular moral responsibility to confront what he called 'cultural indifference'. Said Carey:

'For too long the doctrine of multiculturalism has led to immigrants establishing completely separate communities in our cities. This has led to honour killings, female genital circumcision and the establishment of Sharia law in inner-city pockets throughout the UK. By embracing multiculturalism and the idea that every culture and belief is of equal value we have betrayed our own traditions.'

There will be differing opinions on these issues. What is clear is that we can't afford to assume that a shared culture will somehow spontaneously evolve. Nations such as the United States and France tend to be more assertive than Britain in proclaiming their pride in a shared nationality and cultural history. And while the Scots, Welsh and Irish are passionate about their distinct national identities and heritage, the English authorities are less keen. 'English reserve' seemingly makes them embarrassed to broach the subject for fear of causing offence – being more inclined to celebrate other cultures, or perhaps, to dismiss all cultures as being equally irrelevant.

So when politicians call for us to promote our 'Britishness', many of us are left scratching our heads wondering quite what that might be - other than displaying tolerance of other cultures. So it's all the more important to guard against this tolerance being exploited, leaving the field clear for bigotry and toxic interpretations of theology to take root, spawning angry, undemocratic ideologies. How for example should we respond to a substantial subculture that demands to splinter away entirely from the mainstream, imposing its own laws and values?

We might ask teachers to promote pride in 'British Values' in classroom citizenship lessons, but we need first to consider what those values are (see pages 8 and 140). Greater clarity in the face of muddle-headedness about multiculturalism might at least help sooth the current climate of rising nationalism. As a nation, and as an inclusive society, we need to be far clearer about where we stand on cultural matters. If we fail to do so, we can expect increasingly fractured and alienated communities.

British values

What do you think of as 'Britishness'? Spitfires and Lancasters, green fields and hedges, rain clouds in summer, Victorian terraces, thatched cottages, E-type Jags, Sherlock Holmes, Buckingham Palace, chip butties and chicken vindaloo – there are thousands of images that might spring to mind, along with more specific, perhaps sometimes clichéd, symbols of our home nations – from kilts, cabers and haggis, burns and lochs, to daffodils and male voice choirs; from Celtic and Rangers to TT Races and Orange marches. But what are the *values* behind the symbols?

Like the language, we learn 'British values' by observing those around us throughout our lives and by drawing conclusions from the tales told to us as children. So there are different interpretations of British values. We can't distil a definitive list of what *all* British people hold dear and, in fact, if we try to do so, we're undermining one of those very values – accommodating diversity (although there is a diversity of opinions on whether we should be so diverse!). However, since we are unwilling to accept defeat (a Churchillian

'bulldog' quality) here are ten concepts of 'Britishness' (plus one for luck).

- **The rule of law**: Even a cursory glance around our society indicates we are not all equal in practice – some of us are stronger than others, some have considerably more wealth and power. Yet, in the eyes of the law we are all held to be equal, from Joe Public up to top political and business leaders, and even the head of state. We must all abide by the same set of rules and regulations. Being equal in the eyes of the law is a central pillar of Britishness (but is meaningless if different people face different legal codes).

- **Tolerance**: It's an annoying fact of life that other people sometimes have differing opinions from ourselves (but then we can't all be right). But all parties must tolerate the right of others to hold differing points of view. This is not to say we must all hold the same opinions or like another's point of view – if it did, there would be no need for tolerance. Tolerance means the capacity to accept something we do not like. The only thing of which we should be intolerant is injustice (see point 1). Prime Minister Blair once famously warned: 'Our tolerance is part of what makes Britain, Britain. So conform to it; or don't come here' (it seems the one thing that we won't tolerate is intolerance).

- **Freedom of opinion and speech**: So long as a person is not directly inciting a crime, we ought to have the right to express our point of view publicly. We also require a range of media by which these views might be expressed. Media should be unconstrained by establishment interests and should be capable of expressing our national culture.

- **Individual liberty**: In general, so long as we do not transgress the law, we require our freedom and liberty be maintained against those who would bully us – be they of corporate origin, state sponsored, or friends of the mother-in-law (although times of national emergency may require short-term measures limiting individual freedoms).

- **Democracy**: Parliament is a precious control on power – deriving from the struggles of the people of this island over the course of 800 years. This is not to say that it might not further evolve to better reflect our desires and wishes. Ultimately, the authority of Parliament stems from the people who assent to be governed in this way by their elected representatives (MPs).

- **The monarchy**: Not everyone is a fan, but the monarchy is about as British as dunking tea biscuits, providing a continuity of rule that many nations lack. A weekly meeting of the prime minister of the day with a head of state whose position rather requires her to take a long-term view provides a useful counterbalance to fashionable political ideology. In Britain, the monarch (head of state) comes under the law, the same as the rest of us. Hope she's remembered to pay the TV licence.

- **Social justice and decency**: It's a very British thing to demand 'fair play' (see 'Good sportsmanship' opposite) in society at large – and to bristle when we believe that the rules are being broken. Our recognition of what is fair and our national distaste for injustice has been scientifically proven to exist. Especially when we win.

- **Private property**: It's long been said that 'an Englishman's home is his castle'. The right to own property, to save and invest, to buy, sell and trade, are meat and drink to British people. No one can accuse Britain of being a communist nation.

- **National treasures**: Different things matter to different

Table 13.1 Top 25 UK religions

		Adherents	% of pop
1	CHRISTIANITY	33 200 000	59.3%
2	None	14 100 000	25.1%
3	ISLAM	2 700 000	4.8%
4	HINDUISM	817 000	1.5%
5	SIKHISM	423 000	0.8%
6	JUDAISM	263 000	0.5%
7	BUDDHISM	248 000	0.4%
8	Jedi Knights	176 632	
9	Paganism	57 000	
10	Spiritualism	39 000	
11	Agnosticism	32 382	
12	Jain	20 000	
13	Humanism	15 067	
14	Wicca	11 766	
15	Ravidassia	11 058	
16	Rastafarian	7 906	
17	Heavy Metal	6 242	
18	Bahá'í Faith	5 021	
19	Druidism	4 189	
20	Taoism	4 144	
21	Zoroastrianism	4 105	
22	Scientology	2 418	
23	Pantheism	2 216	
24	Heathenism	1 958	
25	Satanism	1 893	
	2011 Census		

'Heavy metal' is the religion of some 6,242 Brits – more than three times the number of self-confessed Satanists!

people, but many citizens value British institutions such as the NHS, armed forces, the Church, the BBC, Dr Who, free museums, the bobby on-the-beat, red Royal Mail post boxes (there was deep dismay at the loss of our red phone boxes) and of course our beautiful natural habitat – Britain's green and pleasant land (while demanding development to house an ever-growing population). The list could go on. In recent years, however our trust in some of these institutions has been much shaken as they have failed to live up to their high ideals and our expectations.

- **History and culture**: British history is filled with tales of glory, but while we have a great deal to be proud of, there are also moments of reputational stain and shame (which of course is true of all nations). If we fail to understand our past, to build on our triumphs and to address our weaknesses, we will fail to progress. We should bear in mind, 'those who cannot remember the past are condemned to repeat it', falling at the same hurdles. Certainly, a lot of political-economists have apparently forgotten the lessons of the Great Depression of the 1930s.

- **Love of sport and good sportsmanship**: Most of the major sports played around the world originated or were codified in this country. While others fumbled with the ball, we marked out the pitch and the goal posts – and then urged participation, declaring 'It's the taking part that counts' – it's just a shame that we sometimes struggle to win (which might explain why the British love an underdog).

We might add to this list the famed dry British sense of humour – our affection for the subtleties of irony often lost on other nations – not forgetting our interesting range of cuisine. Plus of course the joy of supping a pint or two down the pub and our reputation as a nation of animal lovers. Fortunately there's no shortage of things in which we take pride – things that might draw us together in our vision for our nation and society.

QUIRKY AND PROUD OF IT

Bill Bryson's affection for our 'small island' is infectious:

Suddenly, I realized what it was that I loved about Britain – which is to say, all of it. Every last bit of it, good and bad – Marmite, village fetes, country lanes, people saying 'mustn't grumble' and 'I'm terribly sorry but', people apologizing to me when I conk them with a nameless elbow, milk in bottles, beans on toast, haymaking in June, stinging nettles, seaside piers, Ordnance Survey maps, crumpets, hot-water bottles as a necessity, drizzly Sundays – every bit of it.

What a wondrous place this was – crazy as fuck, of course, but adorable to the tiniest degree. What other country, after all, could possibly have come up with place names like Tooting Bec and Farleigh Wallop, or a game like cricket that goes on for three days and never seems to start? Who else would think it not the least odd to make their judges wear little mops on their heads, compel the Speaker of the House of Commons to sit on something called the Woolsack, or take pride in a military hero whose dying wish was to be kissed by a fellow named Hardy? What other nation in the world could possibly have given us William Shakespeare, pork pies, Christopher Wren, Windsor Great Park, the Open University, Gardeners' Question Time and the chocolate digestive biscuit? None, of course.

Tensions within society

Self-interest

In the 1987 film *Wall Street*, main character Gordon Gecko seemed to capture the 1980s zeitgeist (and, for many, the 21st-century zeitgeist) when he declared that 'greed is good': 'Greed is right, greed works. Greed, in all of its forms; for life, for money, for love, knowledge has marked the upward surge of mankind.' What is clear, however, is that the greed of the powerful isn't good for the rest of us.

Greed certainly turned out to be extremely rewarding for the casino bankers whose recklessness contributed to the 2008–9 global financial crisis. And yet as the *Daily Mail* recently observed: 'It remains extraordinary that no individual banker in this country has received any meaningful punishment for the near collapse of the entire financial system with all the hardship that has inflicted on taxpayers, companies and innocent individuals.'

We may not agree that greed is good, but to work efficiently society does require some pretty large helpings of 'self-interest' (some would say that's all it needs). The great Enlightenment thinker Adam Smith (you can see his likeness on the Bank of England £20 note) is often credited with arguing in favour of rational self-interest as a sufficient motivator of society. However, Smith would certainly have disagreed with Gecko that the *unrestrained* pursuit of self-interest is what is required. On the contrary, he argued in his masterpiece *The Theory of Moral Sentiments* there are three virtues that, in a decent society, we should all act in accordance with:

- **Prudence** This is the best known part of Smith's work. Prudence means 'care for our own person' – *ie* self-interest and having

the foresight to provide for our future. This underpins the widely held belief in the power of markets and competition. It should be noted, however, that prudence is by no means the same as greed.

- **Justice** The virtue of justice requires that we do no harm to others whilst pursuing our own ends. In practice, justice is the basis of the law of the land (hence the 'judiciary'). Importantly, however, for Smith the virtue goes beyond simply obeying the law; it also requires that we behave justly even if we don't think that there's a risk that we'll be caught.
- **Benevolence** This is about kindness. In contrast to justice (which simply requires we do no harm), here we are actually required to do good – things that positively benefit other people. For example, we might donate to charity or register as an organ donor.

Smith argued that no nation could exist without justice as its central pillar. On its own, however, justice is not enough for a truly healthy society. Consider friendship: we might offer friendship to another

when it's in our self-interest to do so and justice would require that we don't steal from that friend. But a strong and deep friendship will result only amongst people who are prepared, on occasion, to put the good of the friendship ahead of their own self-interest. A genuine friendship, in other words, is based on mutual kindness (beneficence) – and the same should be true of society in general.

All of the truly valuable things about our society – politeness, courtesy, respect for others (the very best of British values) – arise from beneficence. But while it's certainly possible to draft laws that demand justice, we can't easily legislate to require people to behave kindly towards one another – and that makes the quality of kindness all the more valuable.

So of Smith's three virtues, the first can be left to self-interest, the second to legislation and the criminal justice system, and the last one (which he regards as 'productive of the greatest good') is up to the individual. Based on a full reading of Smith's work, it's clear that a policy agenda greatly emphasising self-interest over the virtues of social justice, personal beneficence and social responsibility will inflict great damage on the fabric and sustainability of Britain.

The 'classless society'?

Those of a certain age may recall *Citizen Smith*, a 1970s TV comedy centring on 'Wolfie', self-styled class warrior, urban guerrilla and leader of the Tooting Popular Front, doing battle against the state oppressors. But does class still exist today?

For much of modern history, any debate about society, politics, or economics has revolved around the concept of class. In the late Victorian era, Karl Marx's enormously influential theory of society depicted a 'class struggle' between the bourgeoisie (who own the means of production – that is, capitalists) and the proletariat (the wage earners). But by the late 20th century, 'class' seemed to have gone out of fashion.

This was due to a number of things, including the market-based emphasis on individual ambition and the rise of consumerism. Also economic transformations in recent decades led to a reduction in traditional, manual occupations and the rise of the service economy. Many people working in the service sector today might experience economic hardship and be on the rough end of the inequality divide, but they are arguably more likely to see this in terms of their personal situation rather than a class issue. Current debates tend to focus instead on inequality.

However, the early years of the 21st century have seen a renewed interest in class – but the way it's defined is changing. It's no longer simply about your work, or what your father did for a living, and differences of economic opportunity. Now cultural factors – personal tastes and refinement – are also being taken into account.

WHAT CLASS ARE YOU?

In 2003, the BBC's '*Great British Class Survey*' looked beyond the traditional 'upper, middle and working' classes. As well as taking into account the job you do, the survey also looked at:

- **economic capital** – income, and the value of your home and savings;
- **cultural capital** – cultural interests and activities; and
- **social capital** – the number of people whom you know and their own status.

The BBC survey divided Britons into seven distinct classes:

- **Elite (6%)** This is the most privileged class, with high scores in all three of the 'capitals'. Deep pockets, with high amounts of economic capital, set the elite apart from everyone else. Members of this class live predominantly in London and south-east England, and have an average age of 57.
- **Established middle class (25%)** Members of this class have high levels of all three capitals, although levels aren't as high as those of the elite. They enjoy socialising and are a culturally engaged bunch, with an average age of 46.
- **Technical middle class (6%)** This is a small class with plenty of money (high economic capital). They have relatively few social contacts and so are less socially engaged. Like the elite, they predominantly live in south-east England. Their average age is 52.
- **New affluent workers (15%)** This class has medium levels of economic capital and higher levels of cultural and social capital. They are a young(ish) and socially active group, with an average age of 44.
- **Traditional working class (14%)** This class has low scores on all forms of capital, although it's not the poorest group. Members are, on average, older than members of the other groups, at 66.
- **Emergent service workers (19%)** This new class has low economic capital, but high levels of cultural and social capital. Members are quite young (34 on average) and live predominantly in urban areas.

- **Precariat (15%)** This is the most deprived class of all, with low levels of economic, cultural and social capital. The everyday lives of members of this class are precarious: they have little predictability or security. They experience insecure employment, combined with low wages and little access to the means by which they might move to a more secure lifestyle. Their average age is 50.

This fascinating piece of research (by Mike Savage and Fiona Devine) showed that the old stereotypes are out of date. Only 39% fitted into the 'established middle class' and 'traditional working class' categories. Younger generations are more likely to be 'emergent service workers' or the 'precariat'.

THE DEATH OF THE MIDDLE CLASS

So it would seem that class divides are not entirely consigned to history, as some might have hoped. As wages continue to decline and employment becomes more 'flexible', membership of the middle classes is becoming increasingly precarious – at least in terms of economic standing. Incredibly, there are genuine concerns that the middle classes might largely die out in the UK over the next few decades. Without being unduly alarmist, this is already happening in the United States, where commentators have decried their virtual disappearance.

When Britain was promised a 'classless society' in the 1990s, we imagined that it would be one in which affluence would be shared; instead, it seems that many of us will be sinking into the depths of debt, and sharing a future of insecurity and stress. Come back Wolfie, all is forgiven!

Localism and regionalism

In the wake of the Scottish independence referendum, it looks likely that all regions of the UK will benefit from greater independence from Westminster. But this isn't entirely thanks to Alex Salmond and the Scottish National Party (SNP). Even before the referendum, there had been a groundswell of support calling for a reversal of the centuries-long tradition of centralising political power in London.

According to the English Devolution Poll carried out by Survation in 2014:

■ 64% of the English people surveyed agreed that 'Too much of England is run from London' (even the majority of Londoners agreeing with this statement); and
■ 69% agreed with the statement 'London receives preferential treatment over the rest of the UK' (again, even in London, the majority agreed).

While the public doesn't generally support England having the relatively extensive levels of devolved power that Scotland and Wales currently enjoy, there is support for economic powers being delivered at a local or regional level – especially decision-making on local transport.

In considering the newfound English appetite for devolution and greater local power, we should bear in mind that proposals for regional assemblies were rejected when put to referendum in the north-east

in 2004. Likewise, local elections for police and crime commissioners have never managed to capture the public imagination sufficiently to motivate most people even to vote. Moreover, recent Ipsos-MORI polls suggest that people in England believe there to be far more pressing matters for government to sort out, with only 7% of the public considering regionalism/localism to be a matter of major concern.

Devolved government: National Assembly for Wales, Cardiff

LONDON: A WORLD CITY (WITH AN ATTACHED COUNTRY)

In the debate over devolution, the question of whether the rest of Britain benefits from London (and whether London benefits from Britain) is often raised. The well-known north–south divide is nothing compared to the divide between those who argue over whether London supports or exhausts the rest of Britain.

It's understandable that Londoners themselves assume that 'what's good for London is good for the UK', as business lobby group London First puts it. But others are concerned that putting London first means draining the life out of the rest of the country, which is relegated to an afterthought.

Both perspectives have their merits. London does indeed have the greatest concentration of affluence and productivity – but the great regional cities of England (Birmingham, Bristol, Leeds, Liverpool, Manchester, Newcastle, Nottingham and Sheffield) host half of England's leading research universities, are home to almost a third of its population and support around a third of its highly skilled workers. Collectively, these eight cities generate more than a quarter of England's economic output – a greater contribution to national income than London – yet receive considerably less funding for arts and infrastructure.

While it appears that, per capita (head of the population), London is a net contributor to the national tax pot (*ie* puts more in than it takes out), London does an awful lot better than average when it comes to central government forking out money. Compared to the rest of the country, nearly twice as much is spent in the capital per person on things such as transport, skills, and research and development. Taking transport specifically, the contrast is particularly striking: up to 15 times more per person is spent in London and the south-east than is spent in the north.

In other developed countries across the world, larger cities consistently outperform the national economy; this is not generally the case in England. In Germany, for example, all eight of the largest cities outside Berlin outperform the national average; in England, outside of London, only Bristol occasionally does so. Some argue that localism will allow us to do better sharing out the national income.

WHO PULLS LOCAL GOVERNMENT'S STRINGS?

Did you know that local councils are almost entirely funded by Westminster (see Chapter 8)? In return for providing the money, government requires councils to spend most of their budgets on centrally set targets, rather than in accordance with local priorities.

Of course, social problems differ massively from one part of the country to another. The south-east, for example, struggles with affordable housing; the north-east struggles with unemployment. So setting targets centrally is more of a widely scattered shotgun blast than a precise sniper shot. If the Bank of England raises interest rates,

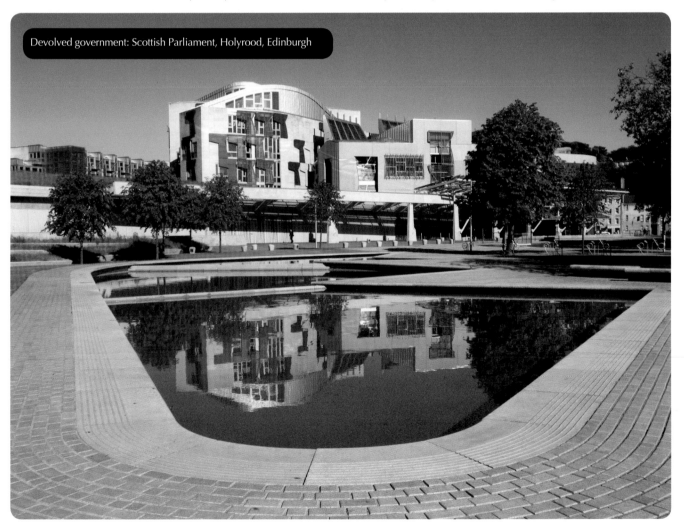

Devolved government: Scottish Parliament, Holyrood, Edinburgh

Devolved government: Northern Ireland Parliament, Stormont, Belfast.

HOT TOPIC: IMMIGRATION

From ancient times, the British Isles have witnessed new arrivals from far and wide, not least Roman, Viking, Saxon and Norman invaders. In the last millennium, however, the population has been relatively stable in terms of its ethnic mix. In the period from the Norman Conquest (1066) to the 1940s, migrant flows were limited, amounting to only an estimated 1% of the population – usually becoming assimilated over time. Towards the end of the period, the UK was generally a net exporter of migrants to Australia, North America and other (former) colonies.

Following the Second World War, in the hope of attracting cheaper labour to the UK, the British Nationality Act 1948 gave all subjects of the British Empire (as was) the right to live and work in Britain. Over the following decade, however, it became abundantly clear that the UK quite simply did not have the room for all those who would like to immigrate, and the pressures resulting from population growth led politicians to rethink. The first major change to policy was the Commonwealth Immigrants Act 1962, which limited numbers. This was superseded by the Immigration Act 1971, when it was assumed that the first wave of immigration had been curtailed. The British Nationality Act 1981 was a further development.

More recently, after EU enlargement and during a period of relaxed migration rules under the Blair government, net migration (those entering the country less those leaving the country) totalled some 1.5 million in the decade ending 2008. According to one former Blair adviser, there was a policy to 'open up the UK to mass migration' to engineer a 'truly multicultural' country – and to 'rub the Right's nose in diversity'. Others have blamed high levels of migration simply on an absence of policy.

The upside

There are many benefits to migration flows. If we assume that a successful economy is a growing economy (an assumption that's by no means universally accepted), migration is required to offset a declining birth rate and increasing life expectancy.

However, as the supply of labour increases, real wages are likely to stagnate or decline in those sectors in which migrants compete; therefore poorly skilled workers are most likely to lose out. The effect on the economy as a whole is not easy to determine as lower wages benefit businesses and employers in terms of their reduced costs. Further, where there are specific skills shortages, it is less expensive and much faster to attract migrant workers, for example medical professionals, than it is to boost training. This adds to the flexibility of the local economy. It might be, of course, that developing nations need their skilled professionals more than does the UK, even if they cannot match the salaries on offer here. However that is, arguably, not our problem.

Current estimates indicate that it costs around £85,000 to educate a child to working age in the UK; the net migration of 228,000 already educated people into Britain in 2013–14 therefore implies that the rest of the world is subsidising the UK to the tune of many billions of pounds. This adds to the flexibility of the local economy and it's therefore possible that migration may boost economic growth in aggregate – it saves us part of the cost of educating our workforce (although workers who find themselves displaced from jobs as a result may have to resort to state support, potentially reducing the overall gains).

Although it's not easy to measure economically, it's also reasonable to assume that many British people feel socially enriched by the cultural and ethnic diversity that migration brings. We celebrate the contribution to culture and sport that the likes of Freddie Mercury (born in Zanzibar), George Michael (born in Greece), Eddie Izzard (born in Yemen) and Mo Farah (born in Somalia) have made, and part of London's appeal as a 'global city' is its ethnic and cultural diversity.

for example, it might ease house prices in one region, but would be likely to exacerbate unemployment in others.

Because so much control lies in the hands of Westminster rather than with authorities close to the people they serve, the provision of local public services is unwieldy. But simply devolving all public service provision to the local level isn't always the best solution. So the question is, which services can be more effectively coordinated and delivered at local level, and which services at the national level?

However this trade-off is resolved, a brisk wave of the devolution wand ('Reparo!') won't instantly provide a magic solution to Britain's rapidly fraying society. The Welsh Assembly, for example, was established in 1998 and has a fair degree of control over the local budget, yet Wales remains the poorest among the home nations. If a balanced prosperity is to be restored to Britain, the size of the budget matters too. Simply having local control of an inadequate budget does not, by some miracle of accounting, increase the amount of resources available. Empowerment to decide locally where spending cuts fall might cushion the blow, and lessen their impact – but they're still cuts.

LOCAL TAXES

It can make a lot of sense to boost local responsibility for the gathering and spending of tax. But such freedom needs to come with an attached health warning: we must not facilitate a 'race to the bottom', with each region seeking to out-do others, luring business investment with ever-lower tax rates – ultimately, to the detriment of all.

Alarm bells should also ring when it comes to deciding where to spend both local and national tax revenues, so people living in the regions don't get cheated. For example, London is a 'net importer' of young educated people and a 'net exporter' of older people. So it would be socially unjust if the UK's regions got lumbered with paying for the education of their young folk out of local taxes, only to see these young people migrate to London, to earn and pay taxes there. Worse, if these people later decide to return home in their retirement years, local tax-payers would also have to shell out for their old age health care bills.

It makes a lot of sense for local taxes to be spent on local infrastructure and the local environment (which cannot be moved around the country). But when it comes to spending on 'human capital' (which *can* move) it should be the national budget which picks up the tab.

If we really are 'all in this together', the more affluent regions of Britain must expect to have to subsidise the less affluent; otherwise devolution runs the risk of becoming disintegration. There is only so far that devolution and local taxation can go before national government eventually becomes impotent and irrelevant – having given away all its powers (but at the moment there's a long way to go before Westminster needs to start worrying!).

The downside

It is, however, by no means clear that a national population can – or should – keep growing, not least because of the constraints of space. England, in particular, is already one of the most densely populated major countries in Europe, and the UK's population continues to grow more rapidly than those of other EU nations. As the nation becomes more crowded, pressures on housing increase; such pressure is likely to feed through to increased housing costs and environmental costs. High levels of immigration (some market towns absorbing increases in population as great as 30%) have inevitably fuelled demands upon schools and doctors' surgeries, stretching services. Understandably, this creates social tensions.

While employers may reap the benefits of lower wages in the form of lower operating costs, workers themselves suffer. While the UK monthly minimum wage is typically around four or five times that in eastern Europe, the costs of living here are high – and ever rising. Economic theory suggests that when workers or skills are in short supply, wages should rise. When instead, immigration is encouraged to meet the shortfall, local wages will either fall or simply stagnate – with poorly skilled workers the most likely to lose out. There are also concerns about the exploitation of young migrants, often living four or five to a room, having to work impossibly long hours whenever they are required for a relative pittance.

Many argue that immigration has eroded the cohesion of British society and that this is particularly true of those communities that don't learn the language. If a society is to thrive it should celebrate a shared culture and history – and certainly it should share a language. Among other things, the increasing challenge of the ethnic and language mix that teachers face in some areas of the country is rarely matched with increased resources; in times of austerity, rather the opposite is true.

It's apparent that some members of the British public feel threatened by some aspects of the cultural and ethnic diversity associated with immigration. Yet there is a tendency for the 'Westminster elite' to dismiss such concerns as reactionary, which is undemocratic and risks pushing them towards extremist and divisive political parties. The main parties are now reconsidering their approach.

In sum

Immigration offers speedy, few-questions-asked economic growth, providing a steady supply of labour, stopping 'ordinary' wages and expectations from getting out of hand. This may be beneficial for employers and the country as a whole in terms of short term economic growth. But it is less good – indeed a threat – to many, particularly the economically vulnerable. The benefits of immigration tend to be reaped by better-off middle classes who are relatively immune to job competition (through professional qualifications etc). The downside is disproportionately experienced by poorer communities competing for work, housing and social services. To compound the problem, the beneficiaries may sometimes bask in moral self-righteousness. There are, in addition, social costs which are poorly understood. We must be very aware that this problem does not arise from migrants themselves – rather from the effects of globalisation.

Ultimately, immigration policy must be designed to serve the interests of existing British citizens, especially poorer ones; this much at any rate seems clear. Perhaps the last word should go to the great British public: nearly two-thirds of participants in a recent poll take a balanced and realistic view, agreeing with the statement that 'Immigration brings both pressures and economic benefits, so we should control it and choose the immigration that is in Britain's best economic interests'. Less clear, however, is how this might be put into practice.

Chapter 14

WHAT'S GOING WRONG?

In the run-up to the 2010 general election, David Cameron talked about tackling 'broken Britain'. He trotted out the same phrase after the 2011 riots, when some UK city streets were left smashed and smouldering. In a single sound-bite this seemed to neatly embrace a whole host of worrying social issues – the breakdown of the family, the widening gulf between rich and poor, social isolation, and the harm caused by drugs and alcohol, to name but a few. If only the solutions were so simple.

Unemployment: Still not working

As the Soviet Union and the Communist bloc teetered towards collapse in the early 1990s, rumours of shops with stocks of bread fuelled queues forming around the block, as citizens desperately sought (and sometimes fought for) simple things that were in short supply – often food. Such 'command economies' suffered from one thing above all – 'under-supply'.

' HE'S DOING HIS OUT-OF-WORK EXPERIENCE '

In the West in the 21st century the situation is somewhat reversed (although, some folk willingly queue all night to get their hands on the latest iPhone). Rather than queues for bread, businesses rumoured to be recruiting will be beset by droves of applicants, desperate to secure what is in short supply – employment. The system seems able to produce everything that we need and more – yet it struggles to generate enough employment opportunities at a living wage.

Put simply, we find ourselves caught in a consumerist culture that's driven by surplus rather than shortage. With the measure of economic success being economic growth – producing ever more – there's simply too much 'stuff' and not enough demand for it. We might seek to solve the problem by selling ever harder – through saturation advertising, credit binges, conspicuous consumption, built-in obsolescence and ever-changing fashions – but it seems that we can't ever offload the excess quickly enough. So businesses cut production and costs; they cut head count – and in doing so, consumption is reduced. It's a damaging downward spiral.

Nations such as Germany and China have gone some way to solving the problem of too few 'good jobs' by developing strong export industries, in effect also 'exporting' their unemployment: German and Chinese workers are busy designing and making products that other countries consume – to the detriment of domestic industries. It's proven to be a successful strategy, allowing them to develop healthy trade surpluses (higher export income than import expenditure), and while naturally not every nation can follow suit (for if all are selling, who's buying?), the UK might adopt at least some elements of the model.

Flexi-people

The classical economic response to a reduction in demand is to cut wages and drive down employment terms and conditions – often described as 'improving labour market flexibility'. As wages fall, they should reach a tipping point at which employers find themselves able

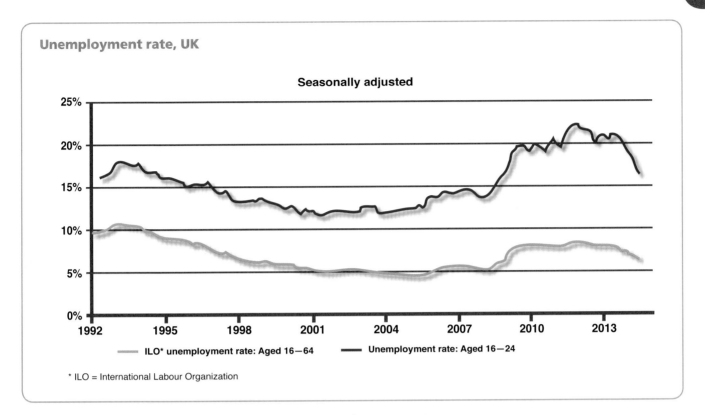

Unemployment rate, UK

Seasonally adjusted

Legend:
— ILO* unemployment rate: Aged 16—64
— Unemployment rate: Aged 16—24

* ILO = International Labour Organization

to offer jobs again – and all will be well. The trouble is that there's no guarantee that the tipping point will be a living wage (currently about 20% above the National Minimum Wage). Moreover, as wages fall, people have less money, so they spend less, thereby reducing demand – which makes the problem of over-supply even worse. And as demand falls, wages fall further, trapping the market in a vicious vortex.

Another issue, of course, is technological development: the loss of skilled and low-skilled manual jobs to automation. Mix this with increased outsourcing and offshoring (to overseas call centres, for example), then sprinkle in workers arriving from low-wage economies (some UK factory jobs like sandwich-making are only advertised abroad), and you've created a recipe for intense competition for even low-skilled jobs.

Given all of these forces, full employment – or at least full employment with a living wage – is less likely now than it has been at any time since the Great Depression of the 1920s and 1930s. There are those who blame the unemployed themselves for this decline in opportunities, but this makes about as much sense as blaming the hungry in the USSR for the shortage of bread. Yet overall, unemployment in Britain has been dropping since 2012. Experts tend to scratch their heads when asked to explain this, but there are a number of possible reasons:

- **Falling real wages** Wage drops and cuts to employment terms and conditions might have allowed employers to recruit new workers.
- **Greater labour market flexibility** People on 'zero-hours contracts' aren't counted. Employers aren't obliged to offer any hours of work under such contracts, yet employees are not technically *un*employed.
- **'Disguised unemployment' and underemployment** The recession saw a rise in people entering into self-employment rather than claiming unemployment benefits, or agreeing to work part-time, when they would prefer to be employed full-time.

- **A fall in labour productivity** Employers keen to retain skilled staff may be reluctant to lay off members of their workforce, even though there's less for them to do, in the hope that there'll be an upturn in demand.
- **Benefit changes** A range of changes to the benefits system have reclassified claimants, or even disentitled them to Jobseeker's Allowance (JSA) or other unemployment benefits. This may force more people into the labour market – thereby placing further downward pressure on wages. Alternatively it is possible that the figures have been massaged so some jobs seekers magically disappear.
- **Housing debt 'bubbles'** Wily politicians know that stoking rising house prices can fuel short-term demand across the broader economy for builders, mortgage and estate agency services, white goods and furnishings etc. (The painful hangover when the bubble 'bursts' is also well known.)

While overall figures may be dropping, youth unemployment in the UK – as is the case across Europe – is especially high, at around 15–20%. Another trend is the rising number of people in low-paid jobs: there are now around 5 million people paid below the living wage (although it may be possible to reduce unemployment by cutting wages, achieving full employment at a living wage is another matter altogether).

Living in poverty

How do we measure poverty? Feeling 'a bit skint' now and again isn't likely to count. Fairly sensibly, it's normally measured in terms of household income. A household is considered to be in poverty if its annual income reaches only 60% or less of the national average (that is, the median income, after taxes have been paid, and adjusting for the size of the household and its composition). This is therefore a *relative* measure of deprivation, because the level at which a household is considered to be living in poverty will change over time as average national income changes. For example, average incomes in the UK have dropped by about 8% from their 2007–8 peak. So this means that 2 million people with low household incomes who used to be classed as being in relative poverty are no longer included today, despite their incomes being the same (or sometimes lower). Even so, a shocking 13 million people in the UK were classed as living in poverty in 2011–12.

However it's not all bad news:

- the proportion of pensioners living in poverty has fallen to 14%, its lowest rate for almost 30 years; and
- the proportion of children living in poverty has fallen to 27%, its lowest rate for almost 25 years.

In the last 30 years or so, there have been some big changes to the sort of people who are suffering deprivation. Back in 1982, the figures for children, pensioners and working-age adults (with or without children) living in poverty were all quite similar. Today, this has changed quite radically:

- 3.5 million children;
- 3 million parents;
- 4.5 million working-age adults without children; and
- 1.5 million pensioners are living in poverty.

One of the biggest changes is the figure for working-age adults without children who are living in poverty – now the highest on record.

There are obviously a number of things in life that can conspire to make you poor – such as unemployment, underemployment (working for fewer hours a week than you would like), low-paid work and changes to benefit payments. And while levels of poverty are important, levels of pay inequality are also a major consideration.

Mind the (wealth) gap...

In 2014, Pope Francis tweeted: 'Inequality is the root of social evil.' There is no doubt that this is one of the most pertinent issues of our time. But this isn't a problem that's easily solved. Part of the problem is human beings have deep-seated psychological responses to the rich. We have a natural tendency to regard outward wealth as a sign of inner worth. So inequality colours how we judge others – and ourselves. Big wealth gaps invoke strong feelings of success or failure, superiority and inferiority, dominance and subordination. In turn this affects the way we relate to and treat each other – and not for the better.

Of course some might well say: 'So what if the richest 1,000 people in the UK have more wealth than the poorest 40% of households – that's the price we pay for living in a consumer paradise, with legal rights and welfare if we need it. Get off your arse and stop whining!'

But rather like booze, too much of a wealth gap is damaging for our health. A certain amount of inequality acts as an incentive – so we aspire to work harder to better ourselves and reap just rewards. But too much becomes a disincentive. If you slog your guts out working all hours and *still* can't make ends meet, you soon become de-motivated; eventually such a system can make honest people dishonest. And if the majority can't meet their essential needs, society starts to unravel.

Research shows that the wider the wealth gap in a country, the lower that country scores on a whole range of health and social

measures, including life expectancy (poorer people die, on average, 12 years earlier than the wealthy) and imprisonment rates. There are also higher rates of infant mortality, obesity, mental illness, drug and alcohol addiction, and violence (including homicide), among other things. Even those at the top of the social ladder can't escape the 'collateral damage' – although the rich can, of course, afford to retreat to live in fear inside guarded ghettos and gated communities, too terrified to answer the door.

The demise of the traditional family

Families are changing. Greater equality between men and women, together with the rising cost of living, means that increasingly both partners want to start a career before having a family; hence the average age of first-time mothers has risen. At the same time more women are choosing to remain childless and infertility rates are rising. For working parents, the cost and availability of childcare is a significant issue – one that governments of all colours like to be seen to support.

Another big change is the number of children being born outside marriage. The numbers have risen sharply across a variety of countries, tripling from 1980 to around a third of all kids today (amongst members of the OECD – Organisation for Economic Co-operation and Development). The risk of parental separation among this group is higher than among married parents. Whether as a result of divorce, separation, or people deciding to start a family without a partner, there have been big increases in the number of children being raised in sole-parent families. In the UK, in 2007, approximately 22% of children lived in sole-parent households – a figure substantially higher than the OECD average. And it's predicted that the proportion of children living in sole-parent families will increase further over the next few years.

Damage limitation

According to the Centre for Social Justice, a right-of-centre think tank, parental separation disproportionately affects the most deprived communities in Britain. Almost half of all children aged 0–5 in low-income households aren't living with both parents – an incredible seven times the proportion among the richest households.

Thankfully, research has found that the majority of such children won't be adversely affected in the long term by their parents' separation – with one important caveat: one thing that everyone agrees is extremely damaging is parental conflict. This is a major cause of 'negative life outcomes' in children (damage done emotionally and psychologically continuing to have an effect into adulthood) regardless of family background. In other words, it's how well a family functions that ultimately has a greater impact on children's outcomes, regardless of how that family is structured. Kids need to be raised in happy homes, not emotional battlegrounds.

Drugs

How many people use illegal drugs in Britain? At last count, the answer was about 2.2 million (estimated from the crime survey of England & Wales). The most common drug of choice was marijuana, with an estimated 800,000 people using cocaine. However, whilst illegal drug use is far more common today than it was 40 or 50 years ago, it now seems to be declining. This trend is clearest among young people aged 16–24: in this age group, the proportion using drugs was about 20% in the most recent survey, down from 30% in 1996.

In contrast, the UK market for 'legal highs' has rocketed over the last few years. These substances, primarily sold over the Internet, offer users a cheaper and supposedly permissible alternative to illegal drugs. The websites describe them as 'research chemicals', 'bath salts', or 'plant food', and stress that they're not for human consumption – but the pictures of clubbers that accompany the descriptions tell a different story. The problem is that most people presume that 'legal' means 'approved' or 'tested', rather than the truth: 'The government hasn't got round to banning it yet'. Even then, when one substance is banned, the chemical composition of other 'designer drugs' can be tweaked to evade the ban – so perhaps we should limit the use of the misleading word 'legal' unless licensed?

When it comes to serious street drugs such as crack and heroin, politicians of all persuasions are keen to declare themselves soldiers in the 'war on drugs'. There's no divisive rhetoric because there's no doubt that hard drugs harm society as a whole, and not only users. For a start, there's the impact of burglary and theft associated with druggies funding their habit; then there's the crime and

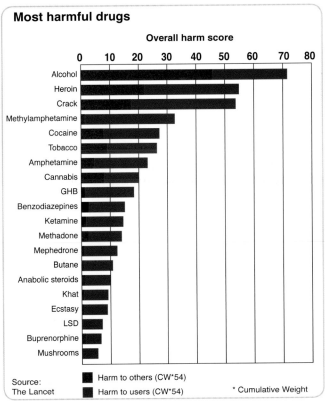

Most harmful drugs

Overall harm score

Source: The Lancet — Harm to others (CW*54) — Harm to users (CW*54) — * Cumulative Weight

DRUG CULTURE

GANG CULTURE

BOOZE CULTURE

GUN CULTURE

K.J.Lamb

MULTICULTURAL SOCIETY

violence associated with illicit dealing; then there's criminal money laundering, and of course the costs to the NHS of drug treatment and rehabilitation. However, some of these costs arise simply from the illegality of the market. Yet when the results of governments waging 'wars on drugs' are analysed, the social benefits tend to be unclear. Research might suggest that policy should be subtly refined, but rarely will ministers respond to evidence that appears to undermine their approach. Indeed on the rare occasions when a government scientist or adviser publicly questions this policy, they tend to be swiftly slapped down.

Bad news for boozers

A study in *The Lancet* assessed 20 drugs according to key measures of harm, covering both users and wider society. Although heroin, crack and crystal meth were deemed worst for individuals, alcohol was estimated to be worst for wider society and worst overall – yet alcohol is the most widespread and socially acceptable of all drugs.

Alcohol use in Britain has increased dramatically in recent decades. Over the last 50 years, consumption of (the equivalent of) pure alcohol per person has doubled, from just over 4 litres a year to over 8 litres – to the increasing alarm of health experts. Yet while politicians talk a lot about wanting to tackle alcohol abuse, they do little in practice – perhaps because of the powerful 'big alcohol' lobby pressurising government, just as 'big tobacco' did successfully for many decades.

Interestingly, alcohol consumption actually appears to be falling among 16–24-year-olds; the opposite is true among women, the middle-aged and the elderly. Whilst we might speculate on the reasons for this apparent boom in boozing, it's intriguing to speculate on why it might be dropping among the young. Lack of money might well be a factor, of course, with increasing financial pressures from student fees and the high cost of housing leaving young adults with less to spend on alcohol. Awareness of health issues surrounding youthful binge drinking might be another factor: after all, who wants to die of liver disease in their 20s? Or perhaps it's partly down to teenage rebellion against the status quo – and shame at the sight of 'my sozzled parents'?

However, before concluding that the problem of alcohol might finally be sorting itself out, there's a possible 'sting in the tail': a reported increase in alcohol consumption amongst very young adolescents aged 11–13. Whether or not such claims by youngsters are skewed by the temptation to brag about being 'grown up', there is an insidious force at work here; alcohol advertising and promotion can be very appealing to young people, sowing the seeds for the development of lifelong drinking.

Debt

Britain is a nation in serious debt – and it's not only the government that's in hock to the bankers; it's also estimated that British people in total personally owe around £1.5 trillion – a figure that's rising annually. The average total debt per household – including mortgages – is around £55,000. Per adult, that's an average debt of nearly £29,000, which is more than the average salary (approximately £24,000). Total credit card debt alone is getting on for £57 billion – more than £2,000 per household.

This level of debt is unsustainable. On average, around 300 people a day are declared insolvent or bankrupt – rising at a rate of about 5% a year. Although house repossessions are down on previous years, when mortgage interest rates finally start to rise, this figure is likely to skyrocket.

Some argue that the debt cloud under which so many people in the UK live is the result of frivolous spending or some sort of character flaw; in fact, when the cost of living increases faster than incomes, the vulnerable are effectively being *forced* into debt. Over the last decade, real average wages haven't increased at all – and yet the costs of just about everything else, including even food, have risen at a hair-raising rate.

One major expense is bringing up children: parents now spend 28% of their annual income on raising a child. The total cost is enough to make most prospective parents take fright: parents are now reckoned to spend a record £227,266 on raising a child to his or her 21st birthday. Working out at £29.65 a day, that's a big jump from previous years. Education and childcare are the biggest expenses, both up substantially since 2003 (rising by 126% and 67%, respectively) – but despite being a boon to the state, children aren't even tax-deductible…

ONE BIG GAMBLE

So-called 'sin taxes' are big earners for government, raking in billions every year in revenue. But there are limits on the sort of activities considered ripe for state plucking. Few politicians today would openly advocate smoking, drug taking, or prostitution, no matter how much tax they could generate. But the rise of instant-access gambling and supermarkets pumping out bargain multipacks of super-strong alcohol are nice little earners for HM Treasury.

Few people have strong objections to the National Lottery (although some regard it as a stealth tax on the poor). Neither are premium bonds, bingo and football pools considered the work of the devil. But then, these hail from a different era, along with the occasional flutter at discreet 'turf accountant' premises of pinstriped 'Arthur Daley' types.

Today's gambling is available round the clock. Pop-up adverts deluge tablets and smartphones, offering adults and children alike what appears to be harmless fun: free bets. The industry spends millions aggressively promoting betting online, with celeb-endorsed adverts screened around major sports matches, setting real-time odds for all possible outcomes in the game. Fixed-odds terminals in betting shops are particularly insidious, allowing players to lose large amounts of money in just a few minutes.

Few would deny that gambling can be dangerously addictive, or that the human consequences are tragic and ugly. More than 350,000 people are known to suffer from a gambling addiction in the UK and there's been a steady increase in recent years, triggered by the misery of recession and the saturation of online gambling outlets. Problem gambling is a stealthy addiction that leaves no physical mark, but steadily corrodes from the inside, not unlike alcoholism and drug addiction.

With only around 1 in 20 problem gamblers seeking help for addiction, the resulting unmanageable debt is a major cause of violence and family breakdown, sometimes exacerbated by payday loan sharks. Perhaps the costs to society of treating the effects of addiction should be balanced alongside the tax revenues it rakes in, boosted by 'light touch' regulation. The trick for government is to get the balance right, minimising social ills, whilst generating reasonable amounts of tax.

Source material: Kevin McKenna and BBC

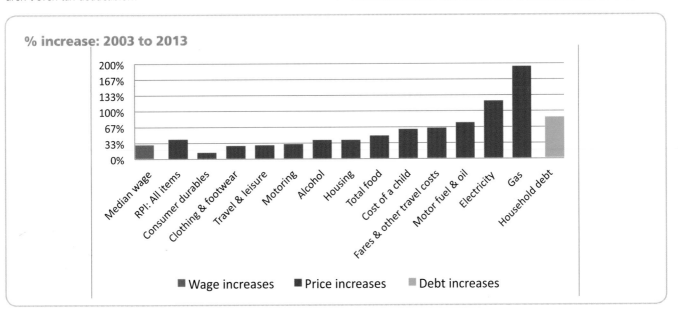

% increase: 2003 to 2013

■ Wage increases ■ Price increases ■ Debt increases

Payday lenders have rarely been out the news recently – for all of the wrong reasons. In recent years, the payday loan market has more than doubled to well over £2 billion; this surging rate of expansion has been accompanied by a major rise in the number of people trapped in serious debt. In the last four years, Citizens Advice reported a shocking tenfold increase in the number of debt cases with payday loan problems. Around 1 in every 3 loans is repaid late, or not at all – clocking up savage fees and fines. One major concern is the routine practice of 'rolling over' – that is, refinancing loans by paying them off with new ones, so that the total amount owed snowballs at ruinous interest rates. About a fifth of payday lenders' income is sourced from just 5% of loans rolled over at least four times.

From January 2015, the Financial Conduct Authority capped payday lenders' interest and fees at 0.8% a day. But this is still nearly 300% per annum, and once other charges are factored in, it could total as much as 2,000% APR – compared to typically less than 5% on a mortgage. Although the total cost of a loan is limited to 100% of the original sum and default fees are capped at £15, many people still end up repaying enormously high amounts, with less consumer protection than citizens have in countries such as Japan, Australia and Canada.

Mental health

In light of the many pressures under which we live in Britain, it may seem small wonder that the most common mental disorder is a mix of anxiety and depression. Of course there are all kinds of things that can get us down, but money problems and social issues in particular are strongly linked to poor mental health.

The numbers are sobering: between 8% and 12% of the population experience periods of depression at least once a year. The good news is that about half of those with common mental health problems recover within 18 months. Unfortunately, those on lower incomes, the long-term sick and the unemployed are more likely to remain affected for longer.

Common mental health problems generally peak in middle age. There is, however, growing concern about the increasing number of young people with mental health problems. The charity Young Minds reports that 10% of children and young people aged 5–16 suffer from a diagnosable mental health disorder – some three children in every school classroom. It's estimated that more than 8,000 children aged under 10 suffer from severe depression. And the longer-term trend is likewise troubling: the number of young people aged 15–16 with depression nearly doubled between the 1980s and the 2000s, with similar increases for those suffering from conduct disorders.

Suicides

There were a shocking 4,513 recorded suicides in England in 2012. The rate is even higher in Scotland than it is for other parts of the UK. The only glimmer of light in the darkness is that this figure is lower now than it was a decade previously.

However, since the 2008–9 global financial crisis and subsequent recession, figures have been on the rise. Around a quarter of suicides are committed by people who've been in contact with mental health services in the preceding year, and clinicians say that the effects of the recession – the financial pressures of unemployment and debt, combined with austerity cuts to state benefits – are leading ever more people to access services. The consequences of mental health services struggling to cope with that rising demand when their own budgets have been similarly cut are therefore potentially devastating.

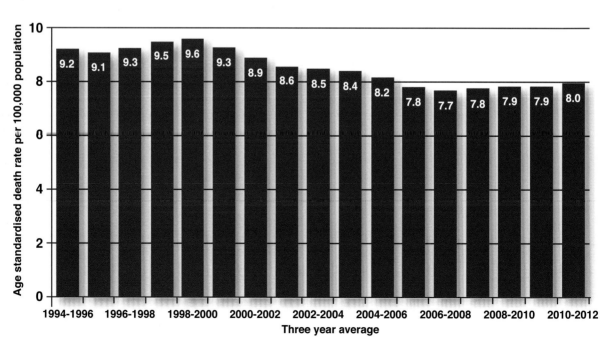

Death rates from intentional self-harm and injury of undetermined intent, England 1994–2012

How long will we live?

The number of older people in the UK is rising. There are 11 million people aged 65 or over in Britain, including more than 13,000 'centenarians' – keeping the Queen busy scribbling 'Congratulations on your 100th birthday' in card after card. By 2034, about a quarter of the UK population will be aged 65 or over (now might be the time to buy shares in stairlift companies?), and life expectancy has increased significantly in the last 80 years. A boy born in the UK between 2006 and 2008 can expect to live to the age of 78 and a girl, to 82 – almost 20 years longer than those born in the 1930s. Nearly one in five people presently in the UK will live to see their 100th birthday (and live to enjoy the royal seal of approval).

For many people, retirement has granted liberating levels of financial and social freedom that previous generations would have found hard to believe. Those aged over 55 control around 80% of the nation's wealth. They're also big spenders, accounting for 40% of the UK's consumption. But not everyone is living the dream – far from it: there are at least 1.5 million pensioners living below the poverty line. Nearly half a million old folk can't afford to keep their homes adequately warm and there are more than 30,000 avoidable winter deaths every year in the UK.

But there's another factor at work that can seriously blight old age: loneliness. Nearly 4 million people over the age of 65 live alone and the charity Age UK reports that:

- more than 1 million older people say that they always, or often, feel lonely;

'IN MY OPINION, HENRY, WE SPEND TOO MUCH TIME WATCHING THE BOX'

K.J. Lamb

AN AGEING POPULATION

The average age of the UK population is rising and this can largely be attributed to the following.

- Overall, the world's birth rates are declining. Given that there are currently more people than the planet can support sustainably, this may not be such a bad thing.
- Improvements in health mean that people are not only living longer, but also living more healthily into old age. This, again, is not a bad thing.

So far, so good… But there are downsides. According to the government, this change in demographics means that state pension provision in the UK is unsustainable. This is because pensions in payment are funded by the tax being paid by those of working age, and for each person aged 65 or over, there are presently only 3.7 people of working age (20–64). By 2050, this is likely to decline even further, to only two people of working age. The government has solved this by implementing phased changes to the age at which we can claim state pension – based on the assumption that if we're living longer, we should also be able to work longer.

But there's a fly in the haemorrhoid ointment – and it's a bit of a whopper. So much depends on our health in old age – and the average disease-free period we can expect to enjoy is not increasing as fast as life expectancy. In fact, the average 65-year-old in the UK today might expect to benefit from some 12 disease-free years (during which they might perhaps have hoped to take a cruise, rather than carry on working). So, if you're unlucky, the pleasure of a longer retirement might be hampered by chronic diseases – and a longer period of poor health means increased health care costs. Also, increasing income inequality is likely to mean greater dependency rates – with the state picking up the tab.

The big question is, can this demographic time bomb be defused? There is an assumption that our ageing population will be supported by (increasingly few) younger people in work. Their taxes should help fund oldies' care costs. But there is a real danger that the sums won't add up – with more elderly people living longer and the costs of care increasing, with the wealth gap growing and state support shrinking, and with fewer young people entering the workplace and youth unemployment (and underemployment) on the rise. So what to do?

Politicians like short-term solutions, such as encouraging immigration to boost the numbers in work and paying taxes. This may mean we don't have to worry about it for the moment (although low paid jobs may not generate much tax revenue) but at the end of the day it's just postponing the problem. To tackle these big issues head on we need to look at ways to increase employment opportunity, not by simply doing more of the same, but by doing something new – by innovating. We also need to empower young people to plug the skills gaps which keep them from finding good jobs. It's no good complaining we don't have enough young people when we're not even employing the ones we already have. We might also look at developing policies that close the wealth gap, so that our young people can rekindle their hopes and dreams. In doing so, we might achieve a win/win situation. Firstly, youth will be more likely to find fulfilling and better-paid employment, generating more tax revenue. And as inequality falls, people will be able to save more for their retirement, and be less dependent on the state. Ultimately, we require policies which will keep us healthy for longer – not merely 'hanging on' for longer.

- some 41% of people aged 65 and over in the UK feel out of touch with the pace of modern life and 12% say that they feel cut off from society; and
- over a third of older people (more than 4 million) say that their TV is their main form of company.

Loneliness matters. Studies have shown that it can be more harmful to our health than smoking 15 cigarettes a day. People who experience a lot of loneliness are twice as likely to develop Alzheimer's disease as people who experience it only occasionally.

Loss of community

When we decry the damage done by drugs and violence, declining mental health, and rising debt, we can easily overlook something simpler that's undermining the social fabric: the breakdown of *community*.

The impact that the breakdown of local communities in the United States has had on ordinary people was graphically captured in an influential book by Robert Putnam entitled *Bowling Alone* (2000) – a reference to how people in small-town America used to go to the local bowling alley with friends and neighbours, yet now increasingly 'bowl alone'. Putnam linked loss of local community to a wide range of adverse trends, such as increasing crime, worsening health and rising poverty.

In the UK, there are signs of a similar decline, for example falling voter turnouts, the drop in trade union membership, and – most evidently – the physical closures of local pubs, post offices, shops, libraries and bus services. The loss of all these local amenities gradually chews away at the fabric of society. A recent study by the Home Office has shown that local areas with a high sense of community, political trust and a sense of belonging have lower levels of crime. Along with the widening wealth gap, there seems to be a growing divide in the community, with the benefits increasingly going to better-off professional and managerial types.

A society of one

In recent decades, Britain has seen significant social and economic changes. Some have affected our attitudes, squashing our aspirations and blinding us to any silver linings. Things such as the death of heavy industry in Britain, the rise of the 'information economy', the breakdown of the traditional family, and a loss of faith in institutions such as the Church and Parliament have stripped us of some of our certainties. On the plus side, being no longer tied by these 'old shackles' means we should have more choice about how we live our lives. We are free to take more responsibility for how well we live our lives, forging new bonds and rebuilding communities; but instead, we seem to have become more individualistic and less willing to contribute to wider society.

What's your view?

Every year since 1983, the British Social Attitudes survey has explored the British zeitgeist. The survey asks respondents which of three options they would want government to pick:

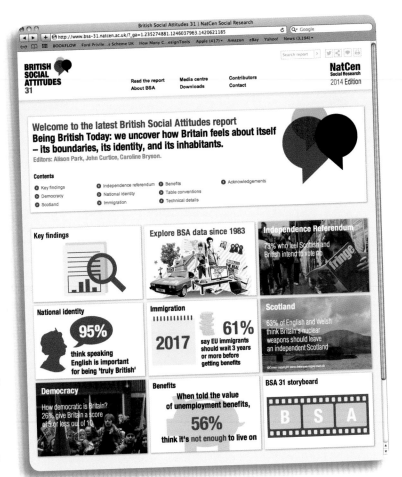

- reduce taxes and spend less on health, education and social benefits;
- keep taxes and spending on these services at the same level as now; or
- increase taxes and spend more on health, education and social benefits?

The first of these options has never been particularly popular, never supported by more than 9% of respondents. Opinion has tended to swing backwards and forwards over time between the other two options, and over the last 30 years the public's views on taxation, spending and social protection haven't changed that much. What has changed, however, is people's attitudes towards social welfare for disadvantaged groups in society, perhaps egged on by populist scaremongering media headlines. Although few would argue with the general proposition that being in work should pay better than receiving benefits, this can sometimes be complex in reality (not least when it comes to affordable housing). Ideally this would be addressed by increasing wages rather than cutting benefits.

TV dinners

The way in which people spend their leisure time is also changing. In 2011, we watched, on average, 4 hours of TV a day, up from 3.7 hours a day in 2004. In contrast, the average number of hours spent volunteering declined by 30% between 1997 and 2007 (per volunteer). A recent survey also provides some insight into the impact of TV on our habits at home. Ten years ago, those aged 18–24 were the group least likely to have TV sets in their bedrooms (just over half had one); today, they are the most likely (almost 80%).

'IF YOU DON'T BEHAVE, I'M SENDING YOU OUT OF YOUR ROOM!'

Nearly three-quarters of people eat at least one of the main meals of the day sitting in front of the box. A European survey in 2004 found that men spend 49% of their free time watching television and videos, 16% socialising and 3% on volunteer work. Women are shown to be more sociable, with figures of 44%, 21% and 5%, respectively.

'Love me do'

There's another worrying trend winging its way across the Atlantic. If the United States is anything to go by (and it normally is), we could be in for a cultural epidemic of narcissism – something that's rather alien to the traditionally self-deprecating Brit.

Research has shown that younger generations are more likely to:

- rate themselves as above average on leadership and drive to achieve;
- score lower on measures of empathy;
- embrace life goals centring on money, fame and image;
- set unrealistically high goals; and
- report higher levels of self-esteem.

Keen viewers of popular TV shows such as *The X Factor* or *The Apprentice* might not find this entirely surprising. Those whose job it is to research such things have evidence of growing individualism and waning collectivism, the rise of 'reality TV' seemingly built on a 'me me me' yearning for celebrity and fame. This is reflected in the decreasing use of moral words in song lyrics and in books written for children. Traditional 'British understatement' has been undermined by popular (rap) culture, brimming with bragging and bravado (which of course might sometimes be ironic). What is surprising is how the stellar self-confidence and boastfulness contrasts starkly with the reality of reduced youth opportunities (the rise of unpaid internships, crippling student debt, lack of affordable housing etc). Might our young folk simply be 'fronting' – with voices raised to drown out the sound of broken dreams and ward off inner doubts?

Chapter 15

FAIR ENOUGH?

Most of us would much rather live in a just society than a blatantly unjust one. But defining precisely what 'social justice' is can be tricky: you might say that you 'know it when you see it'. Another clue might be gleaned from the familiar phrase 'equal opportunities', which strikes at the heart of the matter.

Before we go any further, let's dispel one myth: delivering social justice doesn't mean that everyone and their dog must, by law, be entitled to an equal amount of success; rather, it means that we should each have a place on the starting grid – and that the rest of the race should be up to us. This implies fairness and a mutual obligation in society; it also implies that, as citizens, we have a certain amount of responsibility for ourselves and for one another.

Sadly, there's a mighty long way to go before the box marked 'social justice' can be ticked and everyone can be confident of an equal opportunity to succeed in life. Governments know that 'social injustice' arises as a result of the problems at which we looked in the last chapter – entrenched poverty, coupled with families in crisis, low educational attainment, unemployment, problem debt and addiction – but fixing them is a big ask, to put it mildly.

Does wealth trickle down – or well up?

One of the most influential thinkers on the subject of social justice is John Rawls, whose 1971 *A Theory of Justice* set out two principles:

- the **liberty principle** (individual freedom) – that all citizens should have equal rights before the law, equality of opportunity, and freedom in what they believe, with whom they hang out, what they say, etc (as long as such freedoms don't deprive other citizens of their own such liberties); and
- the **difference principle** (social equality) – that inequality can be justified where it improves the lot of the least well-off members of society.

Fortunately, the first point is largely taken care of, since we already enjoy most fundamental rights and freedoms under the UK

constitution (although they still need to be jealously guarded). But the second principle chucks a hand grenade at the status quo, calling into question so-called 'trickle-down' economics.

Trickle-down theory suggests that economic policy should benefit the economically powerful, based on an understanding that their wealth will 'trickle down' to the rest of us. Left-leaning commentators suggest that it's a bit of a ruse, allowing the super-rich to justify obscene levels of compensation by pretending that it's for the greater good – and the richer the elite become, the harder they try to make us believe that we too benefit. In practice, there's no evidence of the trickle-down effect; rather, the opposite. Because the 'super-rich' tend to invest in assets such as diamonds, gold, paintings and vintage cars, the money stays inside the super-rich bubble rather than converting into jobs in factories, or greater high street sales. And as we saw in Chapter 14, once the wealth gap becomes firmly entrenched, inequality tends to breed only further inequality.

Rawls' principles suggest that a more effective (and socially just) economic policy would be to boost the wealth of the most economically vulnerable. Poorer people have no choice but to spend their money, thereby boosting local economies, rather than squirreling it away in tax havens and investing in global assets. If consumption ('buying stuff') creates demand, and hence new jobs, in a sort of virtuous circle, perhaps we should be pursuing policies that allow affluence to 'well up' instead?

Sheer skill

Delivering social justice is not only morally important; an unjust society is also less efficient. Obviously, not everyone in the UK is capable of being a Premiership footballer or a banker. People have different skills – some of which are more valued than others. But, in a just society, it shouldn't be the case that our potential is curtailed at birth simply because of our postcode or parental income. We're likely to enjoy a higher quality of both football and banking if professionals are selected on the basis of skill rather than parental occupation.

There's a lot that can be done to offset the restricted life chances of those born on 'Skint Street'. For example, society might choose to invest more per pupil in schools in deprived areas. Fairness also dictates that the poorest should pay a lesser proportion of their income in tax than the rich, who – by means of various loopholes – sometimes now pay (as a leading private equity investor recently put it) 'less tax than a cleaning lady'. In other words, tax should be progressive, rather than regressive.

This doesn't mean that promoting social justice requires sacrifice on the part of the affluent. 'Strengthening the weak' is not the same as 'weakening the strong'. It's not likely that we'll ever live in a democratic society in which the rich don't get richer: the rich, in general, *always* get richer. But as John F Kennedy noted: 'If a free society cannot help the many who are poor, it cannot save the few who are rich.' The killer argument is that what is good for the poor is actually, in the long run, also good for the rich. Business, after all, needs customers; millionaire footballers and pop stars need affluent fans; even bankers need borrowers to pay back their loans with interest (and taxpayers to bail the banks out). If an increasing proportion of the population can't afford to flash their cash, the UK's consumer economy will inevitably enter recession. And no one benefits from empty shops, mass defaults, repossessions and bankruptcies – as was made painfully clear in the aftermath of the 2008–9 global financial crisis.

The pursuit of happiness

Although there's still much poverty and inequality in the UK, as the overall wealth of the nation has increased over time some politicians have become preoccupied with the idea of measuring citizens' happiness and well-being. Once we've satisfied our basic survival needs on Maslow's hierarchy (see Chapter 12) – food, drink, shelter – we're free to turn our attention to the next steps: our higher social needs.

'SO – MERRY GENTLEMEN – HOW WOULD YOU RATE YOUR WELL-BEING?'

The secret of happiness

When The Beatles sang 'Money can't buy me love', they voiced a profound philosophical truth. Amazingly enough, despite the difficulties that we encounter day to day, there are indicators that we're generally becoming happier. Not only are alcohol and drug abuse dropping among those aged 16–24 (see Chapter 14), but since 2011 surveys of 'personal well-being' have reported improvements year-on-year. Congratulations are especially due to the good people of Northern Ireland who, on average, report the highest levels of personal well-being in the UK. What's more, at the other end of the spectrum, the lowest average levels were reported by people in London – which is curious, given that average incomes are higher in London and the south-east.

Despite this high-level interest in the subject of 'well-being', there's no universally accepted definition of the concept. Everyone knows that life is hard when times are tough – in other words, that a certain level of income is required to eliminate low mood – but (gasp!) it actually turns out that, above a certain level, happiness does *not* increase with income.

So what *is* the secret? It seems that there's one thing that's more important than any other in determining how we feel about our lives: the quality of our relationships. The things that nourish our individual 'well-being' also appear to be those things that strengthen society (and vice versa) – which, in turn, feed economic growth. In other words, if we focus on improving our well-being and strengthening society, we may well find that we boost our economy by accident. Conversely, if we focus on economic growth to the exclusion of well-being, we might wind up with neither. If we become too focused on money (politicians and hedge fund managers please note), we risk neglecting the other areas of our lives that have been proven to contribute to our higher social selves and our well-being declines. Maslow strikes again.

Where next?

One thing on which all political parties agree is the need to deliver social justice. What they argue about is *how*.

Providing support

The present government's 2012 policy paper *Social Justice: Transforming Lives* set out five principles:

1 A focus on **prevention and early intervention**
2 Where problems arise, concentrating interventions on **recovery and independence**, not maintenance
3 Promoting **work** for those who can as the most sustainable route out of poverty, while offering **unconditional support** to those who are severely disabled and cannot work
4 Recognising that the most effective solutions will often be designed and delivered **at a local level**
5 Ensuring that interventions provide a **fair deal for the taxpayer**

There's much in this strategy that makes sense. Many of the most pressing social problems that our society faces arise because children don't get the support that they need early on in life. It's been demonstrated by child development researchers that early neglect, the wrong type of parenting and other adverse experiences can have a profound effect on how children are emotionally 'wired'. By the

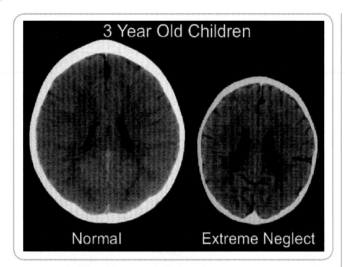

3 Year Old Children

Normal   Extreme Neglect

The CT scan above shows the brain of a healthy 3-year-old child with an average head size; the image on the right is that of a 3-year-old child who has been subjected to severe sensory-deprivation neglect.

age of 3, children's brains are 80% developed. But what's really scary is the fact that, at just 22 months old, a child's 'development score' can often accurately predict how well he or she will do for the next *26 years*. It's no secret that poor educational results can seriously hamper achievements in later life. So it's a 'no brainer' that getting in early – ideally, during the first three years of life – provides the most effective support for the vulnerable.

When, later in life, vulnerable people run into problems, it's obviously important that the authorities try to minimise the harm caused to society, for example damage caused by violent outbursts.

But it's equally important to try to prevent it from happening again, and this means supporting people to help them to recover and to develop a degree of self-sufficiency – offering alcohol or drug treatment to those who are willing to learn to take control of life choices, for example.

CAUSE AND EFFECT

There's a strong link between poverty and substance misuse – but is it the effect of grinding poverty that drives people to the release of hard drink and drugs, or is it the other way around? Does substance misuse make people poor? Plenty of privileged kids have been known to toot away their trust funds; conversely, there are (too) many who seek drunken escape from the hopelessness of homelessness. So trying to tackle a problem such as addiction without seeking to address the underlying causes – looking at the individual's needs as a whole – may never be enough to 'transform lives'.

Likewise, when it comes to schemes to promote work, governments have a tendency to wade into deep and controversial waters, sometimes reflected in critical news coverage. One problem is the sheer number of working families who barely subsist. The extent of 'in-work poverty' is so great that simply promoting other poorly paid work merely perpetuates the problem. Certainly, in many parts of the UK, employment opportunities are limited, but it's also the *quality* of the work that is available that's important: in Britain, there are currently too few jobs that offer a route out of poverty. And the worse inequality becomes, the fewer such 'good' jobs there will be.

Tracking the mythical beast

Government ministers sometimes castigate the unemployed for what ministers describe as an 'entrenched culture of worklessness', supporting their stance with terrible tales of three or more generations of families in which no one has ever had a job. Such

PERSONAL BUDGETS

It's said that allocating money in the form of 'personal budgets' to those who need support can be genuinely empowering. It allows the vulnerable to take some control of their lives, rather than remain passive recipients. With a personal budget, those needing social care know how much money the council will allocate for their use and are able, within parameters, to choose how they spend it. Perhaps an older person who needs personal care might choose to spend the money on provision in his or her own home, rather than in a care home, or a young adult with learning difficulties might use the opportunity to start living independently for the first time.

There are various ways in which a personal budget can be paid. Direct payments are the purest form, giving people direct control over spending, but also all of the associated responsibilities, including employing a carer to provide services. Alternatively, a council can retain partial control over the personal budget or pay it in full to a third-party service provider. Today, there are hundreds of thousands in receipt of personal budgets and over £1.5 billion of public money is spent in this way.

There are many potential advantages to personal budgets. They give people more control over their own care, and can inspire confidence and a greater sense of independence. In some sectors, such as disability care, personal budgets have played an important role in the near-

eradication of long-term, institutional provision. The introduction of personal budgets has also created an entirely new employment market, in the form of registered personal assistants providing care in people's homes.

There are, however, potential downsides.

- Many consumers of care services are isolated, vulnerable and/or grapple with communication challenges. This means that family members and other 'informal' carers will often play an important role in helping to make decisions about the use of the money – and that means that there's potential for financial abuse.
- Some recipients have little experience of the different care options available. They might have become eligible for a personal budget only because of a crisis – say, when an older person has a serious fall and needs long-term personal care as a result – and this will mean that they'll have to make purchasing decisions at a difficult time.
- Some councils appear reluctant to cede genuine budgetary control to individuals, with overly complicated systems demanding a high degree of professional input when choosing services, while others take a laissez-faire approach that leaves service users lost and distressed.

In Britain, there are currently too few jobs that offer a route out of poverty.

beasts have, however, proven elusive in the wild. After months of extensive fieldwork in very deprived neighbourhoods of Glasgow and Middlesbrough, researchers from the respected Joseph Rowntree Foundation were unable to find *any* families in which worklessness had spanned three or more generations. They consequently concluded: 'If such families exist, they can only account for a minuscule fraction of workless people.'

Social innovation

Government strategies for social justice talk about 'local solutions' combined with a 'fair deal for the taxpayer'. It sounds good. But what does it mean in practice?

'Social innovation' is a term that politicians frequently bandy about. There are a number of instances – not necessarily driven by the state – in which this has worked very well. One of the best examples is *The Big Issue,* a magazine sold by homeless people; the cooperative movement in Victorian Britain is another good example. Today, many such ideas harness new technology: Wikipedia, for example.

Clearly, social innovations may be 'local', or they may have national or global reach. The Open University has local reach, but is a national organisation. Social innovations are often delivered *by* local communities *for* local communities – think of Neighbourhood Watch or a self-build cooperative – but social innovation might equally be delivered by the public sector (NHS Direct), or by charities, or even the corporate world (for example the Fairtrade Foundation).

Social investment

Government is committed to supporting ventures that bring the delivery of social justice to life at the local level. 'Social investment' is one such strategy.

Social investment involves more than simply spending money to address vulnerable people's immediate needs. The aim is to give people the tools that they need to take control and improve their own situations, where possible. For example, governments will pay benefits to unemployed people to help them to survive; a more proactive approach would require those people also to acquire new skills to better equip them for new job markets. The distinction here

is between a passive 'cash transfer' and actively 'investing in human capital'. The idea is to get more 'bang for each benefit buck' by creating a lasting impact – an investment that offers returns over time.

Choice and personalisation

Key themes in reforming public services over recent years have been 'choice' and 'personalisation'. The consumer culture in which we live emphasises a tailored, personalised service, rather than 'one size fits all'. So, increasingly, we also expect flexibility from our public services, such as doctors' surgeries, with provision that's:

- accessible 24/7;
- personalised to fit our particular needs; and
- delivered via the Internet (or over the phone, or face to face – whatever your preference).

Politicians also remind us that we want choice, whether that means choice of schools for our children, or of electricity supplier, or of hospitals for an operation.

Both choice and personalisation raise bigger questions. If public services are to reflect the (supposedly high) levels of customer service that we get from the private sector, we might question whether the private sector is better placed to deliver them. But if all of our public service provision were to be marketised, where would this leave the relationship between the state and the individual? What's more, if we're to make our own decisions about service provision, competing services must offer us genuine choice. We must have real choice – not, say, a handful of energy providers huddled into an oligopoly, all offering the same lousy service and high prices.

And there's another big 'but': what protection will be available for those who make the wrong choice? Not everyone's adept at skimming the small print – so what recourse will they have when things go wrong? And if the price of choice is spending half our lives navigating our way through automated call centres (only to get cut off) and tearing our hair out as we struggle to secure the 'best deal', might we prefer our local school and our local hospital simply to be a one-stop shop?

Chapter 16

BUILDING A
BETTER SOCIETY:
WORK, CRIME AND LOCALISM

In the last few chapters, we've talked a lot about what society is – and what it isn't. But the big question is how it works in practice. So let's now take a look at what really matters – the impact on real human beings – ourselves and our fellow British citizens.

Safety nets

As fully functioning adults, it goes without saying that we should be grown up enough to take personal responsibility for our lives. But even the smartest of arses can suffer brute bad luck – perhaps a devastating car crash or a mugging, a stalker, a house fire, or a rogue banker gambling away our savings. If a fall from a horse or a freak skiing accident can leave both *Superman* actor Christopher Reeve and F1 champion Michael Schumacher paralysed, we can only conclude: 'There but for the grace of God go I.'

The blame game

By and large, we try to take full responsibility for those things in our lives that are within our control. However, excessive emphasis on individual responsibility can corrode the way in which we judge social support for those in need and down on their luck. Few would blame the elderly for being old; after all, most of us hope that we too will live a long and happy life. Likewise, the need for social protection for sick and disabled people is widely accepted. But when it comes to the unemployed, many among us take a harsher line, swift to condemn 'idle scroungers' clinging to the social safety net – perhaps choosing to ignore the role that ill-fortune can play in any of our lives: your employer might suddenly go bust, or you might find yourself 'out on your ear' after a run-in with an unreasonable boss. New employment may be in short supply – there may be no decent jobs, or competition might be so intense that you eventually get worn down by rejection after rejection. The unemployment quicksand can soon consume your savings, leading to financial worries, depression – even divorce.

Our tendency to stigmatise the jobless is no doubt shaped in part by stories in the more sensational media, with claimants shamed as

lazy parasites, abusing state benefits. Welfare policies too sometimes seem to echo this same agenda. Certainly, there will always be a few bad apples – the occasional low-life scrounger on whom the media can shine a spotlight, for us all to chuck rotten tomatoes at. But one swallow doesn't make a summer.

So the crux of the matter really is: how much economic vulnerability springs from individual responsibility and how much from bad luck?

Personal lifestyle choices are obviously one aspect of how well or badly we do in life; then again, so is the wealth of our parents. Social background and class (see Chapter 13) remain big factors in determining where we end up in the labour market. If our inheritance is one of brutal poverty, there's a pretty high chance that it will cling to us through life like a damp sea mist; hence the risk of social exclusion is particularly high in impoverished households. But there's another 'individual responsibility' booby trap, and – if we're honest – it's one that could have caught any among us: the folly of youth. Most of us experienced at least one thing in our teens that, only by sheer good luck, didn't explode in our faces: the 'lucky' bike crash, the pregnancy 'false alarm', alcohol poisoning, road rage, fighting, gambling, extreme sports. Who can foresee the long-term consequences of ill-conceived decisions taken in our youth?

And yet our hearts have hardened in recent years. The proportion of the public believing that society ought to provide a decent standard of living for the unemployed has fallen from 81% in 1985 to 59% now (up slightly from 50% in 2006 – before the 2008–9 global financial crisis and subsequent recession bit). While many of us support increases in nearly every type of sickness/disability or in-work benefit – for example Carer's Allowance or Working Tax Credit – only 15% of people support increases in unemployment benefits; in fact, approximately half of us would like to see them cut. Further, in 2013, 54% of people agreed that 'Most unemployed people could find a job if they really wanted one', compared with only a third in the early 1990s.

The 'deserving poor'

Arguments about the 'deserving poor' go back to the days of the Victorian workhouse, if not earlier. In practice economic vulnerability is increasing for the majority of fellow citizens. So should support only be offered to those deemed 'deserving' (nowadays described as the 'working poor')? And is it right to stigmatise those whom we consider undeserving? Who decides? What we do know is that following recent changes to the social security system, many people on means-tested benefits now have reduced incomes. The level of benefits for an out-of-work adult without children actually covers only 40% of what the public considers to be a minimum standard of living; for families with children, this figure is 60%.

Back to work

Government schemes, such as the Work Programme, aim to get people off welfare and into work – hence the tagline 'welfare to work'. But what does this mean in practice? The long-term unemployed are referred to a range of organisations that have contracted with government to make this happen. One of the big innovations with these sorts of schemes is that the contractors are paid partly according to the results that they achieve; those results, however, have proven elusive. The government's Public Accounts Committee – a cross-party group of MPs (see Chapter 8) – reported that, between June 2011 and July 2012, only 3.6% of people referred to the Work Programme moved off benefits and into work. A particular concern is that the Work Programme is apparently failing young people and the hardest to help, such as those formerly on Incapacity Benefit. Fairly predictably, there's been a tendency for such organisations to pick the more profitable low-hanging fruit.

Vocational training

Increasingly, the payment of social support to the vulnerable has been linked to their making efforts to reduce their need for such support, rather than as straight 'handouts'. For example, an unemployed youth may qualify for a benefit only if he or she engages with 'social investment' (see Chapter 15) and takes a 'life course' designed to equip them with the necessary skills to get a job (and hence to improve the young person's position within society).

But it turns out that such active labour market policies only marginally increase the chances of getting a job, because such interventions are rarely tailored to individual needs – and that means that they rarely do much good. Besides, it's not only a lack of skills that afflicts the economically vulnerable; they may also struggle to realise their potential (both in the job market and in life) because

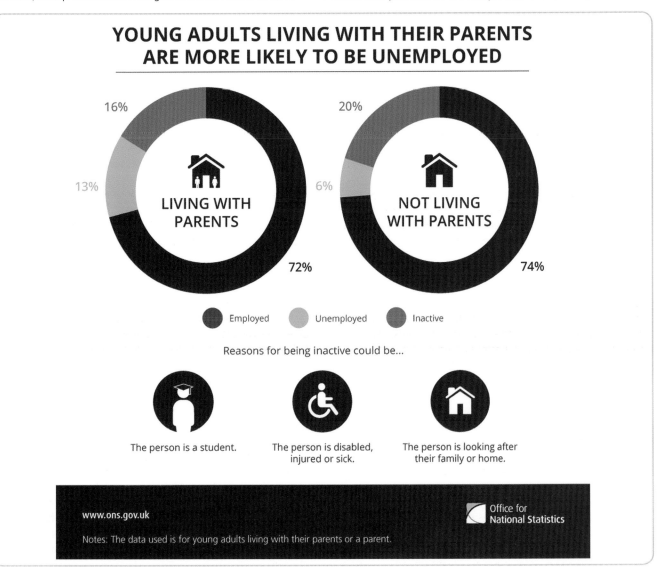

YOUNG ADULTS LIVING WITH THEIR PARENTS ARE MORE LIKELY TO BE UNEMPLOYED

LIVING WITH PARENTS: 16%, 13%, 72%

NOT LIVING WITH PARENTS: 20%, 6%, 74%

Employed · Unemployed · Inactive

Reasons for being inactive could be...

The person is a student.

The person is disabled, injured or sick.

The person is looking after their family or home.

www.ons.gov.uk

Office for National Statistics

Notes: The data used is for young adults living with their parents or a parent.

they lack support from family and friends. Those who are more fortunate find that, in times of need, they can call upon family, old mates or contacts for practical help (such as money), emotional support and solidarity. Those whom the gods haven't blessed with a head start in life, are more likely to encounter anxiety, depression and bad health, rather than help. And to make things worse, because these vulnerable groups lack status in society, they generally lack any influence with which to improve their lot with the 'powers that be'.

In any event, no amount of vocational training can address the underlying issue – the lack of sufficient employment opportunities.

Is there an alternative?

Across Europe, there are different approaches to welfare. Inevitably, poorer nations tend to pay less, and impose greater restrictions on who can qualify for support and for how long.

- The UK follows the Anglo-Irish model. Deregulation of markets and employment regulations was intended to limit the need for welfare. Universal state assistance is provided, but limited, to encourage the economically vulnerable towards self-sufficiency.
- The Nordic/social democratic model assumes that welfare is the

---

A BASIC INCOME GUARANTEE?

What's wrong with the dole?

In a rare display of unity, economists seem to be universally opposed to simple 'dole' payments – that is, doling out money to the workless without seeking to address the cause of unemployment. Where economists differ is when it comes to solutions – that is, whether worklessness results from a deficiency of the system or poor individual life choices.

What are the alternatives?

Many alternatives to the dole have been tried, the following among them.

- The use of means-tested benefits has an especially pernicious impact, the benefit being withdrawn as means increase. While this might seem logical, it leaves the vulnerable caught in a 'benefit trap', in which the small increases in income promised by low-paid employment are wiped out by the resulting withdrawal of benefits. This clearly reduces the incentive to work. Furthermore, means testing can be expensive to administer, requiring authorities to update and analyse ever-changing information on claimants. It also creates a situation in which people can be tempted to tell porkies (commit benefit fraud).
- Where wages are below the subsistence level, the state might subsidise them up to a minimum level, for example through working tax credits. However, subsidising low wages creates a labour market distortion: there's no incentive for employers to pay employees what they're truly worth if they know that the state – that is, the taxpayer – will step in and make up the difference. In effect, any firm that wants to pay its workers a socially responsible wage will be outcompeted by those who pay low wages and can therefore charge lower prices.
- The UK National Minimum Wage for adults is around 20% less than the living wage. Some suggest that the minimum wage should be raised to the living-wage level; others suggest that this might have a counter-productive effect, with classical economists arguing that the number of employment opportunities on offer declines as a minimum wage increases (see Chapter 14). The ideal combination is, after all, a living wage and full employment.
- Where the market has failed to provide sufficient employment at a living wage, the government might step in to create the extra jobs – e.g. by employing more teachers, police or nurses. The drawback of this is that such employment might well distort the labour market; the benefit is that it circumvents the need for minimum wage legislation. If the government is prepared to offer employment at a living wage, the private sector will be forced to offer the same if it's to attract workers.

A 'Basic Income Guarantee': a BIG idea

A simple and feasible way of providing an income level that avoids both the benefit trap and market distortion might be to scrap the means-tested part of the benefits system and guarantee a 'basic income' to *all* individuals legally resident in the UK. (A qualification period could be set to discourage inefficient 'welfare migration'.) Such a system would replace all others – except for disability benefits (which might be more effectively funded through the NHS in any event).

Because the basic income would be paid to all, irrespective of employment or earning status, at a single stroke it could rid us of benefit fraud and stop the stigmatisation of the economically vulnerable. In general, universal benefits are also far more efficient than means-tested benefits, as the superior efficiency of the NHS over private systems indicates (see Chapter 17). Tweaking the tax rate paid on the income by wealthier recipients could help to ensure that 'those who don't really need it' don't benefit unduly, which would also help to offset the overall costs of implementing the scheme.

The level of the basic income should be such that it ensures that everyone who can work will be able to afford to live (avoiding the benefit trap). Further, it would have the advantage of not distorting labour markets, in the way that income support and minimum wage legislation do.

In the 1970s, Manitoba (in Canada) tried implementing a basic income guarantee. The experiment led to many beneficial outcomes for the community and state: hospital visits dropped by 8.5%; there was a reduction in the number of mental-illness-related consultations with health professionals; and there was evidence of a reduction in domestic violence. It was also found that mothers had more time to devote to rearing newborn children. Students showed higher test scores and lower dropout rates than before – plus there was an increase in the number of adults continuing education.

Similar programmes elsewhere have also shown significant improvement in the quality of parenting among those who were economically vulnerable. Basic income guarantee payments have thus been shown to reduce children's early life stress, which feeds through into improving their quality of life and educational outcomes – which snowballs into further improvements in later life. This means that such programmes pretty much pay for themselves, by cutting the costs of criminal interventions and health (including mental health) care.

responsibility of the state. Income compensation is generous, universal and an effective protection against poverty, whilst at the same time support for children, the disabled and the elderly is strong.

- The Continental model, followed in countries such as France and Germany, is based on a mix of employer provision, family responsibilities, dependency on the chief breadwinner (usually male) and dominance of employment-linked social insurance. Unemployment benefits are determined by previous earnings and payments to public insurance providers. A challenge for this model is the lack of security that it offers to people with weak links to the labour market, such as women and workers with irregular careers. Since the late 1990s, however, states following this model have moved towards social investment (see Chapter 15), and away from the traditional family ideal and passive income compensation.
- The southern model followed in Mediterranean countries is less comprehensive than those of their northern neighbours, with lower redistribution and higher poverty levels. The extended family has been essential to absorbing social shocks and providing care for children, elderly and disabled members, as well as for housing.
- The central and eastern member states have undergone much change in recent decades, and their welfare systems tend to adopt elements of both the Anglo-Irish and Continental models, but are less well funded than either.

Different welfare regimes across Europe reflect the differing theories of society adopted by different countries.

In the more individualistic nations, such as the UK, the emphasis is more on individual responsibility. Certainly, as Thatcher noted, people should indeed take responsibility for themselves if they can. The question is how we might sensibly go about determining those who can, from those who cannot.

Crime and criminal justice

First, the good news: across most of the Western world, crime rates have declined over the last 25 years. Despite some debate about how you measure them, crime rates in the UK for 'traditional offences' (homicide, violence, robbery, domestic burglary, motor vehicle theft, drug trafficking) have fallen substantially. Your chances of being a victim of crime in Britain today are historically low. One cloud in this otherwise sunny scenario is that some of this traditional activity has been displaced by the new 'cyber' sort. 'Great Train Robber' style raids seem to have become a thing of the past. In fact, it's rather the reverse: cynics might point to banks rigging markets and fleecing their customers.

So if crime is dropping, what does it mean for policing? The British public often say they want to see more 'bobbies on the beat', but do we really need them?

Now, the bad news: despite this decline in crime, rates of imprisonment are heading in the other direction – and, as a result, so is the cost of running prisons. So what can we do to reverse this trend?

'Disturbances in the force'

It's not widely appreciated that, over the last 20 years in the UK, crime has dropped by around half: an incredible success story for the boys and girls in blue. But, as we all know, money is tight, so as part of its

DIXON OF DOCKED WAGES GREEN

ongoing attempts to cut the budget deficit the government has used this fact to justify a real-terms reduction in police funding in England and Wales to the tune of a massive 20% by 2015. The vast majority of these savings – nearly three-quarters – have been achieved by slashing the workforce. Between 2010 and 2015, the force lost 15,400 police officers – and if you add administrative staff and community support officers, this figure more than doubles, to a whopping 31,600, or 13% of all police employees.

The question is: does this matter? Should we be worried that understaffing is an open invitation for the local bad lads to engage in all manner of wickedness? Thankfully, the evidence suggests not:

- Despite these swingeing cuts, police forces have fought to protect their front-line crime-fighting capabilities. Even with a recession causing economic hardship, crime has continued to fall.
- In surveys, the public mostly reported noticing no major changes to policing in their area. Despite the savings, around half of people polled believed that the number of local police had stayed the same (rather than falling or rising, or 'unknown').
- Surveys also show that public concern about law-and-order issues is at its lowest level for over 20 years.

'There goes the neighbourhood'

Not everyone is relaxed about the 'long arm of the law' being that much shorter, with fewer bobbies on hand to collar wrongdoers. Her Majesty's Inspectorate of Constabulary (HMIC), for example, is concerned that many forces have made savings by broadening the remit of 'safer neighbourhood teams' (SNTs).

Neighbourhood teams are generally regarded as one of the successes of modern policing. The strategy has involved moving away from the traditional, reactive 'flashing lights and sirens' approach toward teams of local people and volunteers engaging with communities to solve underlying problems – getting in early can help prevent crime and antisocial behaviour kicking off in the first place. 'Nipping it in the bud' makes a lot of sense – but there's only so much that SNTs can be expected to achieve.

Government is always looking for savings and one of the big ongoing debates is about how many constabularies we actually need. Of the 43 county forces in England and Wales, some are very small. From an economic perspective, this isn't efficient, because lots of 'back-office' functions are being duplicated and smaller forces have only limited opportunities to make further cuts. So should the smaller forces be merged with their larger neighbours? On the one hand, most people seem to like the idea of localism and self-supporting communities (see Chapter 13) – not to mention the reassuringly familiar blue lamp outside the local nick – somewhere in town that you can get to quickly in an emergency. We fondly imagine that our local 'cop shop' can keep tabs on all of the resident villains in the 'local manor'. And of course different forces have proud traditions and cultures – so merging *Taggart* with *Lewis* might cause a few ructions! On the other hand, as crime changes, the force needs to adapt, so that it can respond to new threats – new criminal activity in cyberspace rather than declining car crime – plus, of course, organised criminals who operate at regional, national and international levels.

The debate on merging police forces reached its peak in 2005, when the Home Office considered proposals to replace the county forces with nine regional 'super-constabularies'. Although it seems that the strategy was shelved, some forces have since shared back-office functions and it's likely that a similar solution may be mooted as budget pressures continue to bite. After all, if there are cost savings to be made, the government rarely turns a blind eye…

The prison crisis

In the last couple of decades, the rate of imprisonment per 100,000 of population has increased more rapidly even than in the United States. With around 148 prisoners per 100,000 citizens (albeit compared with the incredible 716 per 100,000 in the United States), England and Wales have the highest per capita prison population in western Europe.

The Ministry of Justice estimates that the average cost to the taxpayer of keeping someone behind bars is around £35,000. This

H.M. PRISON

IN | OUT | BACK IN

K.J. Lamb

equates to around £3 billion in annual costs in England and Wales. Some argue that this figure would be substantially higher if we were to include the wider social costs, such as extra support for families now without their 'breadwinner'; others point out that there are equally costs in community-based punishment. Either way, it's an awful lot of money – leading some offenders to suggest that it might even be cheaper to offer them £20,000 a year to stay out of trouble than it is to lock them up!

At the end of the day, there are some big questions that we need to ask: does prison work? Is it a cost-effective way of spending money? Given the rocketing rates of slinging those convicted of crimes into the slammer, what evidence is there that our increasing reliance on imprisonment gets results? Does it reduce the crime rate more effectively than alternative methods?

GO STRAIGHT TO JAIL

A majority of the British public believe that 'life should mean life' for murder. Understandably, none of us wants to find ourselves quaking in fear for our very lives, confronted by a rampaging knifeman on the bus home. We naturally want society to be free from the shadow of rapists, predatory paedophiles, violent criminals and similar threats to

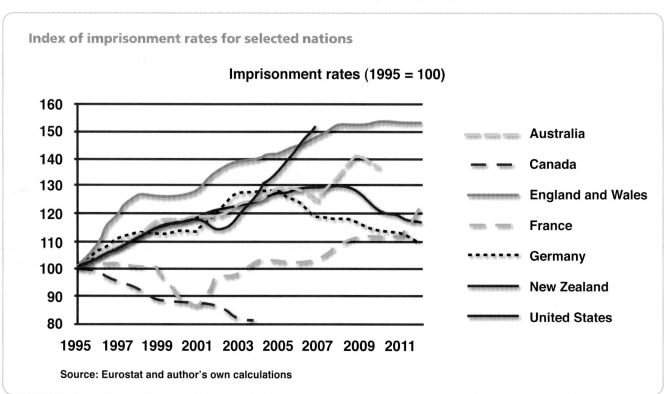

Index of imprisonment rates for selected nations

Imprisonment rates (1995 = 100)

Legend: Australia, Canada, England and Wales, France, Germany, New Zealand, United States

Source: Eurostat and author's own calculations

our well-being, and that of our friends and families. However, at the same time, many recognise that prison is often one of the worst ways of dealing with troubled people. Clearly, a balance needs to be struck.

Imprisonment benefits society in the following three main ways.

- **Incapacitation** Whilst inside, the offender will find it difficult (or impossible) to commit further crime.
- **Personal deterrence** Those imprisoned are assumed to dislike the experience and to be keen, when released, to avoid going back inside any time soon.
- **General deterrence** Those who've not yet offended might not relish the prospect of being 'banged up' and will consequently think twice before committing a crime.

There is, however, another reason why we favour prison-based punishments: not only is it natural for victims of horrendous crimes to want to see the perpetrators punished, but also, as we saw in Chapter 12, dispensing – or even only contemplating – 'just deserts' activates the part of our brain associated with reward. In other words, when we punish those who ignore our social norms, we satisfy a powerful desire for retribution.

THE BAD NEWS: PRISON MIGHT *NOT* WORK

Those who've taken the trouble to assess scientifically whether prison works or not have found that, in practice, it often might not - or at least it might not do so very efficiently. True, it fulfils the basic function of keeping dangerous offenders off the streets and satisfies our need for retribution, but there is conflicting evidence about its effect on overall crime rates: Canada's imprisonment rate declined from 1995, while that of the UK rose – yet Canada's crime rates have fallen more rapidly than those of the UK. Neither did a decline in the rate of imprisonment in the United States since 2007 lead to any apparent increase in crime.

As a cost-effective criminal justice policy, there's little evidence that mass imprisonment works. One drawback is that inmates can become further disengaged from honest life and lose the family connections that might encourage them to desist from future criminal activity. The deterrence value of prison is also somewhat hazy, since only the most intellectual of prospective criminals would conduct a cost–benefit analysis before committing a crime.

What we do know is that nearly three-quarters of the prison population has two or more mental health disorders (with male prisoners 14 times more likely than average to suffer, and female prisoners, a shocking 35 times). To make matters worse, around 20% of the prison population has some form of hidden physical or learning disability, which (combined with a criminal history as an 'ex-con') can severely limit their chances of getting legitimate employment when they get out.

WHAT ARE YOUR CHANCES OF GOING TO PRISON?

If you were to take a random bunch of primary school kids and assess their chances of one day ending up in jail, socio-demographic factors such as sex, race and parental income would come into play. Youth is also a factor. In the UK, black young adults are four times more likely to be in prison than white young adults – and six times as likely as Asian young adults. In general, prisoners are disproportionately drawn from the poorest and most disadvantaged groups in society – and that raises the question: if prison is working, *for whom* is it working?

THE GOOD NEWS: THERE ARE ALTERNATIVES

The cold logic of Winston Churchill goes to the heart of the problem: 'The first real principle which should guide anyone trying to establish a good system of prisons would be to prevent as many people as possible getting there at all.' So is it possible to swoop down like Superman and stop potential offenders in their tracks before an evil deed is done?

The answer is that we already know how to identify those who are socially vulnerable and thus more likely to drift into a life of crime; the trick is therefore to intervene at the right time and offer measures that will improve these people's life chances. Wayward behaviour is often evident in childhood – so engaging with 'community-based interventions' sooner rather than later, with the aim of crime prevention, is surely better for all concerned than having to resort to lock and key. It's also a cheaper and more efficient approach than relying solely on old-fashioned criminal justice. Crime will never be eliminated – but there's no doubt that it can be reduced.

The following are examples of such interventions.

Justice reinvestment (JR)

A relatively new approach pioneered in the United States, it's claimed that 'justice reinvestment' is one of the reasons why US imprisonment rates are beginning to decline.

Geographical research showed that certain residential blocks in US cities were costing a million dollars a year in crime and its consequences (the cost of locking people up etc). Criminal justice agencies began to question whether it might not be better to invest some of this money in tackling the underlying problems that gave rise to the criminal behaviour in the first place and thereby reduce crime. The intervention therefore involves moving some of the money spent on punishing offenders into programmes designed to 'empower' local communities. In this way, not only are the costs of imprisoning offenders saved, but also the reduced rates of offending

mean decreased costs to victims and wider society – a double win. It's a model that the UK might well adopt in the future.

Restorative justice ('say sorry and shake hands')

The two traditional approaches employed in response to crime are:

- **retribution** – punishment such as being sent to jail, perhaps with hard labour (being 'hung, drawn and quartered' was the rather messy medieval approach)
- **treatment** – with a view to reducing rates of reoffending (also known as 'distributive justice').

However there's another approach that's been used successfully in recent years, known as 'restorative justice'. The aim is effectively to 'make up' for the wrong and to 'restore' the people directly affected to the positions in which they were before the offence. Restorative justice is nothing new – you'll find it at the heart of most ancient societies. The traditional wisdom within New Zealand's indigenous Maori society, for example, has always been to maintain balance, to repay kindness with kindness and generosity with generosity, and to seek restoration for injustice. This also forms the basis of our relationships with family and friends, when we sort out arguments and right wrongs by saying 'sorry' and shaking hands, or by 'kissing and making up'.

Obviously, there are limits to what the intervention can achieve in practice: it can't bring people back from the dead, and victims of serious offences such as rape, or even stalking, aren't likely to want to meet with their assailants. Nonetheless, in some cases, restorative justice can be useful and therapeutic. Victim–offender mediation sessions, or family group conferencing, have been shown to help to heal the harm caused by conflict, crime, or victimisation. And there's also evidence that offenders may be less likely to reoffend as a result – recognising for the first time the impact that their actions have had on their victims' lives.

The cautionary note is that the offender needs to be genuinely repentant, rather than simply saying 'sorry' as an easy way of dodging a prison sentence. Moreover, restorative justice can be a waste of time when adopted in a cynical bid to cut prison costs or to meet central police force targets. When *sincerely* adopted, however, this intervention has real potential to heal communities, and to reduce both the level and costs of crime.

The politics

Despite Churchill's perceptive observation, you'd have to be an unusually ballsy politician to stand up in Parliament and announce that you intend to pursue social justice rather than 'put the boot in' with lashings of criminal justice. Appearing to be 'soft on crime' is never going to win votes. Furthermore, investment in communities requires money now – investment up front to prevent crime from being committed – with any payoff realised only some years into the future. Only a pretty amazing political sales pitch could convince people to swallow tax increases to pay for intervention based only on the threat that we'll regret it in the future if we don't – and for most politicians, that's the next administration's problem. But the real stumbling block is this: it's impossible to measure what's been prevented. One reason for the spate of fatal train crashes after rail privatisation was the slashing of engineering, signalling and maintenance expertise by the profit-hungry new owners – because they simply couldn't see any evidence that skilled staff had quietly been averting disaster for years. Likewise, we can hardly expect people to grasp how high crime levels *would have been* had we not implemented social programmes.

In Raymond Chandler's *The Long Goodbye*, detective Philip Marlowe argues insightfully: 'Crime isn't a disease; it's a symptom. Cops are like a doctor that gives you aspirin for a brain tumour.' An economically efficient justice system therefore seeks to cure the underlying disease. Investing in communities rather than prisons might not make for palatable politics – but it does make excellent economic sense.

Restorative justice – traditional wisdom in New Zealand's Maori society.

Period TV dramas set in the 'halcyon days' of the 1950s have a tendency to gloss over reality – and not only the realities of post-war rationing and austerity measures. In the post-war period, crime started rising sharply, consistently, year on year. In England and Wales, some 500,000 crimes were recorded in 1957. The 1 million mark was passed in 1964, 2 million in 1975, 3 million in 1982, and 5 million in 1991. If you were to have talked to expert criminologists in the late 1980s, they'd have seen no reason to assume anything other than that crime rates would continue rising.

Then, in the 1990s, something astonishing started to happen: contrary to expectations, crime started to drop – not only in one country, but across the Western world, from the UK to Australia, and the United States to Germany.

The number of crimes had peaked in 1995; between 1995 and 2005, that number fell by a remarkable 44%. Since 2005, the rate of decline seems to have slowed, but it continues, despite the UK experiencing its deepest recession of the post-war period.

Index of police recorded total crime rates for selected nations

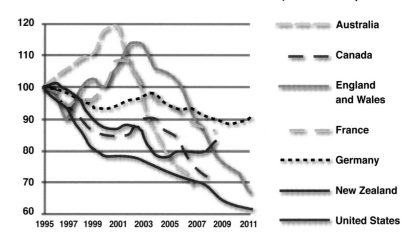

Police recorded total crime rates (1995 = 100)

Legend: Australia, Canada, England and Wales, France, Germany, New Zealand, United States

Source: Eurostat and author's own calculations

Explaining the crime drop: popular theories

This 'crime drop' is one of the intriguing mysteries of our time that has flummoxed experts. There is no glib, single explanation, but the uniform nature of the drop across the Western world suggests that there must be underlying reasons that are common to all such economies.

Certainly, different crimes may have dropped for different reasons, including the following.

- A lot of crime can be attributed to younger people, particularly young men, and most Western economies have ageing populations. Also, young people's lifestyles are changing: they spend less time outside, and more time watching TV and playing computer games. It's been suggested this keeps them out of trouble – and may even provide alternative outlets for antisocial urges.
- Although the crime drop began in the 1990s, before new approaches to policing were widespread, it's suggested that modern policing methods are more effective. The service is moving away from a target-based culture toward one that's more victim-focused. (Obsessing over government targets is said to have historically resulted in some crimes being prioritised over others, such as claims of sex abuse.)
- Perhaps the most obvious explanation is that it's a lot harder to set about stealing from cars with central locking and alarms, or from homes with better security and burglar alarms, etc. There's compelling evidence that car crime has dropped as car security has increased. And if these types of offence aren't so easy, it means that

'learners' can no longer 'cut their teeth' on things like burglary and vehicle theft, and are less likely to become career criminals.
- The recording of crime may also have played its part. The Independent Police Complaints Commission (the 'police watchdog') reported in 2014 that a fifth of crime reported to police wasn't recorded – that is, was dismissed as 'no crime committed' (whether or not this was the case). Inevitably, low-value, time-consuming cases, such as mobile phone theft (often reported only for insurance purposes), in which police aren't likely to get results, won't be prioritised. But some worry that the recording of particular types of offence may be influenced by performance targets.
- Cultural changes in our societies may also have had some effect. Today, we're increasingly likely to work part-time or from home; hence fewer homes are vacant break-in targets. There are also many more single-person households. Some suggest too that crime may have dropped because displays of traditional male aggression are now less acceptable, perhaps linked to the fact that there are more women in the workplace, media and sport, with greater sexual equality.
- Finally, there's the possible impact of lead-free petrol! It may sound bonkers, but there are strong statistical links between a rise in the amount of lead in the environment and rises in violent crime two decades later, and between the removal of lead from petrol and crime levels subsequently dropping. In fact, lead is a very potent neurotoxin that was used in petrol and paint until it was banned in the 1980s and 1990s. Until that time, exhaust fumes contained toxic lead compounds – and studies have shown that lead poisoning in childhood has been proven to increase the likelihood of offending by the time that child reaches late teens.

Localism

In the 1980s, Britain aspired to be a property-owning democracy, according to Mrs Thatcher. And she was right: instinctively we know that people are better citizens and neighbours when they have a real stake in society – and that stake might be home ownership. This is about more than simple pride: there are a number of good reasons why it's often better for people to own the properties in which they live.

Owner-occupier housing

Suppose that, as a tenant, you want to decorate and improve your home; the benefit of that renovation will accrue to the landlord. If you do an especially good job, you might even find that your rent is increased because the house is now so much more attractive in the marketplace. Alternatively, you may not be permitted to decorate in the first place. Then there's the worry about lack of security: the danger of bad landlords failing to maintain the property or evicting you if they get a better offer. If people can't afford to buy their own properties outright, living in housing in which they have a democratic stake, such as shared ownership, is the next best thing.

Owner-occupier communities

A similar logic applies to communities. Suppose that a bunch of tenants begin to build a good, strong community with their neighbours: by volunteering, by maintaining community gardens and by supporting the local society, they make their neighbourhood a more attractive place to live. The problem is that, as their area becomes more attractive, it'll attract the attentions of 'gentrifiers'. As a result of rising demand, rents will rise – and the tenants might wind up being forced out of the very area that they've worked so hard to improve.

For example, less than 50 years ago, London's Notting Hill was described as 'a massive slum, full of multi-occupied houses, crawling with rats and rubbish'. Since the 1960s, those who lived there worked hard to promote the neighbourhood – and as they made the area more desirable, they priced themselves and their children out of it. Ironically, then, they may have been better off neglecting the local community so as to drive down rents (including their own).

Local businesses are similarly influenced by the dynamics of 'owner-occupation'. Those who live, own and work in a local area have an added incentive to contribute to that area – to do more than simply extract profits. The success of one very special local retailer can add to the attractiveness of an entire shopping centre, creating spillover benefits for all of the other shops. Such effects can't easily be maintained by reliance on individual profit orientation.

Consider, for example, the group of independent 'quirky' shops at the western end of Sheffield's 'Gold Route', which takes walkers through the most attractive parts of the central city. The success of local people and the council in turning the area into an attractive part of town is now threatening the viability of the very businesses that co-created the atmosphere of this small 'urban village'. As multinational coffee chains appear and rents increase, some of the businesses – with names and stock that might have come straight out of a *Harry Potter* movie – may well disappear in the not-too-distant future. Out-of-town property developers are also keen to 'invest' and capitalise on the benefits that local people have created, intending to tear down some of the most attractive remaining buildings and replace them with blocks of flats. So, in this case too, perhaps the shopkeepers might have been better off maintaining the area's reputation for antisocial behaviour?

Sadly, the *atmosphere* of a neighbourhood, while important, can't compete with the lure of 'big money'. Is it reasonable to expect people who don't live in an area to sacrifice the potential for a profit simply because of a non-monetisable 'atmosphere'? If property owners aren't local, their 'stake' in society is more likely to be limited to financial considerations; only local ownership is likely to reflect – and preserve – local values.

Owner-occupier nations

As in the home, so in the neighbourhood, town and nation. Local ownership generally works best when it comes to local societies addressing local concerns. It's more efficient. It goes without saying that where a nation has lost the right to rule itself in a way that benefits its citizens – where it's run purely for the purpose of maximising the profits of people who don't live there or multinational corporations headquartered in other countries – the quality of life of locals is likely to suffer. This is no less true of 'economic imperialism' than it is of military imperialism. It also raises concerns where governments have few qualms about selling off successful UK-owned and -operated businesses – the 'jewels in the Crown' – to overseas corporations or anonymous private equity owners looking to maximise short-term profits.

The rise of the blandly homogenous

The law of unintended consequences applies as much to the rise of national and global commerce as it does elsewhere. But the effects are perhaps most plain where it has, unintentionally, undermined the profitability of small, locally owned businesses.

A large national or global franchise generally has far greater marketing and advertising muscle than does a small business. Large businesses also reap huge benefits from economies of scale and may cross-subsidise from one location to another, giving them a major competitive advantage over smaller local business. More insidiously, it would seem that globalised corporations effectively get to choose

'This town is coming like a ghost town'

whether they'll pay local tax. This gives them a further massive competitive advantage over locally owned and smaller businesses.

Somewhat ironically, given the diversity of world cultures, globalised high streets therefore start to resemble each other. The goal of economic efficiency becomes an unstoppable steamroller flattening local culture to produce uniform results – a 'spot the difference' vista for visitors. To wander about Clapham or Hexham, Lancaster or Doncaster means increasingly to encounter the same array of shops – the chain store is king in a globalised world.

As if the bland uniformity of 'downtown anyplace' weren't bad enough, the power that is economic efficiency has another trick up its sleeve: it strips away employment. It's been estimated that local shops employ an average of one person for every £50,000 of annual turnover; for national supermarkets, the figure is £250,000 per job. This is one of the reasons why prices are lower, of course – but what's good news for locals as consumers is bad news for locals as employees.

This wouldn't matter so much if the increased profits from all of this economic efficiency were to be staying in the local area (or country). The money would then simply be spent on something else produced or provided locally, thereby creating new employment somewhere just down the road. But while local business owners tend to spend their profits in local shops and create local prosperity, the profits of globally owned business accrue to the distant owner – and the local community is further impoverished.

The need for community empowerment

However ideal it would be for local business and communities to be owned and operated locally, with a view to benefiting the local community, in practice the world is not like that. On the other hand, the world is what we make it. For example, where possible, communities can take action to shape local markets, to ensure that local people and businesses share in the benefits – ie 'social outcomes' are delivered. Such 'extra-market' actions might include things such as planning controls, setting up community associations, social housing, rent controls and local currencies (such as the Bristol pound), and encouraging consumers to shop locally if possible. Government also has a role to play in levelling the playing field of competition, for example by ensuring that large corporate retailers don't drive out smaller local shops merely by virtue of their size or ability to avoid taxation.

Politicians from both sides of the political spectrum are also starting to recognise that the needs of communities and neighbourhoods may not be met by unfettered market forces or national policy. Recent governments have attempted to empower communities to engage in the improvement of their local areas, for example through the New Deal for Communities (NDC) initiative (under which local people were placed at the heart of achieving improvements in crime, community, housing, education, health and worklessness). Such schemes have produced benefits of between three and five times the costs of running them – clearly good value for money.

More recently, the Localism Act 2011 aimed to empower local communities. The Act is intended to represent a transition from big government to Big Society (see Chapter 12), reforming planning procedure, and providing new freedoms and flexibilities for local government and communities. Unfortunately, in the context of ongoing austerity measures, the tight financial constraints under which local authorities operate mean that they aren't easily able to exploit their newfound powers to the benefit of locals. Freedoms and flexibilities are, after all, more useful when finance is attached.

Vive la difference! Variety may be the spice of life, but it's sadly lacking in today's centrally operated UK. Self-esteem is palpable when we take pride in what we make, grow, or serve, and regional variety makes travel more interesting.

The following are a few suggestions as to how Britain might go about restoring some pride among its local business communities.

- **Food and farming** As in France, we might encourage supermarkets to devote a percentage of shelf space to local produce – both to support the local economy and to breathe some life back into local farms, fisheries and cottage industries. National supermarket chains would be seen to be putting something back into their local communities, whilst making their offerings to customers more diverse and interesting. We ought also to require them to treat suppliers with a certain amount of decency and respect, placing higher value on quality and doing more than simply covering the costs of production. Food and drink should have honest labelling, with county/country of origin and food miles clearly indicated. In France, too, road signs proudly announce the local delicacy or top tipple – so why not here?
- **Quality building materials** From the honey-coloured stone of the Cotswolds to the granite of Aberdeenshire and Cornwall, and the variety of local Victorian bricks that once defined our towns, let's once again take pride in our regional building traditions and the quality of local crafts, and stop erecting soulless 'anywhere' housing developments and bland office blocks. Land is Britain's most precious resource so let's use it wisely.
- **Culture** Britain has a rich heritage of regional cultures, history and accents. Instead of simply swallowing pervasive London-centric and US culture, why don't we give a leg-up to local arts and media?
- **Manufacturing** The Clyde and the Tyne are two among many British rivers once defined by shipbuilding – and pride still resonates today, even though the closure of shipyards and factories ripped the heart out of many local communities long ago. Might it be time for that proud memory to fuel a new 'march of the makers'?
- **Town centres** If you want to kill off a town centre, just permit sprawling food superstores to be built on out-of-town sites. Shoppers might benefit from 'market choice' for a year or so – before the life is sucked out of the old town and the familiar shops are boarded up. The flow might be reversed by making it easy and appealing for shoppers to hit the high street, and creating pleasant social spaces in town with buzzing evening economies fuelled by entertainment, events and easy parking. Retail consultant Mary Portas made 28 recommendations to revive dying town centres, such as zero business rates and easy rental terms for new businesses and 'pop up' shops. At the very least, politicians need to empower planners to breathe life back into 'community assets' – pubs, village halls and churches – and stop closing local post offices.

One last note: to change towns, villages, local economies and communities for the better, we need politicians who are courageous – politicians who won't bow to corporate pressure.

Chapter 17

BUILDING A BETTER SOCIETY:
HEALTH AND EDUCATION

Health and lifestyle

The state of the nation

Throughout the developed world, life expectancy is increasing. Unfortunately, so is the impact of chronic disease. When it comes to health and lifestyle, it's interesting to see how, as a nation, Britain compares with other countries (see Table 17.1).

The good news is that, on many measures, the UK is doing very well – generally, better than average. What really lets us down is 'lifestyle choices' – notably, obesity and alcohol consumption. But

there's one area in which we can really hold our heads high with pride: the quality of our National Health Service.

British is best

Imagine that you're the US president – arguably, the most powerful person in the world – and yet your country is unwell, both economically and medically. The annual federal budget deficit in 2012 was US$1,087 billion. That's one heck of a number: $1,087,000,000,000 *in a single year*. Now, suppose that, in a sudden blinding flash, a great truth were revealed: there's one thing that you could do that would totally eliminate this massive

Table 17.1   UK ranking among OECD* countries for various measures of health

	UK	OECD* average	UK ranking
Life expectancy at birth, 2011 (years)	81.1	80.1	15th
Ischemic heart disease mortality, 2011 (age-standardised rates per 100,000 population)	113	122	19th
All cancer mortality rates, 2011 (age-standardised rates per 100,000 population)	226	211	27th
Infant mortality rates, 2011 (deaths per 1,000 live births)	4.3	3.8	25th
Percentage of adults reporting to be in good health, 2011 (% population)	77.5	69	10th
Prevalence estimates of diabetes, adults aged 20–79, 2011 (%)	5.4	6.9	9th
Obesity among adults, 2011 (% of population aged 15 and over)	24.8	17.6	34th
Daily moderate-to-vigorous physical activity, 15-year-olds, 2009–10 (% of children)	18	15	7th
Healthy life years at age 65, 2011	12	9	6th

* OECD = Organisation for Economic Co-operation and Development

deficit, with no adverse effects. It would even leave you $560 billion in spare change. What's more, adopting this policy would even allow you to eliminate future deficits… You'd jump at the chance, wouldn't you?

The US government could achieve all of this simply by replacing its (largely private sector) health care system with a system equivalent to our NHS. As a welcome side-effect, such a policy could improve US health – reducing the maternal mortality ratio by 70%, for example, and increasing life expectancy by nearly three years. In short: what's not to like?

According to a 2014 report by The Commonwealth Fund, a Washington-based think tank, Britain's NHS was the best health care system in the industrialised world, beating even the Swiss system into second place. Meanwhile, the US health care system came out as the worst of the 11 nations considered (Australia, Canada, France, Germany, the Netherlands, New Zealand, Norway, Sweden, Switzerland, the United Kingdom and the United States).

The democratic NHS ethos

In a market economy, the worth of an individual is largely defined by his or her personal wealth. But for the individual, regardless of their financial well-being, a dignified and healthy life is of enormous value.

At the heart of the NHS ethos is the understanding that provision of life-saving or life-enhancing treatment is based on need, rather than financial clout. In this sense, the NHS is a more socially just institution than the equivalent private sector model.

Even though the NHS is one of the best health care services in the world, most of those among us who use its services have never had the chance to compare it to other systems – so our expectations tend to be fairly high. But by the nature of its 'free at the point of use' ethos, there may naturally be a rise in demand for more services than can sometimes efficiently be delivered. In economics, there's nothing to limit consumer demand for a free service (the usual limit being price). But the solution to the resulting potentially insatiable demand for universal health care services isn't to make people pay (at least not until the day on which we all have the means), but rather to be bold enough to develop and stick to a model of socially efficient health care for all. At the same time, it makes sense to reduce demand by promoting healthier lifestyles.

Of course, in reality, there have to be limits on what can be provided: the original NHS, as set up in 1948, offered a far more restricted range of services. Today the tough task of determining what is and is not socially efficient is taken on by the National Institute of Health and Clinical Excellence (NICE). Sometimes, its

guidance might seem callous when it concerns our own health and that of our relatives – but the alternative is that the system breaks down under infinite demand.

But isn't choice good?

Free market economists often argue (sometimes without reference to any supporting data) that competition and choice in health care will automatically drive down costs and increase efficiency. But if you were to ask Joe Public whether he'd rather have £2,400 a year deducted from his tax to fund the industrialised world's best health service or pay £6,000 to an insurance company for the developed world's worst health care system (with greater choice as to which corporation would treat him), it's unlikely that he'd plump for the latter, more expensive option. Certainly, this is a no-brainer for the average Brit.

There is, however, nothing to prevent us taking out private medical insurance *as well as* paying towards the NHS through our taxes. What's more, the cost of doing so is likely to be cheaper than if private provision were our only option, because the efficiency of the NHS (that is, effective competition) helps to drive down the cost of private provision in the UK.

Perverse incentives

According to free market principles, firms exist for the sole purpose of maximising profits. Corporations prosper if the customer comes back to buy more 'product'. Where the product is medical care, this creates an incentive not to cure illness, but to preserve both life *and* illness, to ensure future profit. In health care, the dead are not customers – but, then again, neither are the healthy.

In order to limit demand, the NHS has an incentive to minimise the causes of ill health in the population as a whole, and it does so by targeting educational campaigns about the damage wreaked by smoking, alcohol, obesity, etc. The NHS is, after all, a facilitator of 'health' rather than of medical treatment.

For the private sector, things aren't quite so clear-cut. It's unthinkable that any private sector medical provider would ever behave so unscrupulously as to prolong illness merely to increase profit (free market principles aren't usually so strictly observed, even in large corporations). But neither does it have an incentive to promote healthy lifestyles in the population at large when this might jeopardise its profits.

The reason why the UK is able to achieve so much in health care with so little funding is not only because of the high quality of NHS staff, but also because of its investment in public health generally. Today, the NHS is seeking to take this ethos one step further: by promoting investment in preventative measures, and by linking health services with local government and social support services. So there are real concerns that the prominence in politics of corporate lobbying and party funding could have serious implications for health

HEALTH AND HEALTHY EATING

It's no secret that the NHS is overstretched, as are doctors' surgeries. One obvious solution is to reduce demand: everyone agrees that prevention is better than cure. So the battle is now on to get us all to live healthier lives. But it would seem that we have our work cut out, since two-thirds of UK adults and a third of children are officially overweight or obese. What's more, diabetes levels have doubled in the past 20 years. This is largely down to excess sugar in soft drinks and food, rather than inactive lifestyles.

It's a sobering fact that it takes about an hour of hard graft in the gym to burn off just 400 calories, but only a few minutes to load it all back on again:

- ■ **Fizzy drink**   140 kcal
- ■ **Cheeseburger**   500 kcal
- ■ **TV dinner**   650 kcal

One of the biggest drivers of the 'obesity epidemic' is sugar, especially when combined with fat. Although all age groups consume more than they should, children and teenagers are particularly at risk. One problem for consumers is that there's currently no clear target for sugar consumption, so even enthusiastic label readers can easily end up puzzled. And added sugars are concealed everywhere in processed food: often, there are no fewer than four teaspoons of sugar in a tin of soup, five in a typical yoghurt or TV dinner, and up to ten in a can of sickly sweet cola. These added sugars have absolutely no nutritional value, and are 'empty calories'. Sugar is processed in the liver into fat, which releases insulin, raising blood pressure. In effect consuming excess sugar can be toxic, leading to type 2 diabetes with the risk of an earlier death from a stroke, heart attack, dementia or cancer.

Opportunity or threat?

Manufacturing and retailing junk food is big business, and understandably the industry isn't over the moon about threats to sales. But change also brings opportunities to develop new, profitable, healthier products. So far, government has meekly followed the 'advice' of industry lobbyists, opting for voluntary 'responsibility deals' and 'nudging' consumers to modify their behaviour – but independent public health scientists argue that such agreements are ineffective. Indeed, recent campaigns have resulted in increasing levels of obesity, with some well-known companies reneging on pledges.

Top trumps: the 'three "A"s' vs the 'three "D"s'

Food processing is the UK's biggest manufacturing sector and health experts claim that the power of the industry is a major obstacle to a

'AND WHAT IS THAT IN EXTREMELY ROUND FIGURES?'

MINIMUM ALCOHOL PRICING

The battles fought for decades by 'big tobacco' are today being re-run by well-funded 'big booze' pressure groups. In 2011, Prime Minister David Cameron firmly pledged that the government would introduce 'minimum unit pricing' to curb super-cheap alcohol, which is linked with violence and high levels of accident and emergency (A&E) admissions. Cameron said that his plan would result in 50,000 fewer crimes and 900 fewer alcohol-related deaths each year by 2020. But, after consultations with alcohol industry pressure groups and with the Home Office struggling to find time to consult with public health experts, government policy took a dramatic U-turn.

The Scottish Parliament actually passed legislation to curb pricing in 2012 – but the corporate alcohol lobby immediately launched prolonged legal action to block it, citing European competition law. This raises an important question: should governments be prevented from democratically introducing public health policies that benefit the health and well-being of citizens because of the power of corporate interests whose loyalty is primarily to shareholders and profits?

policy, on issues such as the pricing and labelling of booze, and foods high in fat and sugar, which are seriously damaging to our health.

Ultimately...

There will always be a role for the private sector in health care provision. Let's not forget that, to make the NHS possible in 1948 and to get doctors on side, they were allowed to carry on treating private patients – a deal which prompted then Minister of Health Aneurin Bevan to famously quip: 'I stuffed their mouths with gold.'

Today, the private sector might become involved as a partner where there are treatments that NICE considers too costly for the NHS to provide. Similarly, the NHS might choose to subcontract out the provision of some of its services to private sector providers and still provide free treatment at point of use. But there remain concerns about the ill-conceived 2012 Lansley reforms and 'internal markets' resulting in costly inefficiencies (as with rail), as well as crippling debt overhangs affecting some hospitals as a result of disastrous private finance initiatives (PFIs) (see Chapter 9).

When it comes to political meddling with the NHS, we should be very careful. If ever a future Minister of Health were to want to tinker, he or she might look to the second-best (Swiss) system for good practice – but certainly no further afield. 'If it ain't broke, don't fix it' seems to be an eminently simple and economically sensible maxim in this instance – and one on which quality of life in Britain depends.

healthier country. The tactics employed are similar to those formerly used by 'big tobacco' and 'big booze' – known as the 'three "D"s':

- **denial** of any health risk,
- **delaying** tactics (such as legal action or funding bogus research); and
- **detours and distractions** (that is, weak and ineffective voluntary deals).

But the powerful tobacco industry was eventually tamed by addressing the 'three "A"s':

- **acceptability** (warning labels and marketing restrictions – such as banning Formula 1 sponsorship);
- **affordability** (higher rates of tax to raise prices); and
- **availability** (smoke-free legislation and licensing).

Solutions

Public opinion is today generally supportive of better sugar regulation. Options include:

- imposing a sugary drinks duty (as planned in Ireland, France and Hungary) which the main medical bodies support, calculating that a 20% tax would lead to significantly fewer cases of diabetes and strokes;
- imposing marketing restrictions – that is, using advertising and branding controls to make sugary foods less attractive to children, and regulating TV advertising to limit youngsters' exposure to aggressive marketing of sugary drinks, sweets and junk food;
- effective labelling, such as mandatory 'traffic light ratings', whilst encouraging supermarkets to locate products away from children;

- setting a clear target for sugar content, as was applied to salt, achieving reductions of up to 50% in some foods in just two years – not least because the government's own Science Advisory Committee on Nutrition recommends that the target for sugar consumption should be reduced to half the current level;
- nudging manufacturers towards reducing sugar and saturated fat in junk food, and slimming down excessive portion sizes;
- ending industry sports sponsorship to break the link between unhealthy food and healthy people;
- coming up with new slogans to build on the widely known 'five [portions of fruit and veg] a day';
- establishing a genuinely independent 'food policy institute'; and
- promoting healthy food alternatives with tax incentives and subsidies.

In relation to the last point, cheap food is often nutritionally bad, with some types linked to obesity and cancer. There are consequently concerns about the impact of taxes on low-income families, but 'sin taxes' on damaging foods could be used to subsidise healthy low-priced 'Jamie Oliver'-style alternatives.

Political will

Despite the looming emergency in public health, politicians remain reluctant to tell people what's good for them and are naturally wary of being too 'nanny state', preferring to see this as an issue that's solely down to 'personal responsibility'. But successfully ending endemic tooth decay in Britain was achieved thanks to public support for adding fluoride to the mains water supply; similarly, to solve the monster sugar-related health problem is going to need more than 'self-help'. There's no dodging the issue: to get real results that cut NHS admissions, the state must step in.

Source material: Simon Capewell, Guardian, Channel 4

Education

"Tain't what you do, it's the way that you measure it..."

'Why can't the English teach their children how to speak?' asked Professor Higgins in the musical *My Fair Lady* – set in the London of 1912. It's certainly not for lack of trying. In 2011, the UK spent 6.4% of gross domestic product (GDP) on education at all levels, compared to the EU average of 5.8% and the Organisation for Economic Co-operation and Development (OECD) average of 6.1%.

Although results vary depending on which 'league tables' you look at, in general the UK performs around average in mathematics and reading, and above average in science, when compared with the 34 OECD countries. The UK is roughly comparable to the Czech Republic, Denmark, France, Germany and Norway in its scores. Other surveys put England 11th out of 45 nations for reading, with similar rankings for maths and science.

In the latest international comparisons, compiled by the Economist Intelligence Unit, the success of Asian education systems is highlighted, with South Korea, Japan, Singapore and Hong Kong rated as the highest-performing. But the UK's performance is also strong, ranking sixth, behind only Finland in Europe and ahead of countries such as Germany, France and the United States. One thing most studies agree upon, however, is that the UK (like most other Western nations) is consistently outperformed by the East Asian nations, which traditionally top such rankings.

In short, we spend about the OECD average on education and our results are about average or better – but there's room for some improvement.

'Could do better'

INEQUALITY

How well children do at school is still heavily influenced by their parents' background. This is more of a problem in the UK than it is among many of our competitor countries. Wilkinson and Pickett's ground-breaking book *The Spirit Level* (2009) showed that the link between children's performance at school and that of their parents is strongest in countries with high levels of inequality – such as the UK (see Chapter 15).

The extent to which kids struggle to break free of their disadvantaged backgrounds isn't limited only to their time in school; it follows children as they grow up, into the workplace. If your income today is significantly higher than your parents' income in their day, then 'well done' – because 'earnings mobility' (the extent to which children's earnings differ from their parents') is particularly low in the UK, as well as in countries such as the United States, France and Italy. (It's much higher in the Nordic countries, and in Australia and Canada.)

DIFFERENCES

Within the UK, there are still significant regional differences in educational performance. Coming from a low-income background in London is less of a barrier to academic success and going on to university than it is in the rest of the country: not only does London have the lowest proportion of schools falling below the GCSE 'floor standard' of any English region, but also 50–100% more poorer young Londoners make it into higher education compared with other regions in the country.

One major factor that affects your chances of success at school is the extent to which your parents value learning. Kids whose home environment is one of encouragement and support with homework and getting good results inevitably have a head start. This isn't necessarily linked to wealth; some cultures are known for setting great store by educational achievement, for example those with African or Asian roots. A stable, secure and loving family home life also provides a sound platform for nurturing young minds; those unlucky enough to come from dysfunctional families will inevitably face bigger hurdles when competing to score top marks in class.

OVERWORKED AND UNDERPAID?

Continual efforts by government to incentivise teaching staff seem to have backfired. Although the UK workforce overall is ageing, the teaching workforce, on average, is getting younger – because so many older teachers are leaving the profession. As a result, almost half of all UK secondary school teachers are younger than 40 – the greatest proportion of young teachers in all of the OECD countries. So what's going on?

In 2009, teaching was judged by the Health and Safety Executive (HSE) to be the most stressful profession in the UK. This is shocking: it suggests that standing up in front of (unruly) kids day after day in our schools is more stressful than life-and-death occupations such as firefighting, nursing, or policing. To add insult to injury, these high levels of stress are inadequately compensated in pay. In England, a typical young secondary school teacher will earn around 15% less than employees in equivalent jobs; in other OECD countries, it averages at about 6% less. (Oddly, at the other end of the scale, mature teachers are paid 7% more than their peers in other industries by the time they retire, while the OECD average is 11% less.)

This combination of stress and inadequate pay may explain the declining appeal of teaching to those who've been doing it for years. In 2013, half of all teachers considered quitting the profession for these reasons, exacerbated by excessive workloads. Each year, something like 40,000 teachers quit mid-career – at a cost of £750 million to replace them – and nearly half of new teachers choose to leave within five years of qualifying. Yet more than two-thirds say that they enjoy the work and only 3% report being bored with their jobs.

REFORM

Government appetite for reforming education never seems to be quenched. One of the flagship initiatives introduced by New Labour was the 'academy'. These are publicly funded independent schools that don't have to follow the National Curriculum (although they must deliver the core subjects) and can set their own term times. But they have to follow the same rules as other state schools on things such as admissions, special educational needs and exclusions. Their funding comes directly from government rather than from the local authority. Some academies are run by educational corporations for profit; many have sponsors, such as businesses, universities and faith, or voluntary, groups. Sponsors share responsibility for improving the performance of their schools.

The coalition government continued the academy programme and added 'free schools' into the mix. These are funded by government and run by not-for-profit groups, rather than the local authority. They therefore have more control over how they do things, including setting pay and conditions for staff, changing the

© Padmayogini / Shutterstock.com

length of the school day and terms, and not following the National Curriculum. A range of different groups have set up free schools, including charities, universities, independent schools, businesses, teachers and local parents.

Free schools are, however, controversial. Some see them as a way of centralising control of education; others are concerned that 'pushy' middle-class parents will set up schools in areas in which they're not really needed, diverting resources away from other local schools. There are also concerns that they might increase social segregation, should all of the pupils come from a very narrow community. The evidence from other countries that have tried similar models is mixed. Sweden is sometimes cited as an example, but the most recent tables indicate that Sweden is underperforming in the key subjects (maths, science and reading) and part of the blame for this decline has been laid at the door of the Swedish free schools.

'Top marks'

In the QS 'top universities' ranking of world universities, the UK does proportionally very well. Some might even go so far as to say that we're 'world-class'. Of the 'top 50' higher education institutions ranked, 8 represent the UK; in the 'top 100', 19 are British. While the United States scores highest (18 in the top 50), it is of course, many times larger than the UK and spends twice as much per student on average. But the inexorable pressures of marketisation have been brought to bear on higher education in recent years. To thrive in this environment, universities will increasingly be forced to adopt business models rather than educational criteria.

One of the most controversial changes in recent years has been the introduction in the UK (and subsequent trebling) of tuition fees funded by student loans. The idea is that those whose future earning power is boosted by a degree should contribute to the cost of providing it. The loans become repayable in the form of a 'tax' levied on future annual income above a certain level (currently £21,000). This scheme doesn't apply to students in Scotland and Wales, but the English student loans scheme means that, by the time a typical English student graduates, he or she is now likely to be in hock for a horrifying £53,000 – well over twice the average amount of debt of a US college graduate.

Ironically, there are indications that many students will be unable to repay these debts at all, leaving taxpayers to pick up the excess (plus interest), thereby penalising diligent students who do pay back their loans. Some consequently question whether this relatively new tuition fees structure will ultimately save the government any money in the long term. For the former student, this overhang of personal debt is likely to make it harder to obtain mortgages in future: welcome to 'Generation Rent' (see Chapter 18).

Given the reality that, in the short-term at least, these high fees are here to stay, one idea worth pursuing is that the government might provide grants to promote those shortage skills that we need as a country to regenerate our economy – picking up the tab for those studying subjects such as engineering, medicine and manufacturing (subject to such graduates working within the UK for a set period of time).

Can we achieve a 'high skill, high pay' economy?

Successive prime ministers have called on schools to play their part in producing a 'highly skilled, highly paid' economy… Surely no one could possibly object to cheerleading for such a noble cause?

Countries such as Germany have long appreciated the importance of manual skills.

There is, however, one problem: the reality of the labour market. The greatest employment growth is occurring at the other end of the spectrum – the so called 'low-skilled sector'. Of course even the most successful economies need people to do basic work such as litter picking, mending potholes and serving the tea. But those who casually bandy around the term 'low skill' tend to forget that socially useful jobs (such as caring for the elderly) require considerable skill and aptitude, and many a highly qualified barrister will openly admit that he or she lacks the practical skills to fix a leak or put up a shelf. So these supposedly 'low-skilled' jobs shouldn't be denigrated (nor poorly paid): those who are employed in them are an integral part of the economy – their contribution would probably be missed the most if they stopped working.

New Labour obsessed about getting kids into university. But this ignores the fact that not everyone is cut out for an academic education, studying quantum physics and ancient Greek. In the 1960s, technical colleges were established to provide training in practical skills such as bricklaying, plumbing, cooking, mechanics and metalwork, and countries such as Germany have long appreciated

the importance of manual skills (the snobbishness of Britain's political class in this regard may partly explain our failure to invest in manufacturing). What is needed, then, is a variety of routes through education, including technical and vocational courses. Bright children from poor backgrounds need to be given the chance to shine.

Selective ('grammar') schools, with their culture of educational excellence, were a way of helping many disadvantaged pupils to get into good universities, the key to highly successful careers. By definition, selective schools meant picking more academically successful kids, with many such schools being abolished under successive governments (leaving only 164 in England, the majority in Kent). Some claim that this has been a key factor behind the subsequent worsening of social mobility, with most places at top universities now going to private school students with wealthy parents. But the bottom line is that while we ought to continue to encourage the 'brightest' academic minds, we must also recognise that vocational skills and ability are invaluable, and ensure that our education system caters to the needs of and inspires young people from all walks of life.

Chapter 18

BUILDING A BETTER SOCIETY:
SHELTER, TRANSPORT, ENVIRONMENT, ENERGY AND DEFENCE

Housing

Despite being a relatively wealthy country, the UK is struggling to house its people in the 21st century. Rocketing rents and unaffordable house prices are evidence of market failure. Periodic property booms stretching back to the 1970s have benefited a lucky couple of generations. But as a result, house buyers in future will have to saddle themselves with enormous mortgages to afford such sky high prices – in effect younger people will be paying for the profits reaped by those who got there first (always assuming they can get a mortgage at all, given the huge levels of student debt). Looking forward, the most likely outcome is that many people will only be able to afford to live in rented accommodation; or live with mum and dad. The golden era of social mobility based on owner-occupation is slowly fading. What we're likely to see instead over coming years is a gradual reversion to Victorian-type tenure, when most people rented privately or lived in shared family homes, even when married.

The fundamental cause of the problem is obvious: too many people chasing too little housing. Supply and demand are out of kilter. But what lies behind these factors?

Demand

The housing market is largely driven by the availability of mortgage finance, which in recent years has been pegged at extraordinarily low rates of interest. Wealthy cash investors add to the demand pressure – once house prices are expected to rise rapidly speculators tend to pile in, hoping to make money. This pushes prices up even further for those (old-fashioned) few who seek merely to buy a house in which they can themselves live. Demand for rental accommodation is fuelled by 'overspill' from those who can no longer afford to buy, and from rapid levels of population growth and household formation. Britain is a densely populated island, with demand greatest in the relatively overpopulated south-east.

Supply

There are some 27 million dwellings in the UK. The number of new homes constructed in a typical year rarely exceeds 150,000, which is about 0.5% of the total stock. In effect, this means supply is fixed in the short term. Even if the number of new homes built each year doubles, price rises could rapidly make them unaffordable for most aspiring homeowners. Supply is affected by limited availability of building land, plus the fact that big corporate developers tend to sit on large amounts of land over many years – 'land banking'. Although much maligned by government, planning laws are necessary to balance demands on the environment and to reflect the fact that existing local populations don't generally welcome new housing developments on their doorsteps, let alone giant 'new towns'.

Government policies

Over the last couple of decades, governments have mostly come up with short-term policies primarily engineered to win votes. For example, as an incentive to buy their rented home the 'Right to Buy' gifts public sector tenants an incredibly generous discount of up to 70% off market value. But selling off publicly owned residential property assets at bargain prices shrinks the supply of houses available for those in need in future; at worst it is open to abuse.

A more sensible, recently introduced policy is the 'Right to Build'. This incentivises councils to release land at market value to self-builders who wish to construct their own homes.

However, the most controversial current government scheme is probably 'Help to Buy'. This involves the state subsidising private buyers of new homes with five-year interest-free loans and also underwrites mortgages. Critics say that this fulfils the dream of owning a new home for a lucky few at the expense of making it even less achievable for the majority, by keeping prices high – that, in effect, it's a 'Help to Sell' scheme for developers. Handing over state subsidies for the purchase of private homes (up to £600,000) also means risking taxpayers' money in the event that buyers default.

PROBLEMS

- **Affordability** In some areas, average house prices have reached more than ten times average income. One factor pushing up prices beyond first-time buyers' pockets is competition from buy-to-let landlords. As a result, the property ladder has been hauled up beyond the reach of millions of hopeful homebuyers. Social trends are emerging in which two or more generations of a family are now living under the same roof, for example where kids can no longer afford to leave home (and because wages have fallen so low some households can no longer function on parental incomes alone and need the additional income that the younger family members bring in.)

- **Housing Benefit** In the 1970s, approximately 80% of public spending on housing was used for constructing new homes, with around a fifth paid out in benefits to assist people with their rents. Today, government is spending 20 times as much subsiding rents as on building new homes. To fill the gap there is a massive Housing Benefit bill. Some make the point that if we're going to pay subsidies for housing, it might at least be used to support publicly owned housing; this way taxpayers get the benefit of rising house prices. And, of course, this means stopping selling off our supplies of social housing (see above).

- **Population growth** Demand from high levels of population growth (including immigration) mean that, even if house-building could exceed 200,000 new dwellings a year, it would still fall short of the number needed to keep up with new household formation. Experts estimate that one new home will need to be built every 7 minutes for the next 20 years simply to keep pace with demand.

- **Hijacks funding for business** Banks like nothing better than lending on property. But tying up too much capital in unproductive bricks and mortar at inflated prices, rather than investing in productive industries, weakens Britain's economic potential. Historically it also tends to stoke up destructive housing booms.

- **Skills shortages** The mobility of the workforce is seriously hampered when people who want work can't easily get to the available jobs unless they're prepared to travel very long distances at considerable cost. This results in a labour and brain drain, with key workers unable to live and work in some towns and cities.

- **Empty homes** There are something like 50,000 vacant dwellings across London – yet as much as 85% of new prime London property is bought with overseas money, usually for investment rather than occupation. During booms, in some new developments as many as half of completed dwellings are left empty, investors paying no Council Tax and creating 'ghost districts'. This doesn't just affect London and the top end of the market. Demand trickles down the chain: at the extreme luxury end of the market, billionaires outbid millionaires, who in turn gazump purchasers who are merely affluent, all the way down to poor old first time buyers. Also, because developers respond to the demands of overseas investors rather than local people looking for somewhere to live, it tends to distort house-building priorities – with luxury flats galore and few affordable homes.

- **Right to Buy** Selling off council homes to former tenants may once have been 'good politics' and highly popular with those who personally benefited – but the housing stock was never replaced. Today, a shrinking number of very lucky council tenants are enriched at the expense of tomorrow's people in housing need. If publicly owned housing stock continues to be sold off at a fraction of the cost of replacing it, the result will be massive shortages – with insufficient revenue to fund new builds – unless, of course, taxpayers are asked to stump up more of their cash to fund those fortunate few who can then benefit by being in the right place at the right time.

- **Corporate builders** Britain is largely reliant on mass-produced housing built by giant corporations; in most other Western countries, self-build is hugely popular and is facilitated by government policies.

SOLUTIONS

Other countries, Germany among them, have stable property prices, spacious high-quality flats and houses, and secure rental tenure. There's no reason why this happy situation shouldn't be achievable in the UK. There are a number of solutions well worth considering before we start smothering our countryside with 'new towns' and concreting over the precious greenbelt 'lungs' around our cities.

- **Rebalance the economy** Politicians have long relied on debt-fuelled housing booms to get the economy moving and create a 'feel-good factor'. Housing is the only basic human need where escalating price inflation is greeted by many as a *good thing*, because homes have morphed into cash machines and pensions rather than simply providing shelter. Part of the solution is to rebalance the economy towards production and exports, and to generate well-paid jobs. Stimulating growth in economically depressed parts of the country where there is lower demand for housing would also help to relieve pressure. Unless the UK prospers as a whole, those who live in London will continue to see the rest of the nation turning up in the south-east, looking for work and pushing up property prices (while pushing down wages).

- **Realign affordability** A few years of stable house prices and rising wages would naturally bring affordability back into alignment with the long-term average, rebooting the market without the need for state handouts.

- **Population growth** See Chapter 10.

- **Boost building** Seven out of ten people in Britain are interested in self-building, but land is in short supply. Developers sitting on 'dead' land banks could be persuaded to release land for self-builders. Previously developed 'brownfield' sites could be made more accessible for new residential use. Councils could be allowed to borrow to build, just like developers. (But remember that local councils have no incentive to build when tenants can legally demand new homes are sold to them at rock bottom prices. If council houses must be sold, it makes sense to do so at market value and invest the proceeds in newbuild constructions.)

- **Level the playing field** Investors outgunning first-time buyers to acquire starter homes have fuelled price rises. In effect, the Bank of England subsidises buy-to-let mortgages, and lending requirements are not so strict for landlords. Investors also benefit from a generous range of tax reliefs. A level playing field would empower people looking to buy a home, enabling them to compete on a fair basis. Also, by dampening demand among spectators looking to make a quick buck, prices could be gently brought back into line with wages.

- **Rich overseas buyers** UK property has, in effect, become a global currency reserve for investors. Civitas, the free market think tank, point out that the property market is an investment vehicle for some of the world's wealthiest people – a 'piggy bank' for the global elite. Because this has driven up prices, millions of UK citizens risk being excluded from home ownership. So how might we solve this?

  - ☐ **Tax incentives** Much of the appeal is down to the UK's exceptionally mild tax regime. Compared to other global hot spots, such as Hong Kong, Singapore and New York, London has no annual tax based on property value. No land value tax is imposed, and the only capital tax on first homes is Stamp Duty paid by purchasers. Inconsistent Council Tax banding means owners of cheap houses are clobbered at a far harder rate relatively than those at the luxury end of the market. Given that property is a lot less easy than many assets to send overseas to a tax haven, a tax on property ought to appeal to a cash-strapped government hoping to reduce the deficit.

  - ☐ **Planning agreements** Conditions applied to (hugely valuable) planning consents could ensure that new houses are occupied as homes, rather than for asset speculation.

  - ☐ **Manage overseas investors** In Australia, no sale can be made to overseas buyers unless it can be demonstrated that their purchase will lead to an increase in available dwellings. The Swiss also limit the number of homes that can be sold to non-residents and overseas buyers must actually live in the home. However, even if such controls were introduced in Britain, EU citizens would still have a right to own and occupy property.

  Source material. RICS, Toby Helm

Transport

A modern nation requires an efficient transport system to move goods and people to where they're required for economic and social output – that is, a system that gets you to work on time and in one piece, and at a reasonable price. Basically, there are two sides to the national transport system: on the one hand, you've got public services, such as railways, taxis, airlines, trams and buses, etc; on the other, there are all of the private methods, such as driving, cycling and walking.

Despite coming a close second to the weather as Britain's favourite topic of popular complaint, by world standards our transport system is both effective and safe (although this comparison includes a fair few impoverished and overpopulated dictatorships). Avid train spotters may relish the statistics: in 2012, our transport system delivered 480 billion passenger miles, of which 83% were in cars, vans and taxis, 9% by rail, and 5% in buses and coaches.

Which is best?

It's no secret that some methods of transport are less kind to the planet than others. For a start, anything featured on BBC *Top Gear* isn't likely to do a lot to prevent climate change. A typical small-family car emits 214g of CO_2 per passenger mile; in comparison, a two-carriage railway sprinter produces only around 78g – and even this pales into insignificance alongside squeaky clean cyclists and pedestrians. But air pollution isn't the only drawback to road use:

GENERATION RENT

There are about 10 million people in Britain living in private rented accommodation and, on average, nearly half of their disposable income is eaten up by paying rent. A quarter of children in England are housed in private accommodation and these families can in most cases legally be moved on with just two months' notice. Yet the main political parties seem to have little to offer large groups of neglected people feeling insecure and frustrated.

Whilst there are many good landlords, a lack of regulation allows rogue operators to flourish, with little chance of being fined. Even then, councils aren't permitted to keep the (relatively low) penalties that they impose. In some areas, exploitation and squalor are rife, having long been allowed to fester. It's not unusual for tenants to be unaware of who their landlord is, and deposits are routinely stolen. Letting agents remain largely unregulated despite the industry itself calling on government to impose minimum standards; instead, cowboy agents are free to levy all manner of bogus fees. Revenge evictions where tenants dare to complain about repairs or hazards are surprisingly common, as is violent harassment. In some inner city areas, landlords subdivide houses, with living rooms becoming bedrooms, and beds placed in insanitary garden sheds. Landlords are often wary of accepting tenants on benefits, because even people in low-paid temporary work can quickly build up debts if Housing Benefit fails to pay the rent in full.

There are a number of ways in which we might fix the lettings market.

- Regulate lettings agents, to weed out the crooks and cowboys.
- Set up a national register of private landlords – to help to banish rogue traders and promote good landlords with star ratings.
- Give tenants the option of a stable rental contract that allows them to stay for a minimum of five years (as homelessness charity Shelter proposes).
- Target tax breaks to reward long-term landlords providing a quality service.
- Encourage professional institutions, such as pension funds and housing associations, to develop quality rented accommodation.
- The government should fund councils to extend and enforce the regulation of 'houses in multiple occupation' (HMOs).
- Finally, what about 'rent regulation'? In New York, 45% of people live in rent controlled accommodation whereby landlords can increase rents only by a certain percentage each year (such as the rate of inflation). Without 'stabilisation', Manhattan would be unaffordable for those on ordinary incomes.

---

additional travel creates congestion because, as each driver joins the flow of traffic, the speed of other road users – and their potential safety – deteriorates.

People who commute by public transport may also feel gratified by the health benefits of their daily commute – boosted by their walk or cycle to and from the local station. It's also claimed that rail users enjoy a cleaner atmosphere than those subjected to road pollution (although anyone incarcerated in cramped carriages reeking of diesel, sweat and old kebabs might beg to differ). Public transport arguably also creates more community cohesion (perhaps because passengers unite in

ROAD RAGE

Britain has the most congested roads in Europe. More than 70% of us regularly commute to work by car, with school runs adding another 25% or so more traffic at peak times. The number of cars on our roads has grown phenomenally in the last 20 years – by as much as a third. As a consequence, the dream of motoring freedom and individual self-expression is rapidly turning sour, with average speeds in cities today sometimes slower than the horse-drawn carriages of Victorian times.

Being caught up in traffic on a regular basis impacts on people's mental health and well-being: stress and blood pressure levels skyrocket when we're late for appointments, 'caught in traffic' (of which we often forget we're part) over which we have little or no control.

There's no easy solution to relieving pressure on city centres, other than fewer numbers of people driving. In the future, we're likely to see a mix of 'solutions', such as toll roads, more cycle hire schemes and perhaps 'sky cycle' flyover carriageways for dedicated bike use. Cars may be rented rather than owned; they may even be communal and driverless, running closer together on autopilot…

---

seething hatred at delayed, overcrowded trains). But there's one statistic that trumps all others: the undeniable fact that trains and planes are both massively safer than automobiles in terms of deaths per passenger mile.

Who pays?

If you were to be given the job of drawing up a new transport policy for the nation, it would make sense to start by comparing all of the different methods that we use to get about. To make sure you're comparing like with like, you'd need to root out any hidden subsidies or costs. At the moment, some methods are subsidised significantly more heavily by the state than are others. All things considered, the effective state subsidy that road users receive is about four times that granted to rail transport. So, to level the playing field, public transport efficiency would need to be given a pretty hefty boost.

In 2013–14, the government subsidised rail travel to the tune of 6.8 pence per passenger mile – a reduction of 40% over the previous four years (with fares rising instead). This is dwarfed by the subsidy of road use: the tab for maintaining the roads and the costs of policing and dealing with accidents, breakdown recovery, etc is largely picked up by the taxpayer. The cost of driving (*eg* road taxes, fuel duty etc) would have to be raised by about an extra 30 pence per mile if all of these issues were to be included (that is, if 'free market' economics were to be applied). The cost would be even higher if you were to factor in the environmental damage caused by 30 million engines spewing out particles and noxious gases.

If, as a nation, we want to move towards a more effective and efficient transport system, it follows that we must rely less on road and more on rail. But this wouldn't necessarily be an easy option: if just 2% of road traffic were to transfer to the railways, train capacity would have to increase by 25% – requiring enormous investment over many years (and we've already noted that, since privatisation, the railway companies have proved reluctant to reinvest their profits). Certainly, long-term investment of this scope is out of the question under the current system (that is, if a franchise expires long before any benefits are seen). There's also the question of whether the public should effectively be investing in the railway network (in the form of government subsidies) when the profits generated won't be returned to them.

A market-based solution would be one not distorted by misplaced 'invisible' subsidies. One way forward might be to increase fuel duty, but at the same time allow road and rail commuters alike to claim back tax on work-related travel. Whichever approach the government adopts, it's clear that the railways require more thoughtful investment if we're to take pressure off the roads.

© Adrian Phillips / Shutterstock.com

Britain invented railways, but today we have a love–hate relationship with them. Much of the current antagonism dates back to the mid-1990s, when state-owned British Rail was privatised. Clearly, something's gravely amiss when right-of-centre newspapers such as the *Daily Mail* run headlines shouting 'Bring back British Rail' – effectively calling for renationalisation… So who exactly is responsible for running our railways?

- **Network Rail** owns the infrastructure, including some 2,500 railway stations, plus all of the tracks, signals, tunnels, bridges and level crossings. Network Rail is classified as a 'government body', which is state-owned and has £30 billion on the books as national debt.
- **Rolling stock operating companies (ROSCOs)** own the trains that run on the rails. They are responsible for maintaining railway engines and carriages.
- **Train operating companies (TOCs)** operate the trains, which they lease from the ROSCOs. They submit bids to government every seven years or so, with the aim of winning the right to run services on specific lines. There are approximately 25 operators of franchised passenger services, plus a handful of freight operating companies (FOCs). Some TOCs are owned by the French and German state railways.
- **The Office of Rail Regulation (ORR)** is the independent regulator that oversees the whole caboodle.

Pros and cons

To be fair, it must be said that British Rail (BR) wasn't universally admired in its day – BR sandwiches were a staple gag of stand-up comedians. More importantly, not being permitted to raise funding in its own right, it suffered from periodic underinvestment under cash-strapped governments. Today, however, it's hard to find anyone keen to sing the praises of the current system, even within government. Railways are a natural monopoly and no other country in the world runs its system in this way.

Experts raise a number of criticisms that could usefully be taken on board to reform the railways in future.

- Fragmentation of ownership – separating the trains from the rails upon which they run and from the people who operate them creates enormous bureaucracy and expense. For example the necessary contracting between all the various parties involved entails extensive legal costs. It also encourages inefficiencies and lack of accountability, with buck-passing and dodging of responsibilities.
- The railways today cost more than double the amount they did under British Rail, with the state subsidy currently totalling around £4 billion a year – comprising about a third of the operators' income.
- The bidding process to win franchises is expensive and complex. Railways thrive on long-term planning, and putting contracts for running railways out to tender has created uncertainty. The private sector tends to be wary of taking risks over extended periods.
- Franchising results in inflexibility and higher costs. For example, train operators can dispute any changes to the timetable that the Department for Transport (DfT) might seek in response to changing demand, resulting in extra costs. They can also claim large sums in compensation in the event that services are disrupted due to engineering works carried out for their benefit.

K.J.Lamb

'YOU ARE GOING ON A LONG JOURNEY, SUBJECT TO DELAYS, CANCELLATIONS, PLANNED ENGINEERING WORKS, SEVERE DISRUPTION, REPLACEMENT BUSES AND ADVERSE WEATHER CONDITIONS'

- Britain has the most expensive train fares in Europe, with a mind-boggling array of complex tickets and tariffs apparently designed to bamboozle passengers (some might say 'exploit').
- Train operators are wary of reinvesting their profits. Most improvements are funded by Network Rail or by the rolling stock owners. Maximising short-term profits has led to extending the lives of old, overcrowded carriages – although new stock is now materialising on a number of lines.
- Train operators bear very little risk since they can hand back the franchise to government if passenger numbers fail to meet expectations. In 2009, National Express did just this, cutting its losses on the East Coast franchise. Once renationalised, this line excelled, achieving excellent punctuality and service levels, whilst generating more than £800 million for the taxpayer.

Other criticisms include the fact that British Rail was a world leader in developing train technology and engineering. This expertise has now been lost, along with most of our train manufacturing industry.

What the public says

YouGov opinion polls show that the majority of the British public (66%), including the majority of Conservative voters, support renationalisation of the railways – that is, taking the franchises back into one state-owned body.
Source material: BBC, Christian Wolmar, ORR

One of the more controversial topics in the crazy world of UK transport is the High Speed Two (HS2) rail link between London and the regions. The cost of the project is estimated to be between £50 billion and £80 billion. Against this cost, we must weigh the benefits – which largely arise from the travelling time saved. The evidence of HS2 in environmental terms is mixed: generally, the faster a transportation method, the more carbon it produces, because wind resistance increases with speed. In other words, conventional trains might have a lower carbon footprint per mile travelled. Also, the building of HS2 appears likely to impact on large swathes of England's green and pleasant land.

There are some who argue that giving firms in the 'north' (primarily Birmingham, Manchester and Leeds) better access to London will help them to compete and generate business, but it's also the case that London firms will have better access to the 'north'. Whichever region will ultimately benefit is subject to debate – and given the general propensity of larger urban areas to outperform smaller ones (economists call this the 'agglomeration effect'), it seems rather more likely that London will benefit at the expense of her northern sisters.

It's also worth recalling that much of the prosperity generated by the canals and railways of the Industrial Revolution was because producers – factories and farmers – could export more efficiently; if today's investment in infrastructure simply facilitates the 'sucking in' of German, Korean and Chinese-made goods, it's arguable who will ultimately benefit the most.

Even if we measure the benefits of HS2 accurately, the real question is surely 'might better use be made of the money?' (known to economists as 'opportunity costs'). In 2006, the Eddington Transport Study warned: 'Do not be seduced by "grands projets" with speculative returns.' It went on to note that 'the evidence on the costs and benefits of new North–South high speed rail lines suggests returns at the lower end of the distribution compared to the returns available from other policy options'. In other words, the money might be better spent on cheaper, but more effective, alternatives.

Environment

In economics, there are two basic ways of considering the value of the natural world:

- the **selfish gene** dictates that the environment exists solely to promote human well-being – defined in terms of money, as the maximisation of real GDP (*ie* 'purely instrumentally'); or
- as **valuable in its own right** – that is, not as human property, but with the same right to survive as the human race.

These are two extremes, and in practice most approaches to the subject fall somewhere in between. The OECD, for example, recognises the reality that human well-being and economic growth depend on a healthy natural world, although their emphasis is centred on human needs – the 'selfish gene' end of the spectrum.

Putting a price on everything

Classical economists encounter problems when they try to consider the world as a 'good' in its own right. This is because one key principle of free market economics is that value is represented by price. For something to be of value, it must be capable of being exchanged and traded – that is, bought and sold. The implication of this is that if the natural world can't be exploited, it's of no value.

One of the big worries with this approach is that the preservation of nature – all the planet's wonderful biodiversity – is justified only where profit can be made from its continued existence. If we want to save the elephants, say free market economists, we have to set up a market in which people can pay to exploit them – even if this involves killing them for their ivory. Similarly, if we wish to preserve the Amazon rainforest, we should give oversight to logging companies.

Applying these principles more constructively, if we become concerned with the level of greenhouse gas (GHG) emissions, we can set up a market to reduce them to optimum levels (carbon emissions trading). If the rainforest is threatened, governments around the world might put their hands in their pockets to pay for long-term ownership to be handed to local tribes, or perhaps to Greenpeace. But how would we put a *price* on the priceless: the lungs of the world, from which we all benefit? In reality, it may mean simply that we have to outbid those who want to pay for a rival (destructive) economic use – unless sanity could be restored by legislative means.

Appreciating true value

An alternative approach might be to accept the obvious truth that human development is constrained by the limits of the environment – rather than the other way around. This sidesteps the crazy notion of trying to pin a price tag on everything green, slithery, or furry. Even if nature can't be monetarised, its value should be at least maintained, if not enriched. The advantage of this approach is that the continued existence of, say, elephants might not be traded off against the short-term benefits that a few greedy humans might accrue through their extinction.

The bottom line is that there are some environmental goods that are simply too large and too important to be assigned to private ownership. Economists shouldn't have the last word on anything as fundamental to the long-term survival of our species as the natural

environment and climate. In any case, most people would agree that natural justice requires one generation to sustain and hand over the unspoilt natural world to the next. In the final instance, the natural world is a public good – that is, it should be freely available for all to enjoy. Simple economic theory indicates that free markets can never provide public goods at an appropriate level; therefore the state has a role to play in applying regulations to ensure that development does not – in the longer term – harm humanity. It also has a duty to ensure that the natural world is conserved for its own sake.

For this reason, we have planning regulations, and things like the National Trust, national parks, sites of special scientific interest (SSSIs) – all with the aim of preserving the environment as a public good. Without such regulations the decision over whether we should protect, for example, the red squirrels and natterjack toads at Formby Point when their habitat is threatened by a leisure development would depend merely on whether the leisure park might generate more short-term revenue than squirrels and toads. In the case of the natural world: 'Once it's gone, it's gone.' Future generations of British people might rather come to regret that, to generate a little extra profit, we allowed the extinction of red squirrels, hares, skylarks and song thrushes, to name but a few of the UK's endangered species.

Globally, we can't accurately predict the ultimate impact of greenhouse gas emissions or the felling of the Amazon rainforest – so the precautionary principle might suggest, therefore, that we adopt an approach of constraint and preservation, rather than exploitation.

Keeping the lights on

In the 1970s, British Gas and the Central Electricity Generating Board were centrally responsible for ensuring that demand for energy would be met. Under this state-owned system, there was sufficient investment, and by the 1980s we had significant surplus capacity. Today, however, as population pressures increase and we demand more power for our electronic gizmos, surplus capacity is running out. Critics say that we seem to be moving towards a complicated situation in which government is ever more entwined in an industry that's supposed to be privately run. The danger is that in seeking to combine the best of both worlds, we could end up with the worst.

How real is the risk of blackouts?

According to National Grid, spare electricity capacity was about 4% over the winter of 2014. This is a huge drop from the margin of 17% just three years earlier. Only the 'good luck' of an economic downturn has bought us an extra few years. Clearly, we're sailing very close to the wind: extra demand from a harsh winter could swiftly eat up spare capacity.

To make matters worse, there's uncertainty surrounding the stability of gas supplies. Although the UK doesn't receive supplies directly from Russia, gas flows to Europe could be affected, which in turn would impact on supplies to the UK. Fortunately, National Grid has a cunning plan: to 'manage supply', including paying big firms to switch off on cold winter evenings. But this has the hallmarks of an expensive remedy that simply papers over the cracks – the lack of long-term planning.

FACING A 'TRILEMMA'

Energy expert Professor Dieter Helm points out that government energy policy is failing on all three of its key objectives.

- **Carbon emissions** Despite being committed to reductions in emissions, we're actually seeing an increase (resulting from coal-fired power stations). Reducing emissions will require less reliance on coal and greater emphasis on reducing demand.
- **Energy bills** Bills have tended to rise rapidly, but fall very slowly in relation to wholesale prices.

- **Trust** in the 'big six' suppliers is at an all-time low. And with 20% of the UK population living in fuel poverty, the government can't afford the political fallout of rising prices.

FUTURE ENERGY CAPACITY

Capacity is insufficient to cope with demand. We need new investment now – and on an ongoing basis. Our need for electricity is rising just as many of our existing coal and nuclear power plants reach the end of their lives. In a nutshell, the problem is this: higher prices may make sense for energy companies and for meeting green targets (cutting demand and making renewables more cost-effective), but the public and politicians want to see declining (or at least stable) prices.

It's long been known that old power stations are reaching the end of their lives – but thanks to a lack of investment over the last 20 years they haven't been replaced. With no clear strategy, government policy has largely comprised small-scale tinkering with short-term measures such as ever-changing 'feed-in tariffs' (FITs) for renewables (solar and wind, etc). Although there's some new investment (in renewables and nuclear power), crucially these projects aren't driven by the market alone; instead, government is involved in setting contracts and has to stump up huge sums to stand behind investments. In effect, this has created two systems: a market-led one, which involves 'sweating' old existing assets; and a state-led one, which pays higher prices to encourage new investment.

UTILITIES ARE DIFFERENT

There is a complicating factor in the utilities market: at minimal levels of consumption, utilities are a necessity, for heating and eating. But, at some point, energy use becomes more 'discretionary' than essential (for watching TV or playing computer games). Then, as consumption increases, it's more of a luxury: for heating the indoor pool, lighting the tennis court, or putting on a truly over-the-top display of Christmas lights…

This wouldn't be an issue if all consumers had the same level of income. In the real world, in which incomes differ widely (see Chapter 15), the unit price needed to discourage the wealthy from overusing a scarce resource might put even simple lighting beyond the reach of the poor.

One way around this problem would be to promote 'differential pricing', similar to mobile phone contracts. As a household chooses to use more gas, water, or electricity, the per-unit price might rise. Indeed, a minimum level might be provided free – or at cost price. Steeper prices might apply for those who use more. Smart meters would allow householders to see how much of their 'cheap rate' remains each day or each week. And increasing tariffs might permit a socially acceptable minimum standard of supply to the consumer, alongside profit maximisation on the surplus for suppliers (albeit that the government may need to incentivise suppliers to promote home insulation).

PUBLIC VS PRIVATE

We have a choice between the market or the state when it comes to who's to dictate investment in energy capacity and prices. Whichever model we opt for, the state needs to set and enforce targets for environmental considerations. Subject to that consideration, the main options can be summarised as follows.

A market solution

In theory, well-functioning markets can deliver new investment. In practice, relying solely on markets may fail to deliver on social goals, for two main reasons.

*For energy companies to be incentivised to invest, prices have to rise. Politicians won't view this as a good outcome. But without increases in prices to achieve profit-maximising levels of investment, there's a risk of blackouts and supply shortfalls. Suppliers competing on price will be reluctant to raise their prices to allow them to invest heavily in future capacity if they see that competitors remain focused on short-term profits.

*In markets for non-essential things, such as chocolate (arguably!), consumers might accept supply occasionally not keeping pace with demand. But when it comes to something as fundamental as energy, this would mean occasional blackouts. So we expect 'wasteful' excess capacity to be maintained to cope with peaks during which demand is higher than normal.

Nationalisation of the industry

Alternatively, the public might opt to invest directly, by funding the renationalisation of the energy industry. This has been successfully achieved in a number of countries, including Wales (see Chapter 9). A 'not-for-profit' public monopoly has the advantage of a longer-term focus, with state (or directly funded) investment in future capacity ultimately benefiting taxpayers rather than the industry's shareholders and directors.

A quasi-market solution

Private profit backed up by public subsidy is, in effect, the current UK model. But taxpayers might query why their taxes are being 'invested' in an industry in which the profits go to private shareholders. One alternative form of subsidised 'direct action' involves declaring our independence by upgrading our properties' insulation levels and generating our own power by means of renewables – but this generally requires state support, such as feed-in-tariffs (FITs).

A NEW WAY FORWARD?

The private and public sectors aren't mutually exclusive. For example, no one would argue that ITV shouldn't exist simply because the BBC also produces TV programmes. Conversely, the BBC has to provide programmes that the public want if it's to compete with ITV. Likewise, in the utilities market, competition might be provided between the public and private sectors.

Where energy price rises are politically unacceptable, rather than proposing 'price freezes' the state might maintain a not-for-profit public supplier that offers a socially optimal tariff – and let competition do the rest. In New Zealand, for example, the public sector has a majority interest in corporations at both the retail and generating levels. In theory, the competition between public and private firms drives efficiency in both. Consumers are free to change providers if they feel that one is overcharging.

Similarly, if the state wishes to invest in extra capacity on behalf of taxpayers, the future profits will accrue to the public purse. This won't prevent private firms from also investing – but to prevent one sector from freeriding at times of high demand, a system of penalties might create incentives to reduce the likelihood of a blackout.

With an appropriate set of environmental constraints, competition between the public and private sector, accompanied by an appropriate tariff structure, could be the solution that delivers the best of all worlds.

See website for pros and cons of gas, coal, nuclear, fracking, wind, solar, wave power etc.

Defence

There's a general perception that the UK isn't spending much on defence – but this rather depends on how you look at it. In terms of the *absolute* amount of money spent (£36 billion at last count), Britain had the sixth largest spend worldwide in 2013, behind only the United States, China, Russia, Saudi Arabia and France. (The United States alone splashed out more defence cash that same year than the next eight highest spenders combined.) But looked at in terms of percentage of GDP, we're not even in the top 20, weighing in at a lowly 34th worldwide – one place lower than we were 25 years earlier.

The fact is that Britain has only intermittently been a highly militarised nation – and, as you might expect, this has predominantly been in times of war. The proportion of GDP that we spend on defence today (around 2.01%) isn't a million miles away from that spent during the inter-war years (for example 2.75% in 1936).

Budget cuts

Further reductions in the defence budget are expected until at least 2020, spread across the army, Royal Navy and the Royal Air Force (RAF). However, spending is likely to be maintained above the magic mark of 2%, which, according to NATO, is the point of balance between those nations that are 'pulling their weight' and those that are not.

Much of the British defence budget is devoted to the purchase of equipment. Based on plans at the time of writing, the navy is likely to get between 8 and 13 'Type 26' frigates and two carriers by 2020, and the RAF and Navy together are sharing in new (American-designed) Lightning II fighter aircraft. However, equipment requires personnel and, in 2013, General Sir Nicholas Houghton, Chief of the Defence Staff, warned that the UK was getting close to a point at which there would simply be too few trained people to make use of what we have. It's not impossible that one of the two new carriers will be mothballed

on completion – with accusations of astounding short-sightedness and waste (following a litany of botched government decisions on Nimrod, Chinook and aircraft carriers without aircraft, etc).

Punching above our weight

British leaders have often argued that whilst we can't hope to match the defence expenditure of the United States, China and Russia, we're more efficient in using what we have, thanks to our strategic alliances. For example, the combined defence expenditure of the four largest European nations (including the UK) is greater than that of either China or Russia. There's also the 'special relationship' – although Washington has questioned whether the UK will be able to continue to play a substantial part in this if our defence budget is slashed further.

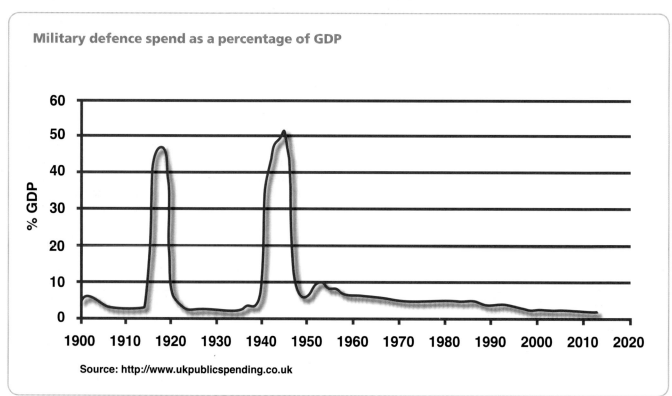

Military defence spend as a percentage of GDP

Source: http://www.ukpublicspending.co.uk

The nuclear option

Britain's nuclear deterrence programme, the submarine-launched Trident missile system, is now 20 years old and will soon be up for renewal. Replacing it would cost an initial £20 billion, with maintenance swallowing another £3 billion a year. On one hand, a Trident upgrade should continue to deter potential attacks and also allow Britain to retain its prestigious seat at NATO's top table; on the other hand, some say, this mindset is rooted in the days of the Cold War. Today, the main threats come from isolated terrorist groups (including home-grown suicide bombers) against whom nuclear weapons offer no protection. What's more, Trident is a US-supplied system and Britain could not realistically use its weapons independently. At a time of financial austerity, might the money be better spent on more effective and affordable conventional weapons and soldiers?

By sea, by land, by air – and in cyberspace

The UK retains the capability to defend against conventional attack, and it's clear that our armed services are world-class, for their size. However, the world of today also faces online threats: so-called 'cyber-warfare'.

There are three main types of threat:

- the influencing of people's beliefs by means of social media, etc (for example jihadist propaganda);
- hackers engaging in military and industrial espionage (stealing secrets); and
- the sabotaging of strategic networks, such as power supplies, to reduce Britain's ability to operate.

Countries such as the United States, Russia, China and the UK have long had the ability to launch cyber-attacks on perceived threats (the United States and Israel being widely thought to be behind the 'Stuxnet' Internet worm that aimed to sabotage the Iranian nuclear programme). However, the UK is the only member of this elite group, which has admitted publicly that it's developing cyber-weapons and investing hundreds of millions in response to the global cyber-arms race.

Past and future threats

Sadly, the world isn't getting any more peaceful. Every year since the Global Peace Index was first published in 2007, the world has appeared to become a less safe place. It would therefore seem that we won't stop investing in defence any time soon – although it follows that the areas in which we invest are likely to evolve in response to perceived threats: no guns and tanks can prevent a cyber-attack, after all.

The violent instability in the Middle East posed by groups such as Islamic State (IS) also means that we need to retain the capability to respond when our allies ask for our help (albeit that we should be mindful both of our national independence and of past disasters such as Iraq). At the time of writing, NATO is assessing the level of threat posed by Russia – a threat that many assumed had been consigned to history. So it seems that we still need guns and tanks after all, along with personnel who know how to use them.

As the Romans observed, 'If you want peace, prepare for war' – or at least 'prepare for defence'.

THE LAST WORD

This has been a hugely ambitious book – perhaps overly ambitious. Hopefully, it will at least spark debate beyond the tribal level of Westminster politics. Now, in the true style of Haynes manuals, we'll distil the preceding pages into a checklist of items needing maintenance, repair or a complete strip down and rebuild.

Global success

The UK needs a vision of globalisation that considers what's best for Britain rather than for global markets. An honest and tolerant discussion is needed about the UK's place in the global economy, including difficult topics like immigration and our vulnerability to global capital flows.

Restore trust in markets

In some sectors, such as the NHS or natural monopolies like water and rail, pure market solutions are inappropriate or inefficient. And markets need trust, which is notably short where authorities have turned a blind eye to market rigging and the abuse of customers. To put morality at the heart of markets needs firm and effective government regulation, not least in the largely unreformed banking system. This should allow good businesses the freedom to excel, innovate and profit, while protecting consumers from exploitation. Regulators need to be sharper and unafraid to impose harsh penalties where it is clear that social good has been compromised by the pursuit of profit. As in sport, sensible rules imposed with effective refereeing make for smoother-running markets and a fairer society.

Promote employment

The UK is desperately short of good jobs: government policy should be judged by its impact on the jobs market as well as on the deficit. The government must boost employment opportunities, not just employability (*eg* by a smart application of the state chequebook with a procurement policy that favours home producers).

More devolution

Regions and local communities need more powers, not necessarily in taxation but certainly in spending priorities. We should also spread central government departments throughout the regions – particularly to those areas short of employment. Government must value the social glue that binds people together and heals fault lines. True localism means putting communities back at the heart of local economies.

Long-term strategies

Governments without coherent plans are prone to losing their way and are open to manipulation and capture by powerful outside interests. As in business, 'joined-up government' depends on consistent long-term strategies that provide a clear roadmap. This is too important to be left solely to tribal MPs with short attention spans focused on the electoral cycle. The first step in achieving an agreed cross-party consensus on key areas like industry, energy, health and housing is to appoint impartial experts. Voters might be asked to give their seal of approval to key national strategies.

Debt and the deficit

No nation can live beyond its means indefinitely. The UK's ballooning trade and budget deficits cannot be resolved by endless borrowing and the sale of national assets. We need to bridge the gap with effective tax collection and a genuine 'march of the makers' regeneration of export industries. Here are some policies to consider:

- **Innovative taxation** Tax is the price of civilisation. The UK requires new taxation policies to ensure that those who benefit most from the civilised nature of our society also contribute their fair share towards its upkeep. We need independent experts to take the reins, people like authors Richard Murphy and Richard Brooks, and the redoubtable head of the Public Accounts Committee, Margaret Hodge, scourge of HMRC bigwigs and tax-avoiding corporate giants.

- **Manufacturing renaissance** To stem the UK's decline, a new spirit of economic patriotism needs to pervade government. This will require a 'Team GB' approach to rebuilding our manufacturing base and overcoming our addiction to short-term fixes such as selling off profitable businesses to competitors. To build a strong new economy centred around resurgent national champions will require enormous energy, ingenuity and resources, backed up by a wartime spirit – along the lines prescribed by the Cambridge professor of economics Ha-Joon Chang. British business leaders who have built world-class brands starting from little or nothing include James Dyson, John Bloor and Anthony Bamford. There is also much to learn from the economic dynamism of countries like South Korea and Germany.

Get real about our place in the world

Policing the globe is no longer Britain's responsibility. The UK is a nation with limited resources and living on credit. It can no longer afford to become embroiled in ruinously expensive overseas military campaigns unless critical for the 'defence of the realm'. Whilst maintaining well equipped armed forces is essential to defend British interests, some might consider the stratospheric cost of replenishing our Trident nuclear weapon capability as an unaffordable luxury. Some of the billions in funding might instead be diverted to investment in industrial resurgence.

Trickle-up economics

As well as increasing GDP, it makes good economic and social sense to improve the position of the most vulnerable in our society – while leaving no one worse off. As the poorest share economic growth, their increased spending will 'well up' throughout the economy, benefiting all.

Value professionalism

Better decision-making requires that we look beyond short-term profit-seeking. We should value the expertise of public servants, and hire good people and encourage them to innovate. To improve efficiency we must value feedback from the people who actually do the job and interface with customers. The success of German industry in part reflects team spirit aided by employee representatives at board level. Wise leaders consult others, welcome constructive criticism, avoid yes-men and yes-women, understand the power of staff motivation and don't rule by diktat.

Addressing shortfalls in public services

We need a debate about bridging the gap between our demands as citizens for public services and the reality of the provision of health care, affordable housing, transport, schools, jobs and so on. To overcome shortages and boost supply to meet future demands will require enormous investment funded in part by more effective taxation. On the other side of the equation, curtailing demand is likely to involve tough decisions such as limiting the range of free services, aiming for more sustainable levels of population growth, the management of immigration, and measures to reduce demand by promoting healthier lifestyles, localism and self-help where practical.

Reduced inequality

Markets must serve society, not the other way about. Both the IMF and OECD are warning about the threat to prosperity caused by spiralling inequality, advising that measures must be taken to spread the fruits of economic growth more evenly. Countries with lower levels of inequality are proven to suffer fewer social problems as well as being more economically efficient. This will require a political culture of openness, for example declaring the relationship between the salaries of company bosses and of their employees. It would also be enlightening to grade jobs by how socially useful they are. We could learn from the success of societies with lower levels of inequality in wealthy countries like Norway, Sweden, Japan and Germany, perhaps adopting the best from each. To quote the OECD, 'Countries that promote equal opportunities for all from an early age are those that will grow and prosper.'

Accountability and transparency

As voters, we should demand more of those in positions of power. The workings of government need to be exposed to greater scrutiny; even the US government is more transparent. Accountability requires openness in areas like political lobbying by powerful outside interests, opaque PFI schemes, creeping NHS back-door privatisation, and potentially corrupting conflicts of interest at the top.

We might also demand greater efficiency and shareholder value among senior management. Good leaders are motivated by more than naked self-interest and personal enrichment; they might rather be driven by a sense of achievement or of public service. Government would do well to set guidelines in the cash-strapped public sector for senior salaries, and banish excessive payouts in the NHS, Network Rail, the BBC, local councils and MPs themselves. To sweep away rewards for failure it might help if those at the top were to abide by the same performance rules as everyone else. Compensation should work both ways, with rewards for ability and success but penalties for poor performance, negligence and corruption. We need an end to the 'iron floor' mentality at the top that prevents failed elites being replenished meritocratically by fresh minds.

The state and its citizens

The relationship between citizens and the state needs to strike the right balance between individual rights and responsibilities – the extent of give and take. Individual rights at the top but personal responsibility at the bottom makes for inefficiency.

The EU

The issue of EU membership is only likely to be resolved with a referendum. If the UK stays in, we need to work from the centre to change the EU in our national interests. If the UK decides to go it alone, in order to prosper we will need a strong independent economy.

And finally

At the end of Part 2, we listed some of the ways politics might be done better. But just for good measure here are a couple more:

A '**none of these**' option on ballot papers. Being better than nothing should be required of all elected candidates.

MPs must **lead by example**, putting country ahead of personal ambition and party loyalties.

To read more – or join the debate – please visit:
www.howtorunbritain.com